CRC Handbook of Ultrasound in Obstetrics and Gynecology

Volume I

Editor

Asim Kurjak, M.D., Ph.D.
Professor and Head
Department of Obstetrics and Gynecology
University of Zagreb
J. Kajfes Hospital
Zagreb, Yugoslavia

CRC Press
Taylor & Francis Group
Boca Raton London New York

CRC Press is an imprint of the
Taylor & Francis Group, an **informa** business

T0262942

First published 1990 by CRC Press
Taylor & Francis Group
6000 Broken Sound Parkway NW, Suite
300 Boca Raton, FL 33487-2742

Reissued 2018 by CRC Press

© 1990 by Taylor & Francis
CRC Press is an imprint of Taylor & Francis Group, an Informa business

No claim to original U.S. Government works

A Library of Congress record exists under LC control number: 89023921

Publisher's Note
The publisher has gone to great lengths to ensure the quality of this reprint but points out that some imperfections in the original copies may be apparent.

Disclaimer
The publisher has made every effort to trace copyright holders and welcomes correspondence from those they have been unable to contact.

ISBN 13: 978-1-138-10545-4 (hbk)
ISBN 13: 978-1-138-55848-9 (pbk)
ISBN 13: 978-1-315-15088-8 (ebk)

Visit the Taylor & Francis Web site at http://www.taylorandfrancis.com and the CRC Press Web site at http://www.crcpress.com

TO IAN DONALD — FRIEND AND TEACHER

PREFACE

It is now 40 years since Ian Donald first started to use ultrasound in obstetrics and gynecology. In a relatively short period of time ultrasound has improved in what seems to be a logarithmic progression, and it can with good reason be said to have changed the way of thinking of our age. The magnitude of this step alone is incalculable. Moreover, more than any other modern technique ultrasound has made it obvious that the fetus is an individual virtually from conception.

The original excitment is, of course, still felt by many of us. One cannot stop wondering how many applications of this relatively simple invention the future is hiding. Even now fetal medicine, prenatal diagnosis, infertility, and assisted conception are totally dependent in expertise on ultrasound screening and the diagnostic horizon is constantly expanding into new areas such as cancer screening and urodynamics. To quote Ian Donald: "We live in an age when today's improbability becomes tomorrow's reality."

The most exciting recent developments are color Doppler and transvaginal sonography. The combination of these two modalities in the same vaginal probe provides for superb simultaneous visualization of structural and flow information and offers new insight in dynamic studies of blood flow within the female pelvis. Our group has been the first to introduce this new technique into the clinical practice and to the best of my knowledge this is the first book containing a chapter on transvaginal color Doppler.

The waves of interest created by present possibilities are spreading rapidly through a large numnber of specialities. We see their solid evidence in the form of hundreds of scientific contributions to almost all major journals. Any interested individual will find it difficult to read or even scan these articles, although he will feel this to be his duty. It is the purpose of this book to offer some relief from this responsibility.

This handbook is the result of my personal efforts to weigh and consider, stemming from my clinical and ultrasonic experience and reading over the years. As such it must be accepted as a personal view with inevitable biases and idiosyncrasies.

A. Kurjak

THE EDITOR

Asim Kurjak, M.D., Ph.D., is Chairman of the Department and Professor of Obstetrics and Gynecology at the University of Zagreb, Zagreb Yugoslavia. He is also Head of the Ultrasonic Institute of Zagreb which is the World Health Organization Collaborating Centre for diagnostic ultrasound.

Dr. Kurjak obtained his training at the University of Zagreb, receiving his M.D. degree in 1966 and his Ph.D. degree in 1977. He served as an assistant professor at the Department of Obstetrics and Gynecology, University of Zagreb from 1968 to 1980. In 1971, as a British scholar he was Research Assistant for one year at the Institute of Obstetrics and Gynecology, University of London under Prof. Stuart Campbell. From 1983 to 1985 he was External Examiner at the University of Liverpool. It was in 1983 that he assumed his present position.

Dr. Kurjak is a member and past president of the Yugoslav Society of University Professors. He is a member of the advisory board of five international scientific journals. He served as Vice President of the European Federation for Ultrasound in Medicine and Biology. He is also the President of the International Society "Fetus as a Patient". He has been the recipient of many research grants from the Scientific Council from Yugoslavia and is currently the WHO coordinator for the use of ultrasound in developing countries. Recently he has been elected as a member of the Executive Bureau of World Federation for Ultrasound in Medicine and Biology. Among other awards, he is an honorary member of the Ultrasonic Society of Australia, Italy, Egypt, and Spain, and of the Society of Obstetrics and Gynecology of Italy, Poland, Hungary, Egypt, Spain, and Chile. He is also an honorary fellow of the American Institute of Ultrasound in Medicine. Recently, he has been elected the Secretary of the International Society for Ultrasound in Obstetrics and Gynecology.

Dr. Kurjak has presented over 90 invited lectures at major international meetings and approximately 100 guest lectures at universities and institutes. He has published more than 200 research papers and 14 books in the English language. Lately, in conjunction with Prof. Kazuo Maeda, he published *Textbook of Ultrasound in Obstetrics and Gynecology* in Japanese. *Ultrasound and Infertility* and *Fetal Growth Retardation—Diagnosis and Therapy,* were published by CRC Press.

His current major research interests include conventional and color Doppler studies of fetoplacental and maternal circulation.

CONTRIBUTORS

Volume I

Željko Andreić, M.S.
Department of Obstetrics & Gynecology
University of Zagreb
Zagreb, Yugoslavia

Branko Breyer, Ph.D.
Professor and Chief
Department of Obstetrics & Gynecology
University of Zagreb
Zagreb, Yugoslavia

Vincenzo D'Addario, M.D.
First Clinic of Obstetrics and Gynecology
University of Bari
Bari, Italy

Davor Jurković, M.D., Ph.D.
Ultrasonic Insitute
University of Zagreb
WHO Collaborating Centre for
 Diagnositic Ultrasound
Zagreb, Yugoslavia

George Kossoff, D.Sc. Eng.
Chief Research Scientist
Ultrasonics Laboratory
Chatswood, NSW, Australia

Asim Kurjak, M.D., Ph.D.
Head
Ultrasonic Institute
University of Zagreb
WHO Collaborating Centre for
 Diagnositic Ultrasound
Zagreb, Yugoslavia

Višnja Latin, M.D., Ph.D.
Department of Obstetrics & Gynecology
University of Zagreb
Zagreb, Yugoslavia

Jadranka Pavletić, M.D.
Ultrasonic Institute
University of Zagreb
WHO Collaborating Centre for Diagnostic
 Ultrasound
Zagreb, Yugoslavia

TABLE OF CONTENTS

Volume I

Volume II

Chapter 1

BASIC PRINCIPLES OF ULTRASONIC IMAGING

Branko Breyer and Željko Andreić

INTRODUCTION

In this chapter we shall describe basic physical and technological principles of ultrasound diagnostic equipment without extensive mathematical treatment, except for some simple and useful formulas. These formulas are usually supported by worked examples and comments relevant for practical use. Ultrasound diagnostic instruments and procedures are developing rapidly, so that mere knowledge of manipulation with the existing instruments is definitely insufficient for sound usage of the instruments to come. On the other hand, the knowledge of underlying physical principles allows one to understand what is actually new in an instrument, what the supposed advantages are, and how they can be exploited in practical work.

PHYSICAL PRINCIPLES

BASIC CONCEPTS OF WAVES AND SOUND

Sound is mechanical vibration which spreads from its source into the surrounding medium. Such spreading mechanical vibrations are called waves, mostly because in many ways they resemble waves on the water surface. For instance, if we disturb calm water, say, with a wooden stick which we move up and down, water waves will form and spread radially away from the stick. In an analogous way, sound waves are produced by disturbing the air somehow, and they spread in all directions away from their source. When we speak about sound waves, we intuitively think about audible sound which we can hear and which spreads in air. Sound waves can also exist in other media and can be totally imperceptible to us. What is common to all "sound" waves is that they can be described by the same laws of nature.

The vibrating object which produces the sound is called the source. This source is somehow made to vibrate, and its vibrations disturb the medium around it. The produced disturbances spread away through the medium around the source in the same way the water waves spread around the moving stick. If we look at the water waves more carefully, we will see that the water itself does not flow. It just moves up and down, and the movements travel from the stick outwards. This can be verified by a simple experiment. If we put a few small chips of wood on the water surface and watch their movements as the wave passes by, we can see the chips moving up and down while the wave is passing by them, but after the wave is gone, they are again at rest at their original positions. So, only the disturbance travels through the water, while water itself stays at rest. This traveling disturbance is called a wave, and under normal circumstances it produces no flow of medium through which it spreads. In audible sound waves, air molecules are moved back and forth around their positions in the direction of wave spreading. Such a wave is called a longitudinal wave. All sound waves in normal circumstances are longitudinal. In some cases, transversal waves or waves with complicated particle motions can exist, but we shall limit our discussion only to the longitudinal sound waves because only such waves are used for therapeutic and diagnostic applications.

TABLE 1

**Speed of Sound and Characteristic Acoustic
Impedances of Some Materials**

Medium	Speed of sound (m/s)	Characteristic acoustic impedance (10^6 kg m^{-2} s^{-1})
Air 20°C	340	0.000411
Water 20°C	1480	1.5
Castor oil	1540	1.46
Perspex	2680	3.17
Steel	5950	46.6
Pyrex® glass	5610	13

The speed with which the wave travels through the medium is called the speed of sound (in that medium). The number of oscillations the wave makes in 1 s is called the frequency of the wave. In our water wave experiment, we can measure the speed of the wave by measuring the time it needs to travel some known distance, between two wooden chips for instance. We can also measure its frequency by counting how many times a particular chip has been moved up and down in 1 s. In a similar manner, we use measuring instruments to measure the speed and frequency of sound in air, water, or other media.

The human ear can hear sound waves with frequencies from about 16 to about 20,000 Hz. The Hertz (Hz) is the unit of frequency; 1 Hz means one full oscillation in 1 s. Larger units used are kilohertz (kHz), 1 kHz = 1000 Hz, and megahertz (MHz), 1 MHz = 1 million Hz = 1000 kHz.

Sound with frequency in the range 16 Hz to 20 kHz is usually called audible sound, and the 16-Hz to 20-kHz frequency span, the audible range. For illustration we can mention that musical tone AO is given by a tuning fork which has the frequency of exactly 400 Hz (Table 1).

If we divide the speed of sound with the frequency of sound, we get the length between the adjacent wave peaks in the traveling wave. This length is called the wavelength of the wave.

$$\text{wavelength} = \text{speed of sound/frequency of sound} \tag{1}$$

or, abbreviated

$$\lambda = c/f \tag{1a}$$

where λ means wavelength, c is the speed of sound, and f is the frequency of sound.

***

The formula $\lambda = c/f$ is a very useful one. It can be used to find one of the three basic sound parameters if we know the other two. Usually, diagnostic ultrasound is described with its frequency. The speed of sound in soft tissues is known to be about 1540 m/s, so we can use this knowledge to find the wavelength of the ultrasound wave. For instance, if we use a probe which generates 2 MHz ultrasound waves, their wavelength in soft tissues will be

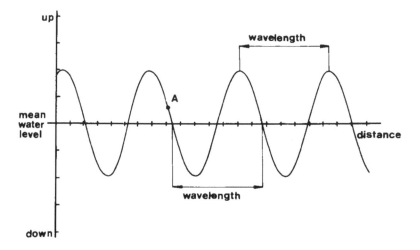

FIGURE 1.   A cut-through of water surface disturbed by a simple water wave shows a characteristic sinusoidal pattern of raised and lowered parts of the surface. The image is frozen in time. In reality, this pattern moves outwards from the wave source with constant speed. Distance between two adjacent wave peaks (or valleys) is called wavelength of the wave.

$$\lambda = c/f = 1540/2000000 = 0.00077 \text{ m}$$
$$= 0.77 \text{ mm}$$

We can also rearrange the formula to find other two parameters:

$$\text{frequency} = \text{speed of sound/wavelength}$$
$$\text{speed of sound} = \text{wavelength} * \text{frequency}$$

or simply

$$f = c/\lambda$$
$$c = f*\lambda$$

***

Suppose that we somehow freeze the water in one moment during the water wave experiment and make a cut through the frozen water surface. We shall get the water wave profile in that moment, as demonstrated in Figure 1.

As this simple picture illustrates, water surface is somewhere raised and somewhere lowered in a sinusoidal pattern. The wavelength is the distance between two adjacent maxima (or minima). The SI unit for wavelength is meter (m), with subunits of cm (1 cm = 0.01 m), mm (1 mm = 0.001 m) and μm (1 μm = 0.001 mm). The speed with which this profile moves away from the source is called the speed of sound (in a particular medium, in our case, water). This speed is constant for homogeneous media and is measured in meters per second.

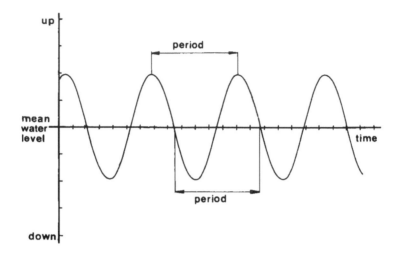

FIGURE 2. Vertical position of a stationary point on the water surface disturbed by a simple wave varies sinusoidally with time. Period of the wave is defined as time needed for one complete oscillation.

Imagine now that we stay at some stationary point on the surface (on one of our wooden chips, for instance) and observe the motions of the surface at that point as the wave is passing by. We shall get a picture very similar to the previous one (Figure 2).

Please note that the value plotted on the abscissa (x-axis) of this graph is time, not distance. While the first graph illustrates wave behavior in space, the second illustrates wave behavior in time. Now, the amount of time between two adjacent wave maxima (in time) is called the period of the wave. As we have said before, the frequency of the wave is the number of oscillations in 1 s, so it is obvious that

$$\text{frequency (Hz)} = 1/\text{period (s)} \tag{2}$$

$$\text{period (s)} = 1/\text{frequency (Hz)} \tag{2a}$$

***

Sound is mechanical vibration which travels through the medium. It is produced by vibrating objects. A sound wave is described with its frequency, or its wavelength, and its amplitude. The speed of sound in a homogeneous medium is constant and the basic relation is

$$\text{speed of sound} = \text{wavelength} * \text{frequency}$$

***

SOUND PRESSURE AND ENERGY

So far, we have said that a sound wave is a disturbance which travels through some medium. As the source vibrates, it pushes and pulls particles of the surrounding medium.

In other words, it exerts some force on the particles. When we describe such a force, we usually talk about force per unit area, the pressure.

***

The SI unit of force is Newton (N). 1 N is the force which in 1 s can accelerate a body of 1 kg mass to the velocity of 1 m/s. When we speak about forces in gases and liquids, we usually talk in terms of pressure. Pressure is the force acting on a unit area perpendicular to the direction of the force. The SI unit for pressure is Pascal (Pa). 1 Pa means the force of 1 N distributed over an area of 1 m². For illustration: mean atmospheric pressure at sea level is about 100,000 Pa. Larger units for pressure are often used:

kilopascal: 1 kPa = 1,000 Pa
megapascal: 1 MPa = 1,000 kPa = 1,000,000 Pa

***

The source of sound produces oscillating pressure variations in the surrounding medium. The pressure oscillations travel through the medium as a sound wave. This wave has a certain amount of energy which is carried with the wave. This amount is proportional to the mean squared pressure variation.

We can describe a sound wave in many ways. We can describe it as a traveling disturbance of the medium or as a traveling pressure wave, etc. All these descriptions are valid and are used in discussions of sound characteristics and effects. Usually, a description which suits the particular problem best is used, although different authors have different definitions for "most suitable". However, for us, it is important to remember that many descriptions are possible. From now on, we shall describe sound waves as pressure waves because many effects of interest depend on the pressure variations. The energy in our case can be defined as ability to do some work. We cannot see or measure the energy itself. We can only detect it by observing the effects which are produced when the energy changes or is spent in some way. The amount of energy spent is equal to the work done.

The amount of energy carried with the wave in 1 s is called power. If some work is done by the traveling wave, the amount of work done in one second is called dissipated power.

***

energy = ability to do some work

work = amount of energy spent

power = energy transfered in unit time

dissipated power = work done in unit time

The physical units for energy and work are the same: Joule (J); 1 J is defined as the amount of work required to accelerate a body of 1 kg to the velocity of 1 m/s. Power is defined as the amount of work done in 1 s, so it is a measure of speed with which the work is done. The SI unit for power is Watt (W); 1 W means 1 J of work done in 1 s. Sometimes, the amount of energy carried with the wave in 1 s is also called power. Then, actual work done in 1 s is called dissipated power to differentiate between the two. We shall use this terminology in discussing sound. If a particular wave carries 10 J of energy in 1 s with it, we say that that wave has a power of 10 W; and if in each second 1 J of the energy is absorbed in the medium, we say that dissipated power is 1 W.

***

As we shall see later, the effects produced by the wave passing through some medium are dependent on the wave power per unit area of the wave cross-section, the intensity. The intensity is defined as

$$\text{Intensity} = \text{power of the wave/cross section of the wave} \qquad (3)$$

or

$$I \ (W/m^2) = P(W)/A(m^2) \qquad (3a)$$

***

Let us compare the intensities of two sound waves; the first one with the power of 1 W and cross-sectional area of 1 m², and the second with the power of 0.001 W, but concentrated on area of 1 mm². The intensities of these two waves can be found by the formula $I = P/A$ as

$$I = 1 \ W/1m^2 = 1 \ W/m^2$$
$$I = 0.001 \ W/1 \ mm^2 = 0.001 \ W/0.000001m^2$$
$$= 1.000 \ W/m^2$$

***

***

Sound waves may be described with variations in pressure traveling through the medium (pressure waves). They possess some energy which is carried by the wave. Physically, the energy carried in unit time is the power. Sound waves are usually described with intensity, which is defined as power of the wave per unit area of the wave cross-section.

***

SOUND BEAMS

So far, we have discussed sound waves which spread in all directions around their source. Such waves are called spherical waves. If we are very far away from the source, a small part of the spherical wave which goes in our direction will look almost straight, and

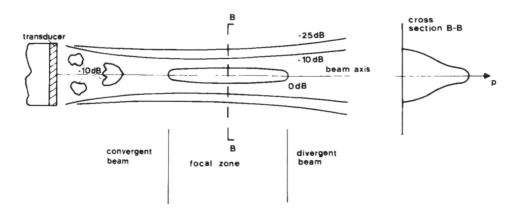

FIGURE 3. A cutaway of a simple ultrasound beam. The beam is represented as a set of isointensity curves (curves which connect points of equal ultrasound intensity). The beam may be divided into three distinct parts: the convergent part in which the beam converges toward the focal point (beam waist), the focal region where beam cross-section is smallest and nearly constant, and the divergent part. Note the intensity irregularities near the transducer (the so-called near field of the transducer).

we shall not be able to see that it is spherical. In such a case, we call the wave a plane wave. If we return to our water experiment, waves spreading around their source are circular, the circle being analogous to the sphere on the two-dimensional water surface. Far away from the source, a small part of the circular wave will look straight, and we would call it a plane wave.

However, in many applications of ultrasound very narrow beams of sound are used. To describe such beams, we need more details than simply stating their wavelength and frequency. In a sound beam, intensity across the beam is not uniform as it was in case of circular or plane waves. Because of that, the distribution of sound intensity across the beam and the position of the cross-sectional plane to which this distribution belongs must be given to completely describe the beam. Such a distribution is commonly called the beam profile (Figure 3).

As the simple drawing in Figure 3 shows, a sound beam is composed of three parts: the convergent part in which the sound wave converges towards the so-called focal point, focal region where the beam has the minimum transversal dimensions, and the divergent part where the beam spreads again. A sound beam which has all these three parts is called a focused sound beam. Sometimes beams without a convergent part and a focal region are used. These are unfocused sound beams.

The laws of nature limit minimum dimensions of the focused beam, and so it is not possible to focus the beam into a point. The diameter of the beam waist (the thinnest part of a focused beam) is approximately given by

$$\text{beam waist} = \frac{\text{wavelength * distance from the source}}{\text{source diameter}} \tag{4}$$

So, by using larger sources or shorter wavelengths it is possible to produce smaller beam diameters in the focused region. There are practical limitations to this rule which we shall discuss later in the section about resolution of ultrasonic images.

Very often literature mentions the so-called near field, or Fresnel zone, and the far field (the Fraunhofner zone) of a transducer, or a sound beam. It is important to know that near field is a part of space from the transducer surface to about a few transducer diameters in which the sound beam is highly irregular and multiple beams are very often present. The far field is the zone far from the transducer in which the sound beam has a regular, smooth shape. The transition between the two zones is gradual and generally cannot be simply defined.

Sometimes a few additional sound beams of smaller intensities exist at the sides of the main sound beam. These beams are called side lobes, and the main beam is, of course, the main lobe. Such beams are responsible for some of the image artifacts in ultrasonic imaging.

***

Sound waves may be spherical, planar, or irregular in shape. In many applications, highly directed sound waves, conformed to a tube-like space are used. Such waves are named sound beams. A beam may be focused or unfocused. A focused beam is composed of a convergent part, a focal zone, and a divergent part. An unfocused beam has a divergent shape. The intensity profile across the beam cross-section is not uniform and usually decreases towards the beam edge.

A part of the beam in the vicinity of its source in which intensity distribution is highly irregular, is called the near field (sometimes near zone or Fresnel zone). The rest of the beam, farther from the source, is named the far field (or far zone or Fraunhofner zone).

***

PULSED SOUND

Very often, short pulses of ultrasound are used in diagnostic applications. Under the term "short" we mean that the duration of the sound pulse is much shorter than the time between adjacent pulses. The duration of pulses used for medical imaging is in order of microseconds (0.000001 s). When we deal with such short sound pulses, we have to describe them differently from continuous sound waves. First, there is no single frequency, or wavelength, with which we may describe the pulse. Instead, the pulse is composed of sound waves of many frequencies. If the pulse is shorter, the spread of frequencies of its constituent sound waves is greater. Therefore, we describe a sound pulse by its frequency spectrum. The frequency spectrum is a representation of intensities of constituent sound waves as a function of frequency. So, when a certain pulsed ultrasound probe is described as a 5-MHz probe, it means that the frequency spectrum is maximal at that frequency, the pulse being composed of many frequencies with a range of about 2 to 10 MHz, or even more (see Figure 4).

***

In diagnostic ultrasound, short pulses of ultrasound are very often used. The ultrasound pulse must be described with its length (or duration) in time and its frequency spectrum. If the pulse is shorter, its frequency spectrum is broader and vice versa. Sometimes the frequency calculated from the zero crossings of sound pressure, or the central frequency of the frequency spectrum, is used as the pulse "frequency".

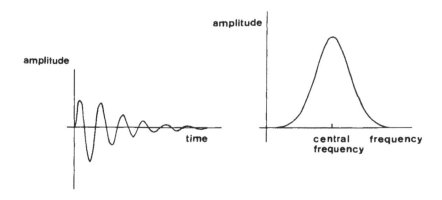

FIGURE 4. A very short sound pulse may have only a few periods. The frequency spectrum of such a pulse (right) is composed of a wide range of frequencies. The pulse is described with its "frequency", which is calculated from the times of zero crossings of pressure oscillations, with its frequency spectrum, and with its duration in time. The so-called central frequency is sometimes used. It is simply the frequency at which the frequency spectrum of a pulse is at a maximum. The number of pulses in 1 s is called the pulse repetition frequency (or rate).

THE DECIBEL NOTATION

The intensities of ultrasound encountered in a single diagnostic examination may have a very broad range, the ratio of 1 to 1 million or more being not uncommon. In such cases, intensities are often expressed in the so-called decibel (dB) scale. The decibel scale is a logarithmic scale in which a value is represented by the number proportional to the logarithm of the value. In such a representation, big numbers are reduced to much smaller ones, which are usually much more meaningful. In reality, the intensity (or any other value or parameter) is expressed on a decibel scale as

$$intensity\ (decibels)\ =\ 10 * \log(intensity/reference\ value) \qquad (5)$$

This means that we convert a value (in our case the intensity) to the decibel scale by first dividing it by some reference value, and then taking the logarithm of the obtained number. Finally, the logarithm is multiplied by ten. It looks rather complicated, but once adapted to it, it is rather simple. The reference value is chosen in such a way that it represents some "normal" or usual circumstance. For instance, in audible sound, we may choose it as the intensity of sound required for good hearing of music or spoken words. In ultrasound we may choose the smallest detectable intensity as a reference, etc. It should be noted here that in medical ultrasound there is no generally accepted reference value, so in almost every device it is different. The factor ten is used to multiply the logarithm of the ratio because by using it, some simple ratios are expressed as a small, simple integer. For instance, ratio 2:1 is expressed as 3 dB, 4:1 as 6 dB, etc. (see Table 2).

Another advantage of the decibel scale is that multiplication of values is converted to simple addition. This is a general property of all logarithmic scales and is very useful if we have to calculate some final values from the product of two or more intermediate values. To illustrate the point, in a normal obstetric examination, ultrasound echoes are amplified by a factor of about 1000. However, as the echoes from the deeper regions of human body pass through a thicker layer of tissue, they are attenuated and are much weaker than the

TABLE 2
Conversion of Ratios to Decibels

Intensity Ratio	dB	Intensity Ratio	dB
1	0	1	0
1.3	1	0.79	−1
1.6	2	0.63	−2
2	3	0.5	−3
2.5	4	0.4	−4
3.2	5	0.32	−5
4	6	0.25	−6
5	7	0.2	−7
6.3	8	0.16	−8
8	9	0.13	−9
10	10	0.1	−10
100	20	0.01	−20
1,000	30	0.001	−30
10,000	40	0.0001	−40
100,000	50	0.00001	−50
1,000,000	60	0.000001	−60
10,000,000	70	0.0000001	−70
100,000,000	80	0.00000001	−80
1,000,000,000	90	0.000000001	−90
10,000,000,000	100	0.0000000001	−100

echoes from the surface and must be further amplified. This is done, and it is called compensation, and it is not unusual to set the compensation of additional amplification to, say, 1000 for the 6 to 10-cm depth. In that case, the total amplification of the echoes is $1000 \times 1000 = 1$ million, a very big number indeed. In the decibel scale, the first amplification will be expressed as 30 dB, the second as 30 dB, and the total amplification will be $30 + 30 = 60$ dB! We may verify in Table 2 that the answer is correct, the 60 dB corresponding to the amplification of 1 million.

***

The decibel notation is used when a great span of numerical values is encountered. The ratio of values expressed in decibels is the logarithm of the ratio of the values multiplied by ten. By using this notation, large ratios are converted to small, simple, and more meaningful numbers which are far easier to deal with. The notation also simplifies calculations, as products of the values are converted to sums of their decibel equivalents.

***

ULTRASOUND PROPAGATION IN TISSUES

Human tissues are not homogeneous in respect to ultrasound properties. Because of that, ultrasound waves traveling through the tissues are reflected, refracted, scattered, and attenuated. The "tissues" in the ultrasonic terminology may differ from the biological tissues. They are different if their mechanical properties, for instance, elasticity, characteristic acous-

TABLE 3
Acoustic Properties of Soft Tissues

Tissue	Speed of sound (m/s)	Characteristic acoustic impedance (10^{-6} kg m^{-2} s^{-1})	Attenuation coefficient (Np/cm at 1 MHz)
Brain	1540	1.58	0.029
Liver	1550	1.65	0.023
Muscle	1585	1.7	0.11
Blood	1570	1.61	
Bone (skull)	4080	7.8	
Soft tissue	1540	1.63	

tic impedance, and velocity of sound, differ from one another. Biologically they may be parts of the same tissue.

Characteristic acoustic impedance is a property of a medium and is defined as the ratio of the instantaneous acoustic pressure and particle velocity. In different tissues, characteristic acoustic impedance and the velocity of sound are generally different. However, differences between different soft tissues are much smaller than between soft tissues and bones or gas. This fact has important consequences in the use of ultrasound in medicine (see Table 3).

REFRACTION AND REFLECTION OF SOUND WAVES

Sound waves are refracted and reflected at every boundary between media of different acoustic properties. If this boundary is much larger than the wavelength, laws of reflection and refraction apply. For boundaries, comparable or smaller in size to wavelength, there is no simple law of reflection on refraction, and wave behavior may be very complicated. In such cases we speak about scattering of sound waves.

We shall first discuss the simplest case of reflection and refraction of a sound wave: the reflection and refraction of a plane wave on a large plane boundary between two media of different acoustic properties. Although this is a very simplified idealization, the results of the discussion basically hold for all cases where the boundary is much larger than the wavelength, regardless of actual wave and boundary shape. The only difference between the plane wave case and other cases is that we must apply laws of reflection and refraction to every point of the boundary, as directions and intensities of the reflected and the refracted part of the wave will differ from point to point of the boundary.

As illustrated in Figure 5, part of the wave energy is reflected and part is transmitted through the boundary. In effect, the sound wave is divided into two waves with different intensities and directions. The angle of refraction depends on the ratio of propagation speeds in the two respective media and is described by the following equation:

$$\sin(\alpha_i)/\sin(\alpha_t) = c_1/c_2 \tag{6}$$

Here, c_1 and c_2 are speeds of ultrasound in the first and second media, respectively, α_i is the angle of incidence, and α_t is the angle of refraction. Note that these angles are measured from the normal to the boundary between the two media.

Amplitudes of reflected wave depend on angles of incidence and reflection and on the characteristic acoustic impedances of the media:

$$\frac{A_r}{A_i} = \frac{Z_2\cos\alpha_i - Z_1\cos\alpha_t}{Z_2\cos\alpha_i + Z_1\cos\alpha_t} \tag{7}$$

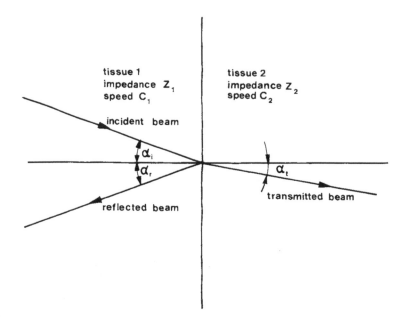

FIGURE 5.   Reflection and refraction of a plane sound wave on a plane boundary between two media of different acoustic properties.

where A_r and A_i are reflected and incident wave amplitude, and Z_1 and Z_2 are characteristic acoustic impedances of the first and second media, respectively. If the wave impinges normally to the surface, this formula reduces to the much simpler one:

$$\frac{A_r}{Z_i} = \frac{Z_2 - Z_1}{Z_2 + Z_1} \tag{8}$$

In many practical cases, when we consider ultrasound waves which are reflected back to the transmitting probe, the second equation gives a fairly accurate picture of what is going on, because in such a situation, relevant waves always transverse boundaries at nearly normal incidence.

We have mentioned before that intensity of the wave is proportional to the square of its amplitude. By using this rule, we can find the ratio of reflected and incident wave intensity as

$$\frac{I_r}{I_i} = \left(\frac{Z_2 - Z_1}{Z_2 + Z_1}\right)^2 \tag{9}$$

If the characteristic acoustic impedances are very different, like in the case of soft tissue and gas (in lungs, for example), virtually all ultrasound energy is reflected at the boundary.

***

As an illustration, let us calculate the ratio of reflected and incident wave intensity for the case of a supposed ultrasonic examination of lungs. The characteristic acoustic impedance of lung is about 400 kg/m/s, and that of surrounding soft tissue about 1.6 million kg/m/s. The wave transverses the boundary at approximately normal incidence.

If we substitute the characteristic acoustic impedances in the formula for the ratio of intensities, we get

$$I_r/I_i = ((1600000 - 400)/(1600000 + 400))$$

$$= 0.999$$

It is clear that practically all ultrasound will be reflected back, and the remaining small fraction of it (0.001 or -30 dB) which enters into the lungs will be far too weak for any practical purposes, as the returning echoes will again be attenuated by another 30 dB at the boundary.

***

A consequence of this is that organs containing gas, like lungs, can not be examined by ultrasound methods, and that gas in stomach and intestines will present serious problems. Another consequence is that some sort of impedance-matching gel (the contact gel), oil, or other coupling agent must be applied between the ultrasound transducer and the body to avoid air bubbles being trapped between the probe and skin. It is interesting to see that ultrasound will be reflected irrespectively of whether it enters from a lower or a higher impedance medium.

The energy which is not reflected will be transmitted across the impedance boundary, so the sum of the reflected and refracted intensities is equal to the incident intensity:

$$Ii = It + Ir \qquad (10)$$

Thus, in many cases the characteristic acoustic impedances are decisive for the intensity of the ultrasound echo. The characteristic acoustic impedance must not be confused with density of the medium by a vague analogy with X-ray imaging. This can be misleading, as it is possible for the two media of similar densities to have grossly different characteristic acoustic impedances. In reality, characteristic acoustic impedance is dependent on the density and the speed of sound:

$$Z = \rho * c \qquad (11)$$

where Z is characteristic acoustic impedance, ρ is the density, and c is the speed of sound in a particular medium.

***

Sound waves are reflected and refracted at boundaries of two different media. The amount of the wave energy which is reflected or refracted at the boundary depends on the characteristic acoustic impedances of the media. If the difference in the impedances is great, almost all energy is reflected. Organs containing gas cannot be satisfactorily examined by ultrasound methods.

***

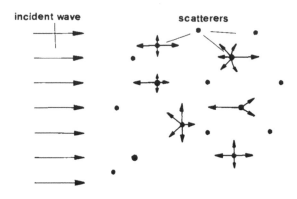

FIGURE 6.   When the boundaries (objects) are similar to or smaller than the wavelength of a sound wave, simple laws of reflection and refraction do not hold. Instead, a small part of the wave intensity is scattered on each object (scatterer) in all directions. The scattered wave is the sum of the contributions from all scatterers.

SCATTERING OF SOUND

So far we have considered the situation where the boundary between the two media is much larger than the wavelength of the sound wave. Such a boundary is called specular (mirror-like) because in many cases it behaves as a mirror. There are many structures in the body which behave as specular reflectors, but there are even more structures in which boundaries between acoustically different media are similar to or smaller than the wavelength of ultrasound. When a sound wave encounters an object which is similar or smaller in dimensions to the wavelength of the wave, the simple laws of reflection and refraction do not hold. Instead, part of the wave passes by the object and part is reflected and refracted (or retransmitted) in all directions around the object (see Figure 6). This disturbed part interacts with the incident wave, and the result of the interaction (or interference, as it is called) is the scattered wave. The scattered wave is basically a spherical wave with the object at its center. The intensity of the scattered wave, however, is not the same in all directions. The body by which the sound wave is scattered is called a scattering center or a scatterer. Usually the total intensity scattered on a scattering center is a small fraction of the wave intensity and can be disregarded. However, in many real situations, there are many scatterers distributed in the medium, and the total energy scattered by all of them can be a considerable part of the whole wave energy. The waves scattered on individual scatterers interfere among themselves, and the resulting scattered wave which returns to the ultrasound probe does not exactly represent each of the scatterers. This has important consequences on our interpretation of echographic images.

***

If ultrasound impinges on objects which are comparable to or smaller than the wavelength of the wave, simple laws of reflection and refraction do not hold. In such a case, most of the wave passes by the object undisturbed. However, a small part of it is intercepted by the objects and ''reflected'' in all directions in space, with intensity strongly dependent on the direction. Such behavior is called scattering, and reflectors at which it occurs scatterers. The observed scattered wave is the sum of all contributions from individual scatterers.

***

ATTENUATION OF SOUND

We have seen that some of the wave energy may be diverted from the beam by reflection at boundaries between different media. The intensity of the wave may be reduced by the wave spreading (e.g., spherical wave or beam in the divergent part). We have also seen that a part of the wave energy can be lost from the beam due to the scattering in inhomogeneous media. Another mechanism of reducing wave energy is absorption. The absorption is present in all media, homogeneous or not, ranging from negligible to extremely large. It is a consequence of interactions between particles of the medium set in motion by a passing wave. As particles oscillate around their rest positions, they collide with the surrounding particles, with the final result being a slight heating of the medium. Thus, the medium is heated by the sound wave, and the energy used for heating is subtracted from the wave energy. The amount of the energy lost in that way depends on the medium and is proportional to the total wave energy, if wave amplitude is not too large. If this is so, the intensity of the wave drops off exponentially with the distance and may be described with a simple equation:

$$I(x) = I_0 * \exp(-\mu * x) \qquad (12)$$

where $I(x)$ is wave intensity at distance x in the direction of wave motion, I_0 is its initial intensity (the intensity at $x = 0$), and μ is the so-called absorption coefficient which is characteristic of a particular medium.

If the density of scatterers in the inhomogeneous media is constant, the reduction of the wave intensity due to the scattering may also be described with an exponential law as

$$I(x) = I_0 * \exp(-s * x) \qquad (13)$$

where s is the scattering coefficient, which is different from the absorption coefficient.

In tissues, ultrasound is at the same time absorbed and scattered, the absorption being the greatest of all factors in reducing ultrasound intensity. The reduction of the ultrasound intensity from initial impulse to the received echo in a diagnostic procedure may easily be greater than 80 or 100 dB! When absorption and scattering are present at the same time, total loss of intensity (or energy) is called attenuation. When the wave amplitudes are small, and exponential laws for scattering and absorption hold, as is the case in practically all diagnostic ultrasound applications, attenuation may also be described with a simple exponential law:

$$I(x) = I * \exp(-k * x)$$
$$k = \mu + s \qquad (14)$$

where k is the attenuation coefficient and is equal to the sum of absorption and scattering coefficients.

***

Sound waves are attenuated as they pass through media, which means that some of the wave energy is lost. The most important attenuation mechanisms are scattering and absorption. The absorption is the greatest factor in reducing intensity in medical ultrasound. It should be remembered that

1. Attenuation   = absorption + scattering.
2. Absorption   = loss of the wave energy due to heating the medium.
3. Scattering   = loss of the wave energy due to scattering the wave at the small inhomogeneities (particles) in the medium.

***

DIAGNOSTIC INSTRUMENTS

Ultrasound waves can be used for medical diagnostics in many ways, and depending on physical phenomena used, one speaks of echography, Doppler measurements, transmission tomography, etc. The most common ultrasonic diagnostic method at present is echography, Doppler being the second in usage frequency, and the rest still being developed for routine practice. We shall deal with these separately.

ECHOSCOPIC SYSTEMS

The principle of echoscopic systems is very simple. One sends out (transmits) into the body short pulses of ultrasound, about 1 μs long, and the echoes from different reflectors and scatterers in the body are detected by the same probe which was used for transmission. Knowing the speed of ultrasound and measuring the time necessary for the echoes to return enables one to calculate the distance from the probe to the reflectors. This procedure is repeated about 1000 times per second. The direction in which the ultrasound pulses have been transmitted is known so that one can determine the position of a reflector in the body in two dimensions. To convert this simple principle into working instruments requires high technology which we shall describe as far as its knowledge is needed for correct usage of the instruments and in acquiring new ones.

The measurement process takes a very short time, so the data contained in the echoes can be processed only by electronic means. The echoes are usually shown on a screen (most often a TV monitor) in the so-called A mode, B mode, and M mode. A and B modes are shown in Figure 7. In A mode (amplitude mode), the echoes returning from along the line of sight of the transmitting-receiving probe are shown as peaks proportional to the pressure of the reflected ultrasound pulses at their respective depths. While this method of display is nowadays rarely applied in practice, we shall describe it in more detail because it helps in understanding the principles of more complicated methods. The procedure is as follows. Approximately 1000 times per second, short pulses of ultrasound are transmitted into the body. At the time of transmission a line is started, being drawn on the CRT screen. The transmitted pulse is 1 μs long, and we have in principle 999 μs at our disposal for detection and registration of the echoes. Whenever an echo returns, it is received by the probe, amplified, and taken to the CRT where the line is deflected proportionally to the echo pressure so that a peak is drawn on the screen. The distance between the peaks on the screen corresponds to the same scale as the actual distance between the reflectors in the body. This basic method of obtaining an A mode display has at present been substituted by more indirect digital technology methods in many instances, but the principle remains the same. The

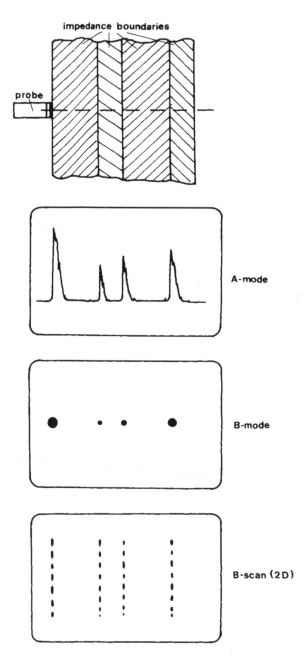

FIGURE 7. An illustration of A and B mode displays. Ultrasound pulses reflect from the tissue boundaries and are displayed as peaks or bright dots on the echoscope screen. If the transducer scans the body interior, the resulting bright dots in B mode sum up into a tomographic image of the scanned area.

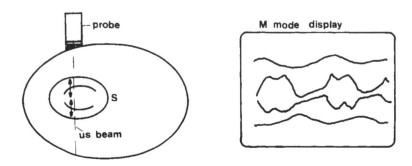

FIGURE 8. In M mode display, the still structures are shown as straight lines and the moving ones as wavy lines. Ordinate is the depth and abscissa the running time.

present description of handling the echo signals is an idealization in which we did not take into account attenuation of ultrasound in the body and the physical properties of the display devices. We shall deal with these problems in more detail later. A mode is still used in neurology, ophthalmology, and indirectly in tissue characterization.

In the B mode (brightness mode), the returned echoes are displayed as bright dots on the screen. The position of the bright dots corresponds to the positions of corresponding reflectors in the body. A pure B mode display simply represents the same data as the A mode image, only the echoes are now displayed as bright dots of different brightness instead of as peaks of different heights. A B mode scan, often referred to as the B mode image, contains data of multiple B mode images obtained by scanning a section of the body and displaying the echo data as a two-dimensional image. The echoscope is built in such a way that it automatically scans the body by steering an ultrasound beam in different and known directions and measures the time needed for ultrasound to travel to reflecting structures within the body and back. In this way one obtains the data needed for reconstruction of a two-dimensional image of body structures. In real-time systems which comprise a vast majority of all echoscopes, the transmitting-receiving probe is automatically moved or angulated, scanning in this way the interior of the part of the body in contact with the probe. In some systems this scanning movement is mimicked electronically using probes which contain many small transducers (transmitters-receivers). The echoes are shown on the screen as bright dots which represent signals which have first been arrayed in the processor memory and then processed (smoothed, interpolated, compressed, etc.). The actual basic data are collected along the beam, i.e., in the line of sight of the scanning probe. The actual (effective) section thickness depends on the probe, tissues, and scanner setting, as we shall describe subsequently. In practice, the tomographic section thickness varies between approximately 2 and 10 mm.

M mode (movement mode) is another way of representing ultrasonic echoes, in particular, the moving structures. Figure 8 illustrates obtaining an M mode display. Here, too, the echoes are represented as bright dots on the screen, but the transducer is continuously aimed in the same fixed direction of interest, for example, a heart valve. The system measures the depths of moving structures and displays these (changing) depths as a function of time. On an axis, usually the abscissa, is thus the running time, the other (usually ordinate) the reflector depth. In this way it is possible to quantitatively show the moving characteristics of structures like heart valve leaflets. M mode plays an important role in echocardiography, and elaborate methods for detailed processing of such data have been developed.

Other methods of displaying echo data have been devised, like C section (a section across the beam), quasi-three-dimensional displays, and mixtures of A and B modes. These methods are not usual and may be used in specialized fields.

***

Ultrasonic echoscopes transmit short pulses of high-frequency ultrasound into the body and measure the time, amplitude, and direction of the echoes returning from the body structures. These data are displayed as images representing either two-dimensional sections of the body or one-dimensional data about distances and amplitudes of movements of body structures.

The frequencies used are usually between 2 and 10 MHz. The ultrasound pulses are approximately 1 μs long and are transmitted at a rate of about 1 kHz.

***

MAIN BLOCKS OF AN ECHOSCOPE

An ultrasound echoscope uses short ultrasound pulses to obtain two-dimensional images in basically the following way.

Short pulses are transmitted from a transducer probe into the body. The echoes reflected from structures in the body are picked up by the same probe and then electronically processed to obtain a section image on a TV screen. Echoes which traveled a longer way return later and are more attenuated. Therefore, one must apply more amplification to the echoes which come from deeper structures in order to compensate for the attenuation. Such amplified signals are taken to the digitizing system which converts the data into a form suitable for digital storage. The procedure is controlled by at least one microprocessor. The content of the microprocessor memory is displayed on the TV screen. A simplified block diagram of a system capable of doing this is shown in Figure 9.

The probe is the crucial element of an echoscope, and its properties dictate many of the system characteristics. We shall deal with probes in some detail later and mention here only as much as needed for understanding of the block diagram. The probe contains one or more transducers which are capable of converting electrical energy into high-frequency mechanical vibrations and vice versa. The same transducers act as transmitters and as receivers. The probes are built in such a way that they can transmit and receive ultrasonic energy from different and well-defined directions.

In the beginning of a transmission cycle, the pulse generator (PG) generates a very short electrical pulse of some tens to some hundred volts in amplitude. This impulse is taken to the transducers in the probe via a control and delay unit which directs the electrical pulse to the appropriate transducer at the appropriate time. This delay and control circuit also handles in the opposite direction the signals generated in the transducers upon the return of the echoes. After the transmission of the short ultrasound pulse, the system waits for the echoes to return from the body. The amplifiers amplify and process the signals to make them suitable for further processing and display. There are several amplifiers, but the one which is of special interest and which can be manipulated with outside controls is the time gain compensation (TGC) amplifier, which has the capability to amplify the signals from deeper structures more than the ones from shallower regions, thus compensating for the attenuation of ultrasound in the body. The amplified signals which represent reflectors within the body are stored in a digital memory together with data on the depth and direction from which they returned. The depth is inferred from the time interval between the transmission

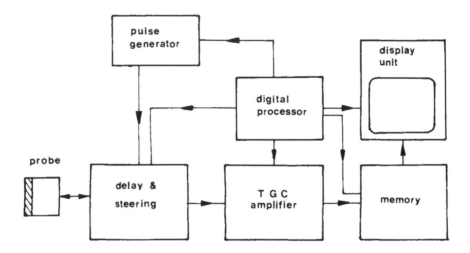

FIGURE 9.   Block diagram of an echoscope. A digital processor directs the pulses from a pulse generator via a delay and steering unit into the probe. Signals (echoes) from the probe are processed in the delay unit, taken to the TGC system, amplified, memorized, and prepared for display. The whole process is synchronized and coordinated by a digital processor (computer) and its software.

of the pulse and reception of the echo, taking into account the average ultrasound propagation speed in soft tissues of 1540 m/s. The direction is known from the probe steering data which are stored in the microprocessor controlling the scanning procedure. The data from the memory are taken to the display unit and shown on the TV monitor screen. One cannot simply display all the data contained in the returning echoes. The processing includes filtering out the carrier wave high frequency and compression of the amplitude range (dynamics) because the TV screen can display a much narrower span of brightness intensities than the actual range of the echo amplitudes. The transfer function which controls the relationship between brightness and echo amplitudes is not linear and can in many scanners interpolate dots between the actually collected data along the lines of sight of the probe. The generated image is better adjusted to human perception characteristics. Although this means "inventing" some data, the images generated in such a way are easier to read than the original images containing only the physical data actually collected.

Until the mid-1970s there was another type of scanner — the static scanner — which played an important role in obtaining good quality images. These systems, now rare, used probes with a single transducer which was hand moved by the operator who had the freedom of choosing the scanning format. The imaging was not real time (fast), but the images were of good quality and with a fixed geometrical relation to the patient couch. The position and the angle of the probe were measured by an electromechanical device from which the probe *was hanging*. This type of scanner requires a degree of manual dexterity not needed for the real time scanners.

TRANSDUCERS AND THE ULTRASOUND BEAM

As already mentioned, the transducer converts ultrasound (mechanical) signals into electrical signals and vice versa. The active element of a transducer is a piezoelectric ceramic element or a piezoelectric plastic foil. The property of a piezoelectric material is to deform under influence of electrical field and, conversely, to generate electrical charge on its faces, if it is deformed by mechanical stress. In echography, electrical pulses are taken to the faces of piezoelectric transducers, inducing vibrations in them which are transmitted into the body as ultrasonic vibrations. Conversely, the echoes from the body induce minute deformations of the transducers so that electrical charge appears at their faces which are covered with conductive layers and taken to amplifiers in the echoscope.

We must pay more attention to the volume in the medium (water, human body, etc.) which is occupied by this ultrasonic energy and which we call an ultrasonic beam. Figure 3 schematically shows the ultrasonic beam in front of a transducer. It is represented by curves which connect points of equal ultrasound intensity — the isointensity curves. A beam like this can be obtained only in nonattenuating media (degassed water is near enough to this for our purposes). In attenuating media, the actual intensity is modified by attenuation, but the echoscope will "see" an equivalent beam like the one in Figure 3 if the TGC amplifier is correctly adjusted.

The intensity is not sharply cut off, but gradually decreases to zero on the edges. If the transducer is focused, then the beam has a narrowing around the focus. Near the transducer, ultrasound intensity is irregular due to interference of ultrasound waves from different parts of the transducer face. Far from the transducer, ultrasound intensity decreases regularly and continuously. The two zones can be mathematically defined.

Ultrasound waves can be focused with lenses, mirrors, curved transducers, and electronically. Figure 10 illustrates the methods of mechanical fixed focusing. The lenses are built of plastic materials, and the shape of a focusing lens can be convex or concave, depending on ultrasound propagation speed in the lens material. Ultrasound mirrors are built as thin structures containing air in order to obtain nearly total reflection. During the production stage, a curved transducer is formed into a focusing shape (for example, paraboloid). All these focusing methods produce fixed focal distances determined by the characteristics of the focusing element. In practice, this means that there should be many different probes as many different foci are needed. Since the focusing zones are fairly long, the number of probes at one frequency would not be more than three, usually two. Electronic focusing is illustrated in Figure 11. One can electronically focus a beam only if the transducer is composed of separate elements which can be individually activated and which can individually receive signals from the body. In our example, the composite transducer consists of three rings, one within another. If we define a focus depth f along the transducer axis, we can see that the distances from different rings to focus f are different, so that ultrasound pulses need different times to reach f. If we now transmit from the outermost ring first, then from the second ring and, after another delay, from the central one, with the delays in transmission adjusted so that they compensate for the different travel times, then the ultrasound pulses from all three rings meet at the same time at point f. This in fact is focusing. The distance f depends on the delays and can be chosen by outside controls. Therefore, such a focusing system is flexible with a broad choice of focusing depths.

So far we have spoken about focusing at transmission. Reception focusing follows basically the same rules. In fixed-focus transducers the transmission and the reception characteristics are equal, and the round trip focusing is the result of both. In electronic focusing these two can be made different; in fact, one can make the receiving focus follow the ultrasound pulse as it transverses the body, thus making a nearly continuous "dynamic" focus.

Lately, a mathematical method for improving the resolving power of echoscopes, previously used only in military applications, has been implemented in medical echoscopes. This computed echography is based on the fact that if the response of a system on a simplest

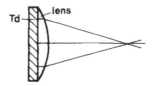

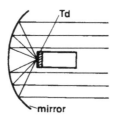

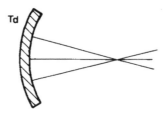

FIGURE 10.   Ultrasonic waves can be focused with lenses, mirrors, or curved transducers and combinations thereof.

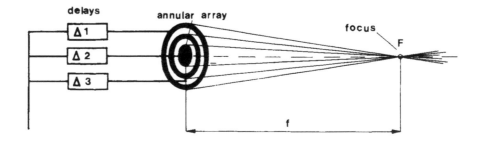

FIGURE 11.   An annular array consists of annuli of piezoelectric material which can be activated separately. The focus of such composite transducers can be adjusted by changing the delays. Larger delays between activations yield a nearer focus.

reflector is known, one can deconvolve (untangle) the effects of the beam shape from the real characteristics of the imaged object.

Properties of the ultrasound beam are very complicated, and we mentioned only the most important and those which are of greater practical importance to the user of modern scanners. Other characteristics of the beam, like side lobes (auxilary beams) and quantitative evaluation of beam properties, can be found in more detailed and dedicated literature.

So far, we have spoken only of the distribution in space; but the time distribution, the pulses, deserve mention. The pulses sent out from the transducer are short, usually two to four cycles long. This means that for higher frequencies the pulses can be made shorter, with consequent better depth (axial) resolving power. The actual length of such pulses is about 1 μs. This means that when defining the intensity of ultrasound, one must clearly state whether it is the average intensity or the intensity during one pulse itself. The difference is large and of utmost importance when considering possible hazards of ultrasound. The time-averaged intensity can be calculated by multiplying the intensity during the pulse with the ratio of "on" time (actual transmission time) to total time. If there are 1000 pulses per second and each of them has a duration of 1 μs, the ratio is 1/1000, i.e., the time-averaged intensity is 1000th of the intensity during the pulse duration. Of course, when considering possible hazards, one must also take into account the space concentration (focusing) by taking the ratio of the surface area of the transducer face and the area of the focal cross-section of the beam. So, when looking at some quoted intensity data, one must be aware of whether it is the so-called time-average-space-average (SATA) or space-peak-time-peak (SPTP) value. Looking at the matter in more detail, it turns out to be more complicated, but the basic logic remains the same.

***

A transducer is an element which generates an ultrasonic beam by converting electrical energy into ultrasound which is transmitted into the body. The same transducer converts ultrasonic echoes into electrical signals for image formation. The ultrasonic beam is of a tube-like shape. Ultrasound intensity in the beam decreases from its axis to the edges. Ultrasound intensity is irregular near the probe due to wave interference. An ultrasound beam can be focused with lenses, curved mirrors, curved transducers, and, when composite transducers are used, electronically. Focusing improves the lateral resolution of an echoscope.

***

ECHOSCOPE PROBES AND SCANNING SYSTEMS

The echoscope probe is a device containing one or more ultrasound transducers used for transmitting and receiving ultrasound. At present, the probes are built in such a manner as to automatically scan the interior of the body with which they are in contact via some coupling agent (oil, gel). They usually operate fast enough to give a real-time image, (i.e., about 20 images per second). Occasionally, the images are composed more slowly with an added quality in detail and resolution. The type of probe determines to a great extent the scanner properties and field of application.

Figure 12 illustrates a number of probes presently in routine use. Probe a is called a linear array. It contains a number of narrow, ribbon-like transducers, all of them separately connected to their cables. There are usually about 64 such transducers in a probe of a length between 5 and 12 cm. Each of the transducers can have additional grooves etched to improve some of the directivity characteristics. The width of the ribbon-like structure is too small to

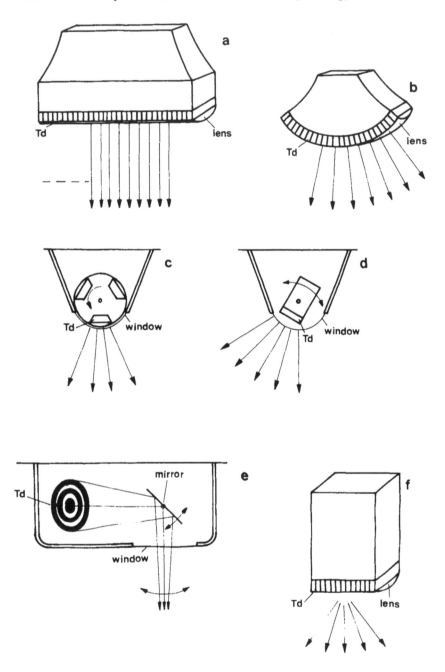

FIGURE 12.   (a) Linear array of probe consists of a series of narrow transducers (Td). A cylindrical lens focuses the beam in one plane; the other plane is electronically focused. (b) The curvilinear (convex) probe has the narrow transducers arrayed along a curved surface so that the image is trapezoidal. (c) The rotating mechanical sector probe contains three to five transducers mounted on a rotating wheel. Each transducer scans the media in front, and the images overlap in the scanner memory. Focusing is fixed with lenses. (d) A rocking sector scanner probe. Here, one transducer scans the interior of the body by rocking on an axis. (e) The annular array with an oscillating mirror. The annular array is used for electronic focusing on transmission and reception, and the oscillating mirror scans the interior of the body. (f) A phased array consists of a series of narrow transducers. Both the beam steering and focusing in the scanning plane are achieved with activation delays. The other plane has a fixed focus.

make a good beam, so that one must activate more than one transducer at a time in order to obtain a composite transducer much larger than the wavelength. A way to do this is to activate groups of transducers. For example, the first group may be composed of transducers 1 to 10, second 2 to 11, then 3 to 12, etc., all the way to the group 55 to 64. In this way, one obtains a shift equal to the width of a single transducer with an apparent composite transducer ten single widths wide. Furthermore, the shifting is actual scanning of the area in front of the probe, without any mechanical movement. In addition to the shifting (scanning), one adds delays to activation of single transducers in a group, thus obtaining electronic focusing as explained previously for the composite ring transducer. Of course, this electronic focusing applies only to one plane. In the other plane there is a fixed-focus lens. This type of transducer is mainly used in obstetrics, breast, and thyroid scanning.

Figures 12b and 12c illustrate the most commonly used mechanical sector scanners. They produce an approximately triangular image. In both types, the transducers are mechanically moved, thereby scanning the area in front of them. Probe b is a rocking probe, i.e., one transducer which is made to rock in front of an acoustical window in order to scan whatever is in front of the window. The rocking movement is not smooth, but stepwise, and the probe spends at each increment angle (step) the time needed for the transmission-reception sequence.

Probe c contains three to five transducers mounted on a turning wheel. Each of the transducers is activated and used only at the time when it traverses in front of the acoustic window. This movement is stepwise too, and the data are gathered along predefined lines with each of the transducers. In fact, the images obtained with the different transducers overlap. The property of the sector transducers is that they have a small acoustic window and can look to the side. Therefore, they are applied in gynecology, upper abdominal scanning, and cardiology. The probe in Figure 12d uses an annular array for focusing and an ultrasonic mirror for scanning. The ultrasound pulses are transmitted onto the mirror, and the echoes return to the annular array transducer via the mirror. The mirror itself is tilting, thereby transmitting the beam in different directions within the body.

The probe in Figure 12e is called a curvilinear probe (sometimes convex probe) and is basically built and activated like the linear array, but yielding an image format between the rectangular (like linear array) and sector format. The image looks like a trapezoid.

The phased array in Figure 12f has the transducers mounted in an array like the linear array, but it is much shorter (1 to 2 cm). In this case, both the focusing and the beam steering (change of its direction) are achieved with delays in activation of the arrayed transducers. The probe produces a sector image without the use of moving parts. For a long time this system was very esteemed in echocardiography, but was used less in upper abdominal scanning due to its problems with beam side lobes. At present, the problem of side lobes has to a great extent been solved in the higher class instruments by improved transducer design.

The probes, as described, are the most common types used in transcutaneous contact scanning. There is a large variety of ways to combine these principles and make adjustments for specific uses.

For ophthalmology and breast scanning, one often uses built-in waterbath probes and water transducers. Special probes for intraoperative use, for transvaginal, transvesical, or transrectal scanning, have been developed. Transesophageal probes for echocardiography have also been developed. Special attachments or holes in probes for puncture needle guidance have been developed in order to keep the needle within the scanning plane at a predetermined angle. All these are adaptations of the above-outlined principles to specific and special needs. To describe them all would require many printed pages, but they can all be understood if the basic principles are clear.

***

Echographic scanning probes contain one or more transducers and scan the interior of the body by changing the direction and the position of their lines of sight, i.e., the lines along which the transmission and reception of ultrasound waves takes place. The scanning can be done by mechanical movements or electronically. The basic formats of scanning are the rectangular (achieved with linear arrays) and sector (achieved with sector probes). There exist scanning modes in between these two formats and combinations thereof. Linear probes are better suited for obstetrics, breast, and thyroid examinations, and sector probes for gynecology, upper abdomen, head, and heart scanning.

***

ATTENUATION COMPENSATION — THE TGC AMPLIFIER

We have already mentioned the TGC system which is used for compensation of ultrasound attenuation in tissues. The TGC stands for time gain compensation (in some scanners the short STC is used). Echoes which return from deeper structures must be amplified more than those coming from shallower regions because they have been absorbed and scattered more. The later the echo returns, the more it is amplified by the TGC system. The gain changes from minimum to the maximum once during each transmission-reception cycle. The echoes decrease approximately exponentially with depth, so the TGC gain must increase approximately exponentially with time for good compensation. The actual attenuation coefficients are not exactly known, and in practice, the compensation is done qualitatively by adjusting the system for an image approximately equally full of detail and echoes at all depths. This is done with outside controls for basically the following aspects of the TGC system:

- Near gain controls the gain of echoes from shallow structures (decibels).
- Far gain controls the gain for the echoes from the deepest structures (decibels).
- Slope controls the rate at which the gain changes from the near to the far setting (decibels per centimeter).
- Overall gain control increases or decreases all gains by the same factor (decibels).
- Delay controls changes at the moment at which the gain starts to rise.

In some systems (usually the more expensive ones), the gain at different depths can be changed separately by a set of sliding controls, i.e., the slope of the compensation curve can be made different from the preset exponential dependence.

The graphical representation of the TGC curve in Figure 13 shows the increase of the gain linearly for simplicity. The possibilities for modification as described are illustrated in this figure.

Figure 14 illustrates some examples of misadjustment and adjustment of the TGC curve. The operator must understand the TGC system well in order to obtain a good image. Some modern echoscopes have a TGC system which automatically adjusts the amplitude of deeper (later arriving) echoes to equal the signal amplitude of shallow echoes. There are different ways of achieving the balance of the signals coming from different depths. The system which operates fairly well in some machines adjusts the gain for each line of sight separately.

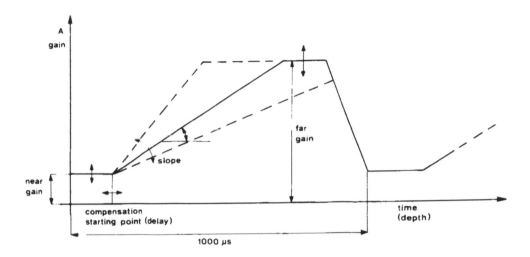

FIGURE 13. An illustration of the TGC amplifier gain variation. The near, the far, and the overall gain can be changed. The compensation slope and starting point (delay) can be adjusted.

While such automatic systems make the operation easier and require less skill, it always produces average images and often obscures some telltale artifacts which are otherwise useful for image interpretation. In the section on artifacts, we shall show the usefulness of these interpretations of the images.

***

The TGC (STC) system allows one to obtain an image which contains an approximately equal amount of echoes at all depths. This is done by adjusting the near and the far gain, the slope between the two, and the starting point of the compensation (delay). In some machines this function is preset and can be additionally adjusted. In others one has to adjust the whole TGC. In addition to this, there is always an overall sensitivity control which acts either on the transmission power or on the overall gain, or both.

***

SIGNAL PROCESSING

Everything we have described so far is signal processing and conditioning which enables us to see in an appropriate form ultrasound reflection phenomena on the body structures. Some of the processing can be adjusted by outside controls, and some of it is inaccessible to the operator. Basically, the signal processing can be divided into preprocessing and postprocessing. The preprocessing is all the manipulations of the signal which are done before it is stored in the echoscope memory. Manipulations with the signal already stored in the memory is called postprocessing and can be done on a displayed frozen image.

Moving frequency filters, which take into account the change of the frequency spectra with the depth, change of the transducer aperture with the scanning depth, and similar processing, are normally inaccessible to the operator.

We have described the main preprocessing methods so far. In addition to these, one can sometimes change the signals by operations like differentiation in order to enhance the

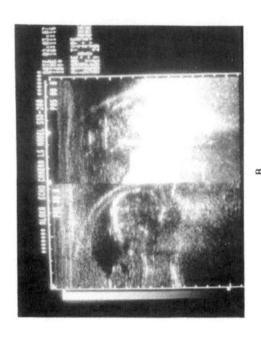

B

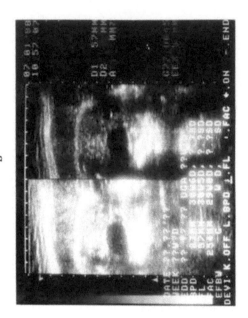

D

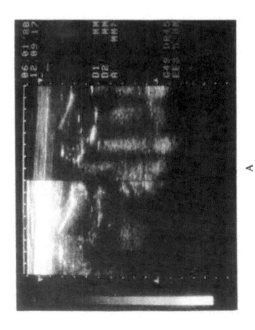

A

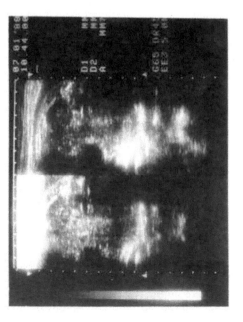

C

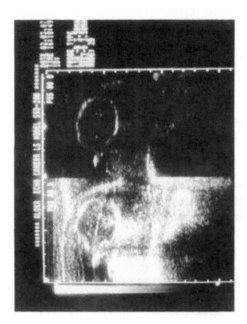

F

E

FIGURE 14. TGC adjustment. (A) Fetal cross-section with the kidney (to the right) and a part of the urinary bladder (left). The left image has too high of a near gain, so the kidney is poorly outlined. The right image is made with too low an overall gain, but the kidney contour is well outlined. (B) Fetal head and heart sagittally. The left image is well balanced; one sees the head and thorax well. In the right image, the far gain is too high — the posterior part of the image is saturated (completely white with no details). (C) Fetal femur. The right image is made with low sensitivity so that bones can be measured satisfactorily. The left image is made with too high a near gain, and the femur is shown too long due to the effective width of the ultrasound beam. (D) Fetal urinary bladder. The left image is made with too high an overall sensitivity (gain and transmitted power), so that the bladder fills in with the electronic "noise". In the right image, the overall sensitivity is too low, so that the urinary bladder is poorly outlined. (E) Fetal cross-section at the liver level with the spine cross-section top left. The left image is made with a low dynamic range (25 dB) so that the outline is very clear. The right image has a broad dynamic range (50 dB) and the outline is less clear. (F) Fetal head cross-section. The left image is made with high sensitivity and low dynamic range. The brain structure is seen, but coarsely, and the skull bone is shown with poor resolution due to too high a sensitivity. On the right image the brain cannot be seen at all due to very low sensitivity and dynamic range, but the skull bones are outlined with good resolution.

boundaries. The basic principle in using preprocessing is to collect all the relevant data and store them in the digital processor memory. Once the data are stored and the image frozen, one can additionally process them to make them more visible or more suitable for registration. These postprocessing functions include the change of the gamma function of the display, boundary enhancement, and windowing. The gamma function is the nonlinear dependence of the brightness of the dots on the screen on the actual echo signal amplitude. Changing this dependence may make the image more pleasing to view, but it is more important for recording and should be adjusted to the particular type of film or printer used for recording. The boundary enhancement is basically a process which brightens the parts of the image where the signal amplitude changes faster and so emphasizes the boundaries and edges. Windowing is a feature which allows one to show on the screen only the echoes within a limited and controllable amplitude span.

A useful method of pre- or postprocessing is rejecting of the lower signals and the displayed echo dynamics control. Some of the previously mentioned processing methods also influence the dynamics. The dynamic range can be defined as the ratio of the largest and the smallest quantity of some kind. So when speaking about the dynamic range of bright dots seen on a TV monitor, we mean the ratio of brightnesses of the brightest and the least bright spot still visible on the screen. On the other hand, one can define the dynamic range of the actual echoes of interest, which include all the echoes which bear some significance in the diagnostic procedure. This dynamic range is much larger than the dynamics of the brightnesses on the screen which represents them. The dynamic range of brightnesses on a common TV monitor is about 20 dB, while we would like to see echoes of dynamic range of 100 dB or more. It is achieved by "squeezing" the larger dynamic range into the smaller by using a compression amplifier. The result is an image in which the brightness increments for larger echoes are smaller if the effective echo dynamics are larger. In practice, this means that a 70-dB dynamics image must be viewed in subdued light, while a 40-dB image can be appreciated at normal room lighting.

RESOLUTION

Resolution is the ability of a system to discern two nearby reflectors. Quantitatively it is the smallest distance of the two reflectors which can be seen in the image. The resolution is a property of the scanner design, of its settings, and of the reflectors. Due to the different mechanisms of measuring the depth and the position of ultrasonic reflectors, as explained before, the resolution in depth (axial) and in width (lateral) is generally not the same, and it is common to refer to the axial and lateral resolution of ultrasonic scanners.

The lateral resolution is the ability to resolve reflectors distributed across the beam, and in this case, the effective beam width is the main parameter which influences resolving power. The axial resolution is resolution along the line of sight of the ultrasonic beam and depends on the ability of the system to correctly detect arrival times of the echoes. In virtually all echoscopes the axial resolution is better than the lateral resolution.

Lateral Resolution

In order to explain the lateral resolution, we shall imagine two adjacent reflectors, as illustrated in Figure 15, positioned side by side so that the scanning beam first images one of them and then, after being moved some steps to the side, it "sees" the other reflector. If the beam were ideally thin, it would image the two reflectors as two dots on the screen. However, since the beam has an effective width, it will start imaging the first reflector when

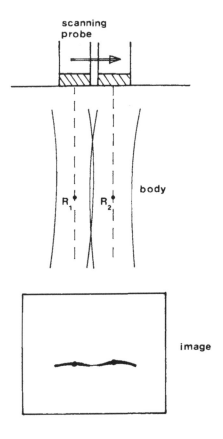

FIGURE 15. If the reflectors are at a distance smaller than the effective beam width, they merge in the echoscopic image.

it first reaches the edge of the effective beam and continue to do so until it leaves on the other edge as the beam is scanned across it. If the second reflector enters the beam before the first has left it, the scanner will have some reflector in the beam all the time and will thus show both reflectors as a single line without a gap between them.

The simplest way to improve the performance of the imaging system is to somehow make the beam narrower. This can be done by taking a better focused transducer, but there are some limitations to this with particular equipment. However, in real situations there may be another way of improving the resolution by manipulation of the existing controls on the scanner. Figure 16 illustrates an effective ultrasound beam at two different settings of the transmitter power with the TGC setting unchanged. If the beam edge is considered to be at -30 dB, the effective beam is narrower at a lower transmitter setting, that is, for all the reflectors which reflect sufficiently to still be detected at this lower setting. Note that the ultrasound intensity in the center is lower as well. However, the faintest reflectors will vanish from the image at this setting. While we spoke about reducing the transmitted power with receiver or TGC gain unchanged, the same logic is valid for reducing the overall sensitivity (gain), i.e., for reducing either or both the transmitted power and gain. If a particular type of reflector can be detected with at least -15 dB of sensitivity, then it will be detected only within the narrow -15-dB area in the center of the beam, while a strong

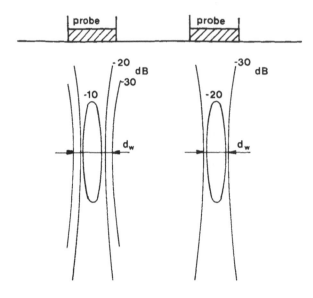

FIGURE 16.   At a lower sensitivity the effective beam width is smaller. The still detectable reflectors are seen with better resolution.

reflector which yields detectable echoes at -30 dB will be shown across the whole beam width. The human body contains both strong and faint reflectors, and so the effective beam width and, consequently, the resolution is different for different types of reflectors within one and the same image. The resolution of fainter reflectors is better. On the other hand, the resolution power of the human eye varies with light intensity and contrast. The eye resolution of faint traces on the screen is so poor that one cannot indefinitely improve lateral resolution by reducing the system sensitivity. In practice, we often image structures containing strong reflectors (fetal bones) and faint reflectors (fetal brain). If the overall sensitivity is sufficient to image the fetal brain, the resolution of the bony structures is poor, i.e., the bones are shown wider than they actually are. When the sensitivity is reduced in order to image the bones correctly, faint reflectors (brain and similar) disappear from the image.

In practice, the imaging is done in two steps: first, inspection imaging at sensitivity which is sufficient to show all structures and organs, and second, at reduced sensitivity for measurement of the bony structures.

Axial Resolution

Axial resolution is the ability of the scanner to separately image two reflectors along the line of sight (the beam). It depends on the length of pulses which represent separate reflectors. If the pulses are too long or the reflectors are too near each other, the pulses will overlap in time, will pile up, and show as one long line along the line of sight instead of as two separate dots, one below the other. The axial resolution can be improved by reducing the effective pulse length. One method would be to use a scanner with shorter pulses. Shortening the pulses of a fixed central frequency results in broadening the frequency spectrum and requires more expensive amplifiers. Increasing the frequency with the same number of cycles in one pulse would be one solution, but this approach cannot be pushed too far due to poorer penetration of higher frequency pulses. The distance along which the ultrasound intensity decreases to one half of its initial intensity (half intensity distance) is roughly inversely proportional to the central frequency of the ultrasound pulse.

However, the axial (depth) resolution can be manipulated. The logic is fairly similar to what we had with lateral resolution, namely, the smaller but still detected pulses are displayed with a better resolution than the larger ones. This improvement is, as before, achieved at a cost of losing the small echoes from the image.

In commercially available scanners the axial resolution is always better than the lateral which in practice means that small blood vessels can be better imaged when perpendicular to the scanning beam. This fact becomes especially important in duplex Doppler scanning.

In the previous illustrations we used a linear scanning for illustration because in this type of scanning it is very simple to separate axial from lateral characteristics, since one corresponds to depth and the other to width. In sector scanning there is still the difference between the axial and the lateral resolution but these notions must strictly be related to the lines of sight, i.e., to the directions in which the ultrasound beam "looks" during the scanning process. Equal depths in the above sense represent points on an arc with the center in the (virtual) center of transducer rotation. So the axial resolution would be used if the tiny blood vessel followed an arc centered at the probe rotation center.

***

The ability of an echoscope to resolve adjacent details is called the resolution. The resolution can be divided into lateral (sidewise) and axial (depth) resolution. Axial resolution is better than the lateral. If strong and faint reflectors are shown in the same image, then the resolution is better for the smaller echoes. Reduction of the dynamics of the image by a separate control or by reducing the system sensitivity (overall gain) improves the resolution of strongly reflecting structures, but removes the weakly reflecting structures from the image. In practice, this means that one must reduce the sensitivity of the system when performing bone dimension measurements, even at the cost of not seeing soft tissue structures at that time.

***

THE DOPPLER EFFECT

The Doppler effect is named after its discoverer J. C. Doppler, an Austrian who lived and worked in Czechoslovakia in the 19th century. The actual effect is the fact that a receiver which relatively moves to a wave transmitter receives a wave, the frequency of which depends on the velocity of the relative movement. This phenomenon is known to us in everyday life as the change of the motor or siren sound pitch when a motorcar passes by.

While the effect is originally related to a separate receiver and transmitter, in present medical use the actual situation is different. The transmitter and the receiver of ultrasound waves are mounted in the same probe and are virtually at the same position, while the reflectors move. The reflectors in this case are usually erythrocytes as one measures the blood velocity. Ultrasound waves are transmitted towards the moving erythrocytes and reflected waves are analyzed and compared to the transmitted wave frequency. If the frequency of the reflected wave equals the transmission frequency, the reflector had no velocity relative to the transmitter-receiver assembly. If the frequency of the received wave is lower than the transmitted wave frequency, the reflectors have been moving away from the probe. A reflected frequency higher than the transmitted one signifies the reflector movement

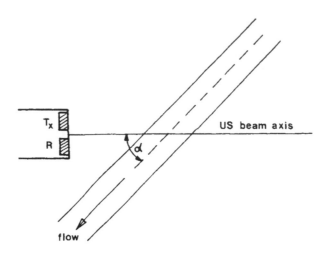

FIGURE 17.   In general, the flow of the ultrasound reflectors (eryth-rocytes) is at some angle α to the ultrasound beam. The Doppler effect exists only if there is a component of flow parallel to the ultrasound beam.

towards the probe. The difference between the transmission frequency and the received frequency is called the Doppler shift. Generally the situation is illustrated in Figure 17. The movement is at some angle to the probing ultrasound beam. The blood velocity v can be calculated from the Doppler shift Δf, transmitted frequency f, ultrasound speed c, and the angle between ultrasound beam and the flow using the following equation:

$$v = \frac{\Delta f \cdot c}{2f \cos\alpha} \tag{15}$$

The transmitted frequency f and the ultrasound speed c are known. The Doppler shift Δf and the angle α must be measured. The Doppler shift measurement is done automatically in the electronic system while the angle must be assessed in some way, usually by measuring the angle between the beam and the blood vessel on an ultrasonic image of the area under examination.

Equation 15 shows that the measurement is not possible if the angle α is 90° (right angle) because the blood velocity turns out to be infinite irrespective of the rest of the parameters. This is a consequence of the fact that there is no component of the velocity towards or away from the transceiver, so the Doppler shift is zero for any velocity. In the present Doppler instruments, this is really so. However, one of the approximations in deriving Equation 15 was that the ultrasound wave is a plane wave, which is not exactly true for wave beams. Some studies show that there exist theoretical grounds for blood velocity measurements even at right angles. In order to use this new principle, some technological modifications must be done to the instrumentation.

So far, we have assumed a single flow velocity within a blood vessel. This is not the case in reality, as we shall see in the next section.

DOPPLER SYSTEMS
Continuous Wave Doppler

This system transmits and receives ultrasonic waves continuously. The transmission and the reception transducers are mounted in a probe side by side. Joint directivities of the transducer and the receiver form the sensitivity volume or the "beam". It is actually a beam of the transmitted ultrasound combined with the area in the body from which the receiving transducer receives the reflected ultrasound. The frequencies of the transmitted and the reflected ultrasound are compared and their difference measured. The difference is the Doppler shift. Any movement along the beam axis will add to the measured Doppler shift. If the beam crosses two blood vessels the measured Doppler shift is a mixture of Doppler shifts from both vessels. This means that the continuous wave (CW) system has no depth (axial) resolution. This system, on the other hand, has no basic limitations to the measured velocity, although for practical reasons the present commercial instruments use a filter which cuts off the lowest frequencies (and thus the lowest velocities).

In practice it is fairly unusual for all the blood across a blood vessel to flow at a single velocity (this is called plug flow). In normal blood vessels of more than 3 mm in diameter the flow velocity increases as we move from its walls towards the center (axis). The dependence is parabolic and the flow is called laminar because it behaves as if the blood stream consisted of thin tubiform flow lamina slipping one over the other. Measuring the Doppler shifts and thus the blood velocities will always yield a spectrum of different velocities at any instant of time. This spectrum yields a spectrum of the corresponding Doppler shifts which can be displayed as a real-time spectrum in which the abscissa is the running time and the ordinate represents the Doppler shifts. Since there are many different velocities at any instant, they are shown as gray scaled dots. Another possibility is to show the average Doppler spectrum over a time interval, in which case the abscissa represents Doppler shifts and the ordinate the fraction of energy contained at particular frequency.

CW Doppler instruments are very useful clinically, but have no depth resolution. If the anatomical situation requires depth resolution, because many blood vessels would overlap along the line of sight, one can use a different type of instrument — the pulsed Doppler system.

Pulsed Doppler Systems

If the Doppler shift is measured on pulses transmitted into the body, we speak about a pulsed Doppler system. If the Doppler shift is measured after the time needed for ultrasound pulses to reach a certain depth and return, the system can separately measure blood velocity in different blood vessels along the line of sight. In this way depth resolution is achieved. When speaking about the Doppler shift of a pulse, one must be aware of the fact that a short pulse has a broad content of different frequencies — a broad spectrum; therefore, the Doppler shift applies to all the frequencies contained, but not to the same extent. A longer pulse has a narrower frequency spectrum, but a poorer axial resolution because it is longer in space as well as in time and therefore the place of measurement is less well defined. This brings us to the first limitation of the pulsed Doppler system — the sensitive volume. This volume is the space occupied by the ultrasonic pulse, its length defined by the (time) length of the transmitted pulse and its width determined by the beam width. Doppler measurements are obtained from within this volume. If we wish to measure the average flow in a blood vessel, the sensitive volume must be larger than the vessel. If the blood vessel to measure is small, a small sensitive volume is needed in order not to include the neighboring blood vessels.

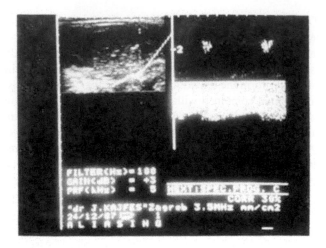

FIGURE 18.   In a pulsed Doppler system, the ability to measure high velocities is limited by the pulse repetition frequency (in this case, 5 kHz). The high blood velocity at systole is too high and the sampling theorem is violated, resulting in the display of the highest velocities as opposite velocities (the two patches in the upper part of the spectrum — right in the image). Compare to Figure 19, where the same spectrum is correctly measured.

Another limitation, and a very serious one, is the Doppler sampling rate needed to measure high blood velocities. A pulsed Doppler system measures the blood velocity by sampling what is going on in the blood vessel at the rate of ultrasound transmission. This rate is limited by the ultrasound speed and by the depth of the blood vessel. As explained earlier, the scanner must wait with transmission of the next pulse until all significant echoes return to the probe, or else the results would be ambiguous. On the other hand, the sampling theorem, a basic physical theorem, requires the sampling rate to be twice as high as the highest frquency contained in the measured phenomenon. This means that if there are Doppler shifts of up to 500 Hz, the sampling rate (pulse transmission rate) must be 1000 Hz at least. Since the pulse rate is limited, the ability of the system to measure high velocities is limited too. The deeper the blood stream to be measured, the more severe the limitation.

If, in spite of the too low sampling rate, we measure a blood velocity too high to satisfy the sampling theorem, the system will show the frequencies higher than the limit frequency as too low, or in terms of flow interpretation as negative flow. Figures 18 and 19 illustrate the failure of a pulsed Doppler system to measure the high-flow velocity in the heart, where the highest (jet) flow velocity is shown as artifactual negative flow (i.e., flowing in an opposite direction). This phenomenon is called aliasing (i.e., spectrum aliasing).

One could increase the sampling rate and intentionally introduce some degree of ambiguity in order to measure higher velocities. If this is done (sometimes commercially called high-PRF Doppler), the solution of the ambiguity, i.e., measurement of flow velocity at two or three different places, rests with the operator who must position the beam in such a way that only one of the positions at which the Doppler measurement is made is actually within the flow.

When actually using the system, one must move the sensitive volume to the depth of interest, adjust its appropriate width, measure the angle between the beam and the flow, and then measure the Doppler shifts.

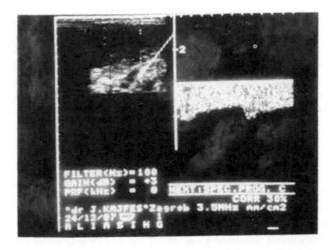

FIGURE 19. A duplex image consists of a B mode scan and the Doppler spectrum. The angle between the ultrasound beam and the flow, the depth, and the blood vessel dimensions can be measured in the section image. The flow characteristics can be appreciated from the Doppler shift spectrum (right in the image). The PRF is sufficiently high (8 kHz) so that there is no aliasing (compare to Figure 18).

Duplex Systems

Doppler systems described so far (CW and PW) can yield useful data if the blood vessel is correctly aimed at. Sometimes, in the neck and peripheral vessels, the aiming can be done on the basis of anatomical knowledge, but in the abdomen the Doppler measurements cannot be done blindly. In this case one uses the duplex systems in which an imaging echoscope is linked with a Doppler system. The Doppler probe is fixed to or integrated into the imaging probe so that a fixed geometrical relation between the image and the Doppler beam is guaranteed. One first obtains the image of the region and blood vessel of interest, and then aims, using electronic indicators on the screen, the Doppler beam into the blood vessel. In pulsed Doppler systems there is an indicator on the screen showing the depth of the sensitive volume (see Figures 18 and 19).

Examples of such duplex images are shown in Figures 18 and 19. There are two basic types of duplex systems. In the first, the imaging and the Doppler transducers are different and the Doppler transducer is fixed to the imaging transducer at a fixed angle. The Doppler beam comes from the side of the imaging transducer. In this system one can well use the good depth resolution of the imaging probe while having the Doppler beam at 50 to 60° from the side (Figures 18 and 19). Its disadvantage is that it needs a relatively large ultrasound window into the body to accommodate both transducers.

The second type of the duplex system uses the transducers in the imaging probe, which is often of the sector type. This system has the advantage of a small ultrasonic window and the disadvantage that it is harder to use the best imaging resolution together with a good Doppler measurement angle.

Mapping Systems (Color Doppler)

The Doppler systems described so far are able to measure the flow at one place in the body (PW) or along a line within the body (CW). The measurement is quantitative, but gives data about the flow at one place at a time. This is useful and sufficient when the measurement place can be defined on the basis of an image or otherwise. If, however, we are not sure about the places where we wish to measure the flow or it is very anomalous like in a heart defect with septal shunts, one first describes a semiquantitative image of flows in two dimensions, only after which may it be of interest to measure some of it quantitatively. During the last 5 years, flow mapping systems have been developed which yield a two-dimensional map of flow, with flow towards the transducer coded in different shades of one color (for example, red) and away from the transducer in shades of another color (for example, blue). The flow with large variance may be indicated green or as a mixture (mosaic) of red, blue, and yellow. The color flow map is overlapped with the gray scale echographic image of the region.

The technological procedure for obtaining the flow images is different from the CW or conventional pulsed Doppler system, but the limitations are those of a pulsed Doppler system since it uses ultrasound pulses to sample the flow. One of the properties is that the present commercial systems cannot measure flow at 90° to the beam, which yields gaps in flow which must correctly be interpreted. At too high velocities for the sampling rate the aliasing occurs as illustrated in Plate 1* for a blood jet.

The absolute values of velocity can be obtained only when the angle is known. The value of average velocity in a blood vessel is important if we wish to measure the volume flow when the volume of blood per second can be obtained by multiplying the average velocity (average over the blood vessel and over at least one heart beat) with the cross-sectional area. Very often one does not wish to assess the volume flow, but the impedance of some vascular system. Namely, if the impedance of some tube is low, the velocity of blood at systole and diastole will be high, and if the resistance to flow is high (for example, due to some obstruction), it will reflect as low flow velocity and sometimes even negative at diastole. For such an estimation, one needs to compare the flow at different parts of the heart cycle in relative terms; therefore, its scaling factor introduced by the angle is immaterial. For such relative measurements angle α does not have to be known, but it must be within about 0 to 60° because at angles near 90°, the measurement error becomes prohibitively large.

Doppler measurements require additional knowledge as similarly extensive as imaging echography itself. Therefore, it cannot be done as a small addition to imaging, even more so because the time needed for Doppler studies may be about the same as for an imaging study.

PUNCTURE AND INTERVENTION GUIDANCE BY ULTRASOUND

All manufacturers offer probes or probe attachments for puncture needle guidance. Such guiding devices are necessary because the puncture needle is imaged only if it is within the scanned (imaged) section. If the needle is only partially within the imaged section of the body, then the end of the needle seen on the screen is not the real end, but the position where the needle leaves the scanning plane. The actual needle tip may be deeper and to the side of what is seen on the TV monitor. In order to keep the needle within the plane of the image, guiding devices have been designed which keep the needle within the scanning plane under some angle to the beam axis or, alternatively, there is a hole in the probe (usually the linear array probe) so that the needle comes into the body along the lines of sight. The

* Plate 1 appears following page 38

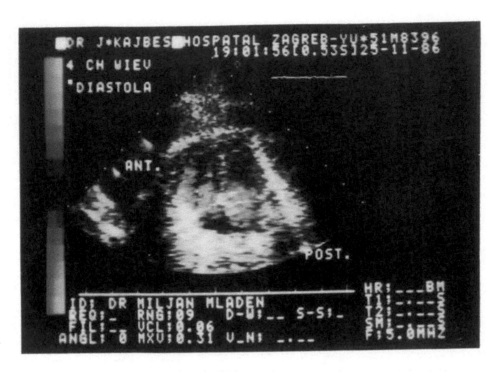

PLATE 1.   Aliasing in a two-dimensional mapping Doppler. Two jets of blood in the right and left ventricle were inflowing from the atria. In the right ventricle (left in the image) a part of the jet is reflected back (blue at far left), but there is a blue patch in the center of the orange-colored jet, indicating that at this position the Doppler shift is too high to be correctly measured and, due to aliasing, is shown as a flow in the opposite direction.

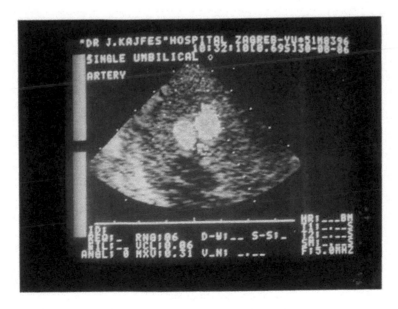

PLATE 2.   A case of single umbilical artery syndrome as seen on color flow mapping. Note almost the same width of flow indication in the artery and vein.

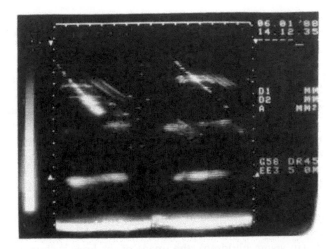

FIGURE 20.   In this waterbath experiment the puncture needle is within
the scanning section along its full length on the left side, but leaves the
imaged section 1 cm from the tip on the right. A situation like this would
cause a missed puncture because the tip position would be misjudged. The
strong sideways and parallel reflections are side lobe and reverberation
effects.

needle is better seen if it comes from the side (Figure 20), but there is a blind area before
the needle enters the imaged section. On the other hand, if the needle follows the lines of
sight, the visibility of the needle is poor, but there is no blind area of this type. In all cases
it should be possible to detach the puncture attachment during the puncture without with-
drawing the needle from the body. The needle visibility is good in liquid media (like amniotic
fluid), while in the parenchema, one sometimes sees only the tip when the needle is moved.
Some experimental systems which make the tip of the inserted device sensitive to ultrasound
promise better solutions to the problem in future. In practice, it is important to bear in mind
that the main cause of missed punctures guided by ultrasound is the noncoincidence of the
imaged section and the needle.

LOOKING AT THE IMAGE, ARTIFACTS

In principle, the whole echoscopic image is an artifact; however, when the image contains
data which do not fit into the basic explanation of the imaging process given so far, we call
these artifacts. Furthermore, looking and interpreting echographic images requires a continuous awareness of the way the image is formed.

1.   The image is a tomographic image of some thickness which varies with depth.
2.   In the majority of the presently used echoscopes, only the amplitude information about
     the echo is used, thus discarding any information about the phase and frequency
     spectrum.
3.   There are two major factors influencing the amplitude: the reflectivity and the atten-
     uation coefficient. Therefore, from one amplitude measurement two unknowns must
     be determined, which requires the operator to estimate or guess one of them and adjust
     the scanner (TGC) accordingly.

4. The scanner shows echoes which arrive later as being deeper along the line of sight and only along the lines of sight, even if they come from another area due to reflection or refraction by specular structures.

Knowing these facts we shall now compare the actual echographic image with an ideal one, i.e., an image in which all the data about reflectors and scatterers in the body are shown with the same imaging quality and where equal structures look equal.

A cyst is shown as an echo-free space if there are no scatterers in the liquid. However, the liquid usually attenuates the waves less than the surrounding tissue, and, therefore, the gain of the TGC will be too high for all the echoes from behind the cyst. Therefore, there is an echo enhancement behind cysts. Furthermore, ultrasound waves meet the side walls of the cyst at a critical angle and are partly reflected out of the beam (lost) or refracted. The result may be side shadows, as seen in Figure 21.

Bones attenuate and reflect ultrasound more than soft tissues, and ultrasound speed is higher than in soft tissues. As a result, it is difficult for ultrasound to image bones, and even if this succeeds (in young children), the image of the bone is shortened along the time measurement axis. Behind bones there is an ultrasonic shadow (Figure 21).

Gas bubbles are very strong reflectors and introduce reverberation and usually obscure everything behind them. Therefore, ultrasonic echography is not very useful for diagnostics in the areas which contain gas or air (Figure 21).

The reverberation artifact occurs not only in such extreme cases as gas bubbles, but always when there are reflective layers orthogonal to the scanning lines of sight. It occurs in the subcutaneous layers and appears in the image in the form of parallel lines behind the actual layers (Figure 21).

Reflection of ultrasound from tilted specular reflectors can result in images of structures to the side of the reflector, to be shown as being behind the reflector, very much in the way a periscope looks around an obstacle.

A strongly reflecting structure surrounded by weak reflectors will look wider than it is and can mimick protruding structures (for example, protruding into the urinary bladder) (Figure 21).

Oval structures, like cross-sectioned muscle bundles, can act as biconvex lenses and can sometimes tilt the beam, thereby causing errors in the direction information.

ACQUIRING A NEW SCANNER

The suitability of the first scanner acquired can prejudice the whole future of an ultrasonic clinic. The basic rule is to buy equipment which will do what is needed and which the presumed operator can become familiar within a reasonable time.

The following basic facts should be considered when acquiring new instruments:

- The generation cycle in ultrasound diagnostic instruments is approximately 2.5 to 3.5 years. This means that within this time from the release of a new modern instrument there may be other instruments in the market which use some qualitatively new technological approach to the diagnostics.
- The training of an ultrasound diagnostician takes 1 to 2 years, but the education never stops.
- The quality of instruments is presently reflected in the price, and there exist approximate instrument classes, both in price and performance. While this may sound obvious these days, only 15 years ago there were too few experts for ultrasonic diagnostics in the world, and the price-quality correspondence was not so real as it is today.

The following data must be known or estimated before acquiring a scanner:

- Which area is to be scanned and scanner usage (obstetrics, obstetrics and gynecology, flow measurement, use of the scanner by other departments in time sharing).
- How many diagnosticians (physicians and sonographers) will do the scanning.
- What is the prevailing pathology to be diagnosed.
- Any administrative (customs, approval, etc.) procedures which lengthen or impede purchase of new instruments.

The basic necessary quality has been well defined in the WHO report no. 723. We shall cite these specifications in short here:

- The scanner should be a combination of linear and sector type, or curvilinear type. The standard transducer should be of 3.5 MHz center frequency with an optional 5 MHz. Fixed in-slice focusing is desirable. The sector angle should be 40° or more, and the linear array should be 5 to 8 cm.
- The linear array is likely to be used more for obstetrics, neck, and breast, and sector scanning is used more in the upper abdomen and in gynecology. The 3.5 MHz gives a fair compromise between penetration and resolution for any scanning depth, but in child scanning, a 5-MHz option can be very helpful.
- Controls must be simple and well arranged. Overall sensitivity (gain or output) control must be built in, and TGC could be preset with the possibility for variation.
- With a well-chosen TGC for obstetrics and one for the upper abdomen, one can do fairly satisfactory examinations in more than 80% of cases by varying the overall gain only. The frame rate should be 15 to 30 Hz for the linear array scanner and at least 5 to 10 Hz for the sector.
- A linear array is likely to be used for fetal heart action detection, and, therefore, it should have a higher frame rate than the sector which is likely to be used in areas where fast motion is not imaged. An exception is echocardiography.
- The frame freeze is necessary at a density of 512 × 512 × 4 bits (16 gray levels). One pair of omnidirectional calipers with quantitative readout is required. Patient identification input onto the screen (e.g., number, date, etc.) should be provided. A hard copy recording facility is necessary, but the choice should be made on the basis of the number of the images made. The cheapest equipment does not always produce the cheapest photographs, but depends on the materials used.

Postprocessing is not included in WHO requirements. Many of the present scanners have too many postprocessing possibilities which are either unused or confusing. A choice of two or three imaging dynamics can be put to good practical use, while a larger number of options is likely to be unused.

The WHO specification is obviously not a description of the simplest scanners available, but one which can be used in roughly 95% of common pathology. For the rest of the pathology more sophisticated instruments are needed. On the other hand, there exist some simpler scanners with only a linear array probe which can usefully be put into use, but are not suitable for gynecology. The vaginal probe can be very useful in gynecological examinations and for early pregnancy, but as a procedure has a smaller throughput (less than half) and can routinely be used in larger departments. Vaginal scanning cannot be used occasionally because of the very different perspective and orientation of the image which may confuse an occasional user.

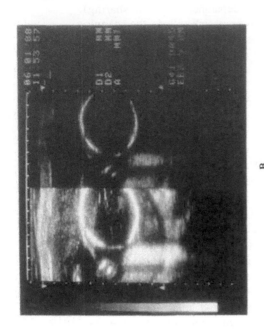

B

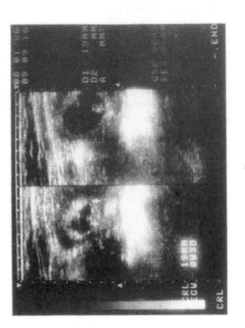

D

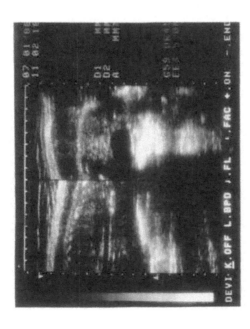

A

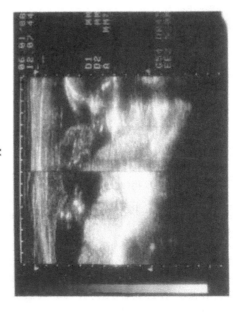

C

FIGURE 21. Artifacts. (A) Liquid-filled structures are imaged as echo-free spaces, as seen in the fetal aorta (left) and the fetal urinary bladder (right). Behind the urinary bladder there is an echo enhancement due to TGC overcompensation because of low attenuation in the bladder. Sometimes, as in the right image, the enhancement can be seen anteriorly, also due to the second order reflections from the flat and parallel surfaces of the liquid-filled structure. (B) Fetal head and arm cross-section imaged with high (left) and low sensitivity (right). There is a second line protruding from the skull which lies parallel to the skin surface. The line is caused by the side lobe of the too wide effective beam imaging the part of the skull which lies parallel to the skin surface. Behind the bones of the arm one can see an ultrasound shadow on the placenta at the bottom. At lower sensitivity (right) the effective beam width is smaller and there is no artifact in the skull bone image. (C) Fetal bones in the legs are shown with "wings" on the left image, which illustrates the effective beam width for strong reflectors. In the right image there are some parallel lines in the amniotic fluid (see also Figure 14E) due to reverberation of ultrasound in the parallel layers below the skin surface. (D) Early pregnancy transversally (left) and sagitally (right). Echoes which can be seen cranially from the uterus on the right image appear all the way to the bottom of the image, but are in fact multiple reflections from gas in the bowel immediately below the abdominal wall.

Distance measurements are mandatory, and area and circumference measurements are used occasionally and may be useful, but the tables of standard values are rare for these parameters.

In ordering probes, one must consider the depths to be scanned. It is important to note that the possibility to change the focus in linear and curvilinear probes acts only in the axial plane, while the lateral plane has fixed-focus with a lens. Therefore, it is of real advantage to have different probes for different depths with appropriate focus distances and frequencies. Annular arrays are focused in both planes.

Biometric tables are presently a regular item in the scanner microprocessor memory and are useful. One should, however, read the original paper on which the table is based, in order to perform the measurement in the original manner. The puncture guidance facility is needed. Puncture attachment must be sterilizable in some way and acquired in sufficient numbers so that more than one puncture per day can be performed.

A hard copy of the image on the screen can be made in different ways with varied quality and price. The requirement for fast development is important when the picture is to accompany the report. In practice, this can be done using instant photography or thermal paper printing. Instant photography can be done with very inexpensive cameras in good quality, while the thermal printer is a considerable investment. On the other hand, the thermal paper is much cheaper than the instant film per copy. Therefore, one is advised to use instant photography for small numbers of hard copies and thermal printers when large numbers of hard copies per scanner are made.

Multi-image cameras which use single-sided X-ray films yield high-quality images with good gray scaling and are best suited for viewing on light boxes.

A good image can be obtained with a common photographic camera directly from the screen of the TV monitor. The quality is good, but the disadvantage is in the time needed for development of the film and print production.

The Doppler measurement facility may be sold as an option, but its price is an essential fraction of the total price. The time and education needed for the Doppler measurement are comparable to those for a thorough echographic B mode examination. Therefore, the Doppler instrument can be put into use only if the additional time and manpower are there. Again, an occasional usage of Doppler measurements may result in serious mistakes. The development of the Doppler instrument is at least as fast as that of the echoscopes, and the technological "scissors" wait here for overeager buyers as well.

The output ultrasound intensity must be stated in the technical data. While the final word on the safety of diagnostic ultrasound has not yet been stated, international professional organizations, like the American Institute for Ultrasound in Medicine and Biology, The European Federation for Ultrasound in Medicine and Biology, The British Medical Ultrasound Society, etc., are publishing carefully studied guidelines on the state of safety knowledge. A manufacturer which does not publish the transmitted intensity data may be withholding vital information.

Service is another parameter in acquiring equipment. It is always a good idea to ask other users of the equipment about the quality of the service and maintenance, because the most expensive instrument is a nonworking one.

SUGGESTED READING

1. **Wells, P. N. T.,** *Biomedical Ultrasonics,* Academic Press, London, 1977.
2. **Woodcock, J. P.,** *Ultrasonics,* Adam Hilger, Bristol, 1979.
3. **Seto, W. W.,** Acoustics, McGraw-Hill, New York, 1971.
4. **Kremkau, F. W.,** *Diagnostic Ultrasound,* Grune & Stratton, New York, 1974.

5. **Rose, A.,** *Vision, Human and Electronic,* Plenum Press, New York, 1973.
6. **The Bioeffects Committee of the AIUM,** *Safety Considerations for Diagnostic Ultrasound,* AIUM Publications, Bethesda, MD, 1984.
7. The Watchdog Group of the European Federation of Societies for Ultrasound in Medicine and Biology, *Eur. Med. Ultrason.,* 6, 8, 1984.
8. **Blackwell, R.,** New developments in equipment, *Clin. Obstet. Gynaecol.,* 10(3), 371, 1983.
9. **Kremkau, F. W.,** Biological effects and possible hazards, *Clin. Obstet. Gyneacol.,* 10(3), 395, 1983.
10. **Kasai, C. and Namekawa, K.,** Real-time two-dimensional blood flow imaging using ultrasound Doppler, in *Recent Advances in Ultrasound Diagnosis,* Vol. 5, Kurjak, A., Ed., Excerpta Medica, Amsterdam, 1985.
11. *Handbook of Chemistry and Physics,* 70th ed., Weast, R. C., Ed., CRC Press, Boca Raton, Fl, 1989.
12. **Kurjak, A. and Breyer, B.,** The use of ultrasound in developing countries, *Ultrasound Med. Biol.,* 12, 611, 1986.

Chapter 2

CURRENT OPINION ON THE SAFETY OF DIAGNOSTIC ULTRASOUND

G. Kossoff

Diagnostic ultrasound has been in clinical use for over 25 years, and during this period it is estimated that tens of millions of patients have been examined by the method. With the salutary experience gained from the early indiscriminate utilization of X-rays, the question of the safety of diagnostic ultrasound has been the subject of considerable attention, and a large number of studies have been undertaken to investigate the biological effects of ultrasound. To date, there has been not one independently confirmed investigation which has demonstrated that ultrasound at diagnostically utilized dosages has any significant biological effect on mammalian tissues, and for this reason, all national and international societies on medical ultrasound advocate that no restriction should be placed on the utilization of the technique when it is indicated on clinical grounds.

Yet controversy continues to surround the application of the method, particularly in the examination of the fetus. Several factors are responsible for this situation. The performance of the equipment continues to improve through the design of more powerful transmitters and more efficient and more highly focused transducers which could lead to greater fetal exposures. As the subject of sonography matures, new scanning techniques and new procedures are being developed. For example, some consider endovaginal scanning as capable of increasing the fetal exposure, while introduction of pulsed Doppler techniques has seen the utilization of pulses significantly longer than those used for imaging, and this potentially could result in larger amounts of energy to be beamed at the fetus. Other procedures change the previously investigated irradiation regimes. Flushing procedures used in oocytes recovery techniques introduce microbubbles of air into the follicle, and the presence of those bubbles, which are not normally present in tissue, could allow different mechanisms of interaction to take place which could ultimately harm the fetus. The question of dosimetry also poses assessment difficulties. While good progress has been achieved in the measurement of acoustic output when it is generated into water, calculation of ultrasonic exposure to the fetus is difficult, and this leads to the uncertainty in estimating the fetal dose. Finally, to date, all ultrasonic biological investigations at diagnostic dosages have been negative in their outcome. The safety of any technique cannot be unequivocally demonstrated by such negative-effect studies in that one can always postulate that a sufficiently sensitive or long-term end point had not been tested. To overcome these limitations some authorities have proposed the establishment of some form of risk-benefit relationships for ultrasonic examinations.[1,2] Unfortunately, there is insufficient information on both these parameters to allow the implementation of this proposal. This climate of relative uncertainty has led a respected administrative authority to set, on an arbitrarily chosen criterion, the upper limit of permissible acoustic output and has encouraged the issue of unscientifically based alarmist statements by investigators not working directly in the field.

The resolution of the question of safety can only come about by analysis of data from studies which have been structured to conform to rigorous scientific standards. Steps are being taken to achieve this aim, in particular, through the activities of various organizations and societies.[3] The issues are, however, complex and will take some time to resolve.

Nevertheless, even today there is a considerable amount of data to allow a reasonable assessment of the relative safety of the technique. This is based on information that has been obtained from epidemiology studies, animal experiments, *in vitro* irradiations, and study of physical mechanisms of interaction of ultrasound with tissue.

Epidemiology investigations into safety of diagnostic ultrasound have been undertaken since 1969. The majority of these have been similar in structure in that they consist of a retrospective investigation of status of children who were exposed *in utero* and who at the time of study ranged in age from 3 months to 12 years. The population sample size has generally been of the order of 500 exposed and an equal number of control children, while the end points which have been investigated range from a search for increased incidence of malformation or of cancer through reduced birth weight to adverse physical and neurological developmental effects.

Since the demonstration of increased incidence of leukemia in infants exposed to X-rays *in utero*, the possibility that ultrasound could do likewise has been of continual concern. Two major studies have, however, failed to identify any increase in childhood carcinoma in a population of 555 and 1731 children, respectively.[3] In Japan, the potential increase in the incidence of congenital abnormalities was investigated by comparing results between periods of 1966 to 1968 when ultrasound was not used, to those of 1978 to 1980 when Doppler and sonography were utilized.[3] Of 3036 deliveries in the first period, 77 abnormalities were found, compared to 53 anomalies in 2492 deliveries in the second period. The incidence of anomalies of 2.54 vs. 2.13% was not statistically different, suggesting that ultrasound does not increase the overall rate of anomalies.

A number of studies have attempted to determine whether ultrasound exposure results in a reduced birthweight. Some of these illustrate the difficulties and the care which must be exercised in the interpretation of the data. One study, for instance, reported a small yet statistically significant difference in the number of low birth weight in children in the exposed group.[3] However, 2 years later, a reevaluation of a subset of that data consisting of 425 exposed children and 381 matched for hospital delivery and previous pregnancy complications found no significance in the birth weights.[3] In another study, 300 pairs of siblings who were matched for sex, birth order, and reason for ultrasound examination were assessed and no adverse effect on the height and weight in children up to 6 years of age was found.[3]

The interpretation of results obtained with epidemiology studies must take into account the limitations of these studies. These include factors associated with uncertainty in estimating and controlling the ultrasonic exposure. No control in any of the studies was exercised over the gestational age at which the fetus was examined. In most instances the examinations were performed in the 2nd and 3rd trimester, while it would be reasonable to expect that the fetus is most at risk in the 6th to 12th week of pregnancy during the most active period of organogenesis. Other difficulties are associated with problems of matching the exposed population with the controls and the relatively short follow-up time used in most studies.

Probably the most serious limitation relates to the relatively small population size examined, which makes statistical analysis difficult. The likelihood of detecting a change depends on the relative increase in the incidence of the effect, and a small but important change requires study of a large population of exposed patients. The minimum sample size N needed to conclude that an observed increase is significant is given by

$$N = Z^2 P_0 (1 - P_0)/(P - P_0)^2$$

where Z is the standard variate at the required level of significance, P_0 is the proportion of cases in which the event occurs naturally, and P is the proportion of cases in which the event occurs after the exposure.

For example, naturally occurring anomalies occur at a frequency of 2.5% and suppose that the exposure by ultrasound increases overall incidence by 0.5 to 3.0%. To detect the presence of an event at a 95% level of confidence, the value of the standard variate must be set at 1.65. The minimum sample size required to observe the occurrence of the increase is

$$\frac{1.652^2 \times 0.025 \times (1 - 0.025)}{(0.03 - 0.025)^2} = 2654$$

which is about two to four times the population sample used in most studies.

If, however, an event such as anencephaly, which occurs more rarely, is to be investigated, then a much larger sample is required. Again, if, for instance, the incidence of anencephaly is increased by 10% from its natural occurrence of 0.10 to 0.11%, then the minimum sample size necessary to detect this increase would be one quarter of a million patients. The example is not trivial in that at this rate of increase the ultrasonic examination of 10 million patients would result in the birth of an extra 1000 anencephalic infants.

From these considerations the results of epidemiology studies indicate that diagnostic ultrasound does not produce any large increase in devastating or life-threatening effects at birth or children up to 6 years of age. Further studies would, however, have to be performed on much larger populations to determine if the examination exercises more subtle physiological or long-term delayed or genetic effects. Because of the difficulties in conducting such long-term studies, they may be impractical to implement, and investigation of such potential effects must be undertaken by other means.

The extensive literature on the effect of ultrasound irradiation on the developmental processes of animals has been reviewed in the report by the National Council on Radiation Protection and Measurements.[4] The results of various experiments on small animals, such as mice, using continuous wave (CW) exposure have shown that above a threshold intensity there appears to be a sigmoid relationship between the incidence of prenatal mortality and exposure intensity, while the incidence of malformations appears to be related to the stage of gestation at exposure. During organogenesis, CW exposure with sufficiently high intensities and durations can lead to a variety of embryotoxic effects. These include decreased fetal weight, which tends to be linearly related to the product of duration and the square of intensity. No clear demonstration of increased incidence of mortality or malformations has been obtained when pulsed ultrasonic regimes were employed.

Animal experiments thus demonstrate that there appears to be a threshold level of intensity below which no effects are obtained, that most of the observed effects seem to be thermal in origin, and that the deleterious effects are noted only at exposure regimes which are much higher than those used clinically. Because of size and species difference, unequivocal statements on safety, however, cannot be made on the basis of results obtained with animal experiments.

The majority of studies on biological effects of ultrasound have been conducted using *in vitro* irradiation of suspensions of cells. These allow the accurate measurement of a wide range of parameters of the irradiating field, ready changes in experimental conditions, and the utilization of sensitive end points to study the effects of the irradiation. Further homeostatic mechanisms which operate *in vivo* to maintain constant cellular environment are not present, and *in vitro* systems are, therefore, more easily perturbed to demonstrate an effect. On the other hand, *in vitro* studies have several inherent disadvantages. The exposure situations between *in vivo* and *in vitro* experiments are very different, and it is highly likely that different mechanisms of interactions dominate. For instance, thermal mechanisms which play such an important role *in vivo* due to absorption of energy by tissue are mostly absent in the nonabsorbing aqueous solutions used *in vitro*. It is also virtually impossible to extrapolate an *in vitro* bioeffect observation to predict a potential hazard *in vivo*. The main value of *in vitro* experiments, therefore, lies in enlarging the understanding of the interaction of ultrasound with living cells and in the identification of effects which may be subsequently demonstrated *in vivo*.

In vitro experiments have demonstrated that ultrasound interacts with cells at clinically utilized exposure. The main mechanisms of interaction which have been identified using CW exposure are associated with gas bubble activities, where radiation pressure forces attract cells to the oscillating bubbles, causing acoustic microstreaming which can disrupt cell content. The only repeatable effects from diagnostic pulsed conditions have been associated with cavitation phenomena in suspensions, where air bubbles are present and have shown effects such as platelet aggregation and the killing of *Drosophila* larvae and eggs. Under normal conditions air bubbles of the type required to allow the initiation of cavitation events are not present in tissue. More recently, diagnostic pulses at the upper limit of intensity have been shown to have a small effect on the nucleus by causing a slight increase in sister chromatid exchange in the chromosomes of irradiated cells. The potential hazard meaning of this observation is not clear, nor is it certain that this effect would be obtained under *in vivo* exposures.

The main mechanism of interaction of ultrasound with tissues are thermal, mechanical, and those associated with stable and transient cavitation. The thermal mechanism is simply the effect of heat due to selective absorption of ultrasound by tissue. The extent of the heating is determined by a number of factors such as the coefficient of absorption by tissues, the heat loss due to conduction and blood flow, and the spatial intensity distribution of the ultrasonic field. The specification of the ultrasonic output is complex, and in the case of pulse excitation, requires measurements which depend on the shape of the pulse waveform. Because of thermal inertia consideration, this is less important in the study of effects due to thermal mechanisms, where the specification of power based on the measurement of the spatial average-time average intensity (I_{SATA}) is adequate.

Various models have been described which describe the likely temperature elevations in tissues, taking into account the typical acoustic and physical properties of tissues. Most of these conclude that irradiation of indefinite duration at an I_{SATA} less than 100 mW/cm² would result in a temperature elevation of under 0.1°C and would therefore be harmless to tissue. The intensity output of diagnostic imaging equipment is generally less than this value, and for this reason most authorities believe that thermal mechanisms do not have an important role in the potential harmful effects of diagnostic ultrasound procedures.

Mechanical effects due to ultrasound result primarily due to radiation forces set up in the ultrasonic field. These can become relatively large if standing waves are set up and can cause blood cells to form corresponding bands in small blood vessels and to impede blood flow. Standing waves can only be set up in quasicontinuous excitation exposure regimes, and effects due to these have not been demonstrated *in vitro* at intensity levels below 10 W/cm². They are therefore considered unlikely to have an important role in any potential deleterious effects of pulsed diagnostic ultrasound techniques.

Cavitation effects require the presence of microbubbles of gas or vapor and are associated with activities surrounding these bubbles. Stable cavitation describes the alternating change of dimensions of gas bubbles which draw the surrounding liquid toward and away from them, setting up strong forces near their surface area. Transient cavitation describes the phenomenon of the rapid collapse of a gas bubble. Associated with this collapse are regions of high pressure and temperatures which can release free radicals which, in turn, can damage cells. Stable cavitation is only set up in continuous excitation exposures, and neither types

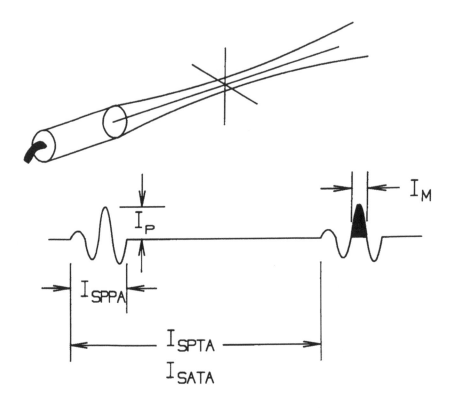

FIGURE 1. Five intensity parameters used to specify acoustic output of sonographic and pulsed Doppler equipment.

have been observed in *in vitro* experiments at intensities below 10 W/cm². Transient cavitation may be set up with short pulses of the type used in diagnostic applications. It has the potential to cause harmful effects, and attention is being focused to study these effects.[5] To date, transient cavitation *in vitro* has been noted only to happen under experimental conditions requiring the presence of nuclei, and no study has yet been able to demonstrate the presence of any of its effects in mammalian tissues at clinically utilized dosages.

One of the positive achievements on the issues of safety has been the good progress that is being attained, at an international level, on techniques to measure the various parameters of acoustic output of pulsed diagnostic equipment. Indeed, progress is being achieved at such a rate that in the reasonably near future, manufacturers will be in a position to provide detailed information on the acoustic output of their equipment and recommend modes of operation to ensure minimum exposure to the patient.

A schematic of a typical pulse generated by sonographic equipment is shown in Figure 1. Five parameters of intensities have been utilized to specify the nature of the pulse. The intensity I_p refers to the peak instantaneous intensity, and it is reasonable to expect that some of the mechanical and cavitational mechanisms are determined by this parameter. At the higher output levels generated by diagnostic equipment, nonlinear properties of water severely distort the transmitted pulse, spiking the positive pressure component while reducing the negative pressure swing. The sharp positive pulse can be difficult to measure accurately because the high-frequency components can set up an oscillatory response in the measuring equipment. For this reason some authorities advocate the specification of the maximum

TABLE 1
Maximum Acoustic Output in Water Generated by
Diagnostic Ultrasound Equipment Commercially
Available in 1976

Intensity	Cardiac	Vascular	Ophthalmic	Fetal
SPTA (mW/cm²)	730	1500	70	180
SPPA (W/cm²)	350	350	110	350
I_M (W/cm²)	550	550	200	550

intensity (I_M), which represents the intensity averaged over the largest half cycle. If this half cycle is sinusoidal, then the I_p is twice the I_M. Some equipment use pulses which are longer than others. The spacial peak-pulse average intensity (I_{SPPA}) is therefore also employed to characterize the amount of intensity associated with the pulse. To take into account the differing repetition rates used by equipment, the spacial peak-temporal average intensity is (I_{SPTA}) is also employed in the specification. Finally, the I_{SATA}, which takes into account the intensity averaged over the beam width, is also used by some in the specification of the output.

In order to restrict the indiscriminate increase in acoustic output of modern equipment, the Center for Devices and Radiological Health of the U.S. Food and Drug Administration has introduced a document entitled the 510(k) Guide for Measuring and Reporting Acoustic Output of Diagnostic Ultrasound Medical Devices. This document specifies the maximum value of three intensity parameters of acoustic output that was generated by commercially available equipment manufactured in 1976. It also states a policy decision that modern sonographic or pulsed Doppler equipment may be introduced on the market in the U.S. without having to undergo investigational approval if the acoustic output of this equipment expressed in terms of these three intensity parameters is below the maximum quoted values.

The FDA maximum acoustic output values as measured in water are shown in Table 1. As illustrated, vascular applications are permitted to employ the highest values, reflecting the low signal strength obtained from flowing blood. The lowest values apply to ophthalmic studies. This should not be taken to imply that the eye is potentially the most sensitive organ to damage by ultrasound, but simply that ophthalmic equipment in 1976 utilized these low outputs. The 510(k) Guide also quotes the maximum value of "*in situ*" values. These are computed from the values which apply as measured in water, subject to changes determined by attenuation by tissue of selected dimensions. The "*in situ*" values are generally a factor of two or more less than the values in water. Care must be exercised to note which values of output are being quoted because of the natural tendency by manufacturers to quote the lower numerical value figures.

The effect of the 510(k) Guide has been to encourage the majority of manufacturers to limit the acoustic output of their equipment to under the FDA maximum values, although there have some notable exceptions. Table 2 shows the typical output of one of the current instruments capable of function in the transabdominal, endovaginal, and pulsed Doppler mode. In the imaging mode, this equipment generates an output approximately half that of the FDA maximum value. Also shown for comparison is the I_{SPTA} of a typical, continuous, 5-MHz Doppler equipment. Because of the continuous nature of the excitation, the sensitivity of the equipment is high and its acoustic output is therefore low. The table also shows the output of the equipment functioning in the pulsed Doppler mode. To keep the sensitivity high, the equipment employs a high I_{SPTA}, but still within the allowable limit. In the Doppler mode, the equipment utilizes pulses which are about ten times longer than those needed for

TABLE 2
Acoustic Output of Typical Modern Sonographic and
Pulsed Doppler Equipment

| | | | Doppler | |
| | | | Pulsed | |
Intensity	Imaging (3.5 MHz)	CW (5 MHz)	Abdominal (3.5 MHz)	Vaginal (6 MHz)
SPTA (mW/cm²)	60	20	110	30
SPPA (W/cm²)	160	—	10	2
I_M (W/cm²)	250	—	10	2

imaging. To keep the temporal average intensity within the allowable limit, the equipment reduces the pulse amplitude, and for this reason employs, as shown, low values of I_{SPPA} and I_M.

Endovaginal scanning, in the first instance, may be considered to be capable of increasing the fetal exposure because less energy is lost in transmission between the transducer and the fetus. An alternate point of view has also been put forward which proposes that endovaginal scanning should allow lower exposures because less energy is lost in reception between the fetus and the transducer and, therefore, less energy is required to return the same strength signal. The table shows that for this equipment this is indeed the case in that a lower I_{SPTA} is employed and even lower I_{SPPA} and I_M are utilized.

In summary, all of the information available to date suggests that at presently utilized levels, diagnostic ultrasound entails a minimal if not zero risk, and there is no scientifically based reason to restrict a sonographic examination when it is indicated on clinical grounds. A number of issues, however, remain to be resolved. For this reason all national ultrasound societies advocate that ultrasound should be used prudently. It should be performed only by qualified personnel using techniques which minimize patient exposure, i.e., minimum output and examination dwell time consistent with acquiring the required acoustic diagnostic information. Frivolous and unwarranted use of the method are considered to be unacceptable and unethical practice and are strongly discouraged.

REFERENCES

1. **Nyborg, W. L.,** Optimization of exposure conditions for medical ultrasound, *Ultrasound Med. Biol.,* 11, 245, 1985.
2. **Wells, P. N. T.,** The prudent use of diagnostic ultrasound, *Ultrasound Med. Biol.,* 13, 391, 1987.
3. **Kossoff, G. and Barnett, S. B., Eds.,** First symposium on safety and standardisation of ultrasound in obstetrics, *Ultrasound Med. Biol.,* 12, 673, 1986.
4. Biological Effects of Ultrasound, Mechanisms and Clinical Implications, NCRP Rep. No. 74, National Council on Radiation Protection and Measurements, Bethesda, MD, 1983.
5. **Carstensen, E. L.,** Acoustic cavitation and the safety of diagnostic ultrasound, *Ultrasound Med. Biol.,* 13, 597, 1987.

Chapter 3

ULTRASOUND IN THE FIRST TRIMESTER

Asim Kurjak and Vincenzo D'Addario

INTRODUCTION

The first trimester of pregnancy is characterized by a dynamic period of both embryonic differentiation and growth. Ultrasound, more than any available technique, can provide objective and reliable information of an early pregnancy at any moment in time. For this reason, diagnostic ultrasound can give direct information about the embryo and fetus itself in the first, most critical period of intrauterine life and, therefore, has a highly important role to play in the assessment of early pregnancy and its complications.

SONOGRAPHIC ASSESSMENT OF THE EMBRYONIC PERIOD

The embryonic period of pregnancy extends from fertilization of the ovum to the development of the fetus, that is to say, to the end of the 7th week after conception or to 9 weeks of menstrual age. At that time all the major structures of the fetus have begun to develop and the fetal period of pregnancy starts.[1] Continuous improvements in the resolution of ultrasonic imagery, and particularly in the introduction of the new high-frequency endovaginal probes,[2] have made a detailed study of this crucial period of pregnancy possible, allowing specialists to recognize some hitherto ignored or misinterpreted structures.[3] For this reason the ultrasonographer must have a good understanding of the embryologic events which can be imaged by ultrasound.

The aim of this chapter is to correlate the main events in the early stages of human development with the normal ultrasonic findings of early pregnancy. When referring to the age of pregnancy the term "menstrual age" (weeks of gestation starting from the first day of the last menstrual cycle) will be used instead of the more precise term "gestational age" (weeks of gestation starting from the day of fertilization), used by the embryologist, because this convention is generally used in clinical circumstances.

BASIC EMBRYOLOGY

Although the earliest stages of human development cannot be visualized by current sonographic equipment, they will now be briefly described in order to enhance a clear understanding of the sonographic findings during the embryonic period of gestation.

Fertilization occurs in the distal third of the Fallopian tube. Fusion of the two gametes produces a zygote, a single cell which, while passing through the Fallopian tube, segments into a number of daughter cells (blastomers), forming a morula. By day 4 or 5 after conception, these cells have arranged themselves in a hollow sphere (blastocyst) which is carried from the Fallopian tube to the uterine cavity (Figure 1). A cluster of cells (the inner mass) now differentiates at one pole of the blastocyst and will later become the embryo proper, while the wall of the blastocyst (trophoblast) will give origin to the placenta.

At the 6th or 7th day, the surface of the blastocyst corresponding to the inner cell mass attaches to the rashly vascularized endometrium (Figure 1) and lies deepest when implantation is complete.

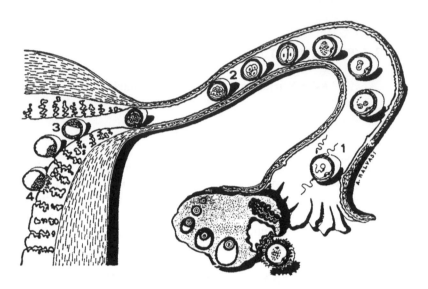

FIGURE 1. Early stages of human development (1 = fertilization; 2 = stage of morula; 3 = stage of blastocyst; 4 = implantation).

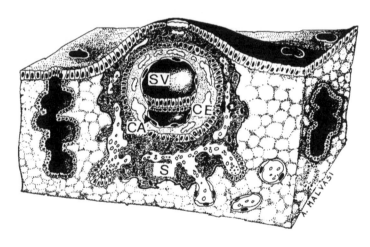

FIGURE 2. Schematic drawing showing the trophoblast differentiated into two layers, syntitial (s) and cytotrophoblast (c), the amniotic cavity, the primary yolk sac (SV), the bilaminar disk embryo between the amniotic cavity (A) and the secondary yolk sac, and the extraembryonic coelom (CE) (12 d of gestation = 4 weeks of menstrual age).

After implantation, the trophoblast becomes thicker, differentiates into two layers (syntitial- and cytotrophoblast) and finally gives origin to the chorionic villi. The inner cell mass differentiates into a bilaminar disc; the outer layer (ectoderm) forms the floor of the primitive amniotic cavity, while the inner one (endoderm) represents the roof of the primitive yolk sac (Figure 2) and later covers the wall of the secondary yolk sac completely (Figure 3).

IMPLANTATION

The earliest ultrasonic sign of a normal intrauterine pregnancy is the visualization of the so-called "gestational sac" inside the uterus during the 5th week of amenorrhea.[4] At this

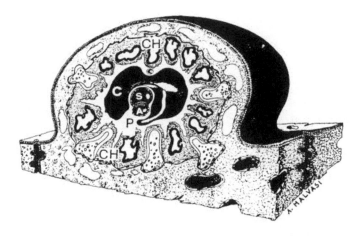

FIGURE 3. Menstrual age of 5 weeks: the developing chorionic villi (CH) cover the entire surface of the chorionic sac; the embryo, interposed between the amniotic cavity (A) and the secondary yolk sac (S), is surrounded by the large chorionic cavity (c) and is connected to the chorion by the connecting stalk (p).

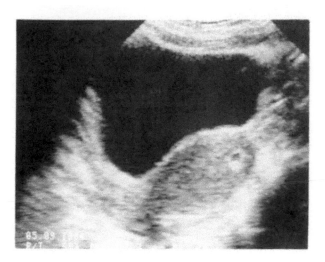

FIGURE 4. Ultrasonic appearance of the gestational sac at 5 weeks of menstrual age. The sac shows a uniformly thick wall due to the developing chorionic villi; the echo-free area inside the sac corresponds to the chorionic cavity (see Figure 3).

stage of pregnancy, the developing villi cover the entire surface of the chorionic sac (Figure 3); for this reason the gestational sac ultrasonically appears as a little ring with a uniformly thick wall (Figure 4).

The gestational sac is usually eccentric within the uterine cavity (Figure 5). This fact can be used as a differential sign to identify centrally located pseudogestational sacs[5] typical of ectopic pregnancies. However, the exact site of implantation, whether on the anterior or posterior surface of the endometrial cavity, can only seldom be identified at a very early stage, when it is possible to recognize the relationship between the gestational sac and the

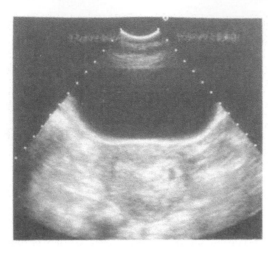

FIGURE 5.   Transverse scan of a 5-week pregnant uterus showing the gestational sac eccentrically located in the uterine cavity.

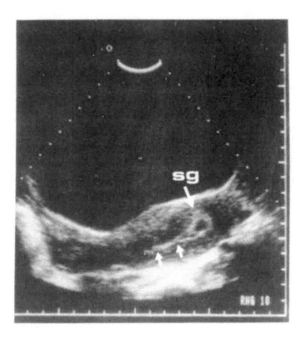

FIGURE 6.   Pregnancy at 5 weeks: longitudinal scan of the uterus showing the correlation between the gestational sac (sg) and the uterine cavity linear echo (arrows).

linear cavity echo (Figure 6). Sometimes the decidua surrounding the central uterine cavity echo can be seen with the gestational sac located deep in the decidual cast (Figure 7).[6]

At this early stage of pregnancy the embryo and the yolk sac cannot be visualized yet and the amniotic cavity is still small, as compared to the extraembryonic coelom (or chorionic cavity) (Figure 8). The echo-free area inside the gestational sac, therefore, corresponds to

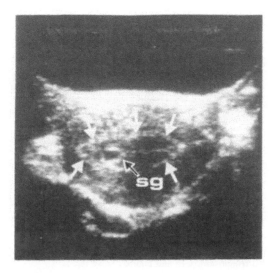

FIGURE 7. Pregnancy at 5 weeks: transverse scan of the uterus showing a very small gestational sac (sg) located deep in the decidual cast (arrows).

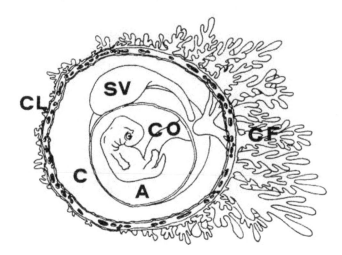

FIGURE 8. Schematic drawing of a 7-week pregnancy showing the differentiation between the chorion frondosum (CF) and chorion laeve (CL); the amniotic (A) and chorionic (C) cavities divided by the amniotic membrane; the fetus in the amniotic cavity; the secondary yolk sac (SV) in the chorionic cavity; and the umbilical cord (CO) connecting the fetus to the chorion.

the chorionic cavity. The large difference in acoustic impedance between the chorionic cavity and the trophoblastic wall explains the strong and uniform echogenicity of the gestational sac wall.

SAC GROWTH

After the 5th week of amenorhea, the chorionic villi corresponding to the embryonic pole increase greatly in size and complexity to the form "chorion frondosum", which represents the fetal component of the placenta. Concurrently, the villi on the opposite side

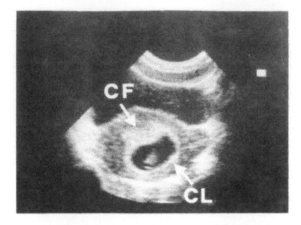

FIGURE 9.   Pregnancy at 8 weeks: ultrasonic appearance of the chorion frondosum (CF) and chorion laeve (CL).

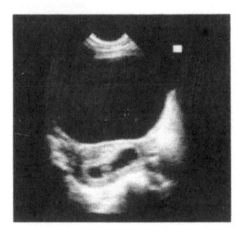

FIGURE 10.   Pregnancy at 8 weeks: the gestational sac is compressed and distorted by an overfilled urinary bladder.

become compressed and gradually atrophize, and differentiation of the chorion frondosum and chorion laeve is ultrasonically identified as a different thickness of the gestational sac wall (Figure 9). This differentiation becomes clearer in the following weeks until the early placenta can be easily identified.

As the pregnancy proceeds, there is a rapid increase in the size of the gestational sac, which reaches a volume of 70 ml at 12 weeks (range 50 to 120).[7] Meanwhile, the shape of the gestational sac varies widely, particularly if it is compressed and distorted by an overfilled urinary bladder (Figure 10). This explains the unreliability of the techniques used to measure the gestational sac volume when assessing gestational age.

THE INTERDECIDUAL SPACE

As the chorionic sac grows and protrudes further into the uterine cavity, the decidua can be divided into three parts: the decidua basalis, the decidua capsularis, and the decidua

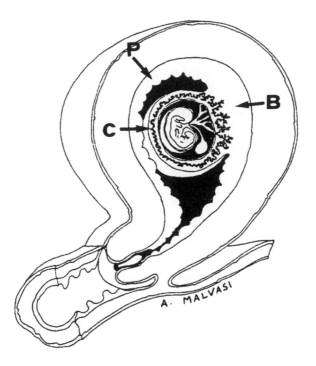

FIGURE 11. Schematic drawing showing the chorionic sac protruding into the uterine cavity, with the subsequent differentiation of the decidua basalis (B) (underlying the chorion frondosum), decidua capsularis (C) (covering the chorionic sac), and the decidua parietalis (P) (covering the uterine cavity). The black area between the decidua parietalis and capsularis represents the interdecidual space.

parietalis. The decidua basalis is a part underlying the embryo and forming the maternal component of the placenta, the decidua capsularis covers the chorionic sac, while the remaining endometrium covering the uterine cavity is the decidua parietalis. The chorion frondosum and the underlying decidua basalis form the definitive placental site. The space between the decidua capsularis and parietalis usually contains mucus and sometimes a small amount of blood (implantation bleeding) (Figure 11). For this reason the triangular space can be ultrasonically visualized as a small, triangular echo-free or echo-poor area adjacent to the gestational sac (Figures 12 and 13), or as an echo-free rim surrounding the gestational sac (Figure 14). The latter appearance, greatly depending on the orientation and angulation of the transducer, is also erroneously called "double sac sign" and can be used as a differential sign distinguishing the normal gestational sac from the pseudogestational sac of ectopic pregnancy.[16]

As the gestational sac enlarges, this space is gradually obliterated, and its ultrasonic visualization becomes more difficult until the sac fills the uterine cavity completely and the decidua capsularis fuses with the decidua parietalis at 15 to 16 weeks.

THE AMNIOTIC MEMBRANE

As the gestational sac grows, the amniotic cavity gradually enlarges, filling the chorionic cavity which reduces in size and surrounds the fetus (Figure 8). The fusion of the amniotic and chorionic membranes becomes complete at about 16 weeks. Before the fusion occurs, the amniotic membrane can be sonographically seen with a careful scanning.[9] Since it is a very thin structure, it can be ultrasonically visualized only when the ultrasonic beam is

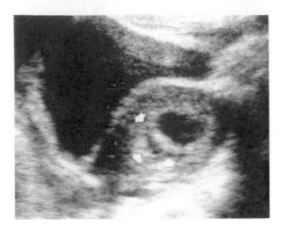

FIGURE 12.   Ultrasonic appearance of the interdecidual space as an echo-free triangular area (arrows) adjacent to the gestational sac.

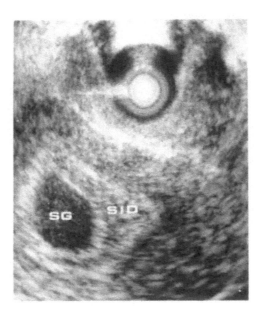

FIGURE 13.   Endovaginal scan in a 6-week pregnancy showing the interdecidual space (SID) as an echo-poor triangular area adjacent to the gestational sac (SG). (Courtesy of Dr. L. Popp.)

perpendicular to the membrane. In this case, although the amniotic membrane is very thin, it acts as a good reflecting surface and appears as a thin linear echo inside the gestational sac, dividing the amniotic and the chorionic cavities (Figures 15 and 16). In a small percentage of cases, the amniotic and chorionic membranes fail to fuse over their entire surface at 16 weeks or separate following an initial opposition. This finding, called acquired chorioamniotic separation, is thought to be of no clinical significance.[10]

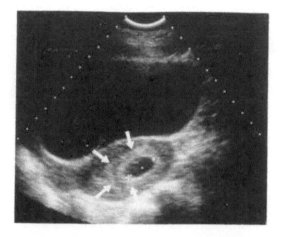

FIGURE 14. "Double sac sign" due to the interdecidual space surrounding the gestational sac as an echo-free rim (arrows).

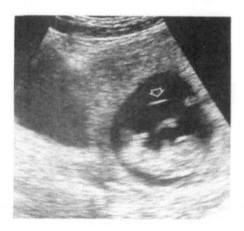

FIGURE 15. A 9-week pregnancy: the amniotic membrane appears as a thin linear echo (arrow) between the chorionic and amniotic cavities.

THE FETAL POLE

During the earliest weeks of gestation, the embryonic disk undergoes deep changes, which, by means of complex histogenetic and morphogenetic sequences, will lead to the formation of a mature human being. At its earliest, ultrasonic visualization of the embryo is possible at 6 to 7 weeks of menstrual age when embryolically it is 5 mm long. At this age, the amniotic sac surrounding the embryo is still small as compared to the chorionic cavity, and the embryo is attached to the chorion frondosum by a short, wide connecting stalk (Figure 8). For this reason, at 6 to 7 weeks, the fetal pole ultrasonically appears as a small, ovoid structure adjacent to the chorion frondosum (Figure 17). During the 7th week, fetal cardiac activity can be seen by real-time instrumentation.[11] From the 7th week onward, cardiac activity should be identifiable in 100% of the cases, and gross fetal body motions can also be seen. At 8 weeks, the head can be easily identified and is approximately the same size as the body (Figure 18). From 9 weeks onward, the fetal extremities can also be recognized (Figure 19). It is possible to assess menstrual age in the first trimester by measuring the long axis of the fetus or crown-rump length (CRL) accurately.

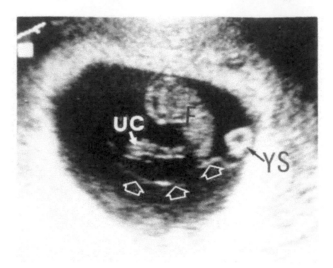

FIGURE 16.   An 8-week pregnancy. Endovaginal sonography: the amniotic membrane is nicely visualized (arrows) as well as the fetus (F), the umbilical cord (UC), and the yolk sac (YS). (Courtesy of Prof. F. Catizone.)

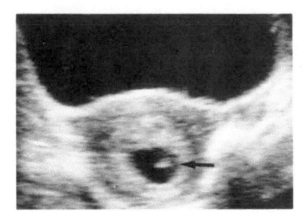

FIGURE 17.   Earliest ultrasonic visualization of the fetal pole during the 7th week of pregnancy.

As the embryo grows, the amniotic sac enlarges and gradually obliterates the chorionic cavity, so that the embryo floats freely in the amniotic fluid, connected to the chorion by the umbilical cord. This derives from the above-mentioned connecting stalk, which in the meantime has grown longer and has been sheathed by the expanding amnion. The umbilical cord may be imaged starting from the 8th week of menstrual age as a trunk-like structure running from the ventral surface of the embryo to the chorion (Figures 20 and 21).

THE SECONDARY YOLK SAC

From 7 weeks of menstrual age onward, it is possible to visualize, almost constantly, a 4- to 6-mm, round cystic structure lying adjacent to the fetus, corresponding to the secondary

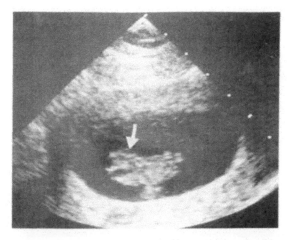

FIGURE 18. Pregnancy at 8 weeks: the cephalic pole of the fetus can be recognized (arrow).

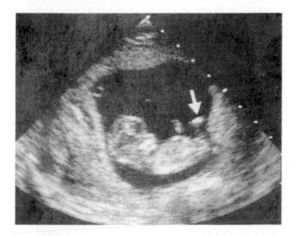

FIGURE 19. Pregnancy at 10 weeks: the lower extremities are easily recognized (arrow).

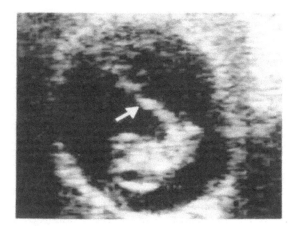

FIGURE 20. Ultrasonic appearance of the umbilical cord during the 9th week of pregnancy. It appears as a trunk-like structure starting from the ventral surface of the fetus (arrow).

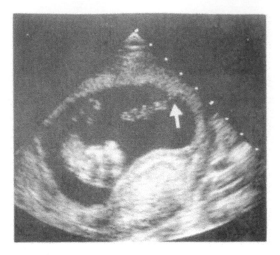

FIGURE 21.   Visualization of the umbilical cord at its attachment to the chorion (arrow).

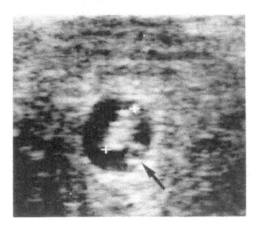

FIGURE 22.   Secondary yolk sac (arrow) adjacent to the fetus at 7 weeks of pregnancy.

yolk sac (Figures 22 to 24).[13] It derives from the primitive yolk sac which develops from the inner cell mass on the side opposite to the amniotic cavity (Figure 3). As a result of the enlargement of the amniotic cavity, and of the transverse folding of the embryo, part of the yolk sac is incorporated into the embryo at the midgut, and the resulting secondary yolk sac is connected to the embryo by the yolk stalk or vitelline duct (Figure 8). With the continuous expansion of the amnion, the elongated yolk sac is embedded into the mesoderm of the umbilical cord, and the yolk sac is pressed against the chorion by the expanding amniotic cavity (Figure 11). It may be found generally near the point where the umbilical cord is attached to the placenta, and it is sometimes possible to confirm its extraamniotic location by visualizing both the yolk sac and the amniotic membrane on the same scan (Figure 25).

The yolk sac may persist until the 5th month of pregnancy, or even throughout pregnancy; however, its ultrasonic visualization is not possible after 11 to 12 weeks of menstrual age.

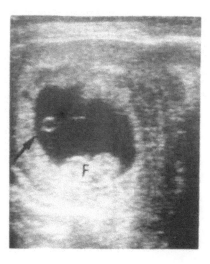

FIGURE 23. Secondary yolk sac (arrow) far from the fetus (F) at 10 weeks of pregnancy.

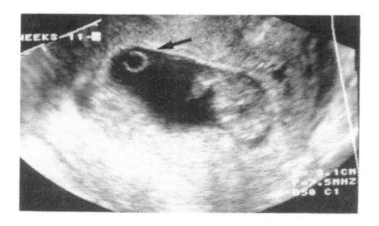

FIGURE 24. Secondary yolk sac (arrow) nicely visualized by endovaginal sonography at 11 weeks of pregnancy. (Courtesy of Prof. F. Catizone.)

CLINICAL ASPECTS OF EARLY PREGNANCY

The clinical problems which must be assessed following a positive pregnancy test include location of the pregnancy, either extrauterine or intrauterine;[14] the type of pregnancy (normal, multiple, molar);[15] the possible existence of pseudohormone-producing tumor of the ovary, such as dysgerminoma;[15] the viability of the pregnancy;[15] and establishment of gestational age.[7]

Pregnant women with poor obstetric histories (intrauterine growth retardation [IUGR], third-trimester bleeding, fetal congenital anomalies, vaginal bleeding, and abdominal cramping) have to be specially examined.

Ultrasound diagnostic methods may be very useful to distinguish normal and pathological

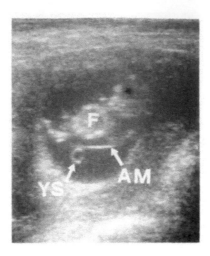

FIGURE 25. Simultaneous visualization of the fetus (F), the amniotic membrane (AM), and the yolk sac (YS). The yolk sac is located in the chorionic cavity.

early pregnancy. Special care should be taken about threatened abortion, molar and ectopic pregnancy, as well as pregnancy with other abnormalities (mioma, cysts, double uterus, multiple gestation).

The sonologist must also recognize the complications of pregnancy, such as failure of pregnancy protection by an intrauterine device (IUD), subsequent combination of a pregnancy with the IUD, and pregnancy associated with a pelvic mass arising either from the adnexal regions or the uterus.[15]

It is generally accepted that it is possible to diagnose pregnancy at the 5th week, recognizing gestational sac inside the uterus. The above results are related to use of a transabdominal probe. It seems that by using a vaginal probe, the diagnosis of early pregnancy becomes possible much earlier.[16] Transvaginal sonography makes it possible to visualize all embryonic structures, including the gestational sac, at an average of 1 week earlier than by the traditional transabdominal route.[17] By 4 weeks and 2 to 3 d of menstrual age, a 6.5-MHz probe can reliably detect a normal intrauterine pregnancy. At this time the serum levels of β-HCG subunits reach level of 500 to 600 mIU/ml (first international reference). A 5.0-MHz probe can detect a normal intrauterine pregnancy at a β-HCG level of 800 to 1000 mIU/ml. This is significantly lower than the "discriminatory zone" espoused by Kadar et al.[18] or the one advocated by Nyberg et al.[19] which are 6500 (first international reference) and 1800 mIU/ml (second international reference), respectively. Pathological pregnancies such as missed abortions or ectopic gestations can also be diagnosed more successfully and earlier than by transabdominal probe. Early recognition of pregnancy is especially important in infertility clinics after the *in vitro* fertilization treatment.[16] In such cases endovaginal sonology may be of tremendous importance.

FETAL BIOMETRY AND GESTATIONAL AGING

The best time to ascertain the gestational age of the fetus is in the first trimester. In 1975, Robinson[7] described a technique for the estimation of maturity in the first trimester by using measurements of the fetal CRL (Figure 26). In a later statistical analysis of 334 measurements made by this very method, Robinson and Fleming[12] showed that in 95% of

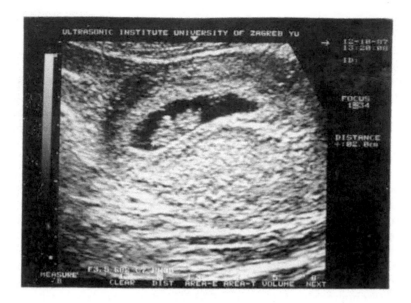

FIGURE 26.   Measurement of the CRL in early pregnancy; markers (crosses) are placed on cephalic and caudal poles of the fetus.

cases a prediction could be made to within 4.7 d with a single measurement and to within 2.7 d with three independent measurements.

The degree of accuracy is made possible by the small biological variations in fetal size and the very rapid rate of growth during this stage of human development. It is during this time interval that the CRL of every fetus is comparable, even if the mother is diabetic. Measurements of fetal CRL have revealed that the fetus grows at an increasingly rapid rate from a mean value of 10 mm at 7 weeks to 82 mm at 14 weeks. The rate of increase in the earliest weeks is approximately 1 mm/d, whereas by the 14th week, the increase is just over 2 mm/d.

The CRL is useful only in the first trimester, and by week 10 to 11, the biparietal diameter (BPD) measurements should also be correlated with the CRL for the increased accuracy. Since the fetus is so mobile at this time, it is often necessary to utilize real-time scanning equipment to establish CRL which is the greatest length of the fetus excluding the yolk sac. A prediction can be made within 5 d by a single CRL, and within 3 d when three CRLs are averaged. We do not recommend the use of the CRL after 12 weeks of gestation because flexion on the spine renders the measurement less accurate.

EVALUATION OF FETAL VIABILITY

Prior to the introduction of diagnostic ultrasound into clinical obstetrics, the differentiation between normal and abnormal early pregnancies posed a difficult problem, principally because of the inaccessibility of the gravid uterus to direct methods of investigation at this stage. Assays of hormones such as estriol, pregnandiol, human chorionic gonadotropin, and human placental lactogen in the maternal blood or urine can indirectly offer some measure of reassurance that everything proceeded well, but on consideration of the site of production of these hormones, it will be appreciated that the information actually relates only to the functional capability of the corpus luteum or trophoblast. The need arose, therefore, for techniques which would provide objective and reliable information on early pregnancy at any moment in time, and for that information to be sufficiently accurate to allow for termination in the event of the pregnancy being abnormal.

Embryologic studies have suggested that the human heart, although not yet completely developed, starts the function about 35 d following the 1st day of the last menstrual period. By using real-time scanning or real-time motion (T-M) equipment, positive findings of fetal cardiac activity are nearly always made from 8 weeks of menstrual age onward and occasionally even as early as 7 weeks. Between 6 and 7 weeks of menstrual age, the success rate is about 50%. By the 8th week of gestation, when fetal age is known exactly, the inability to demonstrate fetal cardiac activity over a time interval of 5 to 10 min is virtually pathognomonic of fetal death. The fetal heart rate (FHR) increases from about 130 beats per minute at 7 weeks to approximately 180 at 9 weeks, followed by gradual decrease to about 140 beats per minute at 15 weeks. The changes in FHR pattern after 9 weeks are comparable with the development of the fetal vagal function. Beat-to-beat variations appear for the first time at 13 to 14 weeks. The fetus, especially if prodded gently by stimulating the uterus exteriorly, should also show some motion. If the fetus sinks slowly toward the posterior-inferior wall of the uterus without showing any cardiac or limb motion, the diagnosis of intrauterine fetal death is definite after the 8th week of gestation.

The major inherent problem, however, is the possibility of the patient being off dates, and thus the ultrasonographer must resort to CRL in order to correlate gestational age with the age ascertained by gestational sac appearance. Fetal movements seldom occur before 8 weeks of menstrual age. From 9 weeks onward, fetal motion is episodic. Slow and inert movements can be distinguished from abrupt violent movements.

VAGINAL BLEEDING

The most common pathologic symptom in early pregnancy is bleeding. It has been established that about 30% of pregnant women will have some type of bleeding in early pregnancy, and 40 to 50% of those patients have an unfavorable outcome.[20,21]

The main problems in the management of these patients are diagnostic ones; after an accurate diagnosis has been made, the selection of possible therapeutic measures is easier. At this moment, ultrasonography is considered to be the best diagnostic method for early pregnancy complications.[21-23]

With the real-time unit, it is possible to obtain very reliable information on the actual state of pregnancy and to predict with adequate certainty the later course of pregnancy at the time of a threatened abortion.

Vaginal bleeding is the most frequent reason underlying referrals to ultrasonic examination; it calls for the verification of fetal life. With such a patient in his consulting room, any obstetrician should like to know several important facts which can radically alter the management. These are

- Is the patient pregnant?
- Is the fetus alive or dead?
- What is the gestational age?
- Are there any signs that the pregnancy may abort?
- Is the pregnancy single or multiple?
- Is there any evidence to suggest that the pregnancy is extrauterine?
- In the event of abortion, is it complete or incomplete?
- Is there any associated pelvic mass?

It is only after such differentiation that control and possible therapeutic measures can be applied in cases where a normal outcome of the pregnancy can be expected. After an accurate diagnosis has been made, the selection of possible therapeutic measures is easier.

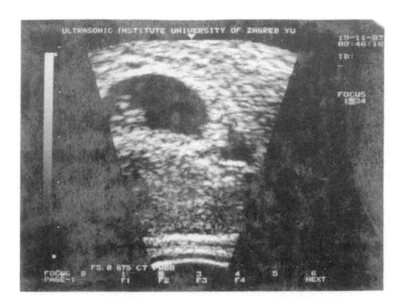

FIGURE 27.   Ultrasonogram in a case of early pregnancy bleeding obtained with a transvaginal probe; triangular anechogenic area on the right side represents implantation bleeding.

In almost 50% of 5- to 8-week pregnancies, implantation bleeding may be observed (Figure 27). It is usually triangular in shape and must not be mistaken for a second gestational sac. Implantation bleeding is a normal finding, and spontaneous abortion is highly probable in situations where a large part of the gestational sac is separated from uterine wall (Figure 28A and B). At present, ultrasonography is considered to be the best diagnostic method for early pregnancy complications. The skill of the ultrasonographer is put to the test, since a verdict of pregnancy failure will often result in surgical intervention.

The results reported by numerous investigators have shown that real-time appliances provide for a correct diagnosis in the vast majority of pregnancies with bleeding in the first trimester at the very first examination.

Ultrasound is the only diagnostic method which can answer the question of whether an early pregnancy with bleeding should be continued with intensive care and therapy at a very early stage.

In a study performed at our institution on a population of 142 pregnant women with bleeding in early pregnancy, in 103 (72.5%) of the cases it was demonstrated that the fetus was alive. In the remaining 39 cases (27.5%) there were no signs of fetal life. In the 39 cases where fetal life was not demonstrated, the most frequent cause was blighted ovum (38.5%), followed by missed abortion (33.3%) and abortus incompletus (25.6%), and just one case (2.6%) of ectopic pregnancy. Out of the 142 women, 82 delivered a live baby, meaning that 58% of cases, regardless of bleeding in early pregnancy, were brought to term. In a very recent paper, Cashner et al.[24] made an analysis of pregnancy outcome in 489 pregnant women after ultrasound documentation of fetal viability at 8 to 12 weeks. Obtained results suggest that if a live fetus is documented by ultrasonography at 8 to 12 weeks of gestation, the risk of spontaneous abortion before 20 weeks of gestation in an uninstrumented population is 2.0%. In a study given by Anderson,[25] 97.3% of pregnancies in which fetal cardiac motion was noted after 7 weeks carried in term. Jouppila et al.[26] observed that in

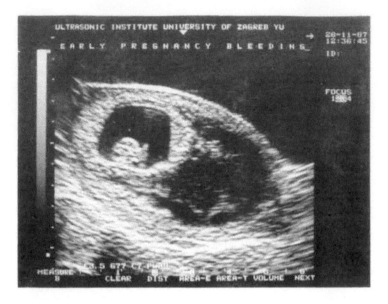

A

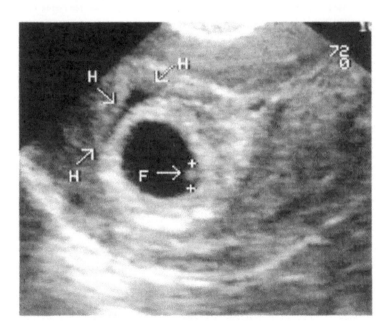

B

FIGURE 28.   Early pregnancy bleeding in the 9th week of pregnancy. (A) The irregular hypoechoic area on the right, adjacent to the gestational sac, represents blood clots in the uterine cavity. Note that chorionic membrane is elevated from the uterine wall, so that spontaneous abortion can be expected. (B) Treatment abortion at 7 weeks; F = fetal pole (2 mm), H = hematoma. Longitudinal scan of the uterus.

patients with threatened abortions, the positive finding of fetal heart action was associated with delivery of a viable infant in 90.0% of the cases.[26]

The prognostic value of ultrasound for women with bleeding in early pregnancy where fetal life has been demonstrated is very great, and we must bear in mind the fact that more than half of such pregnancies will be sustained and brought to term. Aborted pregnancies fall into five categories: blighted ovum, early or late live abortion, missed abortion, and molar pregnancy.

BLIGHTED OVUM

During early pregnancy, embryologic malformations generally escape an ultrasonic diagnosis, but with the use of good ultrasonic equipment it is now possible to detect several types of abnormal embryos. These are not merely of theoretical importance only, because embryonic malformations constitute a large portion of early abortions. The most frequent abnormality in early pregnancy is the blighted ovum (anembryonic pregnancy). In this condition, development of an embryo is altogether absent or arrested at the very early stage (Figures 29A and B). Sometimes some solid echoes may be visualized within the gestational sac. Such an amorphous structure represents the rudimentary embryo (Figure 30).

Blighted ovum may be defined as a pregnancy with a gestational sac volume of ≥2.5 ml at any single examination, but in which no fetus can be identified by ultrasound, or if the volume of the sac is <2.5 ml, and which fails to increase in size by at least 75% over a period of 1 week.

A fertilized ovum develops into a blastocyst, but the inner cell mass and resultant fetal pole never develop. The gestational sac invades the endometrium and acts partly like a normally developing pregnancy. The syncytiotrophoblast invades the endometrium and produces human chorionic gonadotropin, which produces a positive pregnancy test, enlarged tender breast, and other clinical stigmata of pregnancy.

The presence of a small fetal pole with no visible motion of the heart beat would be a missed abortion or truly an anembryonic gestation.

Ultrasonic findings are rather specific and relate to the size, shape, and thickness of the sac and continuity of the trophoblast. The uterus and the sac are smaller than expected for the clinical age, of appropriate size, or even slightly larger, and a common finding is an empty gestational sac. If there is any doubt regarding the gestational age and the patient is relatively free of symptoms, the best way is to repeat the scan in 7 to 10 d. Failure to visualize a fetus within this time improves the diagnosis. If the scan is small, it may be difficult to distinguish this entity sonographically from an ectopic pregnancy.

In serial studies covering 2 weeks, the sac generally does not grow and may in fact get smaller. The outline of the sac may have crenated shape, be angular, or may have a more normal, rounded configuration. Angular irregularities cannot be produced by uterine compression and are presumed to be abnormalities of the primary sac. The echogenic trophoblast is usually of irregular thickness with areas in which no trophoblast is seen. This is a very reliable sign seen in almost all cases. Occasionally, fluid can be observed within the sac, presumably because of hemorrhage. The normal appearances, however, are short lived. The gestational sac fails to grow and develop normally, and the uterus fails to develop as expected.

Generally, one can estimate that about 15 to 20% of all human pregnancies diagnosed before the end of the first trimester terminate in spontaneous abortion.[27] At least one third of these cases are caused by chromosomal abnormalities resulting in very early disorders of embryogenesis or total absence of any recognizable embryonic formation. Among many other aspects these facts support the need for methods which may provide direct criteria of early pregnancy development.

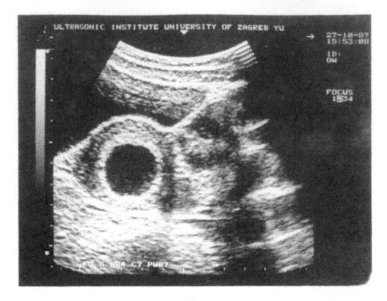

A

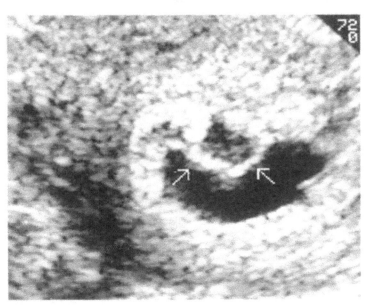

B

FIGURE 29.   (A) The transverse scan through a gravid uterus of a 9-week gestation period with blighted ovum; gestational sac may be seen without an embryonal echo. Note that trophoblast is of irregular thickness, with no clear borderline. (B) Blighted ova at 7 weeks, showing interdecidual bleeding and profusion of hematoma into the cavity of the gestational sac.

The incidence of chromosomal abnormalities among aborted blighted ova is high.[28] In the material of 24 blighted ova examined cytogenetically, Bulic and Singer[29] found 50% chromosomal abnormalities (mainly trisomy, monosomy, and tetraploidy). We have investigated 72 pregnant women with blighted ovum in actual pregnancy.[28] In 26 cases (36.1%) chromosomal aberrations were found, predominantly triploidy, monoploidy X, and auto-

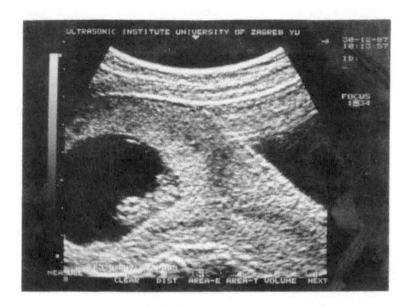

FIGURE 30. Large gestational sac in uterine cavity with a small embryonal rudiment — blighted ovum.

somal trisomies. It is interesting that the two most common trisomies are those also found among live-born children, trisomy of the 18th and 21st chromosome. We were unable to show any significant difference between the obstetric histories, ages, or parity of mothers with chromosomally normal as compared to abnormal blighted ova.[28] In the same studies, 23 parents having blighted ovum in actual pregnancy were analyzed cytogenetically. In 13.6% of them, identical chromosomal aberrations were found as in the aborted material of blighted ova (mainly pericentric inversion of the ninth chromosome and translocations).

Significantly higher incidences of chromosomal abnormalities and fetal malformations in offspring of parents who have had in the previous pregnancy blighted ovum with chromosomal abnormalities were also found.[28] Those results pointed out that each subsequent pregnancy should require close ultrasonic monitoring and early amniocentesis to exclude major congenital malformations and chromosomal abnormalities.[28]

With falling levels of human chorionic gonadotrophin, progesterone and estrogen, the feeling of being pregnant and the associated pelvic fullness and breast tenderness are also lost. The diagnosis of blighted ovum can be made in 100% of cases by two real-time ultrasonography examinations performed at a 1-week interval. The fact that a fetus will never be observed, in spite of very careful study, is of primary importance.

After the first systematic investigations of these problems by Donald and Robinson, several papers confirmed that ultrasound is extremely important and successful in the diagnosis and assessment of anembryonic pregnancies.[30-33]

Jouppila and Herva[32] stated that ultrasound as a direct diagnostic method enables 100% reliability in the differentiation of the blighted ovum and normal pregnancies from 7 to 8 weeks onward. In their analysis of 60 abortions between 8 to 16 weeks of pregnancy, the histopathological findings confirmed that 55% of the cases had pathologic ovum. The evaluated retention time of the uterine contents was 1 week or more in 73%.[32] In a joint paper by Kurjak and Jouppila,[33] 300 blighted ova were analyzed and correlated with histopathological diagnosis. Of the investigated patients, 50% had already experienced one or more spontaneous abortions.

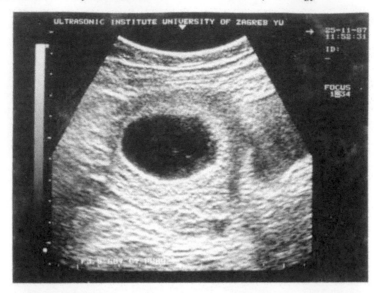

FIGURE 31.   Blighted ovum with initial molar changes.

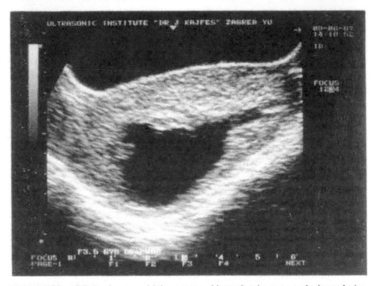

FIGURE 32.   Blighted ovum which progressed in molar tissue; note the irregularity in the shape and thickness of the gestational sac.

MOLAR PREGNANCY

In 1 in 1500 to 1 in 25,000 pregnancies, an abnormality known as the hydatidiform mole develops. These are, however, obsolete statistical data. About half of molar pregnancies are thought to be associated with an embryonic ova development. The incidence of coexisting fetus is between 1 in 10,000 and 1 in 15,000. Successful diagnosis of this condition by ultrasound has been reported.

Two main theories developed about the genesis of hydatidiform mole. The first one considers that hydatidiform mole is a special type of delayed expulsion of pathologic ovum (Figures 31 to 33)

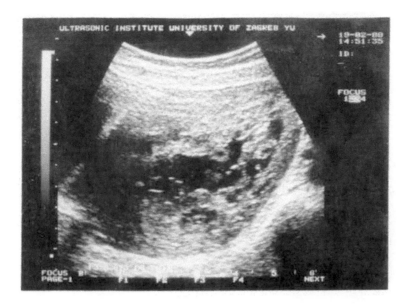

FIGURE 33. Typical picture of hydatidiform mole in a case in which blighted ovum was diagnosed on previous examination and after the patient refused interruption of pregnancy; molar degeneration of gestational sac may be clearly seen; gestational sac wall is thick and irregular, containing numerous anechogenic areas.

In 1940, Hertig and Livingstone[34] examined products of conception in 1027 cases, 74 hydatidiform moles being among them. According to their opinion, the sequence of events in the genesis of a hydatidiform mole commences at about 5 weeks of menstrual age, e.g., in time, when embryonal circulation is normally established; but if the embryo dies in the very early stage of development, it results in failure of establishment of the fetal villous blood vessels. As a consequence, fluid produced by actively secreting trophoblasts, accumulates within a villous stroma because there is no mechanism for its removal. It is suggested that the trophoblastic hyperplasia is due to the stretching by the swollen villi. They regard the classical hydatidiform mole as one end of a continuous spectrum of hydatidiform degeneration, the other end of which is characterized by the spontaneous abortion. This opinion was supported by the fact that pathological ova were aborted at an average menstrual age of 10 weeks, nonpathological ova at 15.5 weeks, transitional moles at 16.5 weeks, and classical moles at 17.5 weeks. This theory is supported by results obtained by Hando et al.[35]

The second theory regarded hydatidiform mole as a primary trophoblastic abnormality, e.g., as a tumor in itself.[36] This theory is supported by the fact that sometimes hydatidiform changes of placenta may be found in the pregnancies with coexistent live fetus. In such cases the genesis of the mole cannot be explained by the failure of establishment of the fetal villous blood vessels caused by fetal death, but acceptable explanation for such cases is the development of hydatidiform mole in placenta of the blighted ovum of a biovular twin pregnancy.

If the theory about hydatidiform mole as a special type of delayed expulsion of pathologic ovum is accepted, it is to be expected that by early diagnosis of blighted ova and consequent interruption of pregnancy, the development of hydatidiform mole and perhaps of choriocarcinoma may be prevented.[37]

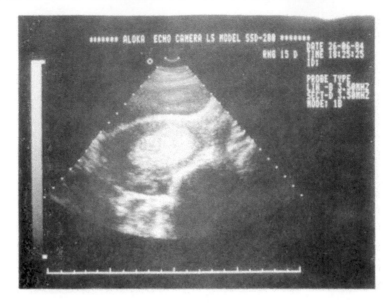

FIGURE 34.   A transverse sonogram of the uterus which is uniformly filled with a mass of uniform echoes presenting a regular speckled appearance. This "snow-storm" effect is a typical finding in cases of hydatidiform mole.

During the past decade, more attention has been paid to chromosome investigation of spontaneous abortions. It is well known that there is a high number of chromosomal abnormalities in specimens of spontaneous abortions, especially in pathologic ova. There are numerous reports about very high incidences of chromosomal abnormalities in molar pregnancies, too. Kajii and Ohama[3] demonstrated that hydatidiform mole results from the fertilization of an "empty egg", e.g., an ovum with no active chromosomal material. According to those authors, the chromosome of the sperm, finding no chromosomal complement from the ovum, reduplicate themselves, resulting in a 46,xx mole. In cases of triploidy, often found in molar tissue, two chromosomes are of paternal origin and the third is of maternal origin.

Degeneration of areas within the mole causes bleeding within or between the vesicles, leading to the classic ultrasonic pattern described as a uterus filled with homogeneous speckled or snowflake echoes (Figure 34). The diagnosis can be made from 7 to 8 weeks of menstrual age. Areas of sonolucency may be seen through the body of a molar tissue and/or along the walls of the uterus, representing areas of degeneration and blood clots. Special care should be taken to evaluate both ovaries for the presence of theca-lutein cysts, which are present in about one third of molar pregnancies.[38] These cystic structures, which have a septated sonoluced and encapsulated appearance, are rare in normal pregnancy, but may be seen in multiple gestations or in glucose intolerant pregnancies.

When both spicule-like pattern and the theca-lutein cyst coexist, the diagnosis of molar pregnancy may be obtained without difficulty. It is also very important to know that presence of theca-lutein cysts has prognostic value, because it increases the chance of the patient requiring chemotherapy for cure. The regression of the cyst can be followed by ultrasound after evacuation of the mole.

Most false diagnoses are false-positive ones, related to the failure to distinguish intra-uterine structures of different origin and quality. It is important to diagnosis, however, to make sure that the patient has had a positive pregnancy test, because other pelvic masses

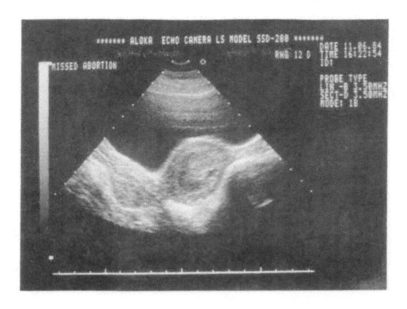

FIGURE 35. Appearance of missed abortion after the resorptive processes have take place; sometimes it is difficult to distinguish such a finding from molar pregnancy.

such as degenerating fibroids or complex benign, cystic teratomas, dysgerminomas, as well as hydropic degenerated missed abortion may mimic the spicule-like pattern.

MISSED ABORTION

The missed abortion is used to describe the lifeless embryo or fetus retained within the uterus for 4 or more weeks. The diagnosis of missed abortion is determined by the identification of a fetus which does not demonstrate any heart activity or motion and the lack of uterine growth or an actual decrease in uterine size. In addition, the amniotic fluid volume may be diminished. In larger fetus the skull will appear collapsed. If an early concept has been dead for some time, it will be a problem to distinguish the fetus and placenta. In this case, a scan will demonstrate an ill-defined collection of echoes within the uterine cavity. This diagnosis is relatively easy and, therefore, can be established during a single examination and with great certainty.

In our patients examined over 10 years, this diagnosis was independent of menstrual or clinical history, and in the series as a whole, there were no false results. In most patients with missed abortion, the volume of the gestational sac continues to increase after fetal death, presumably because of continuous trophoblastic activity. On a few occasions, however, some difficulty may be experienced in distinguishing a molar pregnancy from a very macerated missed abortion, especially if there had been resorption of the liquor (Figures 35 and 36). The differential diagnostic problem may also be with degenerated myoma. In either event there is no question of confusion arising between these and normal pregnancies, and the treatment of both is to empty the uterus. Diagnosis of a missed abortion requires a quick uterine emptying, preferably under local anesthesia. This is the best way to prevent problems with delayed hemorrhage and infection related to retention of necrotic tissue, and also diminishes the chances of disseminated intravascular coagulation (DIC). The emotional stress on pregnant women carrying dead concepts should not be overlooked either.

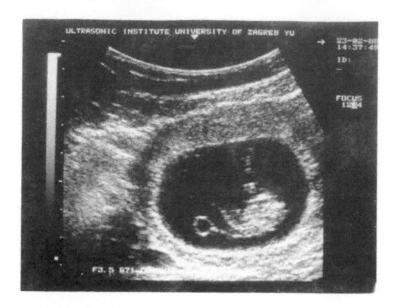

FIGURE 36.   Missed abortion at 10th week: the fetus and fetal parts are demonstrated, but there is no heart action.

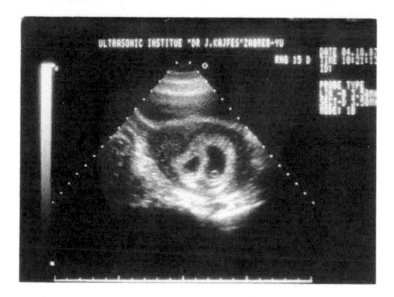

FIGURE 37.   Twin early pregnancy: two gestational sacs inside the uterine cavity may be seen.

MULTIPLE GESTATIONS

Today, a patient with large-for-date uterus will probably be referred to ultrasound examination. A multiple pregnancy will manifest itself by the appearance of two or more gestational sacs (Figures 37 to 43) and may be diagnosed as early as 5 weeks of menstrual age. Since the diagnosis can readily be made by ultrasound at any time during gestation, the unexpected delivery of twins is now unusual except in patients who have had little or no prenatal care.

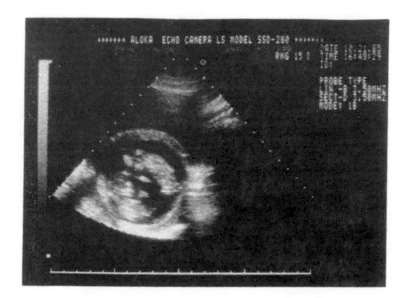

FIGURE 38. Monochorionic, monoamniotic twin pregnancy: inside the unique amniotic cavity two fetuses may be seen.

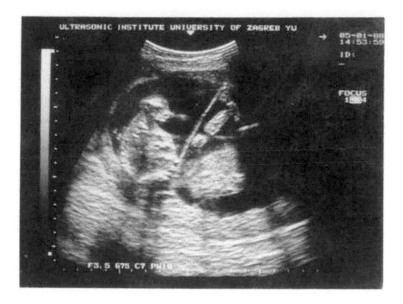

FIGURE 39. Diamniotic, dichorionic twin pregnancy; amniotic membrane clearly divides two amniotic cavities with embryo in each of them.

In several early pregnancy studies, a greater number of multiple pregnancies was observed than ultimately seen at delivery. The second "sac" may be only the collection of blood. Even in cases where there are initially two concepts, if one is grossly abnormal it may be resorbed, with light bleeding being the only sign of a problem (called "vanishing twin"). Therefore, it seems wise, not to inform the parents of the presence of a multiple

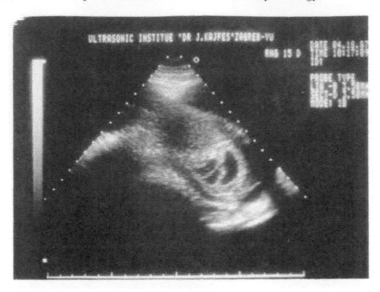

FIGURE 40.   Triplet pregnancy in 7th week of pregnancy: three gestational sacs inside the uterine cavity may be seen.

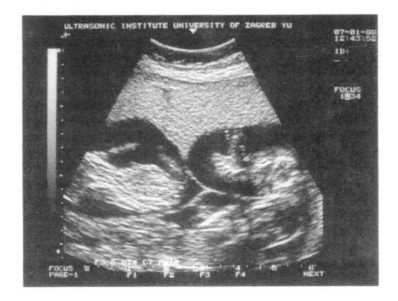

FIGURE 41.   Triplet pregnancy in 10th week of pregnancy: three amniotic cavities are seen, divided by amniotic membrane, with fetus in each of the cavity.

pregnancy before the 10th or 11th week. The concept of the vanishing twin has gained acceptance, and it is now realized that true incidence of twinning is higher than reflected in official birth statistics.[39]

The early diagnosis of multiple gestations has afforded obstetricians the luxury of developing a plan of management based on information concerning the growth, condition, and the maturity of the twin fetuses.

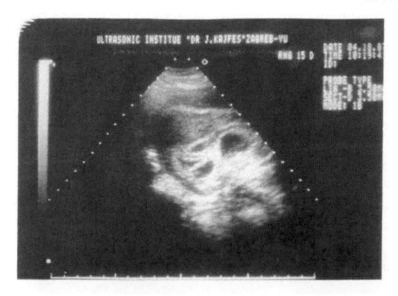

FIGURE 42.   Quadruplet early pregnancy: on transverse scan through the uterus four gestational sacs may be seen.

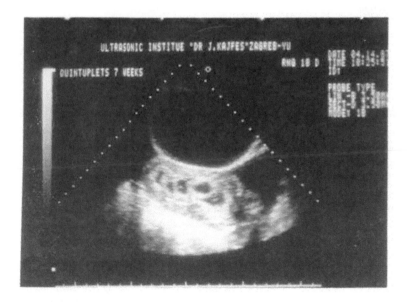

FIGURE 43.   Uterine sonogram of quintuplet pregnancy at 8 weeks: note five gestational sacs inside the enlarged uterus.

About one third of twin gestations are monozygotic. In some monochorionic, diamniotic gestations, the twins share a common placental blood supply through vascular communications on the chorionic plate. Occasionally, this vascular abnormality results in twin-to-twin transfusion. In this situation the donor twin transfers (with each beat of its heart) a very small, but essential amount of its blood volume to the recipient twin. The recipient

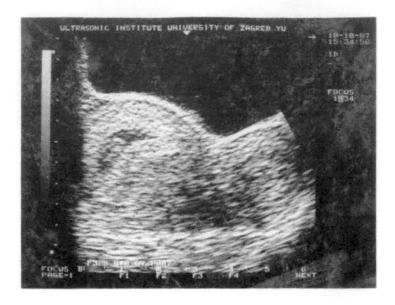

FIGURE 44.   Early pregnancy in bicornuate uterus: gestational sac (left) is situated in one of the uterine horns, the right horn is empty with just signs of decidual reaction.

becomes plethoric and may in time suffer from hypervolemia and cardiac overload, while the donor becomes growth-retarded and anemic. The severity of the condition depends on the magnitude of the vascular communication.

ASSOCIATED UTERINE ABNORMALITIES

Although congenital uterine anomalies are infrequent causes of bleeding in early gestation, pregnancy loss in the subgroup of all women with congenital uterine fusion defects (0.1 to 0.5% of women) is high.[38] Associated uterine abnormalities, developmental or leyomyomata, may cause a confusing picture during pregnancy; but sometimes uterine anomalies are more easily diagnosed in early pregnancy than in nonpregnant women. In cases of uterus didelphis or bicornis (Figure 44), the early gestational sac occupies one horn, while decidual reaction or decidual casts can be noted in the nonpregnant horn. Ultrasonic findings include a bilobed uterine contour on a high-transverse scan. Pennes et al.[41] described this as a dumbbell configuration.

Uterine fibromas are also more easily diagnosed during the first trimester and may be noted with increasing frequency as more women delay childbearing. It is important to evaluate their size and position and to estimate the potential mechanical difficulties which may be caused by myoma during labor (Figures 45 and 46). Evaluation of tumor size is also important, because it can be stimulated by hormone production during pregnancy and be significantly enlarged.

ASSOCIATED ADNEXAL TUMORS

A variety of pathological conditions affecting the ovary can be accidentally diagnosed by routine scanning of the first-trimester pregnancy. The most common finding involves corpus luteum cyst (Figure 47) up to 4 cm large until the 12th week. Occasionally, the cyst

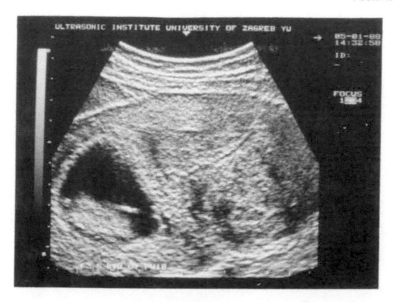

FIGURE 45.   Uterine sonogram of an 8-week gestation showing a normal gestational sac (left) and two myomas in the anterior uterine wall (right).

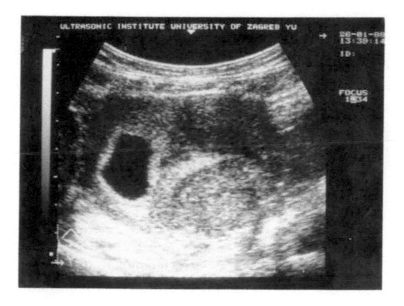

FIGURE 46.   Transverse section through the pregnant uterus containing gestational sac without embryo (blighted ovum) and fibroma in the posterior uterine wall (right).

can become very large and undergo complications such as rupture, hemorrhage, and torsion. Ultrasonically guided puncture of the cyst can be performed in such cases. Besides the corpus luteum cyst, many other pathological tumors may be seen in adnexal regions like cysts or cystic and solid ovarian tumors (Figure 48). Careful examination is required in order to avoid any misinterpretations of normal corpus luteum cyst finding.

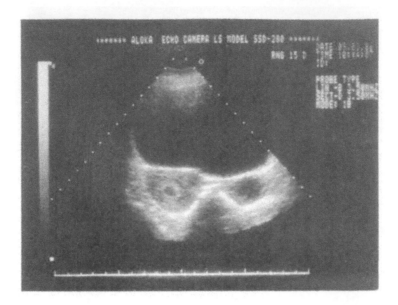

FIGURE 47.   Transverse scan showing a normal 6-week gestational sac within the uterine and corpus luteum cyst (right).

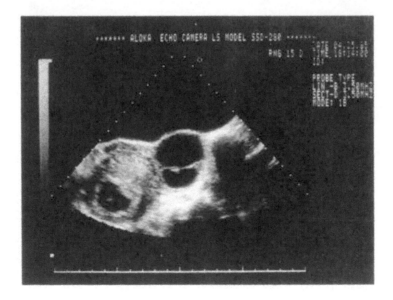

FIGURE 48.   Sonogram of a 10-week gestation showing normal intrauterine pregnancy and a cystic ovarian mass (right). The mass contains well-defined septum characteristic for mucinous cystadenoma. Note the difference between the appearance of this ovarian cystic tumor and the corpus luteum cyst presented on the previous figure.

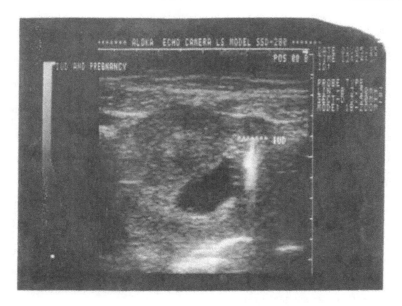

FIGURE 49. Transverse sonogram showing gestational sac and intrauterine device (IUD) within the uterus.

EARLY PREGNANCY AND ASSOCIATED IUD

If an intrauterine contraceptive device and normal early pregnancy are observed (Figure 49), the position of the device in relation to the gestational sac should be evaluated. When the IUD is located far from the implantation site, or even partially expelled, pregnancy can be allowed to progress. In other cases, spontaneous abortions will probably occur.

REFERENCES

1. **Moore, K. L.**, *The Developing Human*, 2nd ed., W. B. Saunders, Philadelphia, 1977.
2. **Catizone, F. A., Pirillo, P., and Marincolo, F.**, L'ultrasonographie transvaginale le premier trimestre de la grossesse: anatomie embryonaire et foetale, *Echorevue*, 5, 6, 1986.
3. **D'Addario, V., Kurjak, A., Miniello, G., and Traina, V.**, Ultrasound and embryology, in *Recent Advances in Ultrasound Diagnosis*, Vol. 4, Kurjak, A. and Kosoff, G., Eds., Excerpta Medica, Amsterdam, 1984, 186.
4. **Batzer, F. R., Weiner, S., Corson, S. L., Schlaff, S., and Otis, C.**, Landmarks during the first forty-two days of gestation demonstrated by the beta-subunit of the human chorionic gonadotropin and ultrasound, *Am. J. Obstet. Gynecol.*, 146, 973, 1983.
5. **Abramovici, H., Auslander, R., Lewin, A., and Faktor, J. H.**, Gestation — pseudogestational sac: a new ultrasonic criterion for differential diagnosis, *Am. J. Obstet. Gynecol.*, 145, 377, 1983.
6. **Catkin, A. V. B. and McAlpin, A.**, The decidua-chorionic sac: a reliable sonographic indicator of intrauterine pregnancy prior to detection of a fetal pole, *J. Ultrasound Med.*, 3, 539, 1984.
7. **Robinson, R. P.**, Gestational sac volume as determined by sonar in first trimester of pregnancy, *Br. J. Obstet. Gynecol.*, 82, 100, 1975.
8. **Bradley, W. J., Fiske, C. E., and Filly, R. A.**, The double sac sign of early intrauterine pregnancy: use in exclusion of ectopic pregnancy, *Radiology*, 143, 223, 1982.
9. **Jeanty, P., Renoy, P., and Van Kerkem, J.**, Ultrasonic demonstration of the amnion, *J. Ultrasound Med.*, 1, 243, 1982.
10. **Kaufman, A. L., Fleischer, A. C., Thieme, S. A., and James, A. E.**, Separated chorioamnion and elevated chorion: sonographic features and clinical significance, *J. Ultrasound Med.*, 4, 119, 1985.

11. **Catkin, A. V. and McAlpin, A.,** Detection of fetal cardiac activity between 41 and 43 days of gestation, *J. Ultrasound Med.,* 3, 499, 1984.

12. **Robinson, H. P. and Fleming, J. E. E.,** A critical evaluation of sonar crown-rump length measurements, *Br. J. Obstet. Gynecol.,* 82, 702, 1975.

13. **Saubrei, E., Cooperberg, P. L., and Poland, B. J.,** Ultrasound demonstration of the normal yolk sac, *J. Clin. Ultrasound,* 8, 217, 1980.

14. **Kurjak, A., Latin, V., Funduk-Kurjak, B., and Miljan, M.,** The current status of ultrasound in diagnosis and assessment of fetal malformations and abnormalities, *Argomenti Ostet. Ginecol.,* 1, 5, 1980.

15. **Kurjak, A. and Kirkinen, P.,** Ultrasonic growth of fetuses with chromosomal aberrations, *Acta Obstet. Gynecol. Scand.,* 61, 223, 1982.

16. **Timor-Tritsch, I. E. and Rottem, S.,** Transvaginal sonography in the management of infertility, in *Ultrasound and Infertility,* Kurjak, A., Ed., CRC Press, Boca Raton, FL, 1988, in press.

17. **Blumenfeld, Z., Rottem, S., Elgali, S., and Timor-Tritsch, I.,** Transvaginal sonographic assessment of early embryonic development, in *Transvaginal Sonography,* Timor-Tritsch, I. and Rottem, S., Eds., Elsevier, New York, 1987, 87.

18. **Kadar, N., DeVore, G., and Romero, R.,** Discriminatory HCG zone. Its use in sonographic evaluation for ectopic pregnancy, *Obstet. Gynecol.,* 58, 156, 1981.

19. **Nyberg, D. A., Filly, R. A., Mahoney, B. S., Monroe, S., Laing, F. C., and Jeffrey, R. B., Jr.,** Early gestation-correlation of HCG levels and sonographic identification, *Am. J. Radiol.,* 144, 951, 1985.

20. **Johansen, A.,** *Acta Obstet. Gynecol. Scand.,* 49, 89, 1970.

21. **Jouppila, P.,** Plasma HCG levels in patients with bleeding in the first and second trimester of pregnancy, *Br. J. Obstet. Gynecol.,* 86, 343, 1979.

22. **Robinson, H. P.,** *Br. J. Obstet. Gynecol.,* 2, 849, 1975.

23. **Jouppila, P.,** Ultrasonic, clinical, hormonal and histopathological aspects of threatened abortion, in *Recent Advances in Ultrasound Diagnosis,* Kurjak, A., Ed., Excerpta Medica, Amsterdam, 1978, 175.

24. **Cashner, K. A., Christopher, C. R., and Dysert, G. A.,** Spontaneous fetal loss after demonstration of a live fetus in the first trimester, *Obstet. Gynecol.,* 70, 827, 1987.

25. **Anderson, G.,** Management of threatened abortion with real-time sonography, *Obstet. Gynecol.,* 55, 259, 1980.

26. **Jouppila, P. et al.,** Early pregnancy failure: study by ultrasonic and hormonal methods, *Obstet. Gynecol.,* 55, 42, 1980.

27. **Kurjak, A., Kirkinen, P., Latin, V., and Rajhvajn, B.,** Diagnosis and assessment of fetal malformation and abnormalities, *J. Perinat. Med.,* 8, 219, 1980.

28. **Miljan, M.,** Komarativno Ultrazvucno-Citogenetsko Ispitivanje Praznog Jaja{ca, masters thesis, Medical Faculty, University of Zagreb, Zagreb, Yugoslavia, 1986.

29. **Bulic, M. and Singer, Z.,** Blighted ovum (hydrovum) — ultrasonic, clinical and cytogenetical aspects, in *Recent Advances in Ultrasound Diagnosis,* Vol. 2, Kurjak, A., Ed., Excerpta Medica, Amsterdam, 1980, 528.

30. **Kurjak, A. and Hinselman, M.,** Nachweiss und Ausshludd von Missbildungen, in *Ultraschalldiagnostic in der Geburtshilfe,* Haller, P. and Hansmann, M., Eds., 1979.

31. **Kurjak, A. and Breyer, B.,** Gray scale ultrasound in obstetric diagnosis, *Gynecol. Obstet. Invest.,* 10, 53, 1979.

32. **Jouppila, P. and Herva, R.,** A study of blighted ovum by ultrasonic and hystopathological methods, *Obstet. Gynecol.,*

33. **Kurjak, A. and Jouppila, P.,** Ultrasonic, biochemical and histopathological assessment of blighted ovum. A collaborative study, *J. Foet. Med.,* 1, 54, 1981.

34. **Hertig, A. T. and Livingstone, R.,** Spontaneous, threatened and habitual abortion: their pathogenesis and treatment, *N. Engl. J. Med.,* 230, 797, 1944.

35. **Hando, T., Hirogami, T., et al.,** in *Gynecology and Obstetrics,* Sakamoto, S., Tojo, S., and Nakayama, T., Eds., Excerpta Medica, Amsterdam, 1980, 548.

36. **Park, W. W.,** *Ann. N.Y. Acad. Sci.,* 80, 99, 1959; as cited in **Kurjak, A., Jouppila, P., Rusinovic, F., and D'Addario, V.,** Choriocarcinoma: possible prevention by early ultrasound diagnosis of blighted ova, in *Ultrasound and Cancer,* Levi, S., Ed., Excerpta Medica, Amsterdam, 1982, 191.

37. **Kurjak, A., Jouppila, P., Rusinovic, F., and D'Addario, V.,** Choriocarcinoma: possible prevention by early ultrasound diagnosis of blighted ova, in *Ultrasound and Cancer,* Levi, S., Ed., Excerpta Medica, Amsterdam, 1982, 191.

38. **Kajii, T. and Ohama, K.,** Androgenic origin of hydatidiform mole, *Nature (London),* 168, 633, 1977.

39. **Longley, J. V. and Sabbagha, R. E.,** Abnormal early pregnancy, in *Diagnostic Ultrasound,* Sabbagha, R. E., Ed., Lippiccott, New York, 1987, 461.

40. **Landy, H. J. et al.,** The vanishing twin, *Acta Genet. Med. Gemellol.,* 31, 179, 1982.

41. **Pennes, D. et al.,** Congenital uterine anomalies and associated pregnancies, *J. Ultrasound Med.,* 4, 531, 1985.

Chapter 4

GESTATIONAL AGE ESTIMATION

Asim Kurjak and Jadranka Pavletic

Accurate assessment of fetal age and evaluation of fetal growth are fundamental to obstetric care. Gestational age can be calculated according to the date of conception, ovulation, first day of the last menstrual period, or first fetal movements. Conceptual age, i.e., the time elapsed from conception, is an absolute value with a single unambiguous definition.[1] Unfortunately, the actual date of conception is usually not known. For that reason menstrual dating, i.e., the time elapsed from the first day of the last menstrual period, has been established in clinical practice. Although satisfactory in studies of large populations, clinical assessment of fetal age based on menstrual history is rather unreliable for individual patients. A questionable menstrual history has been found in 20 to 40% of pregnancies.[2,3] Even when the menstrual history seems reliable, ultrasound dating in early pregnancy more accurately predicts the date of delivery.[3,4] Ovulation can be delayed more than 2 weeks in patients with oligomenorrhea. Moreover, wide variation (-6 d to $+4$ d) has also been reported between the expected time of ovulation predicted by last menstrual period and the actual ovulation time in normal women monitored ultrasonically for assessment of follicular growth.[5] Conception may occur early after birth control medication.[6,7] Bleeding during the time of the first missing period may also cause error in dating the pregnancy.

The feeling of first fetal movement is so subjective, especially in women experiencing it for the first time, that the information is often wrong and seldom of any use. The second group includes physical methods where the gestational age is calculated by measuring uterine size. The oldest method of measurement involves the comparison of the fundus uteri-symphysis distance. By comparing the umbilicus-processus xyphoides distance, gestational age can be calculated within 4 weeks. The method is obviously not very useful because the range is too wide. The fundus-symphysis distance measured in centimeters is also an unreliable predictor of gestational age. A number of various laboratory parameters and amniotic fluid components have also not been efficient because of excessive deviations and complicated usage.[8]

Ultrasound biometry is the most accurate method for gestational age estimation. It is a general rule that the earlier the fetus is measured, the more accurate will be fetal age prediction.

The central issue of almost all quantitative ultrasonic studies is fetal growth. It is dynamic and a very complicated process. In practice, fetal growth is studied by evaluating the way various ultrasonic parameters change over time. When evaluating such data, one has to consider how well the measurement represents the size of the part or, even more important, how the growth of the part selected for measurement corresponds to the growth of other parts of the body.[1]

Table 1 lists various ultrasonic parameters depicting fetal growth.[4,9-37] Some of them have already been widely used in clinical practice either for fetal age estimation or detection of growth abnormalities, particularly intrauterine growth retardation (IUGR). In fact, many reports of fetal dating actually deal with fetal growth, since sonographic measurement has been used as a dependent variable.[38] However, regression models, where gestational age is a dependent variable, i.e., dating curve, may differ substantially from the growth curve (where the ultrasonic parameter is dependent upon gestational age) not only in the appearance, but also in pattern of variability about the regression line.[38]

TABLE 1
Ultrasonic Parameters Depicting Fetal Growth

Ultrasonic parameter	Ref.
CRL — crown-rump length	4,9—12
BPD — biparietal diameter	13—15
FOD — fronto-occipital diameter	16—18
HA — head profile area	17,19,20
HO — head circumference	17,18,21—24
TDap — anteroposterior thoracic diameter	17,18
TDt — transverse thoracic diameter	17
TC — thoracic circumference	17,18
TA — thoracic profile area	17,25
ADap — anteroposterior abdominal diameter	18,21
ADt — transverse abdominal diameter	18,19,21
AC — abdominal circumference	18,21—23,26
AA — abdominal profile area	21,26—29
FL — femur length	30—36
Humerus, radius, ulna, tibia, fibula	30,32,35,36
ThC — thigh circumference	37

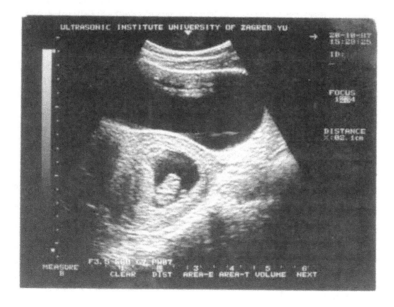

FIGURE 1.   The measurement of the CRL. Calipers mark outer edge of the crown and outer edge of the rump.

The first trimester of pregnancy is the best period for ultrasonically estimating gestational age, for at this stage, biological variations are minimal and there is the best growth rate of the embryo. Measurement of the crown-rump length (CRL), originally described by Robinson,[9] is the most accurate method for determining gestational age, i.e., ±4.7 d (2 SD of the mean).[39] The CRL measurement, which is obtainable by the 7th week of gestation,[40] is the longest length of the embryo, defined as the distance of the crown to the outer edge of the rump. Limbs and yolk sac are not included (Figure 1).

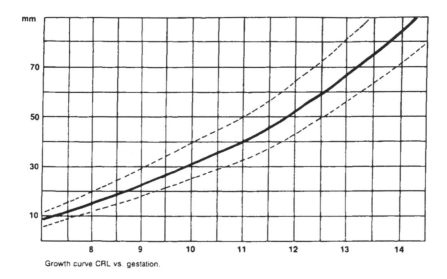

Growth curve CRL vs. gestation.

FIGURE 2.   CRL growth curve.

In an earlier study,[4] we confirmed that during the first trimester of pregnancy it is possible to predict the gestational age within a confidence limit of ±6 d in more than 90% of patients. It is observed that the mean CRL increases from 10 mm at 7 weeks to 84 mm at 14 weeks, i.e., about 10 mm/week. Our own graph is shown in Figure 2. The original study was performed with a static scanner, but similar accuracy can be obtained with real-time equipment.[41]

The results of CRL measurements obtained in five different investigations are presented in Table 2.[4,9-12] The degree of agreement is rather high, indicating an extraordinary consistency in the CRL-MA relationship and the absence of significant dating errors. However, in a recent study, MacGregor et al.[12] reported slight underestimation (3.2 to 3.5 d) of gestational age by conventional CRL dating curves from both Robinson and Fleming[9] and Drumm et al.[10] They performed CRL measurements in 72 previously infertile women with known dates of ovulation and then transformed the data to menstrual age by adding 14 d to the date of ovulation. Such discrepancies may exist in part because conventional CRL values were derived from women with menstrual-timed pregnancies, many of whom have variable preovulatory periods. For that reason the authors suggest using CRL dating curves based on ovulation-timed pregnancies.[12] However, the minor differences in the five studies presented in Table 1 do not appear to be clinically significant.

After the 12th week of gestation, the flexion of the fetal spine significantly reduces the measurement accuracy. Biparietal diameter (BPD) measurement is the standard and most widely used ultrasonic parameter for the estimation of gestational age in the second trimester of pregnancy.[13-15] The BPD is distance between the parietal eminences and is the widest diameter of the skull at right angles to the plane of the faix cerebri. The correct diameter of the head will be measured only when the ultrasound beam enters the fetal head perpendicular to the proximal eminence and exists normal to the distal eminence.[42] The mean rate of growth of BPD is about 3.5 mm/week from 13 to 30 weeks, and 2.2. mm/week between 30 and 34 weeks. Thereafter, it falls rapidly until term, when it is of the order of 1 mm/week.[42]

For reproducibility, a standard image should be measured.[43] This includes the thalamus and cavum septi pellucidi. The occipito-frontal diameter (OFD) and head circumference

TABLE 2
Gestational Age Estimations from CRL in Five Different Studies

CRL (mm)	Gestational age (weeks)				
	Kurjak[4]	Robinson[9]	Drumm[10]	Nelson[11]	MacGregor[12]
10	7.2	7.0	6.9	8.1	7.7
12	7.5	7.4	7.3	8.3	8.0
14	7.8	7.7	7.6	8.5	8.1
16	8.1	8.0	7.9	8.6	8.4
18	8.4	8.3	8.2	8.8	8.7
20	8.6	8.5	8.5	9.0	8.8
22	9.0	8.8	8.7	9.2	9.1
24	9.2	9.0	9.0	9.3	9.3
26	9.5	9.3	9.2	9.5	9.6
28	9.7	9.5	9.5	9.7	9.7
30	9.9	9.7	9.7	9.9	9.8
32	10.1	9.9	9.9	10.0	10.1
34	10.3	10.1	10.1	10.2	10.3
36	10.5	10.3	10.4	10.4	10.6
38	10.8	10.5	10.6	10.5	10.7
40	11.0	10.7	10.8	10.7	10.8
42	11.2	10.8	11.0	10.9	11.1
44	11.3	11.0	11.2	11.1	11.3
46	11.5	11.2	11.3	11.2	11.4
48	11.7	11.4	11.5	11.4	11.7
50	11.9	11.5	11.7	11.6	11.9
52	12.0	11.7	11.9	11.7	12.0
54	12.1	11.8	12.1	11.9	12.1
56	12.3	12.0	12.2	12.1	12.4

(HC) should be measured in the same section. The shape of the skull should be ovoid, and the midline echo which is generated by the interhemispheric fissure should be exactly in the middle. After obtaining the correct section, ultrasonic gain should be reduced (to avoid apparent "thickening" of the skull image). Calipers should be placed at the outer edge of the proximal skull to the inner edge of the distal skull (Figure 3). From 14 to 16 weeks of pregnancy, BPD measurement has a predictive value of ±7 d in 90% of cases. During the third trimester, its accuracy for estimating gestational age decreases to ±21 d in 90% of cases. Accuracy obtained with static scanners is similar to that obtained by real-time equipment.[44]

Predictions of gestational age from BPD in two different studies are shown in Table 3.[14,45] The predicted gestational age values for given BPD are rather consistent prior to the 24th week of gestation, but significant differences are present after that stage of gestation. This is not surprising when we consider differences in methodology used in both investigations. Hadlock et al.[45] used real-time equipment, while Sabbagha et al. used a static scanner. Hadlock et al.'s study was cross-sectional with one datum per fetus. Sabbagha et al. made serial measurements on each fetus. Hadlock et al. used regression analysis to define the relation between the menstrual age and BPD, while Sabbagha et al. did not use this method because of the serial nature of data collection.

After 24 weeks of pregnancy, accuracy of BPD measurement is affected by biological variations, pathological growth (mostly IUGR), head abnormalities (microcephaly, hydrocephaly), and head molding. Excessive flattening of the head, dolicocephaly, is frequently present in breach presentation and can be quantified by the "cephalic index", i.e., the ratio

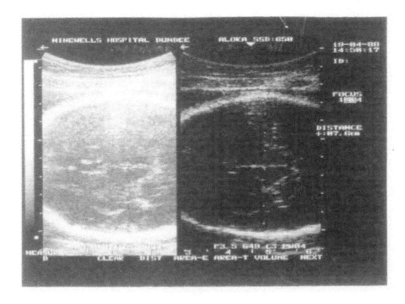

FIGURE 3. The measurement of BPD. Standard plane includes midline echo, thalamus, and cavum septi pellucidi on the same level.

TABLE 3
Gestational Age Estimations from BPD

BPD (mm)	Gestational age (weeks)	
	Sabbagha[45]	Hadlock[14]
35	16	16.5
38	17	17.4
41	18	18.3
44	19	19.2
47	20	20.2
50	21	21.2
54	22	22.5
57	23	23.5
60	24	24.6
63	25	25.7
66	26	26.8
69	27	28.0
73	28	29.5
76	29	30.8
78	30	31.6
81	31	32.5
83	32	33.8
85	33	34.7
87	34	35.6
90	36	37.0
94	37	38.9

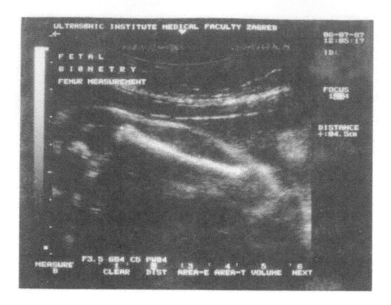

FIGURE 4. The measurement of femur length. Calipers are placed on greater trochanter and lateral condyle.

of the BPD to the OFD.[46] If the cephalic index is smaller than 0.75, dolicocephaly is present and the BPD is not a reliable predictor of gestational age. In such circumstances, a complementary method, i.e., HC[24] or fetal limb bones measurement,[30-36] should be performed.

Fetal limb bones measurements were originally introduced for the detection of skeletal abnormalities.[34,47,48] Subsequently, those measurements also proved useful in the evaluation of gestational age. Fetal femur length (FL) (because it is most easy obtainable) has become the most used parameter, although it appears that other major limb bones are equally good predictors of fetal age.[49] FL measurements have been found to be at least as accurate as BPD in the estimation of gestational age.[49,50] Several authors have found it even superior.[51]

The measurement of fetal FL is obtained from the greater trochanter to the lateral condyle. The head of the femur is not included. When a clear image of the femur is obtained, the freeze frame is employed and the calcified portion of the bone is measured. In the longitudinal section, the entire length of the bone is visualized with characteristic background shadowing (Figure 4). Gestational age estimation based on fetal FL measurements is presented in Table 4.

The relation between menstrual age and HC[24] and menstrual age and abdominal circumference (AC) was reported by Hadlock and co-workers.[52] Jeanty et al. have presented a study of the use of binocular distance (i.e., the distance between the outer margins of orbits) as a dating parameter.[53] Although valuable in some circumstances, all these parameters are not in widespread use for dating purposes.

Experience with ultrasonic measurements has shown that some variation occurs among different populations when the same ultrasound parameters are measured using the same methods. Haines et al.[54] reported a difference of more than 5 mm at term in the measurement of fetal FL, when compared to the study of O'Brian et al.[55] Such a discrepancy could cause a significant error in assessment of gestational age if different normograms are used. Thus, in choosing data from an outside source for use in one's own laboratory, one should consider

TABLE 4
Gestational Age Estimations from FL

FL (mm)	Gestational age (weeks)	
	Hadlock et al.[50]	Jeanty et al.[49]
10	12.8	12.6
12	13.4	13.3
14	13.6	13.9
16	14.5	14.6
18	15.1	15.2
20	15.7	15.9
22	16.3	16.6
24	16.9	17.3
26	17.6	18.0
28	18.2	18.7
30	18.9	19.4
32	19.6	20.1
34	20.3	20.9
36	21.0	21.6
38	21.8	22.4
40	22.5	23.1
42	23.3	23.9
44	24.1	24.7
46	24.9	25.4
48	25.7	26.2
50	26.5	27.0
52	27.4	27.8
54	28.2	28.6
56	29.1	29.5
58	30.0	30.3
60	30.9	31.1
62	31.9	32.0
64	32.8	32.9
66	33.8	33.7
68	34.7	34.6
70	35.7	35.5
72	36.7	36.4
74	37.7	37.3
76	38.8	38.2
78	39.7	39.1
80	40.4	40.0

the equipment and measurement techniques used as well as the demographic characteristics of the population studied.[56]

One of the very important aspects of an analysis of fetal dating is an estimate of the variability that can be associated with a given age prediction. The most common method is a 95% confidence interval representing ±2 SD about the mean value. It was reported that variability in age estimation increases progressively throughout the pregnancy, and it is roughly equivalent using BPD to that using FL measurements.[38]

In order to reduce variability in age estimation, Bovicelli et al.[57] were first to suggest the concept of using more than one sonographic parameter for dating purposes. Using both BPD and CRL measurements, the variability in predicting fetal age (±2 SD) was reduced by 20% in comparison with age prediction based on either BPD or CRL alone.

Later, similar improvements in age prediction were reported by Hadlock and co-workers.[58] They also found that at least five different combinations of various parameters (BPD, AC,

HC, FL) could be considered as an optimal model. These included the following combinations: BPD, FL, AC, BPD, HC, FL, HC, AC, FL, BPD, HC, AC, FL, HC, and FL. The most significant improvements in fetal dating occur in the third trimester, which is of great clinical importance.

REFERENCES

1. **Birnholz, J. C.,** Biological foundations for fetal growth studies, in *Quantitative Obstetrical Ultrasonography,* Deter, R. L., Harrist, R. B., Birnholz, J. C., and Hadlock, F. P., Eds., Wiley Medical, New York, 1986, 49.
2. **Dewhurst, C. J., Beazly, J. M., and Campbell, S.,** Assessment of fetal maturity and dysmaturity, *Am. J. Obstet. Gynecol.,* 13, 141, 1972.
3. **Campbell, S.,** The assessment of fetal development by diagnostic ultrasound, *Clin. Perinatol.,* 1, 507, 1974.
4. **Kurjak, A., Cecuk, S., and Breyer, B.,** Prediction of maturity in first trimester of pregnancy by ultrasonic measurement of fetal crown-rump length, *J. Clin. Ultrasound,* 4, 83, 1976.
5. **Rossavik, I. K. and Gibbons, W. E.,** Variability of ovarian follicular growth in natural menstrual cycles, *Fertil. Steril.,* 14, 195, 1985.
6. **Boyce, A., Mayaux, M., and Shwartz, J.,** Classical and true gestational postmaturity, *Am. J. Obstet. Gynecol.,* 125, 911, 1976.
7. **Funduk-Kurjak, B. and Kurjak, A.,** Ultrasound monitoring of follicular maturation and ovulation in normal menstrual cycle and in ovulation induction, *Acta Obstet. Gynecol. Scand.,* 61, 329, 1982.
8. **Latin, V. and Cecuk, S.,** Gestational age estimation, in *Diagnostic Ultrasound in Developing Countries,* Kurjak, A., Ed., Mladost, Zagreb, 1986, 82.
9. **Robinson, H. P.,** Sonar measurement of fetal crown-rump length as a means of assessing maturity in first trimester of pregnancy, *Br. Med. J.,* 4, 28, 1973.
10. **Drumm, J. E., Clinch, J., and Mackenzie, G.,** The ultrasonic measurement of fetal crown-rump length as a method of assessing gestational age, *Br. J. Obstet. Gynecol.,* 83, 417, 1976.
11. **Nelson, L. H.,** Comparison of methods for determining crown-rump measurement by real-time ultrasound, *J. Clin. Ultrasound,* 9, 67, 1981.
12. **MacGregor, S. N., Tamura, R. K., Sabbagha, R. E., Minogue, J. P., Gibson, M. E., and Hofmann, D. I.,** Underestimation of gestational age by conventional crown-rump length dating curves, *Obstet. Gynecol.,* 70, 344, 1987.
13. **Campbell, S.,** An improved method of fetal cephalometry by ultrasound, *J. Obstet. Gynaecol. Br. Commonw.,* 75, 568, 1968.
14. **Sabbagha, R. E., Barton, F. B., and Barton, B. A.,** Sonar biparietal diameter. I. Analyses of percentile differences in two normal populations using the same methodology, *Am. J. Obstet. Gynecol.,* 126, 479, 1976.
15. **Kurtz, A. B., Wapner, R. J., Kurtz, R. J., Dershaw, D. D., Rubin, C. S., Cole-Beughet, C., and Goldberg, B. B.,** Analysis of biparietal diameter as an accurate indicator of gestational age, *J. Clin. Ultrasound,* 8, 319, 1980.
16. **Deter, R. L., Harrist, R. B., Hadlock, F. P., and Carpenter, R. B.,** The use of ultrasound in the assessment of normal fetal growth, *J. Clin. Ultrasound,* 9, 481, 1981.
17. **Levi, S. and Erbsman, F.,** Antenatal fetal growth from the nineteenth week: ultrasonic study of 12 head and chest dimensions, *Am. J. Obstet. Gynecol.,* 121, 262, 1975.
18. **Hoffbauer, H., Pachaly, J., Arabin, B., and Baumann, M. L.,** Control of fetal development with multiple ultrasonic body measures, *Contrib. Gynecol. Obstet.,* 6, 147, 1979.
19. **Garret, W. J. and Robinson, D. E.,** Assessment of fetal size and growth rate by ultrasonic echoscopy, *Obstet. Gynecol.,* 38, 525, 1971.
20. **Hadlock, F. P., Deter, R. L., Harrist, R. B., and Park, S. K.,** Fetal biparietal diameter: rational choice of plane of section for sonographic measurement, *Am. J. Roentgenol.,* 138, 871, 1982.
21. **Fescina, R. H., Uscieda, F. J., Cordano, M. C., Neito, F., Fenzer, S. M., and Lopez, R.,** Ultrasonic patterns of intrauterine fetal growth in a Latin American country, *Early Hum. Dev.,* 6, 239, 1982.
22. **Campbell, S. and Wilkin, D.,** Ultrasonic measurement of fetal abdomen circumference in the estimation of fetal weight, *Br. J. Obstet. Gynecol.,* 82, 689, 1975.

23. **Campbell, S.,** Fetal growth, in *Medicine,* Beard, R. W. and Nathanielsy, P. W., Eds., W. B. Saunders, Philadelphia, 1976, 271.
24. **Hadlock, F. P., Deter, R. L., Harrist, R. B., and Park, S. K.,** Fetal head circumference: relation to menstrual age, *Am. J. Roentgenol.,* 138, 649, 1982.
25. **Varma, T. R., Taylor, H., and Bridges, C.,** Ultrasound assessment of fetal growth, *Br. J. Obstet. Gynecol.,* 86, 623, 1979.
26. **Woo, J. S. K., Liang, S. T., Wan, C. W., Ghosh, A., Cho, K. M., and Wong, V.,** Abdominal circumference vs. abdominal area — which is better?, *Ultrasound Med. Biol.,* 3, 101, 1984.
27. **Deter, R. L., Harrist, R. B., Hadlock, F. P., and Pointdexter, A. N.,** Longitudinal studies of fetal growth with the use of dynamic image ultrasonography, *Am. J. Obstet. Gynecol.,* 143, 545, 1982.
28. **Wittman, B. K., Robinson, H. P., Artchison, T., and Fleming, J. E. E.,** The value of diagnostic ultrasound as a screening test for intrauterine growth retardation. Comparison of nine parameters, *Radiology,* 134, 30, 1979.
29. **Isel, E. P., Prenzlau, P., Bayer, H. L., Under, R., Schulte, R., Wohlfahrt, G., Weight, M., and Acker, R.,** The measurement of fetal growth during pregnancy by ultrasound (B-scan.), *J. Perinat. Med.,* 3, 269, 1975.
30. **Campbell, S.,** Ultrasonic measurement of fetal limb bones, *Am. J. Obstet. Gynecol.,* 198, 297, 1980.
31. **O'Brien, G. D. and Queenan, J. T.,** Growth of the ultrasound fetal femur length during normal pregnancy, *Am. J. Obstet. Gynecol.,* 198, 297, 1980.
32. **Jeanty, P., Kirkpatrick, C., Dramaix-Wilmet, M., and Stvuyven, J.,** Ultrasound evaluation of fetal limb growth, *Radiology,* 140, 165, 1981.
33. **Hadlock, F. P., Harrist, R. B., Deter, R. L., and Park, S. K.,** Femur length as a predictor of menstrual age, sonographically measured, *Am. J. Roentgenol.,* 138, 875, 1982.
34. **Hobbins, J. C., Bracken, M. B., and Mahoney, M. J.,** Diagnosis of fetal skeletal dysplasias with ultrasound, *Am. J. Obstet. Gynecol.,* 142, 306, 1982.
35. **Seeds, J. W. and Cefalo, R. C.,** Relationship of fetal limb lengths to both biparietal diameter and gestational age, *Obstet. Gynecol.,* 60, 680, 1982.
36. **Merz, E., Kim-Kern, M. S., and Pehl, S.,** Ultrasonic mensuration of fetal limb bones in the second and third trimesters, *J. Clin. Ultrasound,* 15, 175, 1987.
37. **Deter, R. L., Warda, A., Rossavik, J., Duncan, G., and Hadlock, F. P.,** Fetal thigh circumference: a critical evaluation of its relationship to menstrual age, *J. Clin. Ultrasound,* 14, 105, 1986.
38. **Harrist, R. B.,** Regression analysis, in *Quantitative Obstetrical Ultrasonography,* Deter, R. L., Harrist, R. B., Birnholz, J. C., and Hadlock, F. P., Eds., Wiley Medical, New York, 1986, 263.
39. **Robinson, H. P. and Fleming, J. E.,** A critical evaluation of sonar crown-rump measurements, *Br. J. Obstet. Gynecol.,* 82, 702, 1975.
40. **Sabbagha, R. E. and Kipper, I.,** The first trimester pregnancy, in *Diagnostic Ultrasound Applied to Obstetrics and Gynecology,* Sabbagha, R. E., Ed., Harper & Row, New York, 1980.
41. **Adam, A. H., Robinson, H. P., and Dunlop, C. A.,** Comparison of crown-rump length measurement using a real time scanner in an antenatal clinic and a conventional B scanner, *Br. J. Obstet. Gynecol.,* 86, 521, 1979.
42. **Shirley, J. M., Blackwell, R. J., Farman, D. J., and Vicary, R. F.,** *A User's Guide to Diagnostic Ultrasound: Basic Obstetric Procedures,* Pitman Medical, London, 1978, 169.
43. **Shepard, M. and Filly, R. A.,** A standard plane for biparietal diameter measurement, *J. Ultrasound Med.,* 1, 145, 1982.
44. **Daker, M. F. and Setatree, R. S.,** Comparison between linear array real time ultrasonic scanning and conventional compound scanning in the measurement of fetal biparietal diameter, *Br. J. Obstet. Gynecol.,* 84, 924, 1977.
45. **Hadlock, F. P., Deter, R. L., and Harrist, R. B.,** Fetal biparietal diameter: a critical reevaluation of the menstrual age by means of realtime ultrasound, *J. Ultrasound Med.,* 1, 97, 1982.
46. **Hadlock, F. P., Deter, R. I., Carpenter, R. J., and Park, R. S.,** Estimating fetal age: effect of fetal head shape on BPD, *Am. J. Radiol.,* 137, 83, 1981.
47. **Filly, R. A., Golbus, M. S., Carey, J. C., et al.,** Short-limbed dwarfism: ultrasonographic diagnosis by mensuration of fetal femoral length, *Radiology,* 138, 653, 1981.
48. **Filly, R. A. and Golbus, M. S.,** Ultrasonography of the normal and the pathologic fetal skeleton, *Radiol. Clin. North Am.,* 20, 311, 1982.
49. **Jeanty, P., Rodesch, F., and Delbeke, D.,** Estimation of gestational age from measurements of fetal long bones, *J. Ultrasound Med.,* 3, 75, 1984.
50. **Hadlock, F. P., Harrist, R. B., and Deter, R. L.,** A prospective evaluation of fetal femoral length as a predictor of gestational age, *J. Ultrasound Med.,* 2, 111, 1983.

51. **Tse, C. H. and Lee, K. W.,** A comparison of the fetal femur length and biparietal diameter in predicting gestational age in the third trimester, *Aust. N.Z. J. Obstet. Gynaecol.,* 24, 186, 1984.

52. **Hadlock, F. P., Deter, R. L., Harrist, R. B., et al.,** Fetal abdominal circumference as a predictor of menstrual age, *Am. J. Roentgenol.,* 139, 367, 1982.

53. **Jeanty, P., Cantraine, F., Cousaent, E., et al.,** The binocular distance: a new way to estimate fetal age, *J. Ultrasound Med.,* 3, 241, 1984.

54. **Haines, C., Langlois, S. L., and Jones, W. R.,** Ultrasonic measurement of fetal femoral length in singleton and twin pregnancies, *Am. J. Obstet. Gynecol.,* 155, 838, 1986.

55. **O'Brien, G. D., Queenan, J. T., and Campbell, S.,** Assessment of gestational age in the second trimester by real-time ultrasound measurement of the femur length, *Am. J. Obstet. Gynecol.,* 139, 540, 1981.

56. **Hadlock, F. P.,** Evaluation of fetal dating studies, in *Quantitative Obstetrical Ultrasonography,* Deter, R. L., Harrist, R. B., Birnholz, J. C., and Hadlock, F. P., Eds., Wiley Medical, New York, 1986, 33.

57. **Bovicelli, L., Ovsini, L., Rizzo, N.,** Estimation of gestational age during the first trimester by realtime measurement of fetal crown-rump length and biparietal diameter, *J. Clin. Ultrasound,* 9, 71, 1981.

58. **Hadlock, F. P., Deter, R. L., and Harrist, R. B.,** Computer assisted analysis of fetal age in the third trimester using multiple fetal growth parameters, *J. Clin. Ultrasound,* 11, 313, 1983.

Chapter 5

ULTRASOUND IN DETECTION OF GROWTH-RETARDED FETUSES

Asim Kurjak and Jadranka Pavletic

INTRAUTERINE GROWTH RETARDATION

Intrauterine growth retardation (IUGR) continues to represent one of the most significant problems in modern perinatology. IUGR describes the consequences of a complex pathology. Some fetuses grow abnormally because their cells are deprived of nutrients, and some because they have a reduced number of cells. The pathophysiology of IUGR involves the fetus, the placenta, the mother, or a combination of all of these. Growth-retarded fetuses are a heterogenous group that can be classified in two subgroups: (1) constitutionally small fetuses, because of familial or racial factors; the majority of these are "normal" and healthy; (2) growth retarded due to placental insufficiency, genetic disease, intrauterine infection, or toxic damage. These are at increased risk of stillbirth or fetal distress in labor, severe neonatal problems, and difficulties in later development.

Although, there is still no specific treatment, early and accurate diagnosis and intensive surveillance can reduce the hazards of impaired fetal growth by optimal timing delivery.[1,2]

Several attempts have been made to identify risk factors associated with growth retardation, with particular emphasis on maternal hypertension, diabetes mellitus, and renal disease. Women who have a history of growth-retarded infants[3] or who were themselves small for dates at birth[4] are also at increased risk. Unfortunately, such scoring methods[5] are not particularly useful because the traditional high-risk groups account for only a portion of the actual cases of growth retardation.

Clinical evaluation of IUGR is difficult and rather inaccurate.[6] In studies evaluating routine antenatal care, fewer than 50% of growth-retarded infants were clinically suspected.[7] Biochemical methods are also rather unreliable.[8] With sophisticated ultrasonic techniques, the diagnosis of IUGR is now more accurate than ever before. Nevertheless, detection is associated with many problems, and that is reflected in the large number of ultrasonic methods devised for IUGR detection.

Ultrasound screening for IUGR has not been proved to be substantially better than simple serial fundal height measurements.[9,10] However, in selected high-risk groups, ultrasound is the best diagnostic tool for following fetal growth deviation and establishing a diagnosis. It is the only method which can safely provide longitudinal data on fetal growth with reasonable accuracy.

An accurate knowledge of gestational age is essential in order to reliably evaluate ultrasonic measurements in late pregnancy and thereby diagnose IUGR. The optimal method for detecting IUGR is early ultrasonic assessment of gestational age combined with late assessment of fetal size, or preferably, growth rate.

Ultrasound also plays an important role in evaluating fetal activities and functions.[11] A decrease in fetal movements and severe oligohydramnios are often associated with IUGR due to uteroplacental insufficiency. Moreover, its role in detection of fetal malformations (many of which are associated with growth retardation) is irreplacable.[11] Table 1 lists various functions of ultrasound in detection and evaluation of IUGR pregnancies.

The diagnosis of IUGR is associated with difficulties which are partly due to imprecise definition and inconsistent diagnostic criteria. The widely accepted definition of IUGR is

TABLE 1
Functions of Ultrasound in
Detection and Evaluation of IUGR
Pregnancies

Assessment of gestational age
   Crown-rump length (CRL)
   Biparietal diameter (BPD)
   Femur length (FL)
   Combination of multiple parameters
Assessment of fetal size and growth rate
   Fetal weight estimation
   Abdominal circumference (AC) (single,
     serial)
   BPD growth pattern
   Head circumference (HC) to AC ratios
Detection of fetal malformations
   Anatomical
   Chromosomal (karyotyping)
Evaluation of fetal well-being
   Fetal movements
   Doppler blood flow
     (uteroplacental, umbilical, fetal)
   Cordocentesis
Auxilliary diagnostic methods
   Placental maturation
   Qualitative amniotic fluid volume (QAFV)
   In utero ponderal index (PI)
   Distal femoral ossification center

based on birth weight. The newborn whose birth weight is below the tenth percentile for gestational age is classified as small for gestational age, or SGA. This is the most frequently used criterion, but birth weight below the 25th, 5th, and 3rd percentile or 2 SD below the mean, are also reported.[12] Another source of discrepancy is the use of various birth weight standards, and this leads to great differences among newborns classified as an SGA. For example, the 10th percentile values, given by Thompson et al.,[13] are nearly equal to the 25th percentile values of Lubchenco et al.[14] Moreover, all these birth weight curves, often wrongly called growth curves, are rather inaccurate since they have been obtained cross-sectionally and have not been based on a normal population.[15] A recent study from Secher et al.[16] has confirmed that preterm infants, viewed as a group, are smaller than unborn fetuses of the same age. This is not surprising when we consider the fact that many high-risk factors which contribute to fetal growth retardation lead to an increased risk of preterm delivery at the same time. Because of this, the incidence of preterm growth-retarded infants actually exceeds that of term IUGR infants.[17]

In order to overcome this problem, several authors have established intrauterine weight curves based on estimated fetal weights.[16-18] It is obvious that such growth curves are more representative of fetal growth since the measurements have been obtained longitudinally and are based on a normal, healthy population. However, possible errors in weight estimation limit the usefulness of the method. Also, different boundaries between normal and abnormal values of ultrasonic parameters have been reported.[12] It is clear that birth weight criteria alone can lead to an underestimation of the number of infants whose birth weight is (due to the fast growth potential) within the normal range, but who are actually growth retarded at birth. They may be recognized by abnormally rapid weight gain after delivery, by ultrasound during pregnancy (slow growth rate), or by abnormalities of cord blood constituents. Conversely, there are some normal but constitutionally small infants who are wrongly diagnosed as growth retarded.

The term IUGR implies the abnormal restriction of the growth of an infant with greater developmental potential.[19] Hence, IUGR should not be used as a synonym for SGA. The diagnosis of IUGR requires additional information such as the pattern of the fetal growth and, particularly, the rate of fetal growth.

The ultrasound diagnosis of impaired fetal growth has been made by comparing the measurements from individual fetuses to population standards. The limitations of this method have already been mentioned. To overcome this problem, Deter et al.[21] have used Rossavik's growth model[20] to establish individual growth curve standards for various ultrasonic parameters. They reported that individual growth curve models, derived from data obtained before the 28th week of pregnancy, were capable of predicting growth beyond 28 weeks. It is presumed that comparing a measurement to its expected value provides a sensitive indicator of impaired fetal growth. Theoretically, a method of individualized assessment of fetal growth seems to be convenient, but the technique needs further investigation. Another relatively new method, i.e., Doppler flow velocity waveforms,[22] is also very promising, but awaits further assessment.

THE BIPARIETAL DIAMETER

A wide variety of ultrasonic parameters have been used, alone and in different combinations, to diagnose IUGR. At first, cephalometry was probably the most commonly used method of assessing fetal growth.[23] Serial cephalometry identified two patterns of impaired fetal growth.[24] In symmetrical IUGR (type I), the biparietal diameter (BPD) growth pattern was steady, but indicated an abnormally low growth rate ("low profile") which began early in the second trimester. In this group there is a high incidence of congenital malformations and the prognosis is poor. In asymmetrical growth retardation (type II), there is a lengthy period of normal BPD growth which is followed by an abrupt flattening of BPD growth curve ("late flattening") in the third trimester.[24] This type of growth retardation is commonly associated with maternal and placental factors leading to faulty growth support. As there is no strict boundary between types I and II, mixed patterns are also found to occur, and it is not always easy to distinguish one type of growth retardation from another.

Disadvantages of this method include (1) the need for serial measurements, (2) BPD measurements will detect only the symmetrical type of IUGR, which probably includes many healthy genetically small infants,[25] (3) true symmetrically retarded infants constitute only about 20% of all growth-retarded infants,[1] (4) there are intrinsic limitations to the use of ultrasonic cephalometry for the estimation of fetal weight, and (5) the BPD reflects only one dimension of the head and is frequently not truly representative of the total fetal head and brain size. There is also a biological variation in cranial morphology. However, Crane and Kopta[26] reported that BPD measurements can be of value even in detection of asymmetrically retarded infants.

The accuracy of antenatal diagnosis of IUGR based upon BPD data by several investigators ranges from 35 to 70%.[11,27,28] We found that both single and serial BPD measurements showed diagnostic accuracy of approximately 50%.[29] Thus, although the method is simple and reproducible, ultrasonic measurement of the fetal head alone is not a reliable predictor of IUGR. However, a two-dimensional measurement (e.g., fetal head area) similar to that described below may improve the overall assessment.

ABDOMINAL CIRCUMFERENCE

Another relatively old but much more sensitive method for diagnosis of IUGR is the abdominal circumference (AC) measurement, first described by Campbell and Wilkin.[30] The

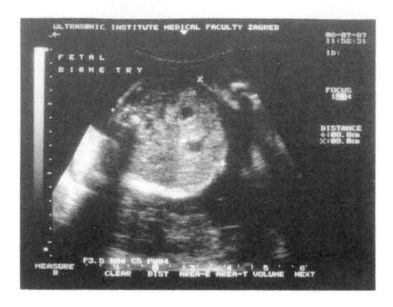

FIGURE 1.   The measurement of AC on the level of bifurcation of the main portal vein into its right and left branches.

measurement should be performed at the level of the fetal liver. As the fetal liver is the most severely affected organ in infants with type II growth retardation,[31] this ultrasound section is of great importance in the assessment of fetal nutrition. There is also a good correlation with fetal weight.[30,32]

The most important criterion in obtaining a proper abdominal section for measurement is that the section should be as circular as possible. The level of the section is also precisely defined as the bifurcation of the main portal vein into its right and left branches.[33] Figure 1 shows a standard plane for AC measurement.

The portal vein should not reach the anterior abdominal wall. The AC can be measured by a map reader, by an electronic digitizer passed along the external circumference (Figure 2), or by multiplying the sum of the two diameters by 1.57.

Lateral resolution is very important for perimetrical measurements. It might be expected, therefore, that perimetrical measurements are less accurate when obtained from linear array images than with compound scanning. In practice, the difference between static and real-time measurements has been reported to be very small.[34] We found the AC to be the best single predictor of IUGR.[1,35] In conjunction with other biometric parameters, its predictive value is greatly enhanced and capable of accurately predicting IUGR in more than 96% of patients.[1,35] Figure 3 demonstrates significantly reduced AC in the growth-retarded twin (left) as compared to the normally growing second twin (right). Recently, Pearce and Campbell[10] reported 83% sensitivity of AC measurements in screening for IUGR. The false positive rate was rather high (up to 61%). However, in selected patients, detailed ultrasonic biometry with repeated examination will reduce this figure to about 15%. Better results (93% sensitivity) were obtained by Neilson et al.[36] They performed a complex measurement involving the product of the CRL and the trunk area in the third trimester, which is not suitable for real-time equipment.

Recently, two new ultrasonic parameters have been reported to be of possible value in IUGR detection. Vintzileos et al.[37] described fetal liver measurements, and determined fetal

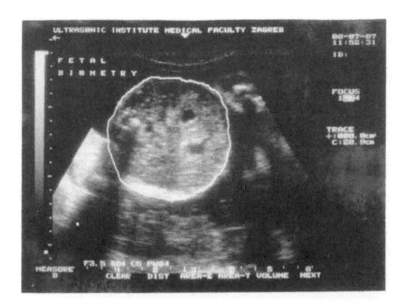

FIGURE 2.   AC measurement by electronic cursor.

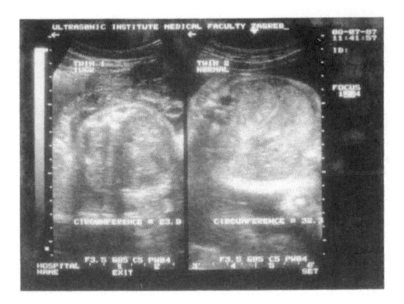

FIGURE 3.   Significantly reduced AC in growth-retarded twin (left) as compared to the normally growing second twin (right).

liver size for each week of pregnancy from 20 weeks. A linear relationship between fetal liver and abdominal circumference measurements was also described. The fetal liver is the most severely affected organ in deprivational IUGR. However, it has a fast growth rate during the critical third trimester, and this is of great importance for the accurate detection of growth abnormalities. In a preliminary study of ten IUGR infants, the authors reported excellent correlation (100%) between IUGR and fetal liver measurement decreasing more than 2 SD below mean.[37]

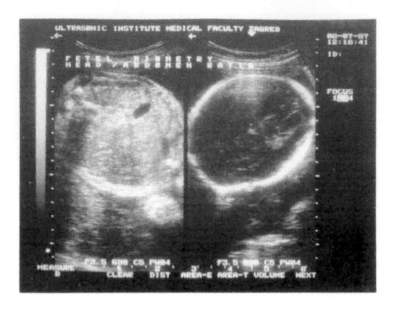

FIGURE 4.   Standard planes for head and abdomen circumference measurement
— normal pregnancy.

Several authors have reported on fetal thigh circumference (ThC), which reflects the
fetal soft tissue mass as a potentially valid parameter for identifying fetuses with IUGR.[38,39]

THE HEAD TO ABDOMEN RATIO

Head to abdomen (H:A) circumference ratio is reported to be valuable not only in
detection of IUGR, but also in the distinction of the symmetrical and asymmetrical[40] types.
Campbell and Thoms[40] first introduced the ratio in the diagnosis of IUGR and established
normal values during the pregnancy. These decline from 1.18 at 17 weeks to 0.96 at 40
weeks of pregnancy. Using this parameter, they were able to distinguish the symmetrical
and asymmetrical type of growth retardation in a group of 33 SFD infants, which may be
of importance in the long-term assessment of growth-retarded infants. Figure 3 shows H:A
ratio in normal pregnancy. Correlation of elevated H:A ratios (Figure 4) and IUGR was
reported by Crane and Kopta.[44] In all of the seven growth-retarded fetuses, the ratio was 2
SD above the mean. Others found this method less successful in diagnosis of IUGR.[42]

In our experience, the accuracy of the H:A ratio is inferior to the AC in the diagnosis
of IUGR. We use the H:A ratio to demonstrate the pattern of growth (i.e., perinatal risk),
rather than the diagnosis of IUGR (Figure 5).

THE ESTIMATED FETAL WEIGHT

Estimation of fetal weight is the most practical step in the diagnosis of IUGR. It is also
an important factor in the management of high-risk pregnancies. A recent survey of over 2
million births concluded that perinatal mortality rates are much more sensitive to birth weight
than to gestational age.[43] Based on ultrasonic measurements of various fetal dimensions, a
number of formulas have been devised for the purpose of estimating fetal weight.

A basic problem in establishing connections between ultrasound measurements and fetal
weight is that weight can only be measured after birth.[44] This fact necessitates the assumption
that the weight of a fetus born shortly after the scanning is similar to that of the fetus with

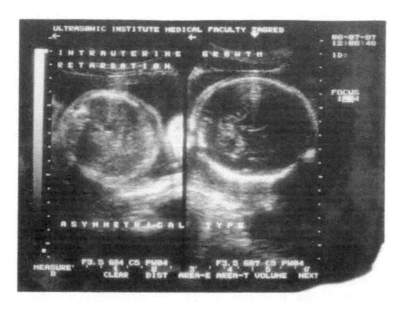

FIGURE 5. Increased H:A ratio in case of IUGR.

the same values of the ultrasound measurement, but remaining *in utero*. Any method for fetal weight estimation should be as accurate as possible. Also, in order to be clinically useful, it should be simple and practical. The efficacy of a formula for weight estimation depends upon how successful the formula describes the relationship between measured parameters and fetal weight, the accuracy of the measurements, and how the formula deals with altered fetal body proportions often present in IUGR.

As a single dimension, the BPD is a poor predictor of fetal weight, especially in cases of type II growth retardation. Better results have been obtained using AC measurements.[30,32] Campbell and Wilkin[30] estimated fetal weight from AC and reported that 95% of actual weights were within 160 g/kg of the estimated weight. Kurjak and Breyer[32] measured two abdominal diameters (the longest and the smallest) and calculated the AC of an ellipse. In 83% of the cases, the difference between the actual and expected weight was within 150 g. The mean error was 105 g.[32] Because the fetal mass is contained mostly in the head and trunk, a accurate assessment of fetal weight has to involve measurements of both. A number of formulas have been devised which use measurements of both the fetal head and fetal abdomen. Warsof et al.[45] reported that a combination of the BPD and AC predicted fetal weight with an accuracy of 106 g/kg. Using Shepard's formula (which also utilized the BPD and AC),[46] Ott and Doyle[47] calculated fetal weight in 595 patients, both low and high risk, who had undergone ultrasound examination within 72 h before birth.[47] The estimated fetal weight was then plotted on a normal ultrasound fetal weight curve.[17] They found this technique to be 89.9% sensitive and 79.8% specific for the diagnosis of SGA infants.[47] Moreover, all of the severely growth-retarded infants (birth weight below the third percentile) were accurately predicted.[47]

The formulas mentioned above do not take into account fetal length, which could have a great influence on fetal weight, particularly in extra long or short fetuses. There is, however, no accurate method for fetal length estimation, but good correlation between crown-heel length and femur length (FL) has been shown.[48] Therefore, it has been suggested that FL should be added to the formula for estimating fetal weight.[49] Weiner et al.[50] were the first to report a fetal weight estimation using head circumference (HC), AC, and FL in low-birth-weight infants.[50] FL was used only to adjust the weight estimate if the FL was greater than 2 SD from the mean for gestational age.[50] By using HC instead of BPD, the problem of dolicocephaly has been resolved. On the other hand, Seeds et al.[51] have suggested the use of a femur equivalent in cases where the BPD is unavailable or distorted.[51] The correlation between FL and BPD has been reported to be linear with only small variability throughout gestation.[49] Using Warsof et al.'s formula,[45] fetal weight was estimated within 10% of actual birth weight[51] in 77.1% of low-birth-weight infants (birth weight between 520 to 1500 g). Using femur equivalent BPD substitution, the estimation was only slightly less accurate.

Evaluating three equatations,[30,45,46] Deter et al.[52] reported that Campbell and Wilkin's formula[30] overestimated fetal weight, whereas Warsof et al.'s formula[45] underestimated fetal weight. They concluded that the best estimates were provided by Shepard et al.'s method. Data from Hill et al. also confirmed underestimation of fetal weight using Warsof et al.'s formula.[53] They also found Campbell and Wilkin's equation most reliable in estimating fetal weight greater than 2000 g, whereas Shepard et al.'s method was more accurate at the ends of the weight scale (less than 200 g and more than 4000 g).[53] Recently, Dudley and co-workers[54] devised a method for estimating fetal weight by calculating an approximate fetal volume from abdominal area, head area, and FL. The new method was then compared to those of Campbell and Wilkin and Warsof et al. in estimating birth weights in 434 cases. It was reported that in the middle range of birth weights, all three methods performed equally, while the new method had greater accuracy in the important low- and high-birth-weight group.[54] Several authors have studied a group of low-birth-weight infants and derived their own formulas for weight estimation.[55-57]

In a recent study, Vintzileos et al.[58] investigated the value of fetal ThC measurement in addition to conventional ultrasonic parameters for fetal weight estimation.[58] They found that addition of ThC to the measurements of head, abdomen, and FL improves the accuracy of fetal weight estimation. However, it is rather time consuming when multiple parameters are included. The same authors also confirmed that as a single parameter AC is the best predictor of fetal weight.

FETAL URINARY PRODUCTION RATE

Oligohydramnios is often associated with severe IUGR.[59] This association probably relates to the diminished fetal urine output seen in IUGR.[1] Campbell and co-workers[60] were the first to describe fetal urine production rates. This is estimated by taking serial bladder volume measurements and calculating the hourly rate of increase. A strong correlation between reduced fetal urine production rate and IUGR was reported.[60] However, this method is rather time consuming, less accurate than others, and, therefore, is not suitable for widespread use.

THE TOTAL INTRAUTERINE VOLUME (TIUV)

A measurement of TIUV is theoretically useful to detect IUGR, since in IUGR pregnancies not only the fetal mass, but also placental and amniotic fluid volume are often diminished. Normal growth curves for TIUV have been reported,[61] and a significantly increased risk of IUGR has been found when the TIUV is below the 2.5% confidence limit.[62] In a nonselected antenatal clinic population of 362 women, Geirsson[63] reported this method to be more sensitive in predicting IUGR than abdominal area and BPD measurements. However, a large number of false positive tests resulted in a lower predictive value for positive tests (mean 34%) than for the abdominal area measurements (mean 54%). Several other authors[64] have also reported high false positive rates with TIUV.

Since measurement of TIUV is rather indirect in relation to fetal size and can be obtained only by a static scanner, it is not convenient for the detection of IUGR and has been supplanted by more accurate and easily obtainable parameters.

QUALITATIVE AMNIOTIC FLUID VOLUME (QAFV) DETERMINATION

Similar to TIUV, a QAFV determination has been reported to be useful for predicting IUGR.[65] QAFV is defined as abnormal if the examiner cannot find one pocket of amniotic fluid at least 1 cm wide.[65] In their study of 120 pregnant women, Manning et al.[65] correctly predicted 85 out of 91 (93.4% accurate) infants to be non-IUGR, while 26 out of 29 patients with decreased QAFV were accurately predicted to have growth-retarded infants (89.9% accurate). Other investigators have not confirmed the same level of correlation.[59,66] Although oligohydroamnios frequently indicates a severe level of fetal deprivation, QAFV is not a useful method for IUGR detection.

PLACENTAL MATURATION GRADING

Kazzi et al.[67] found that ultrasonic placental maturity (grade III placenta), associated with a small fetus, successfully detects IUGR in 62% of patients. As a single method it is not sensitive enough for IUGR detection, but it may be useful in connection with other methods.

Most methods of ultrasonic diagnosis of IUGR are scaled to gestational age, while accurate gestational age may not always be accurately established. Unless the patient is seen in the first trimester of pregnancy, many cases of size-date discrepancy are due to uncertainty concerning dates rather than to IUGR. For that reason, attempts have been made to establish an age-independent predictor of IUGR. For more than 25 years, pediatricians have used ponderal index (PI) in evaluating fetal growth impairment. PI[19] is defined as

$$\frac{\text{birth weight} \times 100}{(\text{crown-heel length})^3}$$

Infants with low PI might not be considered small for dates by weight alone, but could be victims of malnutrition, nevertheless.

Recently, practical methods to establish PI *in utero* have been suggested.[68,69] These are based on fetal FL as representing the fetal length[70] and on the AC, which is known to be closely related to the fetal weight.[30,32,69] In a recent study, Yagel and co-workers[71] found *in utero* PI to be a valuable predictor of fetal outcome in those cases of IUGR in which estimated fetal weight was smaller than 1 SD from the average mean value.[71] In 21 growth-retarded fetuses (out of 51 with IUGR) with an abnormal *in utero* PI, the perinatal outcome was devastating (2 stillbirths, 2 neonatal deaths, 4 cases of intraventricular hemorrhage, 5 newborns with low Apgar score <7). They also found a good correlation of abnormal *in utero* PI with abnormal Doppler-measured umbilical artery systolic/diastolic ratios, decreased amniotic fluid volume, and grade III placenta. *In utero* PI could be used not only as a screening diagnostic procedure, but as a valuable index of IUGR fetuses at high risk.

Zilianti and co-workers[72] proposed the use of the distal femoral epiphyseal ossification center as a screening method for IUGR. After 34 weeks of pregnancy, the epiphyseal ossification center of the femur can be visualized by ultrasound in normal, but usually not in growth-retarded pregnancies. The authors found this method more convenient than other ultrasonic techniques because of the following the advantages: the easy reproducibility of a clear anatomical landmark and the sharp distinction between normal and abnormal findings.[72] There are also no measurements involved, and there are no artificial statistical evaluations and boundaries. However, this method is not applicable prior to the 34th week of gestation.

As described, a wide variety of ultrasonic parameters with various accuracy have been used in IUGR detection. However, when evaluating published results, one has to consider the characteristics (normal or high risk) and size of the population studied and criteria for diagnosis used. When detected (or suspected), IUGR pregnancy needs further evaluation and careful surveillance. The possibilities are now greatly enhanced, owing to new ultrasound methods, particularly Doppler blood-flow measurements[22] and cordocentesis.[73]

To improve diagnostic accuracy of IUGR by ultrasound, we need the following:

1. A precise definition of IUGR based not only on birth weight.
2. An optimal and consistent boundary between normal and abnormal values for various ultrasonic parameters.
3. Normograms of each parameter measured, and these should be obtained by longitudinal studies of the same population or populations with similar characteristics.

REFERENCES

1. **Kurjak, A., Kirkinen, P., and Latin, V.,** Biometric and dynamic ultrasound assessment of small-for-dates infants. Report of 260 cases, *Obstet. Gynecol.,* 56, 281, 1980.
2. **Pearce, J. M. and Campbell, S.,** Ultrasonic monitoring of normal and abnormal fetal growth, in *Modern Management of High Risk Pregnancy,* Laurensen, N. H., Ed., Plenum Press, New York, 1983.
3. **Tejani, N. A.,** Recurrence of intrauterine growth retardation, *Obstet. Gynecol.,* 59, 329, 1982.
4. **Hackman, E.,** Maternal birthweight and subsequent pregnancy outcome, *JAMA,* 250, 2016, 1983.
5. **Hobel, C. J., Youkeles, K., and Forsythe, A.,** Prenatal and intrapartum high risk screening. II. Risk factors reassessed, *Am. J. Obstet. Gynecol.,* 135, 1051, 1979.
6. **Beazley, J. M. and Kurjak, A.,** Prediction of fetal maturity and birth weight by abdominal palpation, *Nurs. Times,* 69, 14, 1973.
7. **Hall, M. H. and Ching, P. K.,** Is routine antenatal care worthwhile?, *Lancet,* 78, 1980.
8. **Campbell, S. and Kurjak, A.,** Comparison between urinary estrogen assay and serial ultrasonic cephalometry in assessment of fetal growth retardation, *Br. Med. J.,* 4, 336, 1972.
9. **Warsof, S. L., Pearce, J. M., and Campbell, S.,** The present place of routine ultrasound screening, *Clin. Obstet. Gynecol.,* 10, 445, 1983.
10. **Pearce, J. M. and Campbell, S.,** A comparison of symphysis-fundal height and ultrasound as screening tests for light-for-gestational age infants, *Br. J. Obstet. Gynecol.,* 94, 100, 1987.
11. **Linn, C. C.,** Intrauterine growth retardation, in *Obstet. Gynecol. Annu.,* 14, 127, 1985.
12. **Deter, R. L., Harrist, R. B., Hadlock, F. P., and Carpenter, R. J.,** The use of ultrasound in the detection of intrauterine growth retardation. A Review, *J. Clin. Ultrasound,* 10, 9, 1982.
13. **Thomson, A. M., Billewitz, W. Z., and Hytten, F. E.,** The assessment of fetal growth, *J. Obstet Gynaecol. Br. Commonw.,* 75, 903, 1968.
14. **Lubchenco, L. O., Hansmann, C., Dressler, M., and Boyd, E.,** Intrauterine growth as estimated from liveborn birthweight data at 24 to 42 weeks of gestation, *Pediatrics,* 32, 793, 1963.
15. **Miller, H. C.,** Intrauterine growth retardation. An unmet challenge, *Am. J. Dis. Child.,* 135, 944, 1981.
16. **Secher, N. J., Hansen, P. K., Thompson, B. L., and Keiding, N.,** Growth retardation in preterm infants, *Br. J. Obstet. Gynecol.,* 94, 115, 1987.
17. **Ott, W. J. and Doyle, S.,** Normal ultrasonic fetal weight curve, *Obstet. Gynecol.,* 59, 603, 1982.
18. **Persson, P. H. and Welchner, B. M.,** Intrauterine weight curves obtained by ultrasound, *Acta Obstet. Gynecol. Scand.,* 65, 169, 1986.
19. **Seeds, J. W.,** Impaired fetal growth: ultrasonic evaluation and clinical management, *Obstet. Gynecol.,* 64, 577, 1984.
20. **Rossavik, I. K. and Deter, R. L.,** Mathematical modeling of fetal growth. I. Basic principles, *J. Clin. Ultrasound,* 12, 529, 1984.
21. **Deter, R. L., Rossavik, I. K., Harrist, R. B., and Hadlock, F. P.** Mathematical modeling of fetal growth. Development of individual growth curve standards, *Obstet. Gynecol.,* 68, 156, 1986.

22. **Trudinger, B. J., Warwick, B. G., Cook, C. M., Bombardieri, J., and Collins, L.,** Fetal umbilical artery flow velocity wave forms and placental resistance: clinical significance, *Br. J. Obstet. Gynecol.*, 92, 23, 1985.

23. **Campbell, S. and Dewhurst, C. J.,** Diagnosis of the small-for-dates fetus by serial ultrasound cephalometry, *Lancet*, 61, 1002, 1971.

24. **Campbell, S.,** The assessment of fetal development by diagnostic ultrasound, *Clin. Perinatol.*, 1, 507, 1984.

25. **Kierse, M. J. N. C.,** Aetiology of intrauterine growth retardation, in *Fetal Growth Retardation*, Van Assche, F. A., Ed., Churchill Livingstone, Edinburg, 1981.

26. **Crane, J. P. and Kopta, M. M.,** Comparative anthrophometric data in symmetric versus asymmetric intrauterine growth retardation, *Am. J. Obstet. Gynecol.*, 138, 518, 1980.

27. **Arias, F.,** The diagnosis and management of intrauterine growth retardation, *Obstet. Gynecol.*, 49, 293, 1977.

28. **Sabbagha, R. E.,** Intrauterine growth retardation: Antenatal dyagnosis by ultrasound, *Obstet. Gynecol.*, 52, 252, 1978.

29. **Kurjak, A., Latin, V., and Polak, J.,** Ultrasonic recognition of two types of growth retardation by measurement of four fetal dimensions, *J. Perinat. Med.*, 6, 102, 1978.

30. **Campbell, S. and Wilkin, D.,** Ultrasonic measurement of fetal abdominal circumference in the estimation of fetal weight, *Br. J. Obstet. Gynecol.*, 82, 689, 1975.

31. **Rosso, P. and Winick, M.,** Intrauterine growth retardation: a new systemic approach based on the clinical and biochemical characteristics of this condition, *J. Perinat. Med.*, 2, 147, 1974.

32. **Kurjak, A. and Breyer, B.,** Estimation of fetal weight by ultrasonic abdominometry, *Am. J. Obstet. Gynecol.*, 1, 962, 1976.

33. **Chinn, D. H., Filly, R. A., and Callen, P. V.,** Ultrasonic evaluation of fetal umbilical and hepatic vascular anatomy, *Radiology*, 144, 153, 1982.

34. **Weiner, C. P., Sabbagha, R. E., Tamura, R., and Dalcompo, S.,** Sonographic abdominal circumference: dynamic versus static imaging, *Am. J. Obstet. Gynecol.*, 139, 953, 1981.

35. **Kurjak, A., Breyer, B., and Olajos, J.,** Ultrasonic assessment of fetal growth and gestational age by measurement of three fetal dimensions, in *Ultrasound in Medicine*, Vol. 3A, White, D. and Brown, R. E., Eds., Plenum Press, New York, 1977, 681.

36. **Neilson, J. P., Munjanja, S. P., and Whitfield, C. R.,** Screening for small for dates fetuses: a controlled trial, *Br. Med. J.*, 289, 1179, 1984.

37. **Vintzileos, A. M., Neckles, S., Campbell, W. A., Andreoli, J. W., Jr., Kaplan, B. M., and Nochimson, D. J.,** Fetal liver ultrasound measurements during normal pregnancy, *Obstet. Gynecol.*, 66, 477, 1985.

38. **Deter, R. L., Warda, A., Rossavik, I., Duncan, G., and Hadlock, F. P.,** Fetal thigh circumference: a critical evaluation of its relationship to menstrual age, *J. Clin. Ultrasound*, 14, 105, 1986.

39. **Warda, A. H., Deter, R. L., Duncan, G., and Hadlock, F. P.,** Evaluation of thigh circumference measurements: a comparative ultrasound and anatomical study, *J. Clin. Ultrasound*, 14, 99, 1986.

40. **Campbell, S. and Thoms, A.,** Ultrasound measurement of the fetal head to abdomen circumference ratio in the assessment of growth retardation, *Br. J. Obstet. Gynecol.*, 84, 165, 1977.

41. **Crane, J. P. and Kopta, M. M.,** Prediction of IUGR via ultrasonically measured head abdominal circumference ratios, *Obstet. Gynecol.*, 54, 497, 1979.

42. **Ellis, C. and Berrnet, M. J.,** Detection of intrauterine growth retardation by ultrasound: preliminary communication, *J. R. Soc. Med.*, 74, 739, 1981.

43. **Williams, R. L., Creasy, R. K., Cunningham, G. C., Hawes, W. E., Norris, F. D., and Tashiro, M.,** Fetal growth and perinatal viability in California, *Obstet. Gynecol.*, 50, 624, 1982.

44. **Morgenstern, J., Burzik, C., Soffke, U., and Bokelmann, J.,** Estimation of birth weight, *J. Perinat. Med.*, 14, 147, 1986.

45. **Warsof, S. L., Gohari, P., Berkowitz, R. L., and Hobbins, J. C.,** The estimation of fetal weight by computer-assisted analysis, *Am. J. Obstet. Gynecol.*, 128, 881, 1977.

46. **Shepard, M. T., Richards, V. M., Berkowitz, R. T., et al.,** An evaluation of two equations for the prediction of fetal weight by ultrasound, *Am. J. Obstet. Gynecol.*, 142, 47, 1982.

47. **Ott, W. J. and Doyle, S.,** Ultrasonic Diagnosis of altered fetal growth by use of a normal ultrasound fetal weight curve, *Obstet. Gynecol.*, 63, 201, 1984.

48. **Fazekas, I. and Kosa, F.,** *Forensic Fetal Osteology*, lleyden, Philadelphia, 1978.

49. **Hadlock, F. P., Harrist, R. B., Carpenter, R. J., et al.,** Sonographic estimation of fetal weight: the value of femur length in addition to head and abdomen measurements, *Radiology*, 150, 535, 1984.

50. **Weiner, C. P., Sabbagha, R. E., Vasirub, N., et al.,** Sonographic Weight Prediction of the Low Birthweight Infants, Abstr. 67, Small Gestational-Age Infants, Meet., Washington, DC, 1983.

51. **Seeds, J. W., Cefalo, L. C., and Bowes, W. A.,** Femur length in the estimation of fetal weight less than 1500 grams, *Am. J. Obstet. Gynecol.,* 149, 232, 1984.
52. **Deter, R. L., Hadlock, F. P., Harrist, R. B., et al.,** Evaluation of three methods for obtaining fetal weight estimates using dynamic image ultrasound, *J. Clin. Ultrasound,* 9, 421, 1981.
53. **Hill, L. M., Breckle, R., Wolfram, K. R., and O'Brien, P. C.,** Evaluation of three methods for estimating fetal weight, *J. Clin. Ultrasound,* 14, 121, 1986.
54. **Dudley, N. J., Lomb, M. P., and Copping, C.,** A new method for fetal weight estimation using real-time ultrasound, *Br. J. Obstet. Gynecol.,* 94, 110, 1987.
55. **Eden, R. R., Jelovsek, F. R., Kodack, L. D., et al.,** Accuracy of ultrasonic fetal weight prediction in preterm infants, *Am. J. Obstet. Gynecol.,* 147, 43, 1983.
56. **Thurnau, G. R., Tamura, R. K., Sabbagha, R., et al.,** A simple estimated fetal weight equation based on real-time ultrasound measurements of fetuses less than thirty-four weeks gestation, *Am. J. Obstet. Gynecol.,* 145, 557, 1983.
57. **Weinberger, E., Cyr, D. R., Hirsch, J. H., et al.,** Estimating fetal weights less than 2000 g. An accurate and simple method, *Am. J. Roentgenol.,* 142, 973, 1984.
58. **Vintzileos, A. M., Campbell, W. A., Rodis, J., Bors-Koefoed, R., and Nochimson, D. J.,** Fetal weight estimation formulas with head, abdominal, femur and thigh circumference measurements, *Am. J. Obstet. Gynecol.,* 157, 410, 1987.
59. **Philipson, E. H., Sokol, R. J., and Williams, T.,** Oligohydramnios-clinical association and predictive value for intrauterine growth retardation, *Am. J. Obstet. Gynecol.,* 146, 271, 1983.
60. **Campbell, S., Wladimiroff, J. W., and Dewhurst, C. J.,** The antenatal measurement of fetal urine production, *Br. J. Obstet. Gynecol.,* 80, 680, 1973.
61. **Chinn, D. H., Filly, R. A., and Callen, P. W.,** Prediction of intrauterine growth retardation by sonographic estimation of total intrauterine volume, *J. Clin. Ultrasound,* 9, 175, 1981.
62. **Levine, S. C., Filly, R. A., and Creasy, R. K.,** Indetification of fetal growth retardation by ultrasonographic estimation of total intrauterine volume, *J. Clin. Ultrasound,* 7, 21, 1979.
63. **Geirsson, R. T.,** Intrauterine volume in pregnancy, *Acta Obstet. Gynecol. Scand. Suppl.,* 136, 1986.
64. **Grossman, M., Flynn, J. J., Aufrichtig, D., and Handler, R. C.,** Pitfalls in ultrasonic determination of total intrauterine volume, *J. Clin. Ultrasound,* 10, 17, 1982.
65. **Manning, F. A., Hill, L. M., and Platt, L. D.,** Qualitative amniotic fluid volume determination by ultrasound-antepartum detection of intrauterine growth retardation, *Am. J. Obstet. Gynecol.,* 139, 254, 1981.
66. **Hill, L. M., Breckle, R., Wolfgram, K. R., et al.,** Olygohydromnios: ultrasonically detected incidence and subsequent outcome, *Am. J. Obstet. Gynecol.,* 147, 407, 1983.
67. **Kazzi, G. M., Gross, T. L., Sokol, R. J., et al.,** Detection of intrauterine growth retardation: a new use for sonographic placental grading, *Am. J. Obstet. Gynecol.,* 145, 733, 1983.
68. **Vintzileos, A. M., Neckles, S., Campbell, W. A., et al.,** Three fetal ponderal indexes in normal pregnancy, *Obstet. Gynecol.,* 65, 807, 1985.
69. **Hadlock, F. P., Deter, R. L., Harrist, R. B., et al.,** A date independent predictor of intrauterine growth retardation: femur length abdominal circumference ratio, *Am. J. Roentgenol.,* 141, 979, 1983.
70. **Hadlock, F. P., Deter, R. L., Roecker, E., et al.,** Relation of fetal femur length to neonatal crown-heel length, *J. Ultrasound Med.,* 3, 1, 1984.
71. **Yagel, S., Zacut, D., Ingelstein, S., Palti, Z., Hurowitz, A., and Rossen, B.,** In utero ponderal index as a prognostic factor in the evaluation of intrauterine growth retardation, *Am. J. Obstet. Gynecol.,* 157, 415, 1987.
72. **Zilianti, M., Fernandez, S., Azuaga, A., Jorgez, J., Maria-Severi, F., and Colosi, E.,** Ultrasound evaluation of the distal femoral epiphyseal ossification center as a screening test for intrauterine growth retardation, *Obstet. Gynecol.,* 70, 361, 1987.
73. **Nicolaides, K. H., Soothill, P. W., Rodeck, C. H., and Campbell, S.,** Ultrasound-guided sampling of umbilical cord and placental blood to assess fetal well being, *Lancet,* i, 1065, 1986.

Chapter 6

PLACENTA, UMBILICAL CORD, AND AMNIOTIC MEMBRANES

Visnja Latin

INTRODUCTION

The placenta is a short-lived organ, but essential for fetal growth and development. It represents the unique connection between the mother and her fetus. Its histological appearances alter profoundly as gestation proceeds, with considerable differences from one area to another.[1]

In the past, a number of methods were used in the placental localization (radiographic placentography or arteriography, termography, scintigraphy) with limited possibilities. Ultrasonical visualization has showed that this technique is superior to all other imaging techniques.

Placentography by ultrasound was first described in 1966.[2] With bistable equipment it was possible to identify the placenta as a white, speckled area between the uterine wall and chorionic plate and as a boundary towards the amniotic cavity. Using this technique, the localization of the placenta was accurate in 95% of cases.[2] However, only after the introduction of gray scale and real-time techniques were physiological and pathological variations in anatomy of the internal structure of the placenta and the retroplacental area demonstrated. The accuracy of the placental localization increased to almost 100%.[3] Real-time technique provides additional information on the dynamics of the placenta and the better display of the umbilical cord with the vessels. Sector probe is superior to linear-array in the placental localization behind the pubis.[4] It allows a better look at the placenta praevia by defining a clearer picture of the bladder and cervical region lying directly beneath the pubic symphysis.

THE NORMAL APPEARANCE OF THE PLACENTA IN EARLY PREGNANCY

The future placental place is first identified by sonography at approximately 8 weeks of menstrual age,[4-8] when the decidua basalis and chorion frondosum are visible (Figure 1). Usually it is clearer between the 9th and 10th week of gestation. By the 10th to 12th week, the sac is elongated and the diffuse granular texture of the placenta is clearly apparent (Figure 2). The specific echoes, which are emitted from the villous tree, result in a characteristic sonographic texture at that stage of pregnancy. The identification of the chorion frondosum is very important in antenatal diagnosis. Using chorion villi analyses, the majority of genetic disorders could be confirmed (Figure 3).

At the end of the 12th week of gestation, the sac is not completely surrounded, but it looks as a completed circle as in the earlier gestational weeks. The chorion frondosum is well defined now, and three main areas can be identified: the basal plate and the chorionic plate with the placental tissue between them (Figure 4). The placental substances produce a homogeneous echogenic pattern. The chorionic plate appears as a continuous line limiting the placenta toward the amniotic cavity because of a strong acoustic interface with the adjacent amniotic fluid.[5,9-11] In routine work it is usually clearer later in pregnancy, around the 19th week of gestation. The basal plate does not have a specific ultrasound visualization, but can be identified late in pregnancy, after the deposition of calcium.

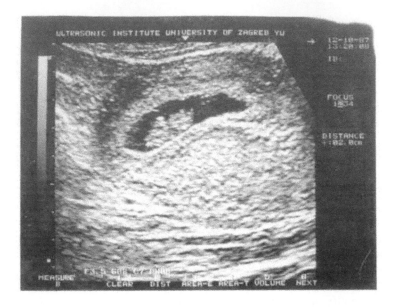

FIGURE 1. Transverse sonogram of the uterus at the 8th week of gestation showing the embryo and gestational sac. The chorion frondosum is seen as an area of increased thickness and echogenicity within the wall of gestational sac.

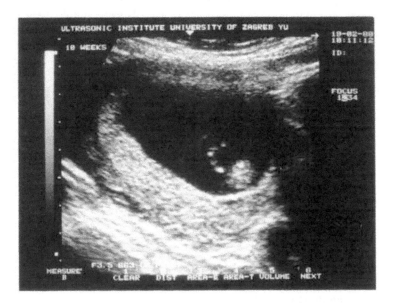

FIGURE 2. Sonogram showing a normal 10-week-old pregnancy. The diffuse granular texture of the placenta is clearly visible on the posterior uterine wall.

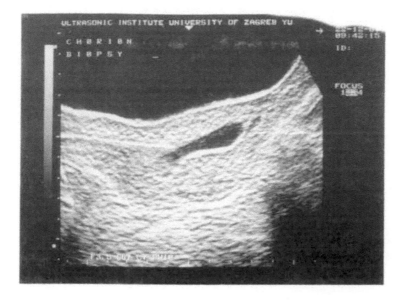

FIGURE 3. Longitudinal sonogram illustrating the chorionic villous biopsy at 9 weeks of gestation. Strong echo of a plastic catheter is well demonstrated, stretching through the cervical canal and reaching the chorion frondosum at its most lower part.

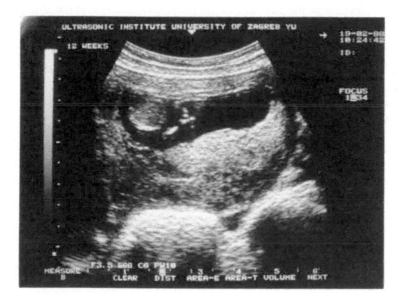

FIGURE 4. Transverse scan of the placenta at 12 weeks. The chorionic plate is well defined and clearly distinguished from the placental tissue.

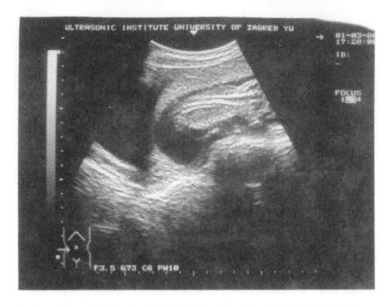

FIGURE 5.   Normal anteriorly located placenta at the 18th week of gestation.

During the 3rd month of gestation, the placental septa develops. It goes from the basal plate toward the fetal surface and divides the maternal surface into 15 to 20 lobes. However, in this period of pregnancy well-structured cotyledons are absent. Comparing it with the anatomical findings in the last 4 weeks of pregnancy, it seems that the reason for the typical sonogram of the placenta in the first half of pregnancy may be due to the absence of well-formed and developed cotyledons.[12]

THE NORMAL APPEARANCE OF THE PLACENTA IN ADVANCED PREGNANCY

Placental examination is a part of routine ultrasound examination. It is possible to obtain a significant amount of information about

1.   Localization of the placenta in relation to certain parts of the uterine cavity.
2.   Maturation of the placenta during different stages of pregnancy.
3.   The placental growth (placental thickness, attachment area, surface area, and volume).
4.   Pathological changes in the placenta and retroplacental space.
5.   Tumors of the placenta.
6.   Umbilical cord and its vessels.
7.   Amniotic membranes.

During the examination, the whole placenta must be visualized combining transversal and longitudinal scans. The differential growth of the uterine wall with the progressive elongation of the lower, isthmic segment, contractions, and flexibility of uterus oblige the examiner to use the uterine and not maternal points of reference in the accurate placental localization.[10]

LOCALIZATION OF THE PLACENTA

The placental localization was one of the first valuable clinical applications of obstetric sonography.[13] Routine obstetric scan will confirm a normal site of the placenta (Figures 5 to 7). Special indications for placental localization are (1) bleeding, (2) any intrauterine

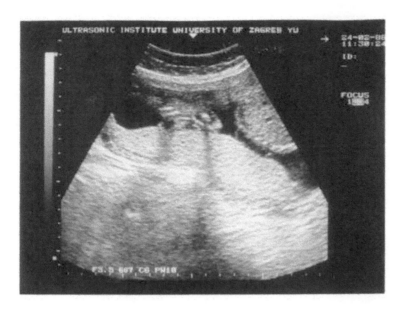

FIGURE 6.   Posteriorly located placenta in an uneventful pregnancy at the 17th week.

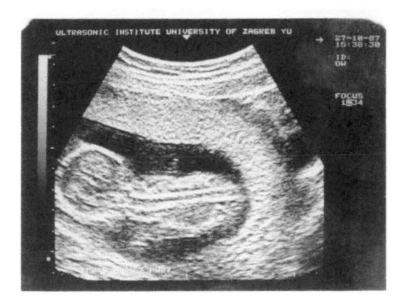

FIGURE 7.   Transverse section through the gravid uterus at the 20th week, demonstrating the placenta located in the uterine fundus.

procedure at any time during pregnancy, (3) evaluation of placental margins and the area of placental attachment to exclude abruption.[14]

The most common reason for placental localization is bleeding. After 20 weeks of pregnancy, that clinical sign is always suspected to be the placenta praevia or low-lying placenta. The diagnosis of placenta praevia is made by assessing the relationship between

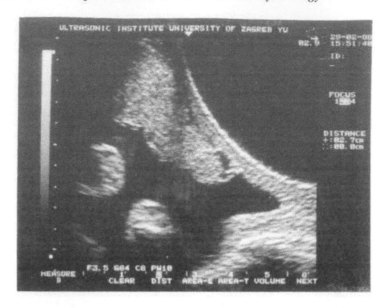

FIGURE 8. Low-lying placenta at 20 weeks of pregnancy. Note the distance between the distal edge of the placenta and internal os.

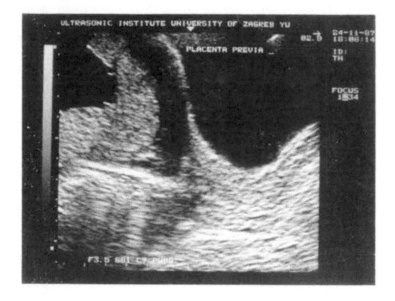

FIGURE 9. Total placenta praevia as seen at the 29th week of gestation. Note that placental tissue is located on both anterior and posterior uterine wall at lower uterine segment completely covering the internal os. Adequate filling of the bladder was a necessary prerequisite for successful ultrasound diagnosis.

the lower margins of the placenta and the internal os. While a low-lying placenta (Figure 8) and total placenta praevia (Figures 9 to 11) can be readily diagnosed, it may be difficult to distinguish the various degrees of placenta praevia by sonographic examination (Figures 12 and 13). To exclude misdiagnosis, several factors should be taken into consideration.

The diagnosis of an abnormal placental localization can be made only if the maternal bladder is well filled. An acoustic window is then created anterior to the lower uterine

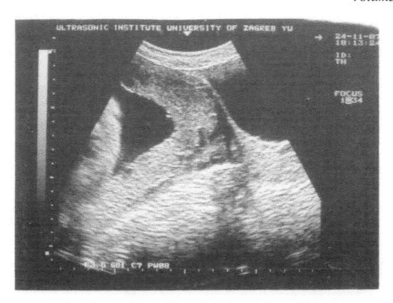

FIGURE 10. Another example of total placenta praevia at the 31st week of gestation. Note an area of nonhomogeneous echoes of triangular shape denoting bleeding above the region of the internal os.

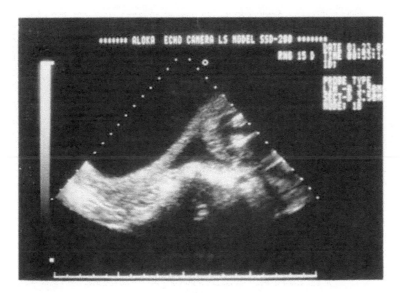

FIGURE 11. A case of total placenta praevia with clinical signs of uterine bleeding, as seen on ultrasound at the 17th week of gestation. Intrauterine bleeding is seen as an anechoic area below the placental tissue which appears partly separated from the uterine wall.

segment, allowing excellent placental, cervical, and bladder margin definition. However, an overfilled maternal bladder may distort the true relationship of the lower margins of the placenta and internal os because of the compression of the anterior uterine wall.[15-20] It will result in an image that appears similar to the placental tissue filling the entire lower uterine segment or even crossing the internal os. Therefore, it is necessary to repeat the ultrasound examination at various stages of bladder filling.

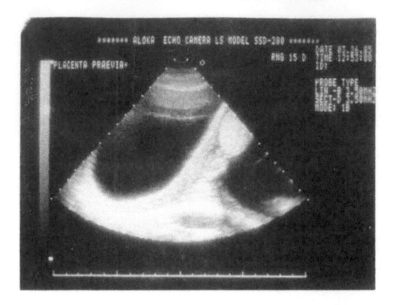

FIGURE 12.   Longitudinal scan showing the lower uterine segment, cervix, and part of vagina at the 22nd week of pregnancy. Echogenic placental tissue is seen close to the internal os, making diagnosis of marginal placenta praevia highly probable. Note full distention of the urinary bladder, which was necessary for an optimal visualization of lower uterine segment.

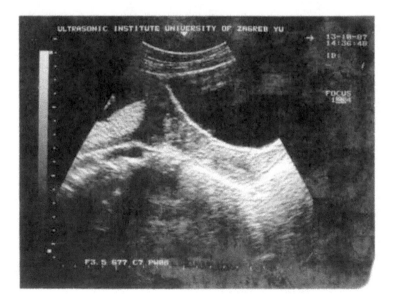

FIGURE 13.   A case of partial placenta praevia. On longitudinal scan, localization of the distal part of placenta over the internal os is demonstrated.

The anterior placenta praevia can be visualized more easily than the posterior placenta praevia because of the shadowing from the fetal skeleton. The posterior placenta praevia should be suspected when the placenta covers the internal os. In that case, the presenting part is usually displaced outside the pelvis, and the distance between the presenting part and the sacral promontory is bigger than 1.5 cm. Better results will be obtained by scanning the mother in a Trendelenburg position and gently moving the presenting part from the lower uterine segment.[21] Thus, the visualization of the posterior wall will be improved.

In each patient it is necessary to examine the lower uterine segment with multiple angled and oblique views, preferably using a sector scanner. This is particularly important for the patients with the lateral placenta praevia, in whom the placental tissue cannot be observed on the anterior or posterior wall. In those cases, a fetal head will be situated very close to the maternal promontorium. Sometimes the uterine contraction or blood above the internal os can be the cause of misinterpretation and misdiagnosis of placenta praevia.[22]

The incidence of placenta praevia is less than 1%.[23-25] If the scan is performed prior to 20 weeks of gestation, the incidence is around 20%, and at the term it is only 0.5%.[23] In a series of 615 consecutive obstetric patients, the low-lying placenta was present in 174 (28%) of them before 24 weeks of pregnancy. Only in 5 cases out of 94 which were rescanned, did placenta praevia persist beyond the 34th week.[26] Some authors explain the difference of findings between early and late pregnancy with the so-called "placental migration".[27,28] A reasonable explanation could be found in the significant growth of isthmus during pregnancy. In nongravide state, the isthmus is around 1 cm in length, making the end point of the cervical channel. During pregnancy, the isthmus changes significantly and increases its size up to 8 to 10 cm. At the same time, it is incorporated in the uterine cavity as a low-uterine segment. With the increasing low-uterine segment, combined with the lateral expansion and slight rotation, the placenta "is going" upwards. Therefore, at the end of pregnancy the placenta is normally localized, except in the case of the total placenta praevia. Gottesfeld[4] pointed out that ultrasound scan should be repeated only in those patients with a recognized placenta praevia who (1) continue to bleed, (2) fail to have engagement of the fetal head by 36 to 37 weeks, or (3) fail to have a vertex presentation or to maintain a polar presentation by the term. However, general agreement is that all patients with suspected placenta praevia in the earlier stage of pregnancy should be rescanned after 36 weeks of gestation.[29-31]

Approximately 5 to 7% of diagnoses are not correct. Although a higher percentage of false positive diagnoses is reported,[15,31,32] less than 2% of false negative findings[15,33] is more important because of a possible catastrophic outcome for both the mother and child. Uterine contractions can be misinterpreted as placental tissue (Figure 14). Usually it is very easy to distinguish between the placental and uterine tissue.

MATURATION OF THE PLACENTA

The maturation process affects the third-trimester placenta image progressively. It is obvious in the three basic anatomic areas: the chorionic plate, the placental body, and the basal layer. Alterations usually occur in the third-trimester placenta and can be classified in four grades (0 to III).[9] This classification is widely used.

Grade 0 is characterized by a straight and well-defined chorionic plate, homogeneous placental substance, and absence of all echogenic densities (Figure 15). In a normal pregnancy, grade 0 is seen during the second trimester until around the 30th week of pregnancy.

Grade I reflects the beginning of the placental maturation at approximately 31 weeks of gestation. In 40% of normal pregnancies, the same appearance of the placenta is seen until the term.[34] The basal area has the same features as in grade 0, the chorionic plate shows

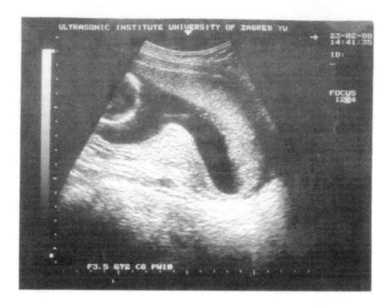

FIGURE 14.   Braxton-Hicks contraction on the posterior uterine wall and anterior placenta. Uterine contraction can be easily distinguished from the placenta because of different shape and echogenicity.

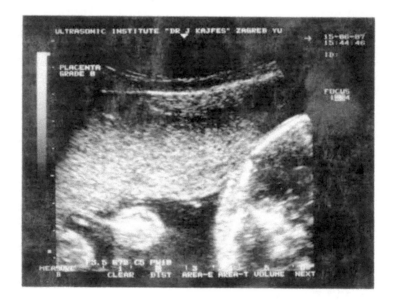

FIGURE 15.   Homogenous placenta with no densities within the placental substance at 25 weeks of pregnancy. The chorionic plate is straight and well defined (Grannum grade 0).

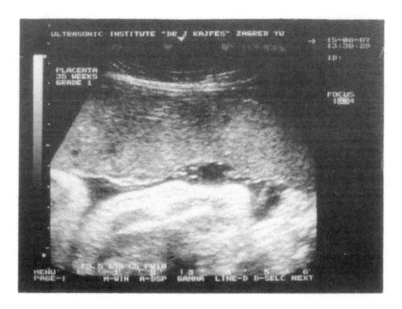

FIGURE 16. Anterior placenta at 35 weeks of pregnancy. Maturation of the placenta can be recognized by the presence of echogenic areas in the placental substance and subtle indentations of the chorionic plate (Grannum grade I).

subtle undulations, and within the substance of the placenta, a few scattered echogenic areas can be identified in the line parallel to the chorionic plate. The areas measure 2 to 4 mm in length (Figure 16).

Grade II is observed usually at 36 weeks and in 45% of normal pregnancies this appearance will maintain until the term.[34] Gottesfeld[4] found grade II changes in 19% of placentas from 31 to 36 weeks of pregnancy and in 30.6% by the term. The ultrasonic image is characterized by comma-like structures extending from the chorionic plate within the placental substance. Echogenic areas within the placental body increase in frequency and size. Along the junction of the placenta and decidua, basilar calcifications can be seen. They are parallel to the long axis of the placenta and may measure 6 mm or more in length (Figure 17).

Grade III changes appear at 38 weeks and maintain the same sonogram in 15% of cases until the term.[34,35] Between 31 and 36 weeks, 9% of the placentas show grade III changes and 31.9% by the term.[4] Grade III represents the so-called ''mature placenta''.[36] It is characterized with widespread calcifications. Linear densities are seen passing through the whole placental substance, from the chorionic plate to the basal area, without a break. The central portions of the outlined area may appear sonolucent and have large, irregular densities with posterior acoustic shadowing (Figure 18). Very similar changes of placental appearance during pregnancy were described in 1976 by an Australian group.[5] The examination of the placenta after the delivery confirmed ultrasound findings. Those findings correspond to the recent paper on spherical high-density areas.[12] They measured 10 to 60 mm and represent fetal cotyledons. All of them were in contact with the basal plate. A reticular space separates cotyledons between themselves and cotyledons to the chorionic plate. An irregularly shaped transonic avascular area (5 to 30 mm) is in the center of the cotyledon. It is connected with the basal plate and filled with the blood from the spiral artery. The spiral artery ends below the center of the cotyledon, and the draining maternal vein in the reticular space between

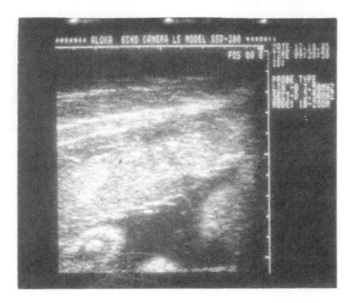

FIGURE 17.   Grannum grade II placenta. Note the basal echogenic and comma-like densities.

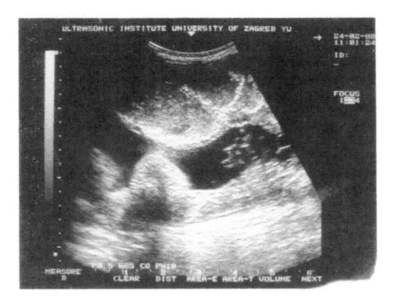

FIGURE 18.   Echogenic placenta at 40 weeks of gestation. Wide-spread calcifications of the placental substance increase the overall echogenicity of the placenta. The cotyledons are seen separated by calcified intercotyledonary septa (Grannum grade III).

the cotyledons. In these two studies ultrasonic findings are confirmed in detail by a histological examination.

Koslowski et al.[37] produced a placental score with a four-point scale:

A. Basal plate:
   1. Visible but interrupted
   2. Solid and thin
   3. Solid and thick for up to 50% of its length
   4. Solid and thick for 50 to 100% of its length, with a formation of arcade-like structures toward the fetal side
B. Peripheral zones:
   1. Poorly defined
   2. Thin and solid
   3. Thickened on one side, echogenic
   4. Thick and solid on both sides
C. Placental substance:
   1. Finely homogeneous
   2. Scattered streak-like echogenic areas up to 5 mm in length
   3. Inhomogeneous with echogenic areas up to 1 cm in length
   4. Scattered plate-like echogenic densities over 1 cm in diameter

These parameters were in good correlation with the outcome of pregnancy.

The correlation between placental and pulmonar maturity showed that the L/S ratio increased with the placental grade.[9] In grade I placenta, 68% of pregnant women had an L/S ratio of 2 or more; in grade II it was in 88%; and in grade III in 100%. Several authors confirmed those results.[35,38,39] In diabetic patients, where the grade III of placenta was present, no case of RDS occurred, although L/S ratio was immature.[40] These results correspond to some other reports.[11,41] However, in a few cases RDS was reported in spite of grade III placental changes.[42,43]

It can be concluded that the correlation between the placental grade changes and fetal maturity exists. However, in spite of the high correlation (95% in uneventful and 90% in high-risk pregnancies),[44] ultrasound estimation of placental maturation cannot replace amniocentesis and L/S ratio or phosphatidyl glycerol in estimations of fetal lung maturity. It seems that placental grading can have clinical importance in cases when the placental grade does not correspond with gestational age. In the cases with fetal growth retardation, severe EPH gestosis, and essential hypertension, grade III placenta can be observed much earlier than in uncomplicated pregnancy, even at the beginning of the third trimester.[14,45-47] The occurrence of "accelerated placental maturation" may be helpful as an additional factor in the diagnosis of intrauterine growth retardation (IUGR) (sensitivity of the method is 66%).[45] Our opinion is that the clinical significance of this sign is to alert the obstetricians to the potential fetal jeopardy.

The presence of grade III placenta before 38 weeks of gestation is good reason for checking the fetal condition, applying the routine methods for the estimation of its well-being.

PLACENTAL GROWTH

Measurements of different placental dimensions were the subject of interest in the past, when ultrasound techniques were not so sophisticated and could not allow such an accurate and precise evaluation of the fetus. Today, these indirect measurements of the placental

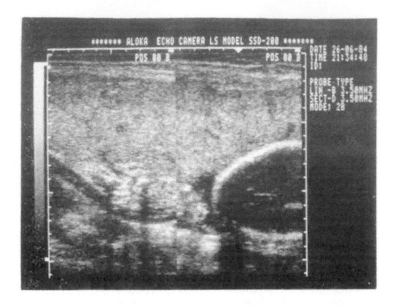

FIGURE 19.   Thick and hydropic placenta at 28 weeks in a case of severe Rh immunization.

thickness or volume are only a small part of a routine ultrasound examination in some high-risk pregnancies (like Rh immunization or diabetes mellitus). However, they are without a significant influence on clinical decisions.

Placental Thickness

In early ultrasound period, an upper normal limit of the placental thickness of 4.5 to 4.7 cm after 34 weeks of pregnancy was reported.[48] Schlensker[49] found that the placental thickness increases continuously up to 36 weeks of pregnancy. The average thickness of the placenta in the 15th week is 2.2 ± 0.3 cm, in the 36th week is 3.6 ± 0.5 cm, and in the 40th week is 3.4 ± 0.6 cm. There is a small suspicion about the accuracy of that measurement concerning the possibilities of the equipment which was used at that time.[14] The problem was the exact recognition of the boundary between the placenta and the uterine wall. It is now generally agreed that a placental thickness greater than 5 cm should not necessarily be pathological,[14,19] except in the cases with Rh incompatibility. Here, a placental thickness greater than 5 cm before the 27th week indicates a poor prognosis. In Rh-immunized patients, the estimation of the placental thickness should be included as a part of the ultrasound examination (Figures 19 and 20). An increase in the thickness of the placenta is usually associated with the increasing severity of disease,[19] but placental findings should always be evaluated in relation to the findings in the liver, skin, and fetal abdomen.

Placentas are usually thicker in those patients with gestational diabetes and insulin-dependent diabetes without vascular complications than in nonimmune hydrops and some congenital anomalies. The placenta is thin in those patients with preeclampsia, IUGR, juvenile diabetes with proliferative retinopathia, and polyhidramnios[14,19] (Figure 21). A glucose tolerance test is recommended in patients whose placentas have matured beyond the grade 0 stage and measure more than 4 cm in thickness.

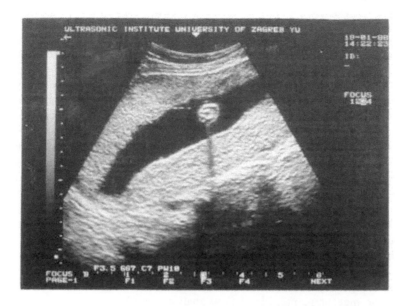

FIGURE 20. The thickness of placenta illustrated in previous figure is more obvious if compared to normally thick placenta in an uneventful pregnancy of the same gestational age.

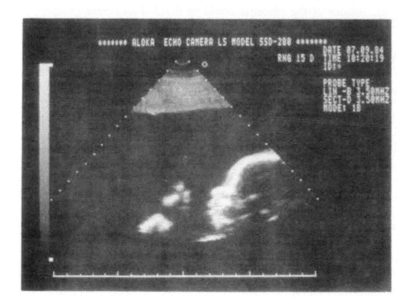

FIGURE 21. Thin, anteriorly located placenta in a case of severe polyhydramnios.

OTHER PLACENTAL DIMENSIONS

In a cross-sectional study, the measurements of the placental volume showed continuous increase of the placental volume until the term.[50] The second study, based on the longitudinal data, showed that the placental volume and the surface of the placenta increased linearly through pregnancy up to 34 to 35 weeks of gestation.[51]

Using a computer program in 171 pregnant women, area of the placental attachment, total placental surface area, and placental volume were calculated.[37] In a normal population the growth curves of all three dimensions are similar. There is no further increase beyond 34 weeks of gestation. Individual measurements of the placental volume showed a greater variation than the area of the placental attachment because of bigger differences in the placental thickness. That was the reason why they introduced the ratio of the volume to the attachment area as an approximate measure of the mean placental thickness. The ratio increases during pregnancy and becomes maximal usually at 32 rather than 36 weeks of gestation. The volumetric values for the diabetic group (B, C, or D) tend to lie above the mean values for a normal population. The increase of the placental volume is mainly due to an increase of the placental thickness. Individual values for the growth of the retarded fetuses were below the mean value in all cases except one. Measurements of the placental surface area showed similar results. If the surface area was 187 cm^2 or less at 150 d of gestation, 50% of fetuses were growth retarded.[52] This measurement was recommended as a screening test for IUGR.

Although some of these measurements can be valuable, their application in a routine ultrasound scanning is not possible because it is time consuming. Today, more reliable and precise ultrasound parameters can be used in the prediction and detection of small-for-date babies (biometric measurements, blood flow analyses, etc.).

PATHOLOGICAL CHANGES IN THE PLACENTA AND RETROPLACENTAL SPACE

Macroscopic Lesions of the Placenta

Macroscopic lesions of the placenta could be divided into three groups:

1. Lesions due to the disturbances of maternal blood flow to or through the placenta: massive perivillous fibrin deposition, subchorionic fibrin deposition, massive subchorial thrombosis, retroplacental hematoma, marginal hematoma, infarct.
2. Lesions due to the disturbances of fetal blood flow: intervillous thrombosis, Kline's hemorrhage, fetal artery thrombosis, and subamniotic hematoma.
3. Nonvascular lesions: calcifications, septal cyst.

Most macroscopically visible lesions of the placenta are of little or no clinical importance. It is true that those lesions which decrease the population of functioning villi, such as infarcts, fetal artery thrombi, retroplacental hematoma, and plaques of perivillous fibrin, diminish the reserve capacity of the placenta, but the vast majority of such lesions are not sufficiently extensive to dissipate that reserve completely and thus impair placental function. Some of these lesions can be visualized by ultrasound.

Subchorionic Fibrin Deposition

Macroscopically, it is a hard, laminated plaque in the subchorionic area, usually roughly triangular, consisting of fibrin. It is found in about 20% of placentas. This incidence is almost entirely unaffected by maternal factors.[53] A subchorionic sonolucent area may be demonstrated in obstetrics sonograms (Figure 22). The laminated collection of fibrin between the chorionic plate and placental villi is a result of pooling and stasis of the maternal blood in the intervillous space beneath the chorion.[53]

Massive Subchorial Thrombosis

This is a red thrombus which measures more than 1 cm in thickness and which separates the chorionic plate from the underlying villous tissue over a big part of its area.[53] The second name for this change is Breus' mole.

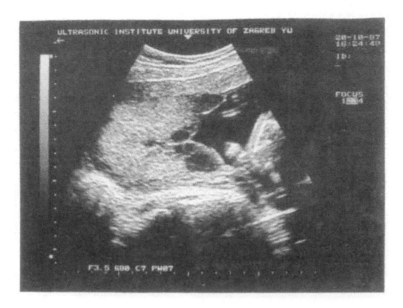

FIGURE 22. Slight elevation of the chorionic plate caused by fibrin accumulation in an otherwise normal placenta.

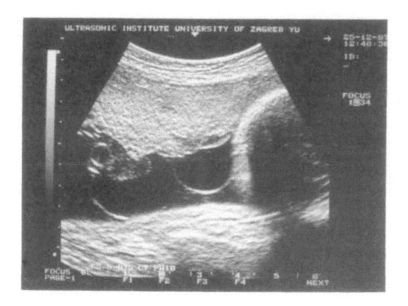

FIGURE 23. Massive subchorial thrombosis causing elevation and distortion of the fetal surface of the placenta.

Macroscopic appearance shows massive subchorial thrombi which are often bulbous or lobulated and tend to elevate and distort the fetal surface of the placenta by forming bulging protuberances into the amniotic cavity (Figure 23). The thrombus may form a single, smooth mass (Figure 24) and sometimes may even reach the basal plate and form transplacental thrombosis. It seems that the cause is extensive venous obstruction leading to massive pooling

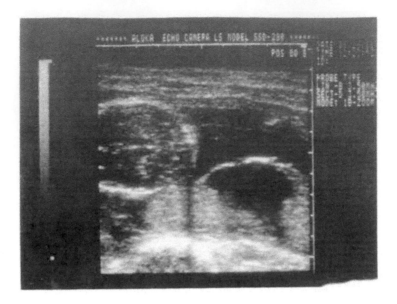

FIGURE 24. Single transonic area caused by thrombosis located below the chorionic plate.

and stasis. The occurrence is around 1 in 2000 deliveries.[54] The condition is connected with a higher incidence of premature labor and high perinatal mortality.

Retroplacental Hematoma

This is a hematoma which lies between and separates the basal plate of the placenta and the uterine wall. A retroplacental hematoma may be large and occupy most, or even all, of the maternal surface of the placenta, but many of them are small, often measuring only 1 or 2 cm across.[53] The freshly formed hematoma is soft, red, and easily separated from the maternal placental surface, while the older hematoma is brown, hard, and firmly adherent to the placental surface.

The incidence of retroplacental hematoma is about 4.5%.[55] In Fox's series,[53] the incidence increased approximately threefold in placentas in women with preeclampsia, but it was not excessive in those patients with essential hypertension. In women with histories of abruptio placentae, retroplacental hematoma is a common finding in no more than in about 30% of their placentas. On the contrary, if a retroplacental hematoma is present, there will be clinical evidence of abruptio placentae in about only 35% of cases.

The etiology of retroplacental bleeding is still uncertain. The majority of the reasons are actually concerned with the etiological factors implicated in abruptio placentae. The retroplacental hemorrhage may manifest in three ways: (1) external bleeding without the formation of a significant intrauterine hematoma, (2) formation of retroplacental or marginal hematoma with or without external bleeding, and (3) formation of a submembranous clot at a distance from the placenta with or without bleeding.[55,56]

The sonogram of the retroplacental or marginal hematoma shows sonolucent or complex mass (Figure 25). If it is localized beneath the placental membranes, the same picture will appear beneath the elevated membranes.[56] Large, dilated draining mural veins are occasionally seen in the retroplacental space, particularly in posterior placentas (Figure 26). They appear as parallel sonolucent channels along the wall of the uterus. This is a normal finding

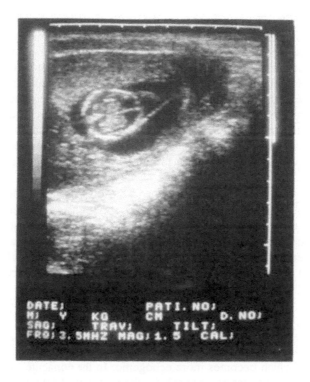

FIGURE 25. Abruptio placentae displaying large extramembraneous clot appearing as an anechoic area on the posterior uterine wall.

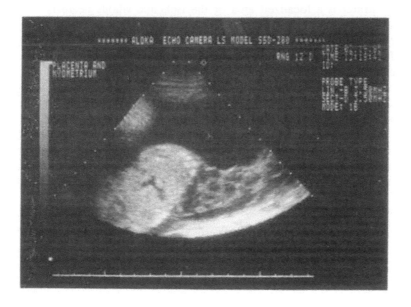

FIGURE 26. Large, dilated veins in the retroplacental space could be easily misinterpreted as the retroplacental hematoma.

and should not be mistaken for a retroplacental hematoma.[57] During early pregnancy, the myometrium thickens under the influence of estrogen and progesteron by hypertrophy and hyperplasia. On ultrasound image, it appears as a relatively sonolucent area behind the placenta and can also sometimes be mistaken for a retroplacental hematoma. Transit Braxton-Hicks contractions change the shape of the uterus and can also be mistaken for the hematoma. In that case, postprocessing ultrasonic appliances will allow the differentiation between the two tissues of different acoustic properties — the placenta and myometrium.

The size of the hematoma may be followed by serial ultrasound examinations, and sometimes it seems that the lesion has disappeared. However, a careful examination of the placenta after the delivery will show a thin layer of organized hematoma along the membranes.[7]

The abruptio placentae is a clinical entity, and the diagnosis is made on the basis of clinical signs. Ultrasound can be useful, because in about 25% of patients with abruptio placentae, the sign of retroplacental hemorrhage will be present.[53,58] In the nonacute cases, serial ultrasound examinations are recommended. In addition to two typical ultrasonic signs (presence of retroplacental clot and an extramembranous clot), some other ultrasonic findings can also be helpful: (1) intraplacental anechoic areas, which can appear deeper in the placental parenchyma, and (2) the placenta is thicker than 5.5 cm.[59]

In the acute cases of abruptio placentae, ultrasound findings do not influence clinical decisions. The management will depend upon the clinical signs and maternal and fetal condition. However, in nonacute patients, serial ultrasound scan can be used to follow the progress of the abruption by measuring the size of the area of the placental separation, or the retroplacental clot, which becomes more echogenic. In the nonacute cases, fetomaternal hemorrhage can occur. It is necessary to check for the presence of fetomaternal hemorrhage, because it can occur in 75% of nonacute cases. The transplacental hemorrhage ranged from no fetal blood cells (with the Kleihauer-Betke technique) to 72 ml of fetal blood cells.[60]

Infarct

A placental infarct is a localized area of the ischemic villous necrosis. Infarcts may occur in any part of the placental substance, but are more commonly seen in the peripheral area. They vary noticably in size (a few millimeters to almost most of the villous tissue) and shape. A fresh infarct is dark red. As an infarct ages, it becomes progressively firmer and its color changes successively to brown, yellow, and white. Fox[53] found infarcts in about one quarter of the placentas from full-term uncomplicated pregnancies, while they are uncommon in the placentas in cases of premature onset of labor. Fox did not find a higher incidence of placental infarcts in patients with diabetes and Rh immunization, but the incidence significantly increased in pregnancies in which the mother suffered from pre-eclampsia or essential hypertension (27 to 70% relating to the severity of the disease).

Placental infarcts result from the coagulation necrosis of villi. Spirt et al.[7] have been able to document, on ultrasound only, a sonolucent lesion which contained fibrin or fluid.

Intervillous Thrombosis

This is a villous-free nodular focus of coagulated blood in the intervillous space. It can occur in any part of the placental substance, ranging in size (from 1 mm to 5 cm) and differentiating in number and shape. Some of them are in contact with the basal plate. In full-term, uncomplicated pregnancy, the incidence of intervillous thrombosis is 36%, ranging from 24 to 48%.[61]

Intervillous thrombosis appears sonographically as a sonolucent intraplacental lesion that varies in size. Thrombosis is seen for the first time at the 19th week of pregnancy.[62] It can be diagnosed by ultrasound in 95% of cases and is probably present in 100% of cases in

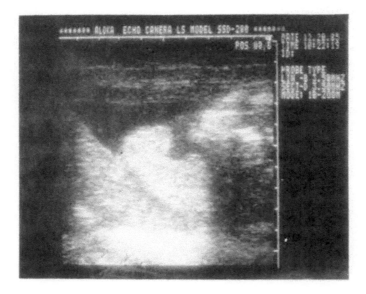

FIGURE 27.   Characteristic marginal ring formed by the decidua and membranes in a case of placenta circumvallata.

large lesions (diameter more than 5 mm) and in 82% of the cases if small lesions (less than 5 mm) are included. In 39% of the placentas, intervillous thrombosis is multiple. The most often detections were from 35 to 37 weeks of gestation. Some lesions increased and/or decreased during pregnancy.[63] It was suggested that intervillous thrombosis might be the cause of immunization of mother during pregnancy.[64,65]

Perivillous fibrin depositions are the result of pooling and stasis of blood in the intervillous space. Calcifications were discussed in detail as a part of the placental maturity.

Other Changes

The placenta consists usually of one main mass. The placenta succenturiata and placenta circumvallata (Figure 27) can be detected by ultrasound.

TUMORS OF THE PLACENTA
Nontrophoblastic Tumors of the Placenta

Primary nontrophoblastic tumors of the placenta are the relatively common hemangioma and the very rare teratoma.[66] Placental hemangioma (known as "chorangioma and chorioangioma") is found in approximately 1% of pregnancies. Usually it is single, but occasionally multiple, with wide variations in size (from a few millimeters in diameter to 780 g) and location.[66] Large hemangiomas are seen most commonly as bulging protuberances of the fetal surface of the placenta, but a substantial minority occur on the maternal surface, where they may appear to replace the whole lobe or a part of it. They can be situated entirely within the membranes, but many of them are not visible on the external placental surface.

Microscopic classification is old,[67] but still valuable in clinical practice. There are three types: (1) angiomatous (numerous blood vessels are set in a loose, inconspicuous stroma containing scanty fibrous tissue, the vessels are usually small, but may be dilated to give a cavernous appearance), (2) cellular (loose, immature, cellular mesenchymal tissue with only a few ill-formed vessels), and (3) degenerate (mixoid change, hyalinization, necrosis or

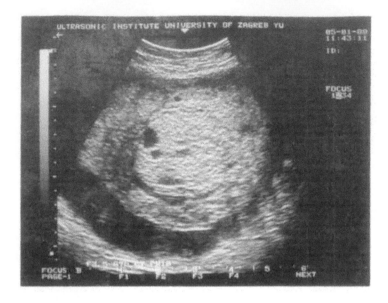

FIGURE 28.   Another example of large hemangioma placentae detected at the 29th week of pregnancy. If compared to the previous case, the tumor appears more solid and is well defined within the placental substance.

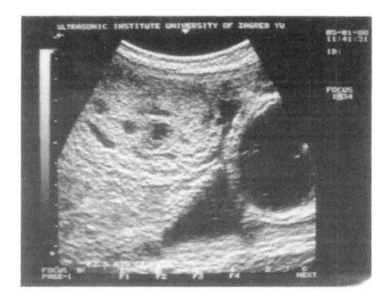

FIGURE 29.   Differently oriented scan in the same case of placental hemangioma.

calcification, and very rare fat). These three types can change the ultrasound appearance. Usually a tumor is encapsulated.

On ultrasound image, the tumor may appear as a weakly echogenic, encapsulated, or sonolucent area within the placental substance (Figures 28 and 29), or as a cystic-solid tumor arising from the placental tissue (Figure 30), and sometimes with multiple internal echoes

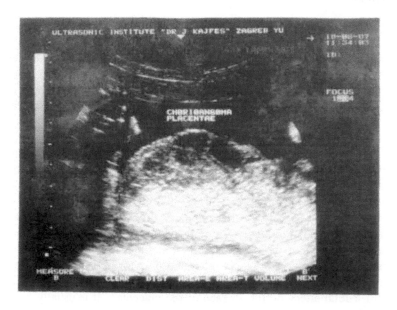

FIGURE 30. Large hemangioma placentae, which is easily diagnosed because of its different echogenicity and structure as compared to the normal surrounding placental tissue. Tumor consists of cystic and solid parts.

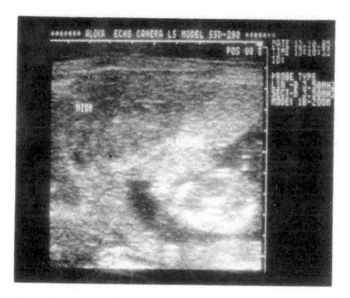

FIGURE 31. Large uterine myoma in the anterior uterine wall on the placental side which can be mistaken for placental hemangioma.

caused by calcium deposition. Care should be taken not to misinterpret uterine fibroma as placental hemangioma (Figure 31).

The vast majority of placental hemangiomata is of no clinical importance whatsoever, but a proportion, particularly those of large size, is accompanied by a variety of complications which may affect the mother, the developing fetus, or the neonate.[66]

A high proportion of hemangiomata (16 to 33%) is accompanied by hydramnios.[68] The cause of hydramnios is obscure. A number of theories have been mentioned (compression of the umbilical veins by the tumor, transudation from vascular channels on the fetal surface of the tumor, thrombosis of the afferent vessels to the neoplasm, peripheral arterio-venous shunt in hemangioma with congestive cardiac failure, etc.), but they have not been confirmed. On the other side, a few cases with chorioangiomata associated with oligohydramnios are observed.[69-70]

In patients with large chorioangiomata, a higher incidence of premature labor (nearly one third of the cases),[68,71] high perinatal mortality (up to 39%), fetal edema and hydrops,[69,72,73] IUGR,[74] retroplacental bleeding and abruptio placentae,[75] cardiomegaly and congestive heart failure,[71,76] and anemia and thrombocytopenia[77,78] is reported. Because of so many possible complications in the patients with large hemangiomas, the hospitalization and intensive control of these patients after antenatal ultrasound diagnosis is mandatory.[79]

The placental teratoma is rare. The tumor always lies between the amnion and chorion, usually on the fetal surface of the placenta, but sometimes in the membranes adjacent to the placental margin. The tumors are smooth, round or oval, and measure between 2.5 and 7.5 cm in diameter. They lack an umbilical cord, and their arterial supply usually comes from a branch of a fetal artery on the surface of the placenta.[67] It is usually benign and of no clinical significance.

Bernischke and Driscoll[80] do not accept these tumors as teratoma. They believe that it represents the extreme of a fetus amorphus. Fox[66] introduced two criteria: the absence of an umbilical cord and the lack of axial organization serve to differentiate a placental teratoma from a fetus acardius amorphus.

Sonographically, a teratoma should appear as a well-circumscribed mass with a complex echo pattern in which echo-free space (cystic part) is mixed with more echogenic parts caused by calcium deposition. Sometimes, it can be difficult to differentiate, as it is on macroscopic examination, a teratoma from a fetus amorphus. Antenatally, it is possible to make a diagnosis, but until now, there have been no reports in the literature on successful ultrasound detection. Teratoma has no influence on the outcome of pregnancy, and the lesion is benign.[81] Regarding secondary neoplasms, an extraplacental malignant disease in pregnant women, although uncommon, it is by no means exceptional. However, metastases have been noticed in a few cases only.[66]

The dissemination of a fetal malignant disease is extremely rare, but a few cases of placenta metastases from fetal neuroblastoma and fetal leukemia with placental villous involvement have been published.

Trophoblastic Tumors of the Placenta
Molla hydatidosa and choriocarcinoma are unfortunately more common placental tumors. This problem is described in detail in the chapter on early pregnancy.

ULTRASOUND APPEARANCE OF THE UMBILICAL CORD
In spite of the statement that the umbilical cord is the "lifeline of the fetus", little attention has been paid to the lesions of the cord, and little clinical importance has been attached to the ultrasound imaging of the umbilical cord. The reason was probably due to the poor visualization of the umbilical cord in the past. Today, with the high-resolution ultrasound machines, it is possible to analyze the umbilical cord in detail — its entire length from the placental surface to the termination in the fetal body. It is also possible to visualize all anatomically normal structures of the umbilical cord: one umbilical vein, two umbilical arteries surrounded with Wharton's jelly, even pulsations of the umbilical arteries with real-

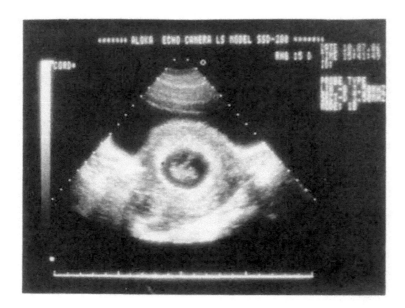

FIGURE 32. Transverse scan of gravid uterus at the 9th week of pregnancy showing the fetal pole and umbilical cord which stretch from the fetus to the chorion frondosum.

time machines. Today, the visualization of the umbilical cord is also an important part of the ultrasound routine examination.

The umbilical cord may sometimes be imaged starting from the 8th week of amenorrhea as a trunk-like echogenic structure (2 to 3 mm in diameter); nevertheless it appears relatively wide as compared to the size of the embryo. It runs from the ventral surface of the embryo to the chorion (Figure 32). The umbilical cord was visualized in 29.6% of all cases up to 13 weeks of pregnancy, with the highest incidence at the 12th week — 66.6% of cases.[82] In the second and third trimester is it more easy to find and visualize the umbilical cord, especially in patients with hydramnios. In patients with oligohydramnios, it may be difficult, even impossible to differentiate the umbilical cord, regardless of the gestational age.

The umbilical cord appears as a complex structure composed of numerous parallel echoes, representing highly echogenic walls of the umbilical cord. To demonstrate one umbilical vein and two umbilical arteries, it is necessary to perform the longitudinal and transverse section. In the longitudinal section within the parallel lines, wider echo-free space represents the umbilical vein, and the next two parallel narrow spaces represent two umbilical arteries (Figure 33). A better visualization of the umbilical cord vessels is due to different colors which are the result of color Doppler machine application. The flow in the umbilical vein is going in one direction and is designed red, while the arterial flow, which is running in the opposite direction, is designed blue. In the transverse section, the arteries and umbilical vein are seen as three separately circular luciencies (Figure 34). The insertion of the umbilical cord into the fetal abdomen is very easy to visualize (Figure 35). In this position, the intra-abdominal part of the umbilical vein and the origins of hypogastric arteries are seen. The insertion site of the umbilical cord on the placental surface (Figure 36) is more often eccentric (up to 75%),[83] less common marginal (1.9 to 6.2%),[84,85] and very rarely velamentous (up to 1.5%).[86] On ultrasound, the insertion site may be demonstrated as a V- or U-shaped sonolucent area adjacent to the chorionic plate.[87] The visualization of the umbilical cord

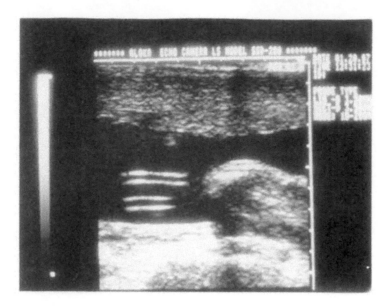

FIGURE 33.   Longitudinal scan through the umbilical cord showing the umbilical vein and, laterally, two thinner umbilical arteries.

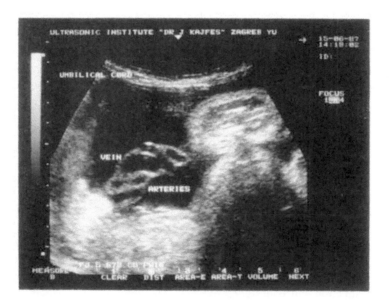

FIGURE 34.   Normal umbilical cord seen floating within the amniotic fluid at the 29th week of pregnancy. Both arteries and vein are demonstrated. Distinction between the vein and artery usually poses no difficulties, mostly due to obvious difference in their diameter.

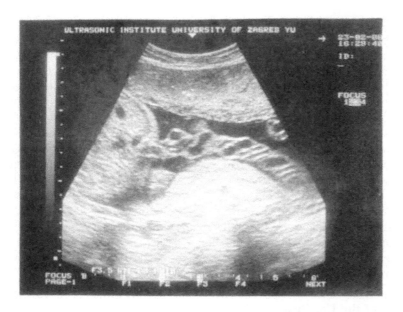

FIGURE 35.   Cord insertion showing the vessels traced into the fetal abdomen.

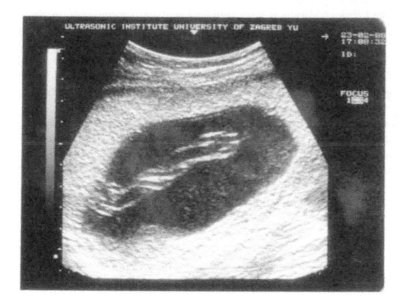

FIGURE 36.   Placental cord insertion in a posterior placenta.

vessels is a part of some new intrauterine-intracanalicular procedures. During the second part of pregnancy, fetal blood sampling is obtained from the umbilical vein (see chapter on interventional ultrasound). Doppler analyses of fetal circulation include the umbilical vein and umbilical artery blood flow (see chapter on blood flow measurements).

Measurement of the umbilical vein diameter was introduced in Rh-immunized patients as a predictor of the severity of the disease.[88,89] In normal pregnancy, a slight increase of the umbilical vein diameter from the 30th week onward was observed.[90] The changes in vein umbilical diameter in some pathological pregnancies were confirmed. In small-for-gestational fetuses, the diameter was below the normal range in 47% of cases. Only 2 out of 11 fetuses with chronic fetal distress had the values of the umbilical vein diameter within the normal range.[90] Apart from the results in two previous studies,[88,89] Jouppila and Kirkinen[90] did not find the enlargement of the umbilical vein diameter in severe Rh disease. The diameters in 18 cases were within the normal range, and blood flow was significantly higher because of higher blood velocity. Witter and Graham[91] found normal values in Rh-immunized patients, but in some normal patients, idiopathic enlargement of the diameter was obtained. Thus, measurement of the umbilical diameter cannot be used as an accurate predictor of the severity of Rh immunization.

Abnormalities of the Umbilical Cord
Developmental Abnormalities

Developmental abnormalities are achordia, abnormal length of the cord, single umbilical artery, and supernumerary umbilical vessels.[92] Theoretically, the achordia can be diagnosed by ultrasound, but this condition is very rare and is usually found only in aborted fetuses which were severely malformed. The average length of the umbilical cord is between 54 and 61 cm.[83,93] The differences in length of the umbilical cord can be associated with a higher incidence of complications. By using ultrasound, it is not possible to measure the entire length of the umbilical cord, but some complications like the descensus of the umbilical cord or coiling umbilical cord, which are associated with its longer length, may be demonstrated.[20]

A single umbilical artery was well recognized and fully described in the 19th century, but precise analyses of that problem started 30 years ago. Since that time, a significant number of papers have been published about the association of a single umbilical artery and fetal malformations. The incidence in unselected pregnancies is around 1%[92] and in malformed fetuses ranges from 7.4 to 48%.[94,95]

In a group of infants with single umbilical artery, perinatal mortality is four times higher compared to other populations.[96] It is probably due to the higher incidence of congenital malformations. In a follow-up study, Bryan and Kohler[97] found out that previously unrecognized malformations became apparent at the age of 10 years. That means that the incidence of malformation associated with single umbilical artery is higher than the incidence found after the delivery.

Prenatal ultrasound diagnosis has been reported in two cases: both of them died.[98] Our group, by applying color Doppler for blood flow analysis, has diagnosed single umbilical artery in a diabetic mother. Her child was normal and alive[99] (Plate 2* and Figure 37). A single umbilical artery can be associated with placental anomalies also.[92]

An increased number of umbilical vessels is not strongly associated with congenital abnormalities. It is possible to diagnose the entity prenatally, but is has not been reported yet.

---

* Plate 2 appears following page 38.

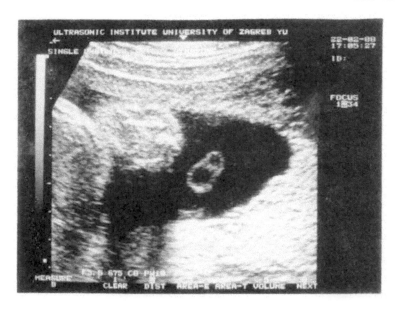

FIGURE 37. Single umbilical artery as seen on B mode scan.

Abnormalities of Insertion

Using ultrasound, the insertion place can be located and approximately estimated in relation to the placental surface. However, there is no need for this, except in the patients with velamentous insertion. This data can be useful when performing the rupture of membranes and probably in the third stage during the maneuver of cord traction.

Mechanical Lesions

In this group, knots, ruptures of the cord, torsions, and strictures are included. These changes are not diagnosed antenatally by ultrasound.

Vascular Lesions

Vascular disturbances can cause hematoma, thrombosis of umbilical vessels, and edema of the umbilical cord.

Hematoma — The hematoma consists of an extravasation of blood into Wharton's jelly. It occurs most commonly toward or at the fetal end of the cord.[92] The size ranges from over 1 cm to even the full length of the cord. In some cases it is possible to demonstrate that the bleeding is caused by a torn or ruptured umbilical vein or, not so often, by a damaged umbilical artery. However, in many cases, no obvious large vessel lesion can be found, so pathogenesis is not clear. The incidence ranges from 1 in 5500 to 1 in 12699 deliveries.[100,101] The perinatal mortality rate in infants with a cord hematoma is 40 to 50%, but it is not clear whether hematoma is responsible for the fetal demise.[92] Prenatal diagnosis of umbilical cord hematoma has been reported in a patient at 32 weeks of pregnancy as a sonolucent, septated intrauterine mass adjacent to the fetal abdomen.[102] In the recent report,[103] the umbilical cord mass has been seen on the sonogram adjacent to and apparently arising from the ventral portion of the fetal abdomen. The umbilical cord runs through the center of the mass. The patient had vaginal bleeding during the first and second trimester, and amniocentesis was performed because of her age. In the amniotic fluid, hemoglobin A was positive. Thus, hematologic studies at the time of the amniocentesis showed that the mass was the result of the maternal bleeding into the amniotic fluid.

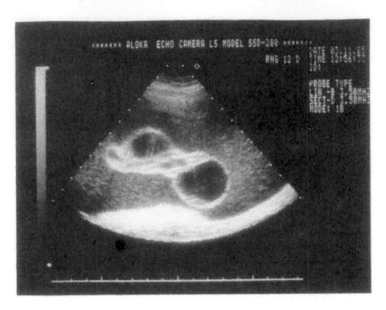

FIGURE 38.   Increased amount of Wharton's jelly with an unusual appearance of
the umbilical cord in a case of hydramnios.

Thrombosis of umbilical vessels — It is a very rare condition, and it seems to be
associated with (or probably it is a complication of) the cord compression, torsion, stricture,
or hematoma.

Edema — Coulter et al.[104] reported the incidence of edema in 10% of all deliveries. It
seems that it happens more often in premature deliveries, in patients with abruptio placentae,
diabetes, hydrops fetalis, and polyhydramnios (Figure 38). They pointed out that possible
factors predisposing to cord edema were a low fetal osmotic pressure, a raised hydrostatic
pressure in the placenta and cord, and an increase in total water content in the feto-placental
unit. In the growth-retarded fetuses and postmature babies, decreased cord Wharton's jelly
is observed. The presence of a good amount of Wharton's jelly in the utero is a pleasing
sign in the exclusion of IUGR.[105] A reduced amount of Wharton's jelly in prolonged pregnancy was associated with the cord compression and higher peripartum morbidity.[106]

Cysts and tumors — Umbilical cord cysts are of several varieties: derived from vestigial
remnants (allantois or omphalomenesenteric duct), derived from amniotic inclusions, formed
by degeneration of Wharton's jelly (a false cyst caused by the mucoid degeneration of
Wharton's jelly), and neoplastic cyst. Sachs and Fourcroy[107] have reported the prenatal
diagnosis of a cystic mass within the umbilical cord, several centimeters from the abdominal
wall, at 21 weeks of pregnancy. To exclude other possible abnormalities, it is important to
visualize the vessels in the lateral wall of the mass and an intact fetal anterior abdominal
wall. Tumors of the umbilical cord are extremely rare. Hemangiomata, teratoma, and mixoma
could be observed.[92] There are no data about prenatal diagnosis of umbilical cord tumors.

AMNIOTIC MEMBRANES

When the amount of the amniotic fluid increases even slightly, it is possible to follow
amniotic membranes crossing the placental rims. In the case of multiple pregnancies, the
division of the amniotic cavity with the membranes can be seen very clearly on the sonogram
(Figure 39). Separation of the two membranes was seen in otherwise normal pregnancy

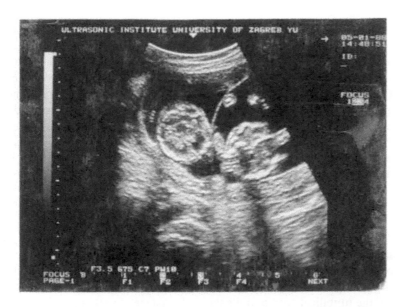

FIGURE 39.   Amniotic membranes separating the two amniotic cavities at 19 weeks in a twin pregnancy case.

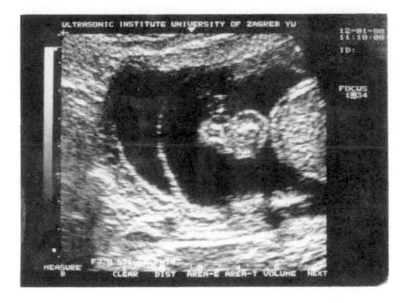

FIGURE 40.   Developmental form of chorio-amniotic separation in a case of an uneventful 19-week-old pregnancy. Amniotic membrane is seen as a thin, well-defined echo separated by an anechoic area from the chorionic membrane.

(Figure 40). Some very rare conditions are extramembranous pregnancy, extra-amniotic pregnancy, and amniotic band syndrome.

If the rupture of the amnion and chorion occur during early or midtrimester pregnancy, the fetus can continue to develop, either partly or completely, outside the membranes. This pregnancy is called extramembranous pregnancy.

If the rupture of the amnion occurs in early pregnancy, the fetus can survive in intact chorion, and this condition is called extra-amniotic pregnancy. The amniotic bands and strings are the consequence of the amniotic rupture during early pregnancy.[108] Following the amniotic detachment, the mesoblastic tissue on the maternal surface of the separated amnion and that of the fetal surface of the denuded chorion tends to be drawn out into thin fibrous strings, which can constrict some fetal part and lead to intrauterine amputation.

Amniotic bands can be demonstrated when fetal parts are seen on both sides of the membranes. It may be hypothesized that in the future, if such a diagnosis is made, one may use a fetoscope to resect the amniotic band either directly or as a guide for a laser beam before fetal damage and/or amputation has occurred.[4]

CONCLUSION

By using diagnostic ultrasound, a significant amount of information about the placenta and umbilical cord can be obtained. In routine work, the most important factor is proper localization of the placenta, which can be ascertained with high degree of confidence. The assessment of placental maturity can sometimes help in detection of fetal jeopardy. Better visualization of the umbilical cord permits the performance of very sophisticated intrauterine procedures. Doppler analyses of fetal blood flow can be used in the assessment of fetal well-being.

The majority of the placental and umbilical cord abnormalities are diagnosed in the antenatal period. Several ultrasound measurements provide information about the progression or regression of the pathological process. These data are important, particularly when the pathological processes that may interfere with the outcome of pregnancy are diagnosed. Therefore, routine scan should include meticulous examination of the total placenta and registration of various abnormalities of the placenta and umbilical cord.

REFERENCES

1. **Fox, H. and Elston, C. W.,** The development and structure of the placenta, in *Pathology of the Placenta,* Fox, H., Ed., W. B. Saunders, Philadelphia, 1978, 1.
2. **Gottesfeld, K. R., Thompson, H. E., Holmes, J. H., and Taylor, E. S.,** Ultrasonic placentography: a new method for placental localisation, *Am. J. Obstet. Gynecol.,* 96, 538, 1966.
3. **Kurjak, A. and Olajos, I.,** Placentography by ultrasound, in *Ultrazvuk u Klinickoj Medicini,* Kurjak, A., Ed., Medicinska Naklada, Zagreb, 1977, 41.
4. **Gottesfeld, K. R.,** The clinical role of placental imaging, *Clin. Obstet. Gynecol.,* 27, 327, 1984.
5. **Fisher, C. C., Garrett, W., and Kossoff, G.,** Placental aging monitored by gray scale echography, *Am. J. Obstet. Gynecol.,* 124, 438, 1976.
6. **Callen, P. W. and Filly, R. A.,** The placental-subplacental complex as a specific indicator of placental position on ultrasound, *J. Clin. Ultrasound,* 8, 21, 1980.
7. **Spirt, B. A., Gordon, L. P., and Kagan, E. H.,** Sonography of the placenta, in *The Principles and the Practice of Ultrasonography in Obstetrics and Gynecology,* Sanders, R. C. and James, A. E., Eds., Appleton-Century-Crofts, New York, 1985, 333.
8. **D'Addario, V. and Kurjak, A.,** Embryologic foundation of the first trimester ultrasonography, in *Diagnostic Ultrasound in Developing Countries,* Kurjak, A., Ed., Mladost, Zagreb, 1986, 59.
9. **Grannum, P. A. T., Berkowitz, R. L., and Hobbins, J. C.,** The ultrasonic changes in the maturing placenta and their relation to fetal pulmonic maturity, *Am. J. Obstet. Gynecol.,* 133, 915, 1979.
10. **Vandenberge, K., Goddeeris, P., and Wolf, F.,** Recent advances in ultrasonography of the placenta, in *Recent Advances in Ultrasound Diagnosis,* Vol. 2, Kurjak, A., Ed., Excerpta Medica, Amsterdam, 1980, 154.

11. **Harman, C. R., Manning, F. A., Stearns, E., and Morrison, I.,** The correlation of ultrasonic placental grading and fetal pulmonary maturation in five hundred sixty-three pregnancies, *Am. J. Obstet. Gynecol.,* 143, 911, 1982.
12. **Vermeulen, R. C. W., Lambalk, N. B., Exalto, N., and Arts, N. F. T.,** The anatomic basis for ultrasonic images in the human placenta, *Am. J. Obstet. Gynecol.,* 153, 806, 1985.
13. **Donald, I. and Abdulla, S.,** Placentography by sonar, *J. Obstet. Gynaecol. Br. Commonw.,* 75, 993, 1968.
14. **Hansmann, M. and Terinde, R.,** The placenta, in *Ultraschall Diagnostic in Gebursthilfe und Gynaekologie,* Hansmann, M., Hackeloer, B. J., and Staudach, A., Eds., Springer-Verlag, Berlin, 1985, 325.
15. **Bowie, J. D., Rochester, D., and Cadkin, A. V.,** Accuracy of placental localization by ultrasound, *Radiology,* 128, 177, 1978.
16. **Goldberg, B. B.,** The identification of placenta praevia, *Radiology,* 128, 255, 1978.
17. **Wiliamson, D., Bjorgen, J., and Baier, B.,** Ultrasonic diagnosis of placenta praevia: value of a postvoid scan, *J. Clin. Ultrasound,* 6, 58, 1978.
18. **Zemlyn, S.,** The length of the uterine cervix and its significance, *J. Clin. Ultrasound,* 9, 267, 1981.
19. **Grannum, P., and Hobbins, J. C.,** The placenta, in *Ultrasonography in Obstetrics and Gynecology,* Callen, P. W., Ed., W. B. Saunders, Philadelphia, 1983, 141.
20. **Japelj, I., Saks, A., and Dukic, V.,** Ultrasonic placentography, in *Diagnostic Ultrasound in Developing Countries,* Kurjak, A., Ed., Mladost, Zagreb, 1986, 104.
21. **Jeffrey, R. B. and Laing, F. C.,** Sonography of the low-lying placenta: value of Trendelenburg and traction scan, *Am. J. Roentgenol.,* 137, 547, 1981.
22. **Laing, F. C.,** Ultrasound evaluation of obstetric problems relating to the lower uterine segment and cervix, in *The Principles and the Practice of Ultrasonography in Obstetrics and Gynecology,* Sanders, R. C. and James, A. E., Eds., Appleton-Century-Crofts, New York, 1985, 355.
23. **Lee, T. G., Knochel, J. R., Melendez, M. G., and Henderson, S. C.,** Fetal evaluation: a new technique for placental localisation in the diagnosis of previa, *J. Clin. Ultrasound,* 9, 167, 1981.
24. **Latin, V., Drazancic, A., Kurjak, A., and Kuvacic, I.,** Fetal growth in the cases with placenta praevia, in *Perinatalni dani 1974,* Drazancic, A., Ed., Medicinska Naklada, Zagreb, 1974, 115.
25. **Japelj, I. and Saks, A.,** Localization of the placenta by ultrasound, *Jugosl. Ginekol. Opstet.,* 12, 17, 1972.
26. **Chapman, M. G., Furness, E., Jones, W. R., and Sheat, J. H.,** Significance of the ultrasound location of placental site in early pregnancy, *Br. J. Obstet. Gynecol.,* 86, 846, 1979.
27. **King, D. L.,** Placental migration demonstrated by ultrasonography: a hypothesis of dynamic placentation, *Radiology,* 109, 167, 1973.
28. **Kurjak, A. and Barsic, E.,** Changes of placental site diagnosed by repeat ultrasonic examination, *Acta Obstet. Gynecol. Scand.,* 56, 16, 1977.
29. **DePalma, R., Santos-Ramos, R., Duenhoelter, J. H., and Sihai, B.,** Total placenta praevia during midtrimester: a failing correlation with placenta praevia at term, in Proc. 24th Meet. AIUM, Oklahoma City, 1979, 179.
30. **Kurjak, A., Olajos, I., Bukovic, D., and Funduk, B.,** The clinical value of ultrasonic placentography: Experience from a series of 1000 obstetric cases, *Elektrofiziologiya,* 5, 28, 1976.
31. **Rizos, N., Doran, T. A., Miskin, M., Benzie, R. J., and Ford, J. A.,** Natural history of placenta previa ascertained by diagnostic ultrasound, *Am. J. Obstet. Gynecol.,* 133, 287, 1979.
32. **Wexler, P. and Gottesfeld, K. R.,** Early diagnosis of placenta praevia, *Obstet. Gynecol.,* 54, 231, 1979.
33. **Reed, M. F.,** Ultrasonic placentography, *Br. J. Radiol.,* 46, 255, 1973.
34. **Levine, L. R.,** Placental Grades and Gestational Age, Ph.D. thesis, Yale University School of Medicine, New Haven, CT, 1981.
35. **Petrucha, R., Golde, S., and Platt, L.,** Real time ultrasound of the placenta in the assessment of fetal pulmonic maturity, *Am. J. Obstet. Gynecol.,* 142, 463, 1982.
36. **Winsberg, F.,** Echographic changes with placental aging, *J. Clin. Ultrasound,* 1, 55, 1973.
37. **Koslowski, P., Terinde, R., and Schmidt, H.,** Bestimmung des Plazenta-wachstums aus Ultraschallschnittbildern, *Ultraschal,* 1, 116, 1980.
38. **Hodek, B. and Klaric, P.,** Correlation between fetal lung maturity and placental changes diagnosed by ultrasound, *Jugosl. Ginekol. Perinat.,* 3-4, 69, 1986.
39. **Podobnik, M., Bulic, M., Bistricki, J., Kukura, V., and Kasnar, V.,** Ultrasound placental grading and fetal lung maturity, *Jugosl. Ginekol. Perinat.,* 5–6, 117, 1985.
40. **Clair, M. R., Rosenberg, E., Tempkin, D., Andreotti, R. F., and Bowie, J.,** Placental grading in the complicated or high-risk pregnancy, *J. Ultrasound Med.,* 2, 297, 1983.
41. **Quinlan, R. and Cruz, A.,** Ultrasonic placental grading and fetal maturity, *Am. J. Obstet. Gynecol.,* 142, 110, 1982.

42. **Kazzi, G. M., Gross, T. L., and Kazzi, S. J. N.,** Noninvasive prediction of hyaline membrane disease: an optimized classification on sonographic placental maturation, *Am. J. Obstet. Gynecol.,* 152, 213, 1985.

43. **Kollitz, J., Dattel, B. J., and Key, T. C.,** Acute respiratory distress syndrome in an infant with grade III placental changes, *J. Ultrasound Med.,* 1, 205, 1982.

44. **Grannum, P. A. and Hobbins, J. C.,** The placenta, *Radiol. Clin. North Am.,* 20, 353, 1982.

45. **Kazzi, G. M., Gross, T. L., Sokol, R. J., and Kazzi, N. H.,** Detection of intrauterine growth retardation: a new use for sonographic placental aging, *Am. J. Obstet. Gynecol.,* 145, 733, 1983.

46. **Radunovic, N., Pilic, Z., and Sulovic, V.,** Ultrasonic signs of placental maturation, *Zdrav. Vestn.,* 54, 327, 1985.

47. **Caroll, B.,** Ultrasonic features of pre-eclampsia, *J. Clin. Ultrasound,* 8, 483, 1980.

48. **Hollander, H. J. and Mast, H.,** Intrauterine Dickenmesungen der Plazenta mittels Ultraschall bei normalen Schwangerschaften und bei Rh-Inkompatibilitaet, *Geburtshilfe Frauenheilkd.,* 28, 662, 1968.

49. **Schlensker, K. H.,** Ultraschallplazentographie, *Gynaekologia,* 9, 156, 1976.

50. **Hellmann, L. M., Kobayashi, M., Tolles, W. E., and Cromb, E.,** Ultrasonic studies on the volumetric growth of the human placenta, *Am. J. Obstet. Gynecol.,* 108, 740, 1970.

51. **Blecker, O. P., Kloosterman, G. J., Breur, W., and Mieras, D. J.,** The volumetric growth of the human placenta: a longitudinal ultrasonic study, *Am. J. Obstet. Gynecol.,* 127, 657, 1977.

52. **Hoogland, H. J.,** *Ultrasonographic Aspects of the Placenta,* Koninklijke Drukkerij, Georg Thieme Verlag, The Netherlands, Nijmegen, Alphen ald Rijn, 1980.

53. **Fox, H.,** Macroscopic abnormalities of the placenta, in *Pathology of the Placenta,* Fox, H. and Elston, C. W., Eds. W. B. Saunders, Philadelphia, 1978, 95.

54. **Shanklin, D. R. and Scott, J. S.,** Massive subchorial thrombohaematoma (Breus' mole), *Br. J. Obstet. Gynecol.,* 82, 476, 1975.

55. **Spirt, B. A., Kagan, E. H., and Aubry, R. H.,** Clinically silent retroplacental haematoma: sonographic and pathologic correlation, *J. Clin. Ultrasound,* 9, 203, 1981.

56. **Spirt, B. A., Kagan, E. H., and Rozanski, R. M.,** Abruptio placente. Sonographic and pathological correlation, *Am. J. Roentgenol.,* 133, 877, 1979.

57. **Yiu-Chiu, V. and Chiu, L.,** Ultrasonographic findings of normal and pathologic placenta and umbilical cord, *J. Comp. Tomogr.,* 5, 136, 1081.

58. **Scholl, J. S.,** Abruptio placentae: clinical management in nonacute cases, *Am. J. Obstet. Gynecol.,* 156, 40, 1987.

59. **Jaffe, M., Schoen, W., Silver, T., Bowerman, R., and Stuck, K.,** Sonography of abruptio placentae, *Am. J. Radiol.,* 137, 1049, 1981.

60. **Cardwell, M. S.,** Ultrasound diagnosis of abruptio placentae with fetomaternal hemorrhage, *Am. J. Obstet. Gynecol.,* 157, 359, 1987.

61. **Wentworth, P.,** The incidence and significance of intervillous thrombi in the human placenta, *J. Obstet. Gynecol. Br. Commonw.,* 71, 894, 1964.

62. **Sprit, B. A., Gordon, L. P., and Kagan, E. H.,** Intervillous thrombosis: sonographic and pathologic correlation, *Radiology,* 147, 197, 1983.

63. **Kurjak, A. and Latin, V.,** Fetal and placental abnormalities, in *Progress in Medical Ultrasound,* Vol. 2, Kurjak, A., Ed., Excerpta Medica, Amsterdam, 1981, 77.

64. **Javert, C. T. and Reiss, C.,** The origin and significance of macroscopic intervillous coagulation hematomas (red infarcts) of the human placenta, *Surg. Gynecol. Obstet.,* 94, 257, 1952.

65. **Hoogland, H. J., deHaan, J., and Vooys, G. P.,** Ultrasonographic diagnosis of intervillous thrombosis related to the Rh isoimmunization, *Gynecol. Obstet. Invest.,* 10, 237, 1979.

66. **Fox, H.,** Non-trophoblastic tumours of the placenta, in *Pathology of the Placenta,* Fox, H. and Elston, C. W., Eds., W. B. Saunders, Philadelphia, 1978, 343.

67. **Marchetti, A. A.,** Consideration of certain types of benign tumors of the placenta, *Surg. Gynecol. Obstet.,* 68, 733, 1939.

68. **Fox, H.,** Vascular tumours of the placenta, *Obstet. Gynecol. Surv.,* 697, 1967.

69. **Resnick, L.,** Chorioangioma, with report of a case associated with oligohydramnios, *S. Afr. Med. J.,* 27, 57, 1953.

70. **Engel, K., Hahn, T. H., and Karschnia, R.,** Sonographische diagnose eines Plazentatumors mit hochgradiger intrauteriner fetaler Mangelentwicklung, Ausbildung eines Anhydramnie und nachfolgendem Fruchttod, *Geburtshilfe Frauenheilkd.,* 41, 570, 1981.

71. **Wallenburg, H. C. S.,** Chorioangioma of the placenta: thirteen new cases and a review of the literature from 1939 to 1970 with special reference to clinical complications, *Obstet. Gynecol. Surv.,* 26, 411, 1971.

72. **Geppert, M. and Bachmann, F. F.,** Über Chorioangiome. 1. Pathologische Anatomie und Schwangerschaftskomplikationen, *Zentralbl. Gynaekol.,* 106, 1937, 1984.

73. **Tonkin, I. L., Setzer, E. S., and Ermocilla, R.,** Placental chorioangioma: a rare cause of congestive heart failure and hydrops fetalis in the newborn, *Am. J. Radiol.,* 134, 181, 1980.
74. **Mahmood, K.,** Small chorioangioms and small-for-gestational age baby, *Am. J. Obstet. Gynecol.,* 127, 440, 1977.
75. **Kohler, H. G., Iqbal, N., and Jenkins, D. M.,** Chorionic haemangiomata and abruptio placentae, *Br. J. Obstet. Gynecol.,* 83, 667, 1976.
76. **Leonidas, J. C., Beatty, E. C., and Hall, R. T.,** Chorioangioma of the placentae: a cause of cardiomegaly and heart failure in the newborn, *Radiology,* 123, 703, 1975.
77. **Bauer, C. R., Fojaco, R. M., Bancalari, E., and Fernandez-Rocha, L.,** Microangiopathic hemolytic anemia and thrombocytopenia in a neonate associated with large placental chorioangioma, *Pediatrics,* 62, 574, 1978.
78. **Stockhausen, H. B., Hansen, H. G., Mönkemeier, D., and Mührer, A.,** Risenhaemangiom der Plazenta als Ursache einer lebens bedrohlichen Neugeborenenanaemie mit Hydrops congenitum, *Monatsschr. Kinderheilkd.,* 132, 182, 1984.
79. **Brühwiler, H., Schneitter, J., and Luscher, K. P.,** Ultraschalbild und fetale Komplikationem bei grossen Chorioangiom der Plazenta, *Ultraschal,* 7, 245, 1986.
80. **Bernischke, K. and Driscoll, S. G.,** *The Pathology of the Human Placenta,* Spring-Verlag, Berlin, 1967.
81. **Svanholm, H. and Thordsen, Ch.,** Placental teratoma, *Acta Obstet. Gynecol. Scand.,* 66, 1769, 1987.
82. **D'Addario, V., Kurjak, A., Miniello, G., and Traina, V.,** Ultrasound and embriology, in *Recent Advances in Ultrasound Diagnosis,* Vol. 4, Kurjak, A. and Kossof, G., Eds., Excerpta Medica, Amsterdam, 1984, 186.
83. **Purola, E.,** The length and insertion of the umbilical cord, *Ann. Chir. Gynecol.,* 57, 621, 1968.
84. **Shanklin, D. R.,** The human placenta: a clinico-pathologic study, *Obstet. Gynecol.,* 11, 129, 1958.
85. **Brody, S. and Frenkel, D. A.,** Marginal insertion of the cord and premature labour, *Am. J. Obstet. Gynecol.,* 65, 1305, 1953.
86. **Foss, I. and Vogel, M.,** Über Bezichungen zwischen Implantationsschaeden der Plazenta und Plazentationsstorungen, *Z. Geburtshilfe Perinatol.,* 176, 36, 1972.
87. **Graham, D., Campbell, J., and Litchfield, K. L.,** Sonography of the umbilical cord, in *The Principles and Practice of Ultrasonography in Obstetrics and Gynecology,* Sanders, R. C. and James, A. E., Eds., Appleton-Century-Crofts, New York, 1985, 369.
88. **Mayden, K.,** The umbilical vein diameter in Rhesus isoimmunization, *Med. Ultrasound,* 4, 119, 1980.
89. **De Vore, G. R., Mayden, K., Tortora, M., Berkowitz, R., and Hobbins, J. C.,** Dilatation of the fetal umbilical vein in rhesus hemolytic anemia: a predictor of severe disease, *Am. J. Obstet. Gynecol.,* 141, 464, 1981.
90. **Jouppila, P. and Kirkinen, P.,** The role of fetal blood flow measurements in obstetrics, in *Measurements of Fetal Blood Flow,* Kurjak, A., Ed., CIC Edizioni Internazionali, Rome, 1984, 139.
91. **Witter, F. R. and Graham, D.,** The utility of ultrasonically measured umbilical vein diameter in isoimmunized pregnancies, *Am. J. Obstet. Gynecol.,* 146, 225, 1983.
92. **Fox, H.,** Pathology of the umbilical cord, in *Pathology of the Placenta,* Fox, H. and Elston, C. W., W. B. Saunders, Philadelphia, 1978, 426.
93. **Walher, C. W. and Pye, B. G.,** The length of the umbilical cord: a statistical report, *Br. Med. J.,* 1, 546, 1960.
94. **Müller, G., Dehalleux, J. M., and Trutt, E.,** L'artere ombilicale unique — a propos de 54 cas, *Bull. Soc. Belge Gynecol. Obstet.,* 39, 333, 1969.
95. **Little, W. A.,** Umbilical artery aplasia, *Obstet. Gynecol.,* 695, 1961.
96. **Froehlich, L. A. and Fujikura, T.,** Significance of a single umbilical artery, *Am. J. Obstet. Gynecol.,* 94, 274, 1966.
97. **Bryan, E. M. and Kohler, H. G.,** The missing umbilical artery. II. Pediatric follow-up, *Arch. Dis. Child.,* 50, 714, 1975.
98. **Jassani, M. N. and Brennan, J. N.,** Prenatal diagnosis of single umbilical artery by ultrasound, *J. Clin. Ultrasound,* 8, 447, 1980.
99. **Kurjak, A., Breyer, B., Jurkovic, D., Alfirevic, Z., and Miljan, M.,** Color flow mapping in obstetrics, *J. Perinat. Med.,* 15, 271, 1987.
100. **Dippel, A. L.,** Hematomas of the umbilical cord, *Surg. Gynecol. Obstet.,* 70, 51, 1940.
101. **Corkill, T. F.,** The infant's vulnerable life-line, *Aust. N.Z. J. Obstet. Gynaecol.,* 1, 154, 1961.
102. **Ruvinsky, E. D., Wiley, T. L., Morrison, J. C., and Blake, P. G.,** In utero diagnosis of umbilical cord hematoma by ultrasonography, *Am. J. Obstet. Gynecol.,* 140, 833, 1981.
103. **Witter, F. R. and Sanders, R. C.,** Maternal hemorrhage into the amniotic sac producing an apparent umbilical cord mass on sonogram, *Am. J. Obstet. Gynecol.,* 155, 649, 1986.

104. **Coulter, J. B. S., Scott, J. M., and Jordan, M. M.,** Oedema of the cord and respiratory distress in the newborn, *Br. J. Obstet. Gynecol.,* 82, 453, 1975.

105. **Picker, R. H.,** A scoring system for the morphological ultrasonic assessment of foetal well-being and maturation, in *Ultrasound,* '82,, Lersky, R A., and Morley, P., Eds., Pergamon Press, Oxford, 1983, 597.

106. **Silver, R. K., Dooley, S. L., Tamura, R. K., and Depp, R.,** Umbilical cord size and amniotic fluid volume in prolonged pregnancy, *Am. J. Obstet. Gynecol.,* 157, 716, 1987.

107. **Sachs, L. and Fourcroy, J. L.,** Prenatal detection of umbilical cord. Allantoic cyst, *Radiology,* 145, 455, 1982.

108. **Fiske, C. E., Filly, R. A., and Golbus, M. S.,** Prenatal ultrasound diagnosis of amniotic band syndrome, *J. Ultrasound Med.,* 1, 45, 1982.

Chapter 7

NORMAL FETAL ANATOMY

Asim Kurjak and Davor Jurkovic

INTRODUCTION

The most important applications of ultrasound in obstetrics are assessment of gestational age and fetal growth, and prenatal detection of fetal malformations. In both fields a basic prerequisite to obtain successful results is a good and accurate knowledge of normal fetal anatomy and its variants. Different anatomical structures like the cavum septi pellucidi or the intrahepatic portion of the umbilical vein serve as useful landmarks to define reference planes for biparietal diameter (BPD) or abdominal circumference (AC) measurements, thus enabling reproducible studies of fetal biometry. The importance of understanding normal fetal anatomy is also emphasized by the nonspecificity of sonographic findings in the majority of detectable fetal abnormalities. Diagnosis of a fetal abnormality is primarily based on absence or distortion of normally present anatomical structures, rather than on meticulous analysis of an apparently abnormal structure.

Therefore, every examination, regardless of its initial indication, includes a rapid and systematic evaluation of fetal anatomy. However, possibilities of sonographic visualization of certain anatomical details largely depend on gestational age and fetal size. At the beginning of the fetal period during the 9th week of gestation, most of the fetal organs are developed and located in their final anatomical position. In spite of that, ultrasound studies at this gestational age enable clear distinction between the head, body, and limbs only, and recognition of heart pulsations, while other anatomical details cannot be depicted. This is quite understandable with respect to the size of the fetus of approximately 20 mm at this gestational age and the 1-mm maximum resolution capabilities of modern commercially available ultrasonic equipment.

Because of this there is a general agreement that sonographic studies of fetal anatomy including measurement of BPD and femur size should start from the 13th or 14th week onward.[1,2]

TECHNIQUE OF EXAMINATION

The routine evaluation of fetal anatomy is made possible by the state-of-the-art, high-resolution real-time scanners, either linear, curved linear, or sector ones, which provide for a quick examination of the fetus without significant loss of resolution. The most significant advantage of real time is the ease of maneuverability, whereby one can quickly change scan planes and rapidly survey the uterus, getting a three-dimensional impression of the structure under investigation. Another advantage of real time is the visualization of vascular pulsations and fetal movements. This enables easy documentation of fetal viability and facilitates examination, even in hyperactive fetuses.

Sonographic evaluation of the fetal anatomy presumes performance of numerous scans in different scanning planes which should follow certain logical scheme. It is necessary that each person involved in obstetric sonography develop his own examination regime which can be easily modified depending on fetal position and lie, but should always include visualization of all relevant anatomical details. In our experience, the examination is best

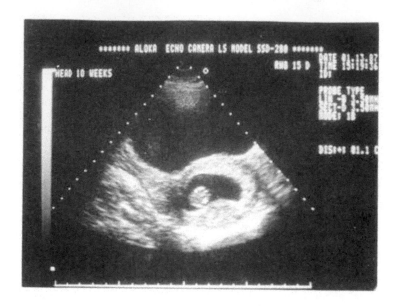

FIGURE 1.   Longitudinal scan through the pregnant uterus at 12 weeks. The fetal head is clearly seen as an ovoid structure floating within the amniotic fluid. BPD measurement is also illustrated.

to start by wide and slow scanning of the whole uterine content from the symphysis to the uterine fundus. This enables easy orientation about fetal position, number of fetuses, amount of amniotic fluid, and placental position. This way prevents overlooking of the second twin or placenta praevia that may occur if examination starts by BPD measurement or assessment of minor anatomical details. The first step in the sonographic visualization of the fetus is orientation about its position and lie. This problem is easily solved by documentation of the position of the head and spine. Transverse scans are then helpful for getting a clear three-dimensional impression of the fetus and the orientation about its anterior and posterior and right and left sides. Distinction between right and left may be facilitated by visualization of the fetal stomach, which is normally located in the left hemiabdomen, and the heart, which is also orientated to the left, After completing data about fetal position, subsequent steps in the assessment of fetal anatomy include visualization of the skull, intracranial structures, and face, spine, neck, thorax (with particular attention to the heart and great vessels), diaphragm, intra-abdominal structures, genitourinary system, and finally limbs.

HEAD

The fetal head can be visualized ultrasonically by the 8th menstrual week, whereas the examination of fetal cranium may begin from the 11th or 12th week of gestation[3,4] (Figure 1). From this gestational age until term, the fetal BPD serves as the primary measurement for determining gestational age. The best plane of scanning to detect the most details is the axial one, obtained at different parallel levels, starting at the vertex of the fetal head. This kind of examination is best done when the fetal head is in an occiput-transverse position. If the head is in an occiput-anterior or occiput-posterior position, visualization of intracranial anatomy is poor (Figure 2). In such situations the probe should be placed laterally on the abdominal wall and directed towards the fetal head in an attempt to send ultrasound waves

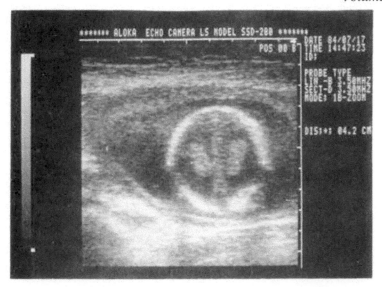

FIGURE 2. Intracranial anatomy as seen on transverse scan through the uterus with the fetal head in occiput posterior position. Midline echo and echogenic choroid plexi are the features recognizable in this position, while other details cannot be seen.

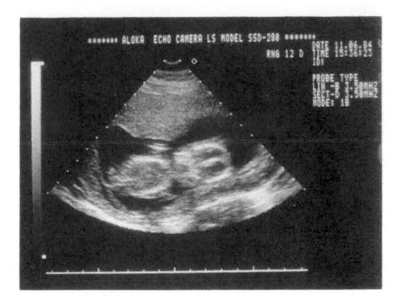

FIGURE 3. Frontal section through the fetal head at 12 weeks. The lateral ventricles are seen as fluid-filled, echo-free cavities which occupy most of the cranial vault.

perpendicularly to the midline echo. Difficulties in intracranial anatomy visualization may also be encountered when the head is situated low within the lesser pelvis. Putting the patient in the Trendelenburg position might be helpful in these cases. By the 12th week, the lateral ventricles are recognized as fluid-filled cavities occupying most of the cranial vault and containing an echogenic choroid plexus (Figure 3). In transverse terms, the choroid plexus

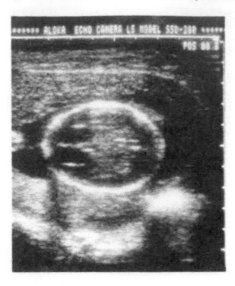

FIGURE 4.   The anterior horns on transverse scan through the fetal head at 16 weeks are demonstrated as prominent, fluid-filled cavities. Note the absence of any echoes, suggesting the presence of choroid.

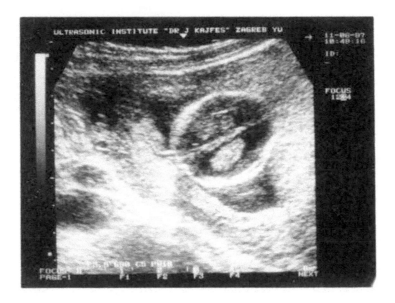

FIGURE 5.   Transverse scan through the fetal head showing marked echogenicity of the choroid plexus at 16 weeks.

fills the lateral ventricles almost completely from the 12th to the 17th week of gestation. The anterior horns are devoid of choroid plexus and have a fluid appearance (Figure 4), while the bodies and atria of the ventricles appear solid because of choroid. Strong echogenicity of the choroid plexuses at this gestational age is primarily attributed to their rich glycogen content, which may represent an energy store for the developing cerebrum[5] (Figure 5).

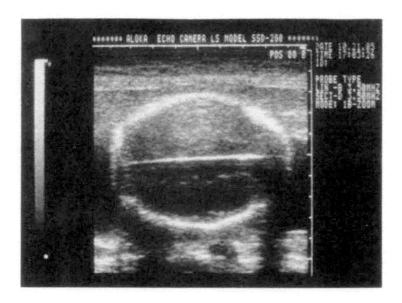

FIGURE 6.   Axial scan below the vertex of the cranium shows continuous echogenic line representing the falx cerebri.

From the 17th week of gestation, a more detailed analysis of neuroanatomy can be performed. Owing to the rapid proliferation of the cerebral cortex, the separation of the lateral ventricles from the calvarium can be recognized. The echogenic choroid still fills the lateral ventricles. The anterior and posterior horns may be visualized, but the former are of relatively smaller size than earlier. Between the 20th week and term there is little structural change of the fetal brain. As mentioned before, the neuroanatomy is most often evaluated on the transaxial or transverse planes.[6]

Beginning at the vertex of the cranium, the first structure to be identified is the falx, which appears as a continuous echogenic line (Figure 6). Progressing caudally, the bodies of the lateral ventricles are seen as two anechoic structures divided by midline echo. The lateral walls of the ventricular bodies are imaged as linear echoes paralleling the central midline echo (Figure 7). The falx and the interhemispheric fissure account for the midline echo at this level.[6]

Scans performed caudally to the bodies of the lateral ventricles demonstrate the brain stem. Beginning at the highest level of the brain stem, the thalami are seen as oval hypoechoic structures on each side of the midline (Figure 8). The lateral walls of the anterior horns of the lateral ventricle are also observed at this level. They are seen as two short, linear echoes paralleling the midline, and the width of the anterior horns can be easily measured (Figure 7). The anterior horn width to hemispheric width ratio can be calculated, and it serves as a sensitive parameter for sonographic diagnosis of hydrocephalus.[7-9]

Posteriorly to the anterior horns, there are two echoes of similar appearance that are placed very close to the midline echo. They represent the medial walls of the posterior horns of the lateral ventricle. The lateral walls of the posterior horns are not visible, but its size may be estimated by measuring the distance between the medial wall and lateral edge of the choroid plexus, which normally occupies a part of the posterior horns[8] (Figure 9). By moving the probe slightly lower, anteriorly in the midline one encounters an echoic rectan-

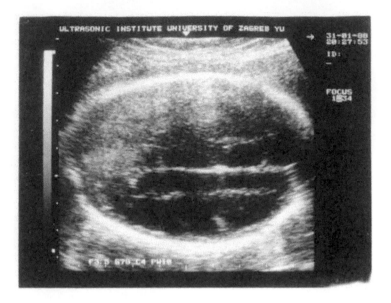

FIGURE 7. By moving the probe a few millimeters lower, anechoic bodies of the lateral ventricles are becoming apparent as two anechoic structures parallel to the midline echo.

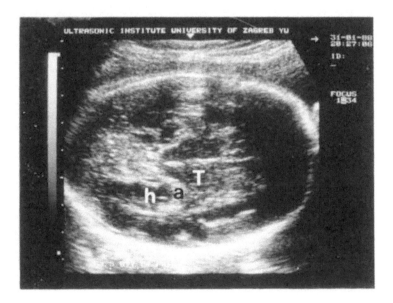

FIGURE 8. Transverse scan through the fetal head showing the thalami (T) which appear as two hypoechoic structures in the center of the head. Posteriolaterally to the thalami, the ambient cysterns (a) are seen as echogenic structures that denote the anterior border of the hypocampus (h).

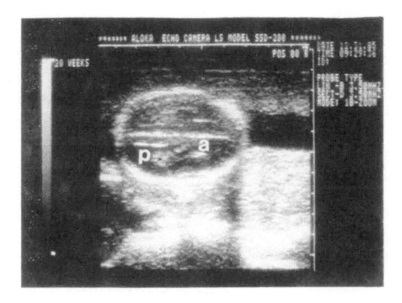

FIGURE 9.   Transverse scan showing the anterior (a) and posterior (p) horns of the lateral ventricles. The lateral walls of the anterior horns are seen as two short echoes parallel to the midline. The medial walls are placed closely to the midline and, therefore, cannot be visualized. The width of the anterior horns is measured from its lateral walls to the midline. Posteriorly to the anterior horn, medial walls of the posterior horns are seen as two longer echoes placed 5 mm from the midline echo. The lateral walls of the posterior horns are rarely seen, and their width can be, in most situations, estimated by measuring the distance between the medial wall and lateral edge of the choroid plexus, which partly occupies the posterior horns.

gular area as the first break in the continuous midline echo (Figure 10). At first, it was mistakenly considered to represent the third ventricle. Some investigators attribute it to the cavum septi pellucidi, and others to the trunk of the corpus callosum.[10,11]

When the scan is moved a few millimeters caudally, a central echo appears in the middle of this anechoic area (Figure 11). A possible explanation for such structure is that it represents the region of the lower tract of the midbodies of the lateral ventricles with the interposed septum pellucidum.[12] The third ventricle is located slightly posterior and caudal to the region of the septum pellucidum. Since it is a very narrow cavity, its lateral walls can be occasionally visualized as two very closely parallel lines. It is placed between the thalami and continues posteriorly and caudally with the aqueduct of Sylvius. This plane which demonstrates both the cavum septi pellucidi and the third ventricle is recommended for measuring the BPD[13] (Figure 11).

The hypoechoic area located posteriorly and laterally to the thalami represents the hypocampus. The strong echoes between the thalamus and the hypocampus are thought to represent ambient cisterns. The lateral border of the hypocampus is formed by the trigone of the lateral ventricle, where two lines can occasionally be seen, corresponding to the medial and lateral borders of the trigone. At the same level, the insula with the overlying Sylvian fissure is usually visible in the lateral aspect of the cerebral hemisphere. On real time it can be easily recognized by the vascular pulsations of the middle cerebral artery (Figure 12).

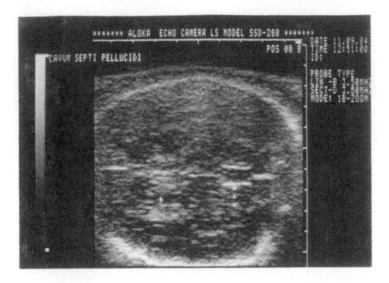

FIGURE 10.   Sonogram of a normal 37-week-fetus at the level of the cavum septi pellucidi. Note the break in the continuous midline echo and the typical parallel echo of the cavum septi pellucidi.

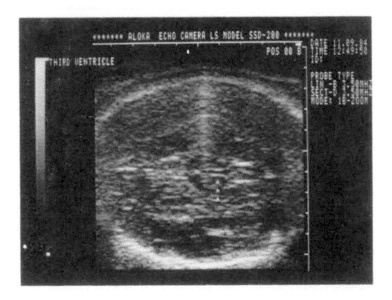

FIGURE 11.   Axial sonogram of the same baby performed slightly caudally in relation to the previous one shows the appearance of the third central echo within the cavum septi pellucidi which most probably represents the septum pellucidum. The third ventricle is located posteriorly to the cavum septi pellucidi (arrows) and continues posteriorly and caudally with the aqueduct of Sylvius. The thalami are also seen along the third ventricle.

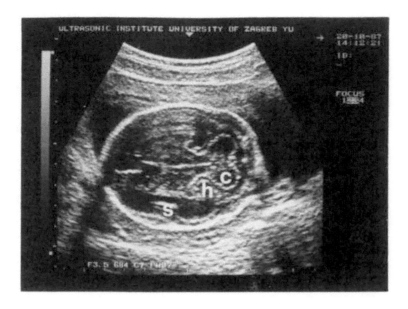

FIGURE 12. An oblique scan showing the ambient cisterns hypocampus (h), Sylvian fissure (s), and posterior fossa with cerebellar hemispheres (c).

By performing an axial scan obtained 1 to 3 cm caudally to the region of the third ventricle, one can visualize the upper brain stem which appears as a heart-shaped structure of low echogenicity with the apex pointing posteriorly. Anterior to the brain stem, the pulsations of the basilar artery can be identified. The posterior cerebral arteries can be imaged around the brain stem in the perimesencephalic cistern. Anterior to the basilar artery, the pulsating circle of Willis can be imaged, but individual vessels cannot be identified. The posterior cerebral fossa can be visualized by oblique or coronal scans. Its superior margin is the tentorium cerebelli which is strongly echogenic. Most of the posterior fossa is occupied by the moderately echogenic cerebellar hemispheres, and the vermis can be recognized in the middle, owing to its strong echogenicity (Figure 13). Besides standard transaxial scanning, fetal intracranial anatomy can be analyzed in sagittal, parasagittal, and coronal planes. Sagittal section may be employed for better visualization of the corpus callosum, which appears as a relatively hypoechoic structure located above the cavum septi pellucidi and thalami[14] (Figure 14).

Sagittal scan also provide a clear demonstration of the tentorium cerebelli, which is seen as an echogenic line denoting the upper border of posterior fossa. Parasagittal scans rarely provide significant diagnostic data, but can be occasionally employed for the purpose of demonstrating the body and anterior and posterior horns of the lateral ventricles in a single plane. The lateral ventricle is seen in this plane as a semilunar anechoic formation, partially filled with echogenic choroid plexus covering the thalamus from its superior aspect.[14] (Figure 15).

Coronal scans are particularly useful for the detection of intracranial pathology that disturbs symmetry of brain anatomy. A well-known limitation of transaxial scanning is its inability to clearly demonstrate brain anatomy in the hemisphere proximal to the probe, particularly during the third trimester. This is due to the reverberation phenomenon which is caused by multiple reflections of the ultrasonic waves within the fetal skull.[15] By performing

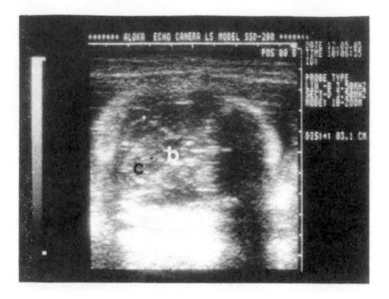

FIGURE 13. An oblique sonogram showing the brain stem (b) and the posterior fossa. The fourth ventricle and the cerebellar hemispheres (c) are clearly recognizable.

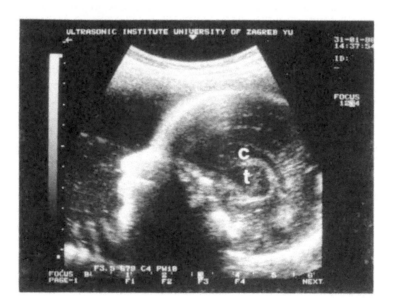

FIGURE 14. Sagittal scan of the normal 24-week-fetus showing the thalami (t) and corpus callosum (c). Fetal profile is best seen in this section.

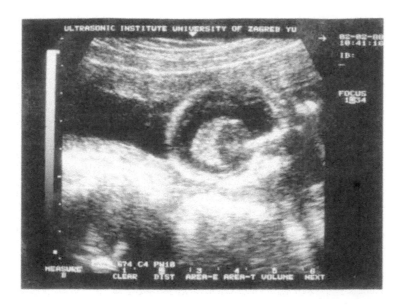

FIGURE 15. Parasagittal scan of the head, demonstrating the lateral ventricle and echogenic choroid plexus within it.

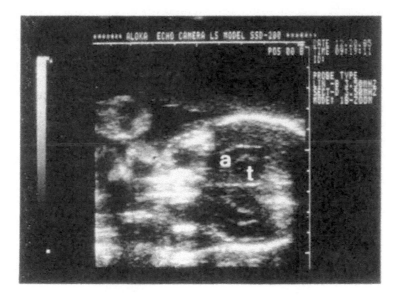

FIGURE 16. Coronal anteriorly angled scan showing the orbits, anterior horns (a), thalami (t), and midline echo in a normal 27-week-old fetus.

the coronal scan, both hemispheres are equally clearly seen, and this may be helpful for reliable diagnosis of unilateral brain pathology (Figures 16 and 17).

The bones of the calvarium are examined in the same sections which are employed for the assessment of intracranial anatomy. In transaxial scans they are seen as continuous, regular, ovoid echogenic lines that surround the fetal brain. During the second trimester, a

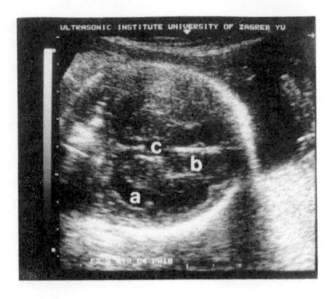

FIGURE 17.   Coronal scan through the cavum septi pellucidi (c) clearly shows interposed echo of the septum pellucidum within it. The bodies (b) and anterior horns (a) of the lateral ventricles are also demonstrated.

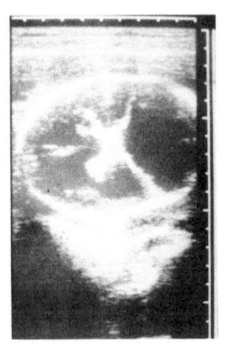

FIGURE 18.   Sonogram of the base of the fetal skull at 28 weeks. The greater wing of the spheroid bone and petrous bones is demonstrated.

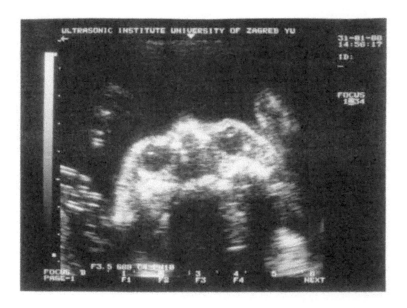

FIGURE 19. An oblique sonogram showing the fetal orbits and lens oculi.

linear echo closely parallel to the inner fetal skull table can be often visualized. The 1- to 3-mm sonolucent space lying between that line and the skull is thought to represent the fetal subarachnoid space.[16]

The base of the skull is usually demonstrated by performing a low axial scan. It appears as an X-shaped structure; the anterior branches of the cross correspond to the spheroid wings, the posterior ones to the petrous pyramids of the temporal bones (Figure 18).

The fetal orbits are easy to identify, and the lenses appear as bright dots in the anterior portion of the orbits (Figure 19). Measurements of the inner and outer orbital diameters may be useful in the diagnosis of suspected congenital syndromes, which include ocular hyper- and hypothelorism, microphthalmus, and anophthalmus.[17,18]

The maxilla and mandible are seen as echoic structures below the orbits and are best visualized in coronal section. Echoes of the teeth may be also seen within these two bones.[19] By slight angulation of the probe, the fetal nose, eyelids, and lips are visualized (Figure 20). This scan is routinely performed in our practice. It provides exceptionally clear visualization of the rim of the lip and nose, which is useful for detection of cleft lip or cleft palate. Lip movements are also frequently seen in this plane during fetal swallowing of the amniotic fluid. The last structures that may be visualized on the fetal head are the ears. They can be easily depicted during transaxial scanning of the fetal head, but are more clearly seen in the parasagittal plane. In this section, even abnormalities of the outer ear may be diagnosed[20] (Figures 21 and 22).

SPINE

The fetal spine is routinely visualized by the 11th week of gestation. In the second trimester, three ossification centers are seen in the fetal spine. The anterior ossification center is located in the posterior aspect of the vertebral body, while two posterior centers develop in the posterior laminae. The fetal spine can be adequately examined only when the fetus is lying aside or in occiput anterior position, while occiput posterior position is particularly

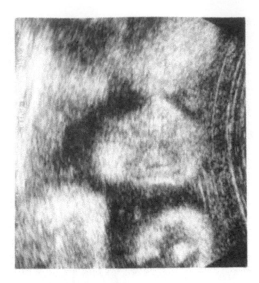

FIGURE 20.   Frontal scan showing the fetal face. The eyelids, nose, and lips can be easily seen in this section.

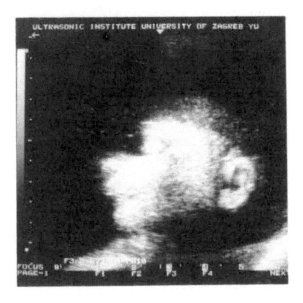

FIGURE 21.   An oblique scan clearly demonstrating fetal face and outer ear in a case of polyhydramnios.

unfavorable. A simple rule which should be strictly followed when examining the spine is that the probe should always be placed directly over the spine, i.e., the spine should be as close as possible to the probe. Only in this way can the integrity of the skin over the spine be checked during examination and symmetry of posterior ossification centers properly assessed. The spine is routinely examined in longitudinal and transverse sections, *while*

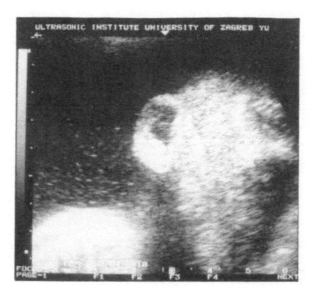

FIGURE 22. Minor details of the outer ear can be seen by orientating the probe to the lateral part of the fetal skull.

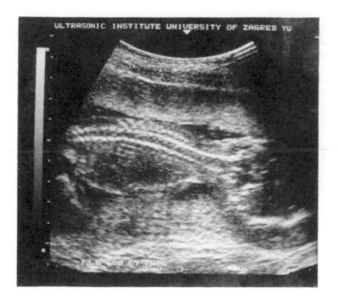

FIGURE 23. The entire length of the fetal spine as shown on the longitudinal scan of a 16-week-old fetus.

scanning in the frontal plane may be employed when confirmation of spinal defect presence is necessary. A longitudinal scan through the spine gives the typical appearance of two strongly echogenic parallel lines[19] (Figure 23). It is difficult to visualize the fetal spine entirely in a longitudinal section after 20 weeks. Using real time, however, one can image the different segments of the spine by moving the transducer along the longitudinal axis. In

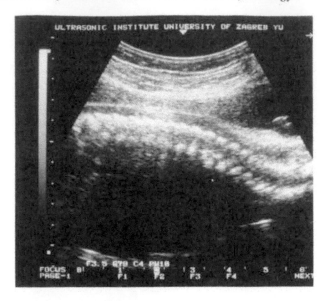

FIGURE 24.   Longitudinal sonogram of the cervical and thoracic part of the normal fetal spine at 34 weeks.

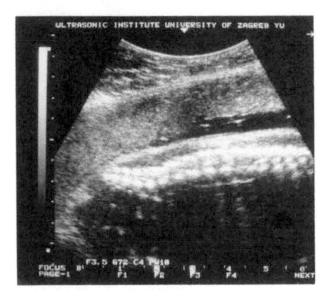

FIGURE 25.   Longitudinal sonogram of the lumbosacral part of the spine of the same fetus.

this way, the spine can be followed up to its attachment to the base of the skull where the spinal canal shows normal widening, or up to the sacrum where it shows a normal gradual tapering (Figures 24 and 25). In the transverse section, the fetal spine shows a typical closed circular appearance. To diagnose spina bifida, it is a good practice to evaluate the spine completely, both in longitudinal and multiple transverse scans throughout the length of the spine[21] (Figures 26 and 27).

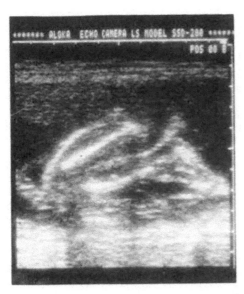

FIGURE 31. Fetal leg in flexed position as seen at 32nd week of pregnancy. The femur, tibia, and foot are easily recognizable.

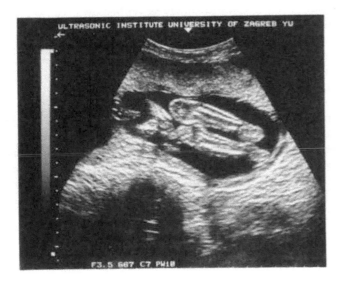

FIGURE 32. Both tibia-fibula complexes at the 37th week of gestation.

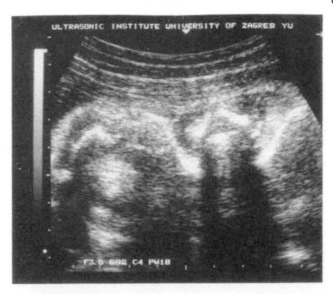

FIGURE 26. Transverse section through the cervical spine shows typical appearance of three ossification centers. Both clavicles are also clearly seen.

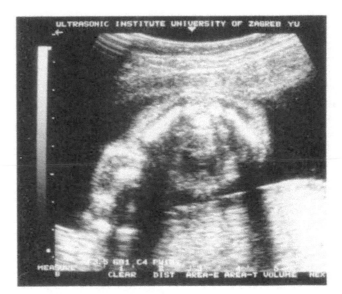

FIGURE 27. Transverse scan through the lumbar spine showing ossification centers and iliac wings.

OTHER PARTS OF FETAL SKELETON

Fetal limbs and the bones within them can be detected ultrasonically from the 10th week of gestation (Figures 28 and 29). Fetal long bones are highly contrasted to other intrauterine structures and can be accurately measured from the 14th week onward.[22] Fetal fingers are easily identifiable as of 16 weeks of gestation (Figure 30). By using real-time equipment,

During routine evaluation of fetal anatomy, the fetal heart is assessed by performing a transverse scan through the fetal chest. Due to the almost horizontal position of the heart during the fetal period, this section shows the long axis of the heart and enables visualization of both atria and ventricles, interatrial and interventricular septum, the tricuspid and mitral valve, and foramen ovale. This so-called four-chamber view is relatively easy to obtain and

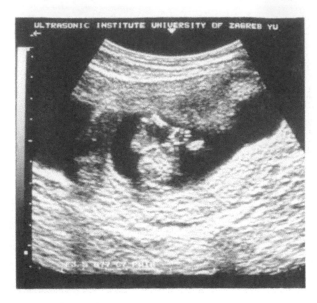

FIGURE 28.   Sonogram of a 13-week-old fetus showing the left arm. Radius-ulna complex and all fingers are demonstrated.

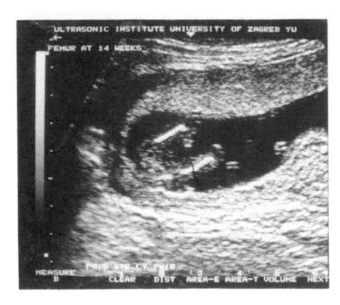

FIGURE 29.   Ultrasound demonstration of both fetal femurs at the 14th week of gestation.

one can visualize limb movements and gain a rapid orientation of limb position, making the examination much easier and faster than with static scanners. A complete examination of fetal limbs in a fetus at risk of having skeletal dysplasia should include all long bone measurements on both sides. When examining the hand and foot, one should be aware that metacarpal bones are ossified at 16 weeks, whereas carpal and tarsal bones (except for the talus and calcaneus) are cartilaginous until term and are not demonstrable by ultrasound.[23]

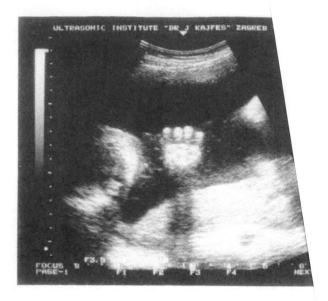

FIGURE 30.   The fetal hand at 19 weeks of gestation. The metacarpal bones and fingers are clearly seen.

The long bones of the arm are most simply recognized by a scan which short axis of the limb. The sonogram of the upper arm will then reveal on section through the forearm two bones. The overall length of a particular b in longitudinal section by rotating the transducer 90°. Foreshortening of l easily occur, and to avoid this, the characteristic posterior shadowing has to soft tissue must be seen beyond both ends of the bone.[8]

The legs are examined best in longitudinal section, which demonstrates bot the thigh. In extended leg position, the calf with the tibia and fibula is seen l the long axis of the extremity in the same section. In the flexed position, the tibi are examined in the same way as arm bones (Figures 31 and 32). Measurements a performed by placing calipers at the lateral edges of the bone. The only exceptio measurement, which is performed from the distal epiphisis to the beginning of neck. Accuracy of measurement is improved if the angle between the beam and lo axis of the bone is about 90° (Figure 33). Numerous standards for long bone l gestational age have been reported and are used for the detection of bone shor various types of skeletal dysplasia.[24] Femur length (FL) measurement is usually mad routine scanning and serves as a good parameter for gestational age confirmation.

Other parts of the fetal skeleton that are consistently seen during routine scanr the clavicles, scapula, illiac wings, and ribs (Figures 26, 27, and 34). Although recognizable, demonstration of these parts of fetal skeleton is, by far, less importan a clinical standpoint.

CHEST

The most prominent organ within the fetal chest is the heart. Visualization of the h is facilitated by its pulsality, which is immediately detected by real-time instrumentati Although fetal heart motion can be detected as early as the 7th week of gestation, evaluat of intracardial anatomy becomes possible at 17 weeks.

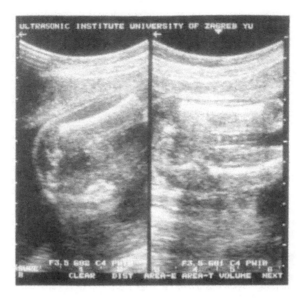

FIGURE 33. Clear demonstration of the fetal femur at the 27th week (left). However, the measurement of its length would be much more accurate if performed when the ultrasound beam comes perpendicularly to the long axis of the bone. It can be relatively easy to achieve this by simple angulation of the probe (right).

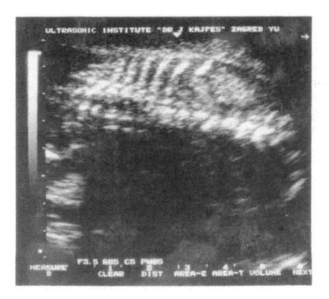

FIGURE 34. An oblique scan through the fetal thorax demonstrating the posterolateral thoracic wall and echogenic ribs.

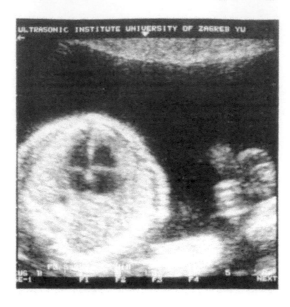

FIGURE 35. A four-chamber view of the fetal heart at 31 weeks of gestation. Numerous structures within the heart can be observed at this section, e.g., both atria and ventricles, the interventricular and intra-atrial septum, foramen ovale, and the mitral and tricuspid valves.

should be checked always, because the majority of congenital heart anomalies affect its normal appearance[25] (Figure 35). However, definite diagnosis of cardiac defect should be made only after meticulous analysis of heart anatomy in four to five different scanning planes. Description of complete heart examination technique is beyond the scope of this chapter and is extensively discussed elsewhere in this book (see Volume II, Chapter 1).

In a four-chamber view, the right ventricle can be distinguished from the left, as it lies more anteriorly, close to the chest wall. An additional guide for distinction between the right and left side of the heart is the fluttering of the valve of the foramen ovale which opens into the left atrium. The appearance of heart structures changes during diastole and systole. During the systole, ventricular cavities become smaller and ventricular walls thicker, while the atria enlarge, being filled with blood.

The fetal aorta is easily recognized on longitudinal scans, and its different portions (aortic root with brachycephalic vessels, the descending aorta and its bifurcation into the iliac vessels) can be identified (Figures 36 and 37). The inferior vena cava can be seen as a large vessel entering the right atrium just above the confluence of the hepatic veins (Figure 38). The lungs appear as two moderately and homogeneously echogenic areas on either side of the heart. In longitudinal section, the diaphragm can be recognized between the lungs and liver as a relatively transonic sliver moving during respiratory excursions (Figure 39). Lung echogenicity increases after 35 to 36 weeks, approaching that of the liver. The significance of increased lung echogenicity for ultrasonic estimation of fetal lung maturity is still being investigated[26] (Figure 39).

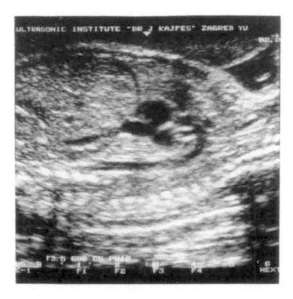

FIGURE 36.   Aortic view of the fetal heart. The ascending aorta, the aortic arch, and descending aorta are demonstrated. Note the head and hand branches arising from the arch. The diaphragm is seen below the heart and appears as a thin anechoic line because of ultrasound beam refraction.

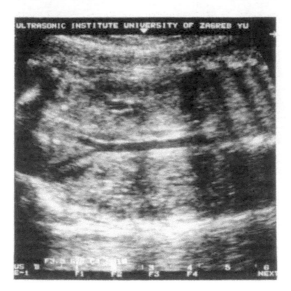

FIGURE 37.   Longitudinal sonogram of the abdominal aorta. The bifurcation and both common iliac arteries may also be seen.

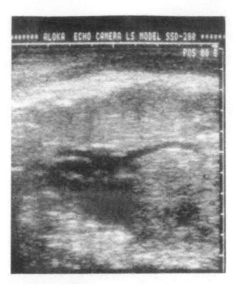

FIGURE 38.   Real-time sonogram of the inferior vena cava reaching the right atrium.

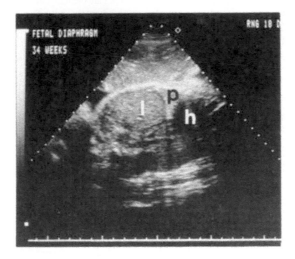

FIGURE 39.   Longitudinal sonogram showing the fetal heart (h), lungs (p), and abdominal viscera separated by the diaphragm. Note increased echogenicity of the lungs as compared to the liver (l).

FETAL ABDOMEN

The upper portion of the fetal abdomen is occupied by the liver, which shows a homogeneous echogenicity, usually higher than that of the lungs. The most commonly obtained section through the fetal abdomen is the transverse section through the liver at the level of the intrahepatic portion of the umbilical vein. The umbilical vein can be followed from its

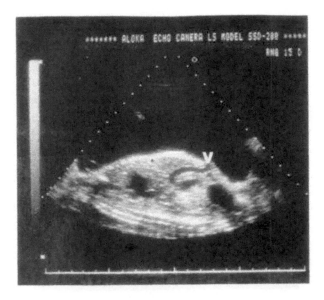

FIGURE 40. The entire length of the umbilical vein (v) from its entrance into the fetal abdomen to the portal sinus is shown on this longitudinal sonogram.

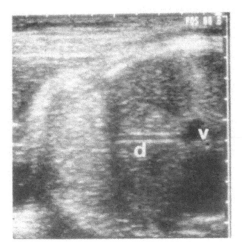

FIGURE 41. An oblique scan of a 34-week-old fetus, demonstrating the ductus venosus (d) entering the inferior vena cava (v).

entrance into the fetal abdomen in the midline and in the cranial direction through the liver tissue until the portal sinus. The entire length of intra-abdominal umbilical vein can be demonstrated either in oblique section or in sagittal section with the fetus lying supine (Figure 40). A smaller part of umbilical vein blood is directed through the liver tissue into the inferior vena cava. The ductus venosus may be visualized intrahepatically in the oblique scan[27] (Figure 41). On the right side of the umbilical vein, the gallbladder can be recognized

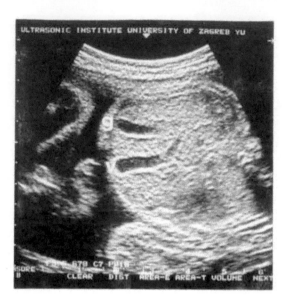

FIGURE 42.   Transverse scan through the fetal abdomen showing the umbilical vein (v) and gallbladder (g). Note the position of the vein, which is located directly opposite to the spine, while the gallbladder is located more to the right.

by its characteristic pear-shaped appearance (Figure 42). Occasionally, these two structures can be confused. This problem can be easily solved by applying differential diagnostic criteria that include their position (umbilical vein is the midline structure, regularly placed opposite to the spine, while the gallbladder is placed more to the right), height (the gallbladder is typically located below the level of the umbilical vein), and shape (the umbilical vein is a tubular structure that can be traced until it curves into the portal sinus, while the gallbladder always finishes blindly).[27]

The fetal stomach can be identified in the left upper quadrant of the abdomen. It appears as a fluid-filled structure, the size and shape of which vary according to the ingestion of amniotic fluid and active peristaltic movement (Figure 43). Occasionally, in a normal stomach, incisura angularis may be unusually prominent, thus giving the impression of the well-known "double-bubble" sign, pathognomonic of duodenal obstruction (see later). This so-called "pseudo-double-bubble" sign should not be confused with true obstruction, and the far position of the right cyst to the gallbladder and absence of hydramnios are helpful guidelines for correct diagnosis[28] (Figure 44). The other two organs which are infrequently clearly outlined in the upper fetal abdomen are the spleen and pancreas. The spleen may be seen behind the fluid-filled stomach and is slightly hypoechoic as compared to the surrounding tissue (Figure 45). Directly behind the stomach lies the fetal pancreas, which is more echogenic as compared to the liver, but in spite of this it is rarely seen. Useful landmarks for pancreas visualization are the mesenteric and splenic veins.[29]

Most of the abdomen below the liver is filled with the gut. Gut is more echogenic as compared to the liver, presumably due to high glycogen content within its lumen.

Intestinal loops are rarely seen during the second trimester, but become more prominent and can be clearly outlined as the fetus approaches its full maturity. Slightly dilated intestinal

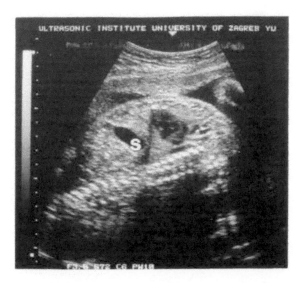

FIGURE 43. Typical ultrasonic demonstration of the fetal stomach (s), which is regularly seen as a fluid-filled structure in the left upper part of the abdomen.

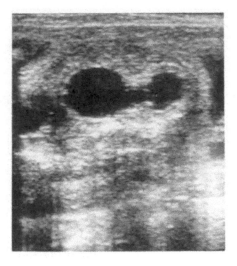

FIGURE 44. Fetal stomach with a prominent incisura angularis separating the body and the antrum of the stomach. This so-called "pseudo-double-bubble" sign should not be confused with duodenal obstruction.

loops represent a normal finding near term and should not be misinterpreted as a sign of intestinal obstruction.[12] (Figure 46).

Sonographic visualization of the fetal kidneys is a regular and important part of routine examination. The kidneys are frequently affected by various developmental anomalies, which emphasizes the importance of familiarity with their normal appearance. Most authors agree

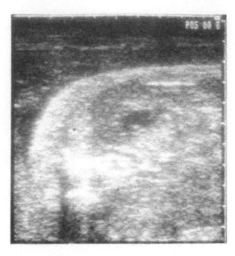

FIGURE 45.   The spleen on the transverse sonogram located posteriorly to the stomach. It appears as a hypoechoic structure of semilunar shape. Unfortunately, the spleen can be visualized only in optimal conditions for ultrasound examination and with the appropriate fetal position.

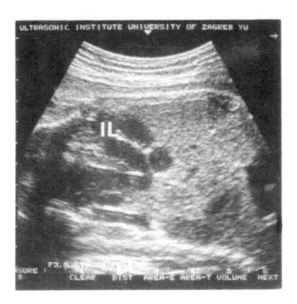

FIGURE 46.   The intestinal loops (IL) are filled with fluid near term and are considered to be one of the ultrasonic signs of fetal maturity. This finding should not be mistaken for intestinal obstruction.

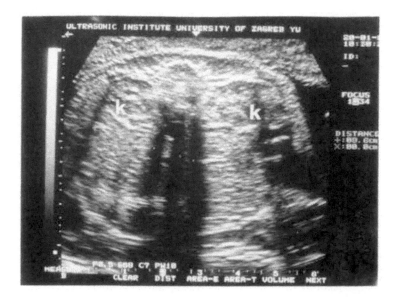

FIGURE 47.   Transverse scan of an 18-week-old fetus showing normal kidneys (k). From this gestational age it is possible to visualize fetal kidneys by ultrasound and to evaluate their morphology with precision. The kidneys appear as two circular structures on either side of the spine and are generally hypoechoic, except for the capsule and collecting system which are strongly echogenic.

that fetal kidneys become sonographically detectable by the 12th or 13th week, but anatomical details cannot be readily depicted before the 18th to 20th week of gestation.[30,31] The kidneys are best seen by performing the transverse scan through the fetal abdomen (Figure 47).

The kidneys are demonstrated as paired, hypoechoic, ovoid structures, being located close to the spine. When the fetus is lying on its side, the proximal kidney is usually well demonstrated. However, the distal one, being located below the spine, is hardly seen due to spine shadowing. That can almost always be overcome by placing the probe on the lateral part of the uterus, directly over the spine. On transverse scan, the kidneys are generally hypoechoic due to low echogenicity of normal renal parenchyma. The capsule and collecting system are, on the contrary, markedly echogenic, and their visualization is helpful for differentiation between the kidneys and other structures that may resemble kidney appearance in renal agenesis, like hypertrophic adrenal glands or intestinal loops.[32] Slight dilation of the renal pelvis might be seen quite frequently and should be interpreted as a normal finding. Kidneys are then separately analyzed by performing a longitudinal parasagittal scan close to the spine (Figure 48). In this section, the fetal adrenal glands may be seen after 30 to 32 weeks. The adrenals typically appear as hypoechoic triangular structures located on the upper renal pole.[12] Their visualization is facilitated by fetal breathing movements and are clearly seen, particularly during inspiration.

Other parts of the urinary system are the ureters, which are not sonographically detectable in normal conditions, and the urinary bladder. The bladder is easily recognized as a small, ovoid, cystic structure within the fetal pelvis (Figure 49). It can be visualized as early as 14 to 15 weeks. From the 20th week onward, it is possible to measure its three-diameter size and calculate its volume. Measurements of the hourly fetal urine production rate have

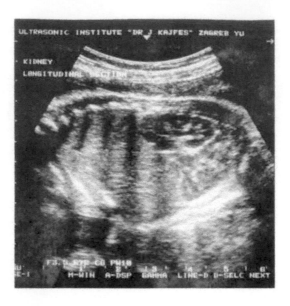

FIGURE 48. Longitudinal section through the fetal kidney near term showing the typical bean-shaped appearance.

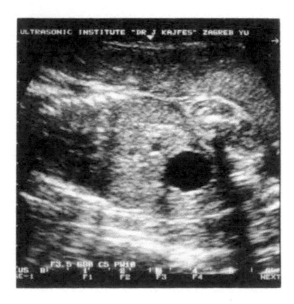

FIGURE 49. Typical ultrasonic appearance of the fetal bladder at 28 weeks. It is visualized within the fetal pelvis as an anechoic structure of regular shape and varying size.

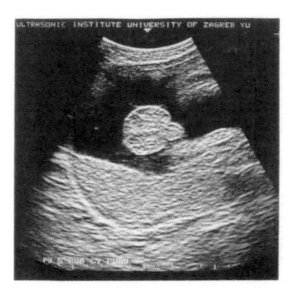

FIGURE 50. The fetal penis and testicles at 25 weeks of gestation. The sex of the baby is identified most easily by performing a longitudinal scan from the site opposite to the spine.

been shown to be helpful in the evaluation of fetal well-being in normal and complicated pregnancies.[33,34] Occasionally, one may observe an unusually dilated urinary bladder which occupies most of the lower fetal abdomen. Although the finding may be quite impressive, suggesting the diagnosis of low urinary tract obstruction, in a vast majority of the cases, it represents an overfull, but normal, urinary bladder. The diagnosis of abnormality is easily ruled out by repeating the examination within 30 min, which shows significant reduction in the urinary bladder size. The process of voiding the bladder may also be directly followed by visualization of the fresh urine stream within the amniotic fluid. Different osmolality and specific gravity of the urine and amniotic fluid enables visualization of this phenomenon by ultrasound.

FETAL GENITALIA

Detection of the fetal sex should be accepted as a part of routine examination in the late second and third trimester pregnancy. However, the sex of the baby should be reported only to those mothers who are interested in it. In our experience, there are about 30% of mothers who do not like to be informed about the sex prior to delivery.

The fetal sex is best demonstrated by performing a longitudinal scan opposite to the spine. The male genitalia are more easily seen and can be clearly detected as early as 14 weeks by demonstration of the penis and scrotum floating freely in the amniotic fluid (Figures 50 and 51). Being much less prominent, the female genitalia are more difficult to see early in the second trimester. In most cases, female sex cannot be established with certainty before

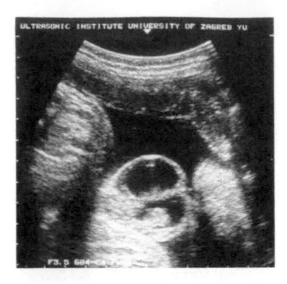

FIGURE 51.   Hydrocele in a male fetus near term represents a frequently seen, normal finding.

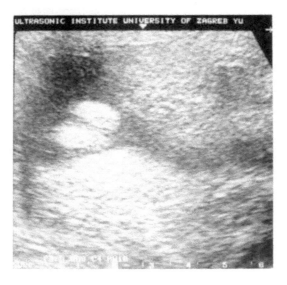

FIGURE 52.   Visualization of the labia majora enables reliable diagnosis of female sex.

17 to 18 weeks. Diagnosis of the female is based on visualization of the labia majora. In most cases, the labia minora can be also demonstrated (Figure 52). Although the detection of the fetal sex is considered to be less important from a clinical standpoint, familiarity with the ultrasonic appearance of the genitalia enables antenatal diagnosis of its malformations and is of particular importance in estimating of the risk of sex-linked diseases.

REFERENCES

1. **Campbell, S.,** An improved method of fetal cephalometry by ultrasound, *J. Obstet. Gynaecol. Br. Commonw.,* 75, 568, 1968.
2. **Queenan, J. T., O'Brien, G. D., and Campbell, S.,** Ultrasound measurements of fetal limb bones, *Am. J. Obstet. Gynecol.,* 138, 297, 1980.
3. **Sanders, R., Miner, N. S., and Martin, J.,** Fetal anatomy, in *Principles and Practice of Ultrasonography in Obstetrics and Gynecology,* Sanders, R. and James, A. E., Eds., Appleton-Century-Crofts, New York, 1985, 123.
4. **Sarti, D. A., Crandall, B. F., and Winter, J.,** Correlation of biparietal and fetal body diametrics: 12—26 weeks gestation, *Am. J. Roentgenol.,* 137, 87, 1981.
5. **Crade, M., Patel, J., and McQuown, D.,** Sonographic imaging of the glycogen stage of the fetal choroid plexus, *AJNR,* 3, 345, 1981.
6. **D'Addario, V. and Kurjak, A.,** Ultrasound investigation of the fetal cerebral ventricles, *J. Perinat. Med.,* 13, 67, 1985.
7. **Denkhaus, H. and Winsberg, F.,** Ultrasonic measurement of the fetal ventricular system, *Radiology,* 131, 781, 1979.
8. **Campbell, S. and Pearce, J. M.,** The prenatal diagnosis of fetal structural anomalies by ultrasound, *Clin. Obstet. Gynecol.,* 10, 475, 1983.
9. **Fiske, C. E., Filly, R. A., and Callen, P.,** Sonographic measurement of lateral ventricle width in early dilatation, *J. Clin. Ultrasound,* 9, 303, 1981.
10. **Johanson, N. L., Dunne, M. G., Mack, L. A., and Rashbaum, C. L.,** Evaluation of fetal intracranial anatomy by static and real-time ultrasound, *J. Clin. Ultrasound,* 8, 311, 1980.
11. **Hadlock, F. P., Deter, R. L., and Park, S. K.,** Real-time sonography: ventricular and vascular anatomy of fetal drain in utero, *Am. J. Roentgenol.,* 136, 133, 1981.
12. **D'Addario, V. and Kurjak, A.,** Normal fetal anatomy, in *Ultrasound in Developing Countries,* Kurjak, A., Ed., Mladost, Zagreb, 1986, 174.
13. **Hadlock, F. P., et al.,** Fetal biparietal diameter: a critical re-evaluation of the relation to menstrual age by means of real-time ultrasound, *J. Ultrasound Med.,* 1, 97, 1982.
14. **Pasto, M. E. and Kurtz, A. B.,** The Prenatal Examination of the Fetal Cranium, Spine, and Central Nervous System, Seminars in US, CT, MR, 5, 170, 1984.
15. **Breyer, B.,** Basic physics of ultrasound, in *Ultrasound and Infertility,* Kurjak, A., Ed., CRC Press, Boca Raton, FL, 1988, in press.
16. **Laing, F. C., Stambler, C. E., and Jeffrey, R. B.,** Ultrasonography of the fetal subarachnoid space, *J. Ultrasound Med.,* 2, 29, 1983.
17. **Mayden, K. L., Tortora, M., and Berkowitz, R.,** Orbital diameters: a new parameter for prenatal diagnosis and dating, *Am. J. Obstet. Gynecol.,* 144, 298, 1982.
18. **Jeanty, P., Dramaix-Wilmet, M., Van Gansbeke, D., et al.,** Fetal ocular biometry by ultrasound, *Radiology,* 143, 513, 1982.
19. **Christie, A. D.,** Fetal anatomy: normal and abnormal, in *The Fetus as a Patient,* Kurjak, A., Ed., Excerpta Medica, Amsterdam, 1985, 116.
20. **Birnholz, J. C.,** Advanced ultrasound assessment of growth retardation, in *Recent Advances in Perinatology,* Maeda, K., Okuyama, K., and Takeda, Y., Eds., Excerpta Medica, Amsterdam, 1986, 199.
21. **Fiske, C. E. and Filly, R. A.,** Ultrasound evaluation of the normal and abnormal fetal neural axis, *Radiol. Clin. North Am.,* 20, 285, 1982.
22. **Jeanty, P., Kirkpatric, C., Dramaix-Wilmet, M., et al.,** Ultrasonic evaluation of fetal limb growth, *Radiology,* 140, 165, 1981.
23. **Filly, R. A. and Golbus, M. S.,** Ultrasonography of the normal and abnormal fetal skeleton, in *Ultrasonography in Obstetrics and Gynecology,* Callen, P. W., Ed., W. B. Saunders, Philadelphia, 1983, 81.
24. **O'Brien, G. D., Queenan, J. T., and Campbell, S.,** Assessment of gestational age in the second trimester by real-time ultrasound measurement of the femur length, *Am. J. Obstet. Gynecol.,* 140, 165, 1981.
25. **Wladimiroff, J. W., Stewart, P. A., and Tonge, H. M.,** Ultrasonic assessment of fetal cardiovascular anatomy and function, in *The Fetus as a Patient,* Kurjak, A., Ed., Excerpta Medica, Amsterdam, 1985, 231.
26. **Hadlock, F. P.,** Normal fetal anatomy, in *Ultrasound in Obstetrics and Gynecology,* Athey, P. A. and Hadlock, F. P., Eds., C. V. Mosby, St. Louis, 1985, 16.
27. **Kurjak, A.,** *Atlas of Ultrasonography in Obstetrics and Gynecology,* Mladost, Zagreb, 1986.
28. **Gross, B. H. and Filly, R. A.,** Potential for a normal fetal stomach to stimulate the sonographic "double bubble" sign, *J. Can. Assoc. Radiol.,* 33, 39, 1982.

29. **Hattan, R. A., Rees, G. K., and Johnson, M. L.,** Normal fetal anatomy, *Radiol. Clin. North Am.,* 20, 271, 1982.
30. **Grannum, P., Bracken, M., Silverman, R., et al.,** Assessment of fetal kidney size in normal gestation by comparison of ratio of kidney circumference to abdominal circumference, *Am. J. Obstet. Gynecol.,* 136, 249, 1980.
31. **Kurjak, A., Latin, V., Mandruzzato, G., D'Addario, V., and Rajhvajn, B.,** Ultrasound diagnosis and perinatal management of fetal genito-urinary abnormalities, *J. Perinat. Med.,* 12, 291, 1984.
32. **Dubbins, P. A., Kurtz, A. B., Wapner, R. J., et al.,** Renal agenesis: spectrum of in utero findings, *J. Clin. Ultrasound,* 2, 189, 1981.
33. **Wladimiroff, J. W. and Campbell, S.,** Fetal urine production in normal and complicated pregnancy, *Lancet,* 1, 151, 1974.
34. **Kurjak, A., Latin, V., and Kirkinen, P.,** Ultrasonic assessment of fetal kidney function in normal and complicated pregnancies, *Am. J. Obstet. Gynecol.,* 141, 473, 1981.

Chapter 8.1

GENERAL CONSIDERATIONS

Asim Kurjak

Most areas in modern perinatal medicine have been thoroughly examined, except for the field of fetal malformations. Data on this subject are provisional and inadequate, beginning with its definition and diagnostic criteria to the undetermined etiology and pathogenesis, the unsatisfactory therapeutic procedures, and insufficient preventive measures. At the same time, fetal malformations continue to represent a significant and relatively increasing problem in perinatal mortality. Although congenital abnormalities are present in only 2 to 4% of births, they are the causative factors in, or are associated with, about 20 to 25% of all perinatal deaths. For the surviving infants, they are responsible for long-term physical and mental handicaps. Even with the most advanced treatment teams and resources, many seriously malformed children cannot be habilitated to any reasonable degree. It is therefore obvious that the future of these types of disorders lies ultimately in their prevention. Unfortunately, preventive measures are almost impossible, and the only realistic approach is accurate and reliable early antenatal diagnosis.

Numerous publications[1-3] have appeared on the ultrasound diagnosis of fetal and placental abnormalities. This should not be surprising if we take into account that ultrasound today has improved to the point where the delineation of intrafetal structures has become a reality very early in pregnancy. This has significantly enhanced the possibility of successful ultrasound diagnosis of abnormalities. Consequently, many patients who have either delivered a fetus with a deformity or whose pregnancies are complicated by conditions known to be associated with fetal anomaly are being referred to those centers with experience in this diagnostic procedure. It should be stressed, however, that the request for an examination seldom specifically asks the ultrasonographer to rule out a fetal malformation, and it is therefore imperative for him or her to ensure that a complete study is performed and to be aware of the appearance of the fetus *in utero*. During each examination, the ultrasonographer must have an "abnormality consciousness".

HISTORY

Fetal malformations and mental retardation have been reported since man learned to write. One of the earliest of these records is from Chaldea (2800 B.C.) about abnormal fetuses of the ancient Babylon found on the brick tablets of Koyngik near the Tigris River. The Babylonians correlated the birth of a monster to the position of the stars, and the malformed infant was supposed to convey the stellar meaning.[4,5] In the 5th century B.C., the prevailing theories were that variations in the paternal element (Empedocles of Agrigentum in Sicily) or abuses of coitus (Democritus of Abdera) could result in monster infants. None of these theories ascribed any importance for the reproduction to the mother and regarded her merely as an "incubator". Aristotle (384 to 322 B.C.) strongly opposed such theories, believing that the mother contributed to the fetus and that the changes in the female element could lead to malformations. He even rejected the hybrid theory, i.e., that intercourse between human beings and animals could result in monsters. In spite of this, such theories existed until the 18th century.[4,5] During the following centuries, severely malformed infants were regarded as divines and messengers from the Gods; but later, the general belief changed, and malformed infants were thought to be the devil's creation which should be destroyed. The Spartans threw their malformed children into the abyss, and often the mother as well. During the Middle Ages this was still the prevailing belief, and many unfortunate women were burned at the stake. During the 16th to 17th centuries, several publications on monsters appeared, e.g., Lycostenes, 1557, Licetus, 1616, and Aldrovandus, 1642, and the flysheets with illustrations of various monsters were scattered among common people.[6-8] During the same period, imagination and fantasies of the pregnant woman were considered decisive for the origin of a malformation. Even the mere sight of certain animals would induce abnormalities, such as harelip after regarding a hare, or marked growth of the hair after regarding a bear. In 1727, J. A. Blondel stated in his book, *The Strength of Imagination in Pregnant Women Examined*, that conception, growth, and sexual determination of the embryo were entirely outside the power of the mother's will. Nevertheless, the old beliefs were not changed until the beginning of the 20th century. In the 18th century, the embryologist, Caspar Friedrich Wolff (1733 to 1794), introduced a more systematic, scientific approach to fetal malformations. He stated that formerly regarded as expressions of influences contrary to nature, malformations were explicable by the application of definitive laws of development. Around 1820, the German pathologist, Johann Friedrich Meckel (1781 to 1893), who identified Meckel's diverticulum, published his *Atlas of Human Abnormalities*. In 1829, Charles Robert Darwin's (1809 to 1882) book, *The Origin of Species*, appeared. An important experimental work was published in 1826 by the zoologist Geoffroy-St.-Hilaire on the manipulations of chicken eggs by which he could cause a large number of anomalies, e.g., spina bifida.[4,5,7] Although teratology was developing as a science, the popular amusement at the courts in Europe, to collect dwarfs and giants, still persisted even in 19th century. Malformed individuals were also exhibited on markets, and probably the most famous were the Siamese twins Chang and Eng Bunker. They were rich, married two sisters, had five and six children, respectively, and they died in 1874 at 63 years of age.[6,8,9] In the first half of the 20th century there was an increased interest in fetopathology. Thus, in 1902, Ballantyne, from Edinburgh, published his *Antenatal Pathology*,[10,11] and in 1906, Ernst Schwalbe published a book on morphology of malformations. In his thesis on "Symmelias and Sirens" in 1914, Paul Barutaut concluded that the etiology was completely unknown, the pregnancy normal, and that the malformations caused the death of the newborns a few hours after delivery.[12]

Indeed, congenital malformations and mental retardation were reported in the earliest recordings in history, but teratology did not become a modern science until the middle of the 20th century. It was the development of modern genetics that influenced scientists and physicians during the first half of the 20th century because it provided a simple explanation for the etiology of human malformations. Furthermore, in the last 40 years, many explanations important for the etiology of fetal malformations were given. In 1941, Gregg showed an increased rate of congenital cataract and heart diseases in children whose mothers had had German measles during the first 3 months of pregnancy.[10-13] The teratogenic effects of toxoplasmosis were described in 1958.[14] In 1952 to 1954, the first reports of the radioactive effects on fetal development from the atomic bomb explosions over Hiroshima and Nagasaki appeared.[15,16] In experimental animals, cortisone and vitamin D deficiency were found to be teratogenic, with increased frequency of cleft palates in the offspring.[17,18] In 1952, Ford, and Hsu in 1958, described the karyotype in man.[19,20] In 1959, Jacobs et al. demonstrated that mongolism was characterized by having trisomy 21 chromosome abnormality.[21] Malformations in connection with trisomies 17-18 and 13-15 were described during the years

1960 to 1962.[22,23] In 1961, Fraser organized the first international conference on congenital malformations, and in 1961, the Thalidomide catastrophe happened.

Thalidomide embryopathy, first suspected in 1961 by McBride in Australia and Lenz in Germany[24] as the cause of phocomelia, provides a number of lessons in our approach to the teratogenic potential of drugs. The extent to which a similar tragedy can be avoided in the future may depend upon how well these lessons have been learned and assimilated. Thalidomide was introduced in the late 1950s in West Germany, England, and several other countries as a tranquilizing agent and as a hypnotic. Around the 1960s, some scattered reports indicated that patients receiving this drug for prolonged periods sometimes developed neurologic disturbances, mostly peripheral neuropathy. Because of its perceived therapeutic properties and advantages, the drug was marketed, and pregnant women comprised one of the selected target populations for distribution. It seemed safe and guaranteed tranquility and uncomplicated sedation for the anxiety produced by pregnancy. Shortly after its introduction, however, there was an increase in the number of infants born with phocomelia, a shortening or complete absence of the limbs. An initial small cluster of cases was reported from Australia, but the University Pediatric Clinic in Hamburg provided the major source of material as it observed a sudden rise in the incidence of a previously almost unheard of malformation. Thus, although not a single case of phocomelia was seen between 1949 and 1959, one case was reported in 1959, 30 cases in 1960, and 154 cases in 1961. Comparable increases in the frequency of the anomaly occurred simultaneously in many parts of the world where thalidomide was used and led to the suspected association between phocomelia and the ingestion of thalidomide by the mother. Subsequent investigations indicated that in virtually every case of phocomelia, the mother had taken thalidomide between the 3rd and 8th week of pregnancy. Thalidomide was withdrawn from the market at the end of 1961, and the outbreak of phocomelia subsided promptly. In the U.S., the drug had not been approved by the Food and Drug Administration, primarily because of the concern for its potential neurotoxic effects. In contrast, the drug had been approved for use in Canada, and its availability both there and to Canadian military personnel stationed in Western Europe at that time resulted in an appreciable incidence of the disorder.[25]

TERMINOLOGY AND ETIOLOGY

A simple and arbitrary terminology has evolved for describing malformations. A *major malformation* has serious medical, surgical, or cosmetic consequences. A *minor anomaly* and a *normal variation* have no serious consequences and are differentiated on the arbitrary basis that a minor anomaly occurs in 4% or less of children of the same race, whereas a normal variation is more common.

A *syndrome* refers to a recognized pattern of malformations considered to have a single and specific cause, such as the Holt-Oram syndrome, an autosomal dominant disorder with malformations of the heart and upper extremities. *Association* is used to indicate a pattern of malformations for which no specific etiology has been identified, such as the VATER association of vertebral, anal, tracheal, esophageal, radial upper limb, and renal anomalies. A *morphogenic complex* (which has also been called an *anomalad*) comprises a primary malformation and its derived structural changes, but does not specify a cause.[26]

Most analyses conclude that a definite etiology for 60 to 70% of human malformations is unknown. All agree that drugs and chemicals account for a very small percentage of malformations. At the conclusion of the 50,000-patient collaborative perinatal project, Heinonen et al. concluded that there was "no common drug analogous to thalidomide." Their results say in a very sophisticated manner that we will never be able to prove with the

TABLE 1
Radiation Exposure to the Fetus

	mrad
Roentgenogram of	
Chest	1
Thoracic spine	11
Abdomen	221
Pelvis	210
Hips	124
Roentgenographic contrast studies	
Upper GI series	171
Barium enema	903
Cholangiogram	78
Intravenous pyelogram	588

From the U.S. DHEW, Gonad Doses and Genetically Significant Dose from Diagnostic Radiology, U.S., 1964 and 1970, U.S. Department of Health, Education and Welfare, Washington, D.C., 1976.

certainty of laboratory experiments that a drug is absolutely safe in the human population.[27] That degree of risk reduction is not available for any potential environmental hazard.

Accidental exposure of pregnant women to radiation is a common cause for anxiety among women, their families, and their physicians, usually about whether the fetus will have birth defects or genetic abnormalities. Fortunately, it is unlikely that exposure to either diagnostic or therapeutic radiation will cause gene mutations. Thus far, no increase in genetic abnormalities has been identified in the offspring exposed as unborn fetuses to the atomic bomb explosions in Japan in 1945.

A more realistic concern is whether the exposed human fetus will show birth defects or a higher incidence of malignancy. The recommended occupational limit of maternal exposure to radiation from all sources is 500 mrad for the entire 40 weeks of pregnancy. Estimates of the gonadal exposure for the mother and the whole body exposure of the fetus from several common roentgenographic examinations are shown in Table 1. The limited data on human fetuses show that large doses of radiation (10,000 to 30,000 mrad) are harmful to the central nervous system. For that reason, therapeutic abortion is often recommended when exposure exceeds 10,000 mrad.

It is much more likely that a human fetus will be exposed to 1000 to 3000 mrad, an amount not shown to cause malformations. There is controversy as to whether this level of exposure is associated with an increased risk of developing cancer or leukemia.[26]

No one can deny the great importance of genetics to this problem. McKusick reports the dramatic explosion in genetic information in the past 20 years. According to McKusick, the number of cataloged genetic diseases has increased 6-fold between 1958 and 1975 — from 412 to 2336.[28] Nature does eliminate most abnormal embryos spontaneously, and it is very likely that by the year 2000, biomedical science will have available electronic, biochemical, and genetic techniques to evaluate the status of every human embryo at very early stages of gestation. What society will do with this information is yet to be determined, because the controversy over the appropriateness and/or the appropriate use of therapeutic interruption of pregnancy has not been resolved in many societies.

Here is ample evidence to indicate that many environmental and genetic factors account for only a small portion of all human malformations.

In a prospective study of 30,681 newborn infants, Holmes found 810 major malformations (2.6%), 57% of which were attributed to genetic abnormalities. The 30,681 infants had 0.2% malformations attributed to chromosomal abnormalities, 0.1% to single mutant genes, 0.7% to multifactorial inheritance, and 0.5% to uncertain patterns of inheritance. The number of chromosomal abnormalities is less than the 0.6% incidence of all types of chromosomal abormalities in newborn infants because many of the common disorders, such as 47, XXY, and 47, XXX, have no detectable physical characteristics in the newborn infant. Teratogens and other environmental factors were identified as a cause of malformations in 0.4% of the infants of 16.0% of all malformations, an incidence lower than many clinicians expect. Teratogens include drugs and maternal conditions such as diabetes mellitus; other environmental factors include amniotic constrictive bands and oligohydramnios. Twinning is associated with a higher incidence of malformations than that in singletons; arcadiac infant syndrome occurs only in monozygous twins. The causes of 27% of the 810 major malformations were not detected.[29] Pitt[30] estimated that 60% of all malformations had no known cause. In 80.8%, the family history was not helpful. Even during epidemic years, rubella accounted for only 0.59% of all malformations. This means that the majority of malformations have no definite etiology, resulting rather from a combination of unknown, environmental, or genetic influences. It is also possible that many malformations result from errors of growth and differentiation in the embryo that are unrelated to exogenous or hereditary factors. There is a statistical probability that a small percentage of embryos will fail to accomplish the intricate processes that are necessary for the normal differentiation. Thus, it is possible that malformations may result from predictable but rare biologic errors of embryonic growth and differentiation, comparable to predictable spontaneous mutation rates occurring at specific gene loci. The problem of multiple etiologies is compounded further by the fact that malformations are relatively common on the order of 25 to 40 malformed infants per 1000 births.[31]

Furthermore, a similarly appearing malformation may be genetically determined, environmentally produced, or have no known etiology. We have now spent many decades with several hypotheses in an attempt to explain the etiology of a large group of human malformations. Although we have more information and some of these hypotheses appear more likely to be correct, we must recognize the tremendous inertia that exists in the field of teratology with regard to these hypotheses. Thus, the high incidence of malformations, the multiplicity of etiologies, and the variety of malformations all complicate the evaluation process.[32]

Although congenital malformations are most readily induced in the first trimester, one must remember that malformations can be induced in all three trimesters. Warkany and Kalter[33] discuss the sensitive period in an excellent monograph dealing with congenital malformations. They emphasize the difference between the "determination" period and the "termination" period for congenital malformations. It is frequently stated that the younger the embryo, the greater is its sensitivity to teratogenic agents. Actually, there is ample evidence to indicate the mammalian zygote is quite resistant to teratogenic agents during the first weeks of gestation. Furthermore, syphilis and toxoplasmosis are more likely to inflict permanent damage to the embryo late in gestation. Growth failures in the latter part of pregnancy can result in certain types of digital abnormalities, even though the original hand formation was normal. Central nervous system (CNS) malformations can be produced in the latter part of pregnancy. Furthermore, one must consider that inflammatory or degenerative processes can occur in the fetus, resulting in destructive lesions that can mimic first-trimester-induced malformations. Therefore, each individual case should be evaluated separately and should not be based on broad generalizations that have become embryologic dogma.[31]

INCIDENCE

There is marked variability of reporting congenital malformations. The frequency varies considerably from country to country and, within countries, from area to area and social class to social class. For example, neural tube malformations are five times more common in England and Wales than in Japan and nearly three times more common in the coal mining valleys of south Wales than along its coastal plain. In Scotland, they are three times more common in infants born into social class V in than infants born into social class I and II.[34] Evidence is accumulating that prenatal elimination may perhaps be the rule rather than the exception, with the implication that in the world of early embryos, malformation may be the norm rather than the exception. In 1956, Hertig and others published the results of examining 34 fertilized ova in the first 17 d of development, recovered after hysterectomy performed on 210 women of proven fertility. Of these 34 very early embryos, 10 were grossly abnormal and would have been lost early in pregnancy, perhaps even before the women themselves had realized that they were pregnant.[35] If we relate this observation to the observation that at least one third of fetuses lost early in pregnancy are chromosomally abnormal, we can conclude that around one half of all postimplantation conceptions are aborted. A suggestion is that in England and Wales, married women aged 20 to 29 years may, on a conservative estimate, abort 78% of their conceptions.[34] In a very large series of surgical abortions, Nishimura has reported a prevalence of neural tube malformation of 13 per 1000. This is 10 times greater than their prevalence at birth, which in Japan is very low (a little over 1 per 1000), and suggests that perhaps 90% of all neural tube malformations in that country are lost early in pregnancy.[36] A study of 3418 fetuses (974 spontaneous abortions and 2444 hysterotomies) undertaken at the tissue bank at the Royal Marsden Hospital, London, showed malformations to be 3 times as frequent in spontaneously aborted fetuses as in fetuses from artificially interrupted pregnancies.[34] Roberts and Lowe studied neural tube malformation rates in all the infants born in south Wales over the 3-year period from 1964 to 1966. They have been able to relate those rates to the frequency with which the women reported previous spontaneous abortions. Women who gave birth to a malformed infant reported slightly, but not consistently, higher previous spontaneous abortion rates than women who gave birth to infants without neural tube defects.[34]

PRENATAL DIAGNOSIS

Prenatal diagnosis was developed to avoid the birth of malformed children and is one of the instruments of the policy of prevention that dominates the present development of medical observation of pregnancy. By means of ever more sophisticated techniques, like echography, medicine is now trying to throw light on what remains hidden, for the moment at least, in the depths of the mother's body. In an effort to make this body transparent, the medicine of today is explicitly dedicated to the aim of eliminating risks and, therefore, perhaps, doubts and, why not, fears.

The era of intrauterine diagnosis started around 1899 when it became possible to demonstrate the fetal head, spine, pelvic bones, and long bones by X-ray pictures.[37] In 1917, the first scientific report on intrauterine diagnosis of fetal malformations was published by James T. Case from St. Lukes Hospital, Chicago.[37] He found this kind of diagnostics important to avoid Cesarean section in pregnancies with monstrous fetus, and that it could be used safely in all kinds of pregnancy complications.

In 1942, Dussik[38] for the first time made attempts to use unidimensional ultrasound as a diagnostic tool for intracranial processes. In 1950, Ballentine[39] was able to discover intracranial pathology. These investigators, together with others, started the use of echo-encephalography for diagnosis of dislocation of the cerebral midline and measurement of the lateral ventricle width. In the field of echocardiography, Edler and Hertz were pioneers and described in 1954 a unidimensional method for investigation of the movement pattern of some heart structures.[40] Howry and Bliss[41] demonstrated a gallbladder containing stones *in vitro* using a two-dimensional system in 1952. In the late 1950s, two-dimensional ultra-sound became the leading diagnostic method. In 1958, Donald and MacVicar[42] introduced the two-dimensional ultrasound method for investigations in obstetrics and gynecology. Sunden, who introduced this method in Sweden in 1960, described his thesis in his book.[43,44] As early as 1963, fetal echoes in the 8th to 9th week of gestation[45] were demonstrated by MacVicar and Donald. In 1964, Sunden found heart activity in the 13th week of gestation.[44] Donald and Brown[46] described the now well-known concept of biparietal diameter (BPD) in 1961. In 1964, a correlation between BPD and fetal weight was demonstrated by Willocks et al.,[47] and in 1969, Campbell[48] introduced the original method of biparietal cephalometry. The first fetal malformation (hydrocephalus) was diagnosed by ultrasound in 1961 by Donald and Brown.[46] Sunden[44] described the intrauterine diagnosis of anencephaly in 1964. The first ultrasound image of a polycystic kidney was presented by Garret et al. in 1970.[49] The first termination of pregnancy because of anencephaly diagnosed by ultrasound was reported by Campbell et al. in 1972.[50] Undoubtfully, the clearest pictures of fetal anatomy have been produced by Kosoff and his team from Sydney. Robinson et al.[51] in 1968 and Flanigan et al.[52] in 1977 described in detail the normal fetal anatomy. Gray-scale and real-time techniques opened new possibilities of diagnostic ultrasound. The rapid development of technical equip-ment in the 1970s and 1980s enabled the observation of the fetus in detail during the first part of the second trimester of pregnancy. A review of the literature made by Stephenson and Weaver[53] in 1981, showed that around 90 different fetal conditions had been diagnosed by ultrasound and that the amount of papers was overwhelming.

Early antenatal diagnosis and selective abortion are extremely important for the individual family who has a child with a fatal, untreatable disease or is at risk of producing one. It is now generally accepted that diagnostic ultrasound, especially with its recent improvements, should be used as the initial test in the management of high-risk patients. The specific indications for examining a patient by ultrasound to rule out congenital anomalies include (1) prior amniocentesis, (2) amniotic fluid abnormalities, such as oligohydramnios or hy-dramnios, (3) elevation of α-feto-protein (AFP) in maternal serum or in amniotic fluid, and (4) a history of a structural birth defect that can be diagnosed by ultrasound.

An elevated level of AFP in maternal serum or in amniotic fluid is associated with many congenital anomalies. Before an abnormality is implicated, however, a distinction should be made between a true and false elevation of AFP. This distinction is dependent, in part, on the results of the ultrasound examination. For example, an apparent elevation of AFP is quickly corrected if twin fetuses are visualized ultrasonically or if the pregnancy is less mature than entertained by the obstetrician. Many fetal malformations can be detected within the first 20 weeks of pregnancy by combining the ultrasonographic examination with the karyotyping of fetal tissues. Furthermore, confirmation of the existence of a normal preg-nancy relieves the parents of a great emotional burden. Owing to the above-mentioned factors, the flow of information on the ultrasound diagnosis of fetal malformations and abnormalities is rapidly growing.[1-3]

PREVENTION

Only one topic in the areas of prevention and treatment will be discussed, namely, the regulation of drug and chemical exposure. The big problem that has not been and may never be solved is the high frequency of the random association of frequently used medications and the occurrence of congenital malformations. Actually, there is a general concern regarding the liberal administration of drugs during pregnancy and the overall incidence of malformations.

Masculinization of the female fetus by administration of androgens or synthetic progestogens and estrogens to the mother for the treatment of habitual or threatened abortion had been reported by the late 1950s.[54] The 1971 report by Herbst et al.[55] recorded the occurrence of adenocarcinoma of the vagina in seven girls between the ages of 15 and 22 years whose mothers had received diethylstilbestrol during pregnancy for prolonged vaginal bleeding. The analogy to the thalidomide report is once again apparent. Adenocarcinoma of the vagina is not common at any age, but its occurrence in girls and young women is rare still. The unusually young age at which adenocarcinoma occurred led more easily to its identification as a specific drug-related effect than would have been the case with either a more common reproductive tract malignancy or its appearance in an older, more appropriate age group.

The critical period for each kind of malformation produced in the human fetus has been established by careful retrospective analysis.[56] When thalidomide was taken 35 to 36 d after the last menstrual period (approximately 21 to 22 d of gestation), absence of the external ears and paralysis of the cranial nerves resulted. Ingestion 3 to 5 d later (about 24 to 27 d of gestation) produced the maximal phocomelia effect, affecting principally the arms. A day or two later, a similar defect of the legs occurred. The sensitive period terminated 38 to 50 d after the last menstrual period (34 to 36 d of gestation) with the production of hypoplastic thumbs and anorectal stenosis. It seems likely that variations in metabolic pathways are a major cause of the species differences, as well as of the differences in sensitivity among humans. Thalidomide is metabolized extensively, and it is believed that one or more of the metabolites, rather than thalidomide itself, is the proximate teratogenic agent.[57] It must rank as a great misfortune that this knowledge became apparent only after an effect of epidemic proportions that may have afflicted as many as 10,000 infants worldwide. The difficulties of preventing such an occurrence again, however, are still with us. What role drugs may play in the overall problem of fetal wastage is difficult to detect in the absence of a teratogenic marker, but that such a relationship may exist seems likely in the absence of a malformed but living fetus or at the level of spontaneous abortion or unexplained death *in utero*. These concerns raise the question of a proper risk-benefit ratio for both mother and fetus for the administration of any drug to the pregnant women. For example, in the case of toxicity to the fetus from administration of phenytoin to the mother,[58] the maternal indications for administration may outweigh the fetal risk. Conversely, the wholesale administration of agents to banish every minor symptom from the body and psyche of the pregnant women seems not only inappropriate, but potentially disastrous. It should not be forgotten that thalidomide was originally offered as a sedative particularly suitable to allow a good night of sleep to the pregnant woman. That thalidomide was responsible for the outbreak of phocomelia is beyond reasonable doubt, but it is still uncertain what degree of risk was attached to the ingestion of this drug by a pregnant woman. The percentage of pregnant women given thalidomide during the critical period who had malformed or affected infants is not known. Obviously, a woman and her embryo present a special and extremely difficult problem where medications are concerned. Several generalizations can be made about teratogens. None are harmful to every exposed fetus; some drugs (e.g., phenytoins) and maternal conditions, such as diabetes mellitus, may cause only a two- to threefold increase in the overall incidence of malformations. Since the increase caused by a teratogen may be relatively small, harmful effects may be difficult to demonstrate. In general, exposure during the first trimester of pregnancy is probably the most harmful. The exact age of the fetus when a particular drug is most harmful has been established for only one drug, thalidomide (days 34 to 50). Even less information is available on the effects of exposure during the second and third trimesters.

If a child has multiple structural malformations, such as polydactyly, cleft palate, meningomyelocele, or absence of a long bone, it is inappropriate to consider intrauterine infections as a possible cause. It is true that rubella infection *in utero* causes cardiac anomalies, but its other effects, such as microcephaly, cataracts, and deafness, are the results of infection of the tissues concerned, not structural malformations. Likewise, congenital toxoplasmosis may cause hydrocephalus, and intrauterine infection with cytomegalovirus may cause cerebral cysts. However, none of these intrauterine infections cause multiple major and minor structural malformations, as can be caused by chromosomal abnormalities, single mutant genes, and teratogenic drugs.

Other conditions are also teratogenic, such as amniotic constriction bands, oligohydramnios, and uterine constraint. Bands of amniotic tissue cause either amputation or constriction of 1 or more extremities in about 1 in every 5000 pregnancies. Oligohydramnios may result from bilateral renal agenesis, severe polycystic kidney disease, chronic leakage of amniotic fluid, and extrauterine pregnancy. Its consequences are lung hypoplasia, clubfoot deformity, a flattened face, and amnion nodosum.[26] An association between diabetes mellitus and fetal congenital anomalies is well known.[59,60] Despite improved management of the diabetic pregnancy, the incidence of fetal congenital anomalies still remains a major cause of illness and death among diabetic infants. Congenital abnormalities have now replaced respiratory distress syndrome as the leading cause of death in some centers caring for diabetic pregnancies.[59-61] These anomalies are reported to be responsible for approximately 40% of all perinatal deaths.[62,63]

The current view regarding the pathogenesis of congenital malformations in diabetes is that organogenesis is disrupted by the hyperglycemia. In animal models, the teratogenic effect of maternal glucose has been demonstrated by the experimental production of hyperglycemia during organogenesis.[64-67] In humans, there is suggestive evidence of similar pathogenesis. Glycosylated hemoglobin (HbA_{16}) is a normal minor hemoglobin distinguished from hemoglobin A by the nonenzymatic addition of a glucose moiety to the amino terminal valine of the beta chain.

Of the major congenital anomalities observed, 5.1% were associated with HbA_{16} determinations between 7.0 and 8.5%, and 22.4% of these malformations were associated with an HbA_{16} level equal to or greater than 8.6%.[68]

Finally, there is widespread belief that many congenital malformations are caused by drugs and chemicals in the environment. This belief has been popularized in the lay press and even by some physicians. The magnitude of the problem is represented by the exponential rise in negligence litigation involving malformed children. Although we have solved some of the problems of teratology, new ones have appeared. Teratology was an isolated clinical and research field 30 years ago, and today it has immense value. Misinformation appears to be a major problem and, in reality, has created major health problems where none existed. Whatever technology is available and on whatever scale it is applied, the basis of prevention remains early detection and careful counseling of mothers at risk. They should be properly informed about the various alternatives of prevention. Every couple must be able to make their own choice in freedom and, once they decide to undergo or to refuse fetal diagnosis, they should be given all support. Teratology needs input from many fields. Undoubtfully, diagnostic ultrasound, with its wide advantages and possibilities, has much to offer.

REFERENCES

1. **Kurjak, A.,** Fetal abnormalities in early and late pregnancy, in *Progress in Medical Ultrasound*, Vol. 1, Kurjak, A., Ed., Excerpta Medica, Amsterdam, 1980, 107.
2. **Kurjak, A.,** Fetal and placental abnormalities, in *Progress in Medical Ultrasound*, Vol. 2, Kurjak, A., Ed., Excerpta Medica, Amsterdam, 1981, 77.
3. **Kurjak, A., Latin, V., and d'Addario, V.,** Abnormalities of the fetus, placenta and umbilical cord, in *Progress in Medical Ultrasound*, Vol. 3, Kurjak, A., Ed., Excerpta Medica, Amsterdam, 1982, 87.
4. **Coffey, V.,** Congenital abnormalies, *J. Ir. Med. Assoc.*, 38, 43, 1956.
5. **Glenister, T. W.,** Fantasies, facts and fetuses. The interplay of fancy and reason in teratology, *Med. Hist.*, 8, 15, 1964.
6. **Broman, I.,** Vidunder och missfoster i fantasi och verkelighet, *Bonniers sma Handboecker i Vetenskapeliga Aemnen*, 1926.
7. **Gruber, G. B.,** Studien zur historik der teratologie, *Zentralbl. Allg. Pathol. Pathol. Anat.*, 105, 219, 1963.
8. **Hollaender, E.,** Wunder, Wundergeburt und Wundergestalt, in *Einblattdrucker des 15-18 Jahrhunderts: Kulturhischtorische Studien*, Verlag von Ferdinand Enke, Stuttgart, 1922.
9. **Shrewsbury, J. F. D.,** A contribution to the historical records of monstrous births, *J. Obstet. Gynecol.*, 56, 67, 1949.
10. **Gregg, N. M.,** Congenital cataract following German measles in mother, *Trans. Ophthalmol. Soc. Aust.*, 3, 35, 1941.
11. **Schmidt, W. and Kubli, F.,** Early diagnosis of severe congenital malformations by ultrasonography, *J. Perinat. Med.*, 10, 233, 1982.
12. **Beck, A. D.,** The effect of intrauterine urinary obstruction upon the development of the fetal kidney, *J. Urol.*, 105, 784, 1971.
13. **Langman, J.,** Medical embryology, in *Human Development — Normal and Abnormal*, Williams & Wilkins, Baltimore, 1963.
14. **Feldman, H. A.,** Toxoplasmosis, *Pediatrics*, 22, 559, 1958.
15. **Plummer, G.,** Anomalies occurring in children exposed in utero to atomic bomb in Hiroshima, *Pediatrics*, 10, 687, 1952.
16. **Yamasaki, J. N., Wright, S. W., and Wright, P. M.,** Outcome of pregnancy in women exposed to atomic bomb in Nagasaki, *AMA Am. J. Dis. Child.*, 87, 448, 1954.
17. **Fraser, F. C., Kalter, H., Walker, B. E., and Fainstat, T. D.,** Experimental production of cleft palate with cortisone and other hormones, *J. Cell. Comp. Physiol.*, 43, 237, 1954.
18. **Kalter, H. and Warkany, J.,** Experimental production of congenital malformations in mammals by metabolic procedure, *Physiol. Rev.*, 39, 69, 1959.
19. **Ford, C. E., Jacobs, P. A., and Lajtha, L. G.,** Human somatic chromosomes, *Nature (London)*, 181, 1565, 1958.
20. **Hsu, T. C.,** Mammalian chromosomes in vitro: the karyotype in man, *J. Hered.*, 1431, 167, 1952.
21. **Jacobs, P. A., Baikie, A. G., Court Brown, W. M., and Strong, J. A.,** The somatic chromosomes in mongolism, *Lancet*, 11, 710, 1959.
22. **Edwards, J. H., Harnden, D. G., Cameron, A. H., Crosse, J. M., and Wolff, O. W.,** A new trisomatic syndrome, *Lancet*, 1, 787, 1960.
23. **Patau, K., Smith, W. D., Therman, E., and Inhorn, S. L.,** Multiple congenital anomalies caused by an extra autosome, *Lancet*, 1, 790, 1960.
24. **Lenz, W.,** Thalidomide and congenital abnormalities, *Lancet*, 1, 45, 1962.
25. **Stern, L.,** Drug therapy of the fetus, in *Fetus as a Patient*, Kurjak, A., Ed., Excerpta Medica, Amsterdam, 1985, 70.
26. **Holmes, L. B.,** Teratogenus, in *Nelson Text Book of Pediatrics*, W. B. Saunders, Philadelphia, 1983.
27. **Heinonen, O. P., Slone, D., and Shapiro, S.,** *Birth Defects and Drugs in Pregnancy*, Littleton, 1977, 516.

28. **McKusik, V. A.**, *Mendelian Inheritence in Man*, 4th Ed., Johns Hopkins University Press, Baltimore, 1975.
29. **Holmes, L. B.**, Inborn errors of morphogenesis, *N. Engl. J. Med.*, 291, 763, 1974.
30. **Pitt, D. B.**, A study of congenital malformations. II, *Aust. N.Z. J. Obstet. Gynaecol.*, 2, 82, 1972.
31. **Brent, L. B.**, The law and congenital malformations, *Clin. Perinatol.*, 13, 505, 1986.
32. **Brent, L. B.**, The complexities of solving the problem of human malformations, *Clin. Perinatol.*, 13, 491, 1986.
33. **Warkany, J. and Kalter, H.**, Congenital malformations, *N. Engl. J. Med.*, 265, 993, 1961.
34. **Roberts, C. J. and Lowe, C. R.**, Where have all the conceptions gone, *Lancet*, March 1, 498, 1975.
35. **Hertig, A. T., Rock, J., and Adams, E. C.**, Abnormal ova, *Am. J. Anat.*, 98, 435, 1956.
36. **Nishimura, H.**, in Proc. of the Third Int. Conf. on Congenital Malformations, Fraser, F. C. and Kusick, A., Eds., Amsterdam, 1970.
37. **Case, J. T.**, Anencephaly successfully diagnosed before birth, *Surg. Gynecol. Obstet.*, 24, 312, 1917.
38. **Dussik, K. T.**, Uber die Moeglicheit hochfrequente mechanische Schwingungen als diagnostisches Hilfsmittel zu vewerten, *Z. Neurol. Psychiatr.*, 174, 153, 1942.
39. **Ballantine, H. T., Bolt, R. H., Heuter, T. F., and Ludwig, G. D.**, On the detection of intracranial pathology of ultrasound, *Science*, 112, 525, 1950.
40. **Edler, I. and Hertz, C. H.**, The use of ultrasonic reflectoscope for the continuous recording of the movements of heart walls, *K. Fysiogr. Saellsk. Lund Foerh.*, 24, 5, 1954.
41. **Howry, D. H. and Bliss, W. R.**, Ultrasonic vizualization of soft tissue structures of the body, *J. Lab. Clin. Med.*, 40, 579, 1952.
42. **Donald, I. and MacVicar, J. B.**, Investigation of abdominal masses by pulsed ultrasound, *Lancet*, 1, 1188, 1958.
43. **Suden, B.**, Ultraljudskdiagnostik i obstetrik och gynekologi, *Sven. Laekartidn.*, 57, 769, 1960.
44. **Sunden, B.**, On the diagnostic value of ultrasound in obstetrics and gynecology, *Acta Obstet. Gynecol. Scand.*, 43, 7, 1964.
45. **MacVicar, J. and Donald, I.**, Sonar in the diagnosis of early pregnancy and its complications, *J. Obstet. Gynaecol. Br. Commonw.*, 70, 387, 1963.
46. **Donald, I. and Brown, T. G.**, Demonstration of tissue interfaces within the body by ultrasonic echo sounding, *Br. J. Radiol.*, 34, 539, 1961.
47. **Willocks, J., Donald, I., Duggan, T. C., and Day, N.**, Fetal cephalometry by ultrasound, *J. Obstet. Gynaecol. Br. Commonw.*, 71, 11, 1964.
48. **Campbell, S.**, The prediction of fetal maturity by ultrasonic measurement of the biparietal diameter, *J. Obstet. Gynaecol. Br. Commonw.*, 76, 603, 1969.
49. **Garret, W. J., Gruenwald, G., and Robinson, D. E.**, Prenatal diagnosis of fetal polycystic kidney by ultrasound, *Aust. N.Z. J. Obstet. Gynaecol.*, 10, 7, 1970.
50. **Campbell, S., Holt, E. M., Johnstone, F. D., and May, P.**, Anencephaly: early ultrasonic diagnosis and active management, *Lancet*, 2, 1226, 1972.
51. **Robinson, D. E., Garret, W. J., and Kossoff, G.**, Fetal anatomy displayed by ultrasound, *Invest. Radiol.*, 3, 442, 1968.
52. **Flanigan, D. and Butny, J.**, Ultrasonic imaging of normal intrauterine fetal anatomy, *J. Clin. Ultrasound*, 5, 334, 1977.
53. **Stephenson, S. R. and Weaver, D. D.**, Prenatal diagnosis — a complication of diagnosed conditions, *Am. J. Obstet. Gynecol.*, 141, 319, 1981.
54. **Jackson, H.**, Antifertility substances, *Pharmacol. Rev.*, 117, 135, 1959.
55. **Herbst, A. L., Ulfelder, H., and Poskanzer, D. C.**, Administration of the vagina: association of maternal stilbestrol therapy with tumor appearance in young women, *N. Engl. J. Med.*, 284, 878, 1971.
56. **Lenz, W.**, Epidemiology of congenital malformations, *Ann. N.Y. Acad. Sci.*, 123, 228, 1965.
57. **Keberle, H., Loustalot, P., and Maller, R. K.**, Biochemical effects of drugs on the mammalion conceptus, *Ann. N.Y. Acad. Sci.*, 123, 252, 1965.
58. **Mirkin, B. L.**, Diphenylhydantoin: placental transport, fetal localization, neonatal metabolism and possible teratogenic effects, *J. Pediatr.*, 78, 329, 1971.
59. **Mills, J. L.**, Malformations in infants of diabetic mothers, *Teratology*, 25, 385, 1982.
60. **Mills, J. L., Baker, L., and Goldman, A. S.**, Malformations in infants of diabetic mothers occur before the seventh gestational week. Implications for treatment, *Diabetes*, 28, 292, 1979.
61. **Soler, N. G., Walsh, C. H., and Malins, J. M.**, Congenital malformations in infants of diabetic mothers, *J. Med.*, 178, 303, 1976.
62. **Karlsson, K. and Kjellmer, I.**, The outcome of diabetic pregnancies in relation to the mother's blood sugar level., *Am. J. Obstet. Gynecol.*, 112, 213, 1972.

63. **Pedersen, J., Molsted-Pedersen, L., and Andersen, B.,** Assessors of fetal perinatal mortality in diabetic pregnancy. Analysis of 1,332 pregnancies in the Copenhagen series, 1946—1972, *Diabetes,* 23, 302, 1974.
64. **Baker, L., Engler, J. M., Klein, S. H., et al.,** Meticulous control of diabetes during organogenesis prevents congenital lumbosacral defects in rats, *Diabetes,* 30, 955, 1981.
65. **Beard, R. W. and Lowry, C.,** Commentary. The British Survey of Diabetic Pregnancies, *Br. J. Obstet. Gynecol.,* 89, 783, 1982.
66. **Horii, K., Watanabe, G., and Ingalls, T. H.,** Experimental diabetes in pregnant mice. Prevention of congenital malformations in offspring by insulin, *Diabetes,* 15, 194, 1966.
67. Editorial, Abnormal infants of diabetic mothers, *Lancet,* 1, 633, 1980.
68. **Merkatz, I. R. and Adam, P. A. J.,** *The Diabetic Pregnancy. A Perinatal Perspective,* Grune & Stratton, New York, 1979.

Chapter 8.2

CRANIAL AND FACIAL DEFECTS

Asim Kurjak

Cranial and spinal anomalies constitute 10% of the major fetal defects, and their diagnosis is still the most successful application of ultrasound. Although there are still papers reporting on the successful diagnosis in the third trimester, most of these anomalies can be detected during the second trimester of pregnancy.

ANENCEPHALY

Anencephaly, the most common anomaly of the fetal central nervous system (CNS), is characterized by the absence of the brain and cranial vault. Some functioning brain tissue is always present at the level of the brainstem and mesencephalon, and vital functions are therefore present during pregnancy. The defect is covered by a thick stroma membrane, but never by skin or bone. The absence of the cranial vault is readily detected by ultrasound from 12 weeks of gestation. The inability to identify normal brain and bony structures above the orbits is a finding pathognomonic of anencephaly (Figures 1 to 3). A common finding associated with anencephaly is the presence of hydramnios, while oligohydramnios is rarely present. Ultrasound diagnosis is simple and accurate and can be made after a single examination. Differential diagnosis may be of importance in distinguishing between anencephaly and the amniotic band syndrome, which is characterized by partial absence and asymmetry of the cranial vault.

Ultrasound seems to have solved the problem of antenatally diagnosing this serious defect.[1] There were no false results in the diagnosis of 44 cases of anencephaly after 13 weeks of pregnancy.[2] In the group paper presented by Hansmann et al.,[3] over 100 anencephalics were correctly diagnosed, with no false positive findings and, up to now, no missed diagnoses. Robinson[4] examined 321 high-risk patients for having a fetus with a neural tube defect; 33 anencephalics were detected, and in no case did the diagnosis by ultrasound pose any problem. While a confirmatory amniocentesis was always undertaken, this was really only of academic interest and was performed to accumulate amniotic fluid α-fetoprotein (AFP) data from abnormal cases.

In Campbell's series,[5] 409 pregnancies were examined between 14 and 24 weeks menstrual age. There were 17 anencephalics, and all were successfully diagnosed. Campbell stressed that the diagnosis can be made as early as 12 weeks of menstrual age, although to avoid the occasional mistake, the definite diagnosis should be delayed to between 14 and 16 weeks. It must always be remembered that due to flexion, the fetal head is quite frequently in a different linear plane to that of the body, and early engagement of the fetal head can occasionally give a false impression of anencephaly. Experienced investigators, however, rarely have any trouble in making the diagnosis.

Acrania should not be confused with anencephaly. In this anomaly there is partial or complete absence of calvarium, but abnormally developed brain tissue is always present (Figure 4).[6]

HYDROCEPHALUS

Fetal hydrocephalus is not a disease, but rather a manifestation of a variety of diseases. It is characterized by abnormal accumulation of cerebrospinal fluid in the ventricles or, in

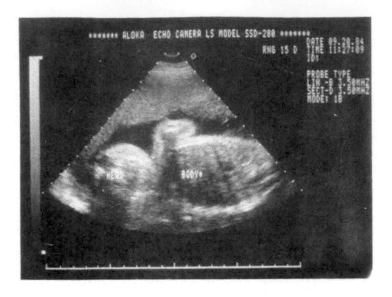

FIGURE 1.   Transverse scan of anencephalic fetus.

FIGURE 2.   Ancephalic fetus after termination of pregnancy.

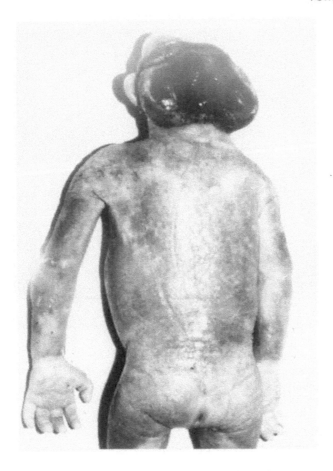

FIGURE 3.   Same fetus as in Figure 2 from the back.

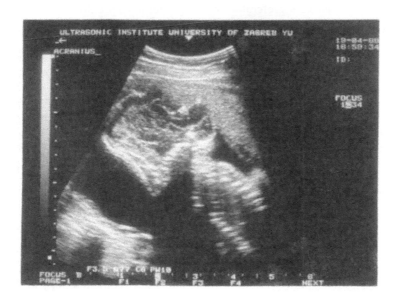

FIGURE 4.   Typical distortion of intracranial anatomy in acrania. Note complete absence of calvarium.

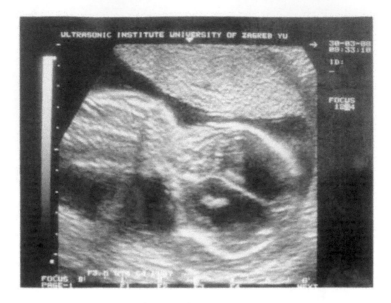

FIGURE 5.   Early ventriculomegaly. Note the relative shrinkage of the choroid plexi.

case of external hydrocephaly, in the subarachnoidal spaces. There are at least three possible causes of hydrocephaly:

1.   Excess production of cerebrospinal fluid
2.   Obstruction of circulation
3.   Defective resorption of cerebrospinal fluid

It is easily identified on ultrasound due to the abnormal enlargement of the cerebral ventricles. Since the finding is ventriculomegaly and the etiology and prognosis are generally not known at the time of diagnosis, it is preferable to use the term ventriculomegaly rather than hydrocephaly.

Because ventricular size can be measured with ultrasound, it is possible to diagnose fetal ventriculomegaly before there has been any increase in biparietal diameter (BPD). Johnson et al.[7] pointed out that the fetal ventricles are relatively large early in gestation and rapidly decrease in size relative to the head between the 16th and 26th weeks. At 16 weeks, the lateral ventricular width to hemisphere width (LVW/HW) ratio can normally be as high as 0.7. After 26 weeks, the mean normal ratio is 0.3 and the upper limit of normal is approximately 0.4.[8] Clearly, some fetuses have enlarged ventricles in early pregnancy, and then demonstrate either no progression or even a gradual improvement in the ventriculomegaly. Serial observations are important in evaluating fetal ventriculomegaly in order to document progressive worsening of the LVW/HW or at least failure to decline in the second trimester of pregnancy.

Before an early diagnosis of hydrocephaly is made, consideration should be given to (1) normal variations in ventricular size and (2) the results of weekly sonar examinations performed to monitor the rate of change, if any, in ventricular dimensions.

Recently, it has been suggested that the first recognizable aberration is a relative shrinkage of the normally prominent choroid plexus within the body of the lateral ventricles (Figure 5). As long as choroid plexus can be seen filling the lateral ventricular body in its transverse dimension, hydrocephaly is not likely to be present.

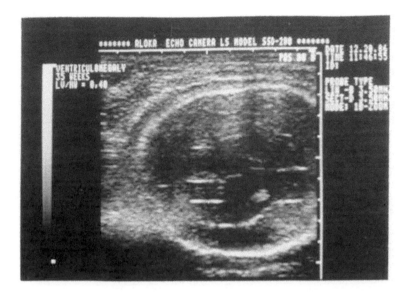

FIGURE 6.   Borderline ventriculomegaly in a 35-week-old fetus. LV/HW ratio is
0.4

According to our experience, to obtain an early and definitive diagnosis of hydrocephaly,
the most useful parameter is a serial measurement of the LVW/HW ratio. The lateral wall
of the frontal horn is undoubtedly the most easily identifiable part of the lateral ventricles;
for this reason the ventricular measurement is to be taken at this point or in the most anterior
part of the lateral wall of the ventricular body. The distance between this lateral wall of the
lateral ventricle and the midline echo is then measured. The greatest hemispheric width is
also measured at the same level as the ventricular width. These measurements should be
taken from the inner edge of the midline echo to the inner edge of the distal parietal bone,
respectively.

A higher value of LVW/HW ratio is the clear evidence of a pathological dilatation of
fetal ventricles, but one must be very careful when making the diagnosis prior to 20 weeks
of gestation, because the lateral ventricles are usually disproportionally large at this time.
Moreover, the ratio measurement accuracy suffers from a wide standard deviation which
renders it insensitive to identification of an early dilatation. For this reason, it is necessary
to repeat the ultrasound examination; if the ratio increases, the diagnosis of hydrocephaly
can be established with great certainty (Figure 6).

As the pregnancy proceeds and the ventricular dilatation increases, the ultrasound diagnosis of hydrocephaly becomes much easier. Lateral ventricles are extremely dilated, and
the LVW/HW ratio is much higher than it normally is (Figures 7 and 8). Furthermore, real
time makes it possible to recognize the midline echo floating, two dilated ventricles, and
the choroid plexi hanging in the cerebrospinal fluid inside the dilated ventricular cavities.
It has already been mentioned that in obstructive hydrocephalus intrauterine operative therapy
may be of some value. This is discussed in the chapter on fetal therapy.

Our team does not have any experience in ventriculo-amniotic shunting because more
than half of our hydrocephalic babies were detected before 24 weeks of pregnancy, and after
the decision of the mother and the agreement of our ethical committee, all of those pregnancies
were interrupted. Therefore, we had no suitable patient for intrauterine surgery.

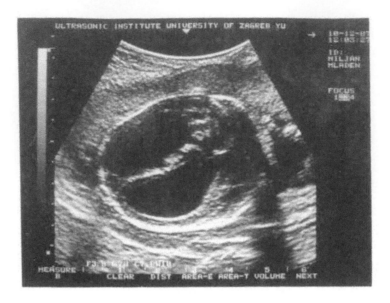

FIGURE 7.   Hydrocephaly with clear evidence of significant ventricular dilatation.

FIGURE 8.   Hydrocephalic fetus after termination of pregnancy.

In 14 cases, pregnancy was left to proceed until the fetus reached a gestational age between 33 and 34 weeks of pregnancy, by which time it should be able to exist independently outside the uterus. Immediately upon delivery, those hydrocephalic babies were handed to our neuro-surgeons who considered further treatment. The Pundenz ventriculo-atrial shunt was performed in ten cases, Hakim ventriculo-atrial shunt in two, while the Pundenz ventriculo-peritoneal shunt was performed in two babies with porencephalic arachnoidal cyst. Mortality and morbidity rate, even in the very early detected hydrocephalic babies, were high, and we feel that much experience and research is still needed in this field.

Apart from anencephaly and hydrocephaly, there are at least a dozen other malformations detectable *in utero*. Unfortunately, for the vast majority of them, the termination of pregnancy is still the only rational management. Numerous publications have appeared on normal fetal intracranial anatomy and the successful early diagnosis of hydrocephaly.[5,7,9-21] Recent improvements in ultrasound technology have now made it possible to differentiate the fine structural detail within the fetal cranium. Since high-resolution real-time instrumentation allows the demonstration of vascular pulsations, it is now possible to visualize fetal intracranial arterial anatomy. Many neural structures can also be identified accurately. This is important for precise and reproducible cephalometry and for the *in utero* diagnosis of intracranial pathological conditions. Johnson et al.,[7] in an excellent paper on intracranial anatomy, analyzed 196 scans of normal fetuses from 15 weeks of gestation to term. They measured the lateral fetal ventricular width and cerebral hemispheric width and calculated the ratio of the LVW/HW. The values steadily decreased from a mean of 56% at 15 weeks of gestation to 28% at term, indicating the more rapid growth of cerebral hemispheres as compared with the cerebral ventricles. This technique permits the detection of hydrocephalus long before the cranium itself has enlarged. The authors showed in two cases that in early congenital hydrocephalus, the occipital horns dilate prior to the enlargement of the bodies of the lateral ventricles. Campbell[5] had 14 cases of early hydrocephalics. To diagnose this condition, he stressed the importance of recognizing the lateral border of the lateral ventricle. This is seen as a discrete line running parallel to the midline echo, approximately half-way between the lateral wall of the skull and midline echo. When this line has been visualized and a Polaroid® photograph taken, the ratio between the distance from the lateral border of the ventricle to the midline (V) and the maximum width of the hemisphere (H) is then estimated. The ventricles of 47 normal fetuses were measured, it was found in these normal fetuses that the V/H ratio was always greater than 0.5 before the 17th week: after this time it was always less than 0.5. The length of the ventricle was also measured and compared to the distance between the occiput and sinciput. It was found that there was no definite constant relationship between these two measurements, probably because it was often difficult to visualize the full length of the ventricle on a single scan. In all 14 hydrocephalic cases, V/H ratios were much greater than 0.5 between 17 and 24 weeks of menstrual age. Here it is important to stress that in all of these cases, the BPD and head circumference (HC) were within normal limits for the gestational age. This, again, indicates that the diagnosis of hydrocephalus is not made on the basis of the increased head size at this stage of pregnancy and can only be made on the finding of dilated ventricles.

An excellent paper was published by the Garret and Kossoff group of Sydney.[13] The width of the bodies of both lateral ventricles was studied in 833 children with B mode echography. The accuracy of the measurement decreased with age, but as the results showed, this is not a serious problem in children under 6 years of age. The authors present their results of the lateral ventricular ratio, the size of the atria of the lateral ventricles, the transverse diameter of the third ventricle, and the HC greater than the 98th percentile. These measurements allowed the correct diagnosis of some intracranial disturbances, and excessive ionizing radiation can be avoided. The ultrasonograms obtained with the UI Octoson illustratively represent these results. With its water-delay system, the machine provides first-rate tissue detail and is particularly suitable for pediatric practice.

The LVW/HW ratio was measured in 200 normal pregnancies.[22] A curve was constructed with the 5th and 95th percentiles as limits. Ultrasonic pictures have been correlated with an anatomical section of the fetal head. It was demonstrated that the LVW/HW ratio can be detected much earlier than abnormal BPD growth. It can be assumed that by 24 or 25 weeks, the abnormality will have been detected, and a significant abnormality of this ratio appeared 2 months before classical hydrocephalus could be suspected. An interesting physiological point was noted. The hydrocephalic process squeezed the brain and enlarged the skull. This is an active mechanism, and arrest of fetal activity resulted in the loss of intracranial pressure with the resulting onset of the Spalding sign.

In a very recent paper, Vintzileos et al.[23] reported their experience with the antenatal diagnosis, management, and outcome of fetal ventriculomegaly. They analyzed 20 consecutive cases with somewhat late ultrasound detection (mean gestational age at the time of diagnosis was 30 weeks). Based on postnatal evaluation, hydrocephalus was the only abnormality in 30% of cases and was associated with other abnormalities in 70%. Spina bifida was the most common associated anomaly and occurred in six cases (30%). There were two chromosomal abnormalities (10%), one case of trisomy 13, and one of trisomy 18. Altogether, there were 78% of patients in which fetal structural and/or chromosome abnormalities were diagnosed antenatally. Ventriculo-amniotic shunt placement was not part of the management, but atraumatic delivery by Cesarean section, once pulmonary maturity was determined, was performed in all cases with isolated fetal ventriculomegaly. The outcomes were induced abortion in four patients (20%), intrapartum death in two patients (10%), postnatal death in five patients (25%), and, currently alive, nine patients (45%).

MICROCEPHALY

Microcephaly is defined as an abnormally small head measuring more than 3 SD below the normal. The etiology of this anomaly is unknown. It has been described in fetuses with chromosomal abnormalities, mostly trisomies, and as part of the Meckel-Gruber syndrome including microcephaly, encephalocele, polycystic kidneys, and polydactyly. True microcephaly caused by intrauterine damage during embryogenesis is regularly associated with severe mental retardation.

In some cases, distortions of intracranical anatomy have been observed, including the formation of the brain stem only, a large cystic area without a midline echo, or well-formed, enlarged lateral ventricles in a small head. All these are associated with underdevelopment of the cerebral hemispheres. Apart from BPD measurement, it is necessary to calculate the head to body ratio in order to exclude intrauterine growth retardation. The diagnosis is most difficult in borderline cases, requiring serial examinations and careful finding interpretation.

Controversy has always surrounded the findings of microcephalic fetuses. Since many women are not sure of their menstrual dates, and others are sure but in error, the degree of confidence with which one can diagnose microcephaly is really limited. Therefore, the paper published by Kurtz et al.,[24] giving an ultrasonic criteria for the *in utero* diagnosis of microcephaly, is very helpful.[24] They stressed that microcephaly (small head) is clinically important only if there is concomitant microencephaly (small brain) (Figure 9A and B). Of 8000 patients examined by ultrasound, Kurtz et al. found 7 cases of microcephaly and reviewed 6. On the basis of these cases, they divide microcephaly into abnormalities of the calvarium and brain. Three definitions are proposed: pseudomicrocephaly — an abnormally

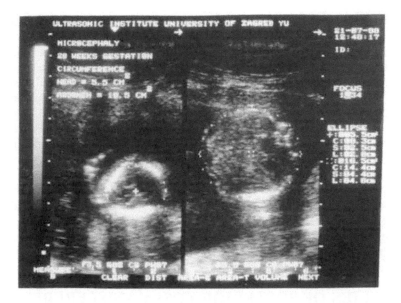

A

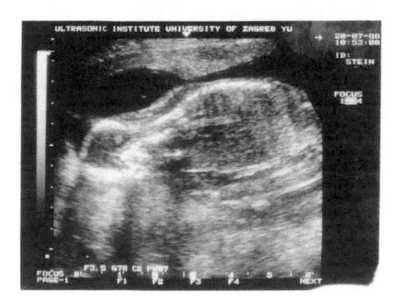

B

FIGURE 9. (A) True microcephaly with obvious disproportion of head to body ratio. (B) Longitudinal scan of the same fetus.

small BPD secondary to an unusually shaped fetal head; the head area and circumference measurements are normal. Relative microcephaly — an abnormally small head, between 1 and 3 SD below the norm. True microcephaly — an abnormally small head, more than 3 SD below the norm; the biparietal diameter, growth rate, and head to body ratio (first thoracic and then abdominal circumference) were measured in all patients. The head area and total intrauterine volume were also estimated. Kurtz et al. conclude that when gross abnormalities exist within the fetal head and the fetal head measurement is more than 3 SD below the norm, the likelihood of true microcephaly and mental retardation is great. However, when the measurements are between 1 and 3 SD below the norm, without internal abnormalities of the fetal head, there is reasonable hope that these fetuses will develop normally. This information may help relieve the anxiety of the clinician and the expectant parents.

Normal sonographic findings are extremely useful in ruling out microcephaly in patients at high risk for this abnormality. It must be remembered, however, that the fetal abdomen may be abnormally enlarged due to edema, ascites, or visceromegaly, as seen in infants of diabetic mothers. If several ultrasound scans are carried out during a given gestation, then the growth pattern of the fetal cranium and abdomen may be followed and the diagnosis of microcephaly made with more confidence.

ANOMALIES OF POSTERIOR FOSSA AND CEREBELLUM

In order to demonstrate possible anomalies of the posterior fossa and cerebellum, an oblique transverse view (suboccipitobregmatic) of the fetal cranium should be obtained. Although abnormalities of this area are rare, they should not be overlooked, as they usually produce spastic diplegia or other motor disorders. These anomalies are often cystic in nature and they may be easily identified sonographically.

Dandy-Walker malformation is a syndrome of unknown etiology which consists of cystic dilatation of the posterior fossa and agenesis of dysplasia of the cerebellar vermis, through which the cyst communicates with the fourth ventricle. Although the hydrocephalus of the variable degree is often present postnatally, it seems that this association is not frequent in the fetus.[25,26]

In Arnold-Chiary syndrome, the posterior fossa is reduced in size, since a portion of the brain stem and cerebellum are displaced downward into the upper portion of the spinal canal.

The enlarged cisterna magna and echo-free space between the cerebellar hemispheres allow the antenatal diagnosis of Joubert syndrome to be made.

Campbell and Pearce[27] have suggested the useful criteria in ultrasound diagnosis of these anomalies. According to them, the measurement of each cerebellar hemisphere should be compared to each other in order to exclude unilateral hypoplasia, and then the distance from the posterior aspect of the cerebellum to the inner table of the skull should be measured.

INIENCEPHALY

In iniencephaly, a severely deformed fetus shows the extreme retroflexion of the head with fusion of occiput to the cervical vertebrae (Figures 10 and 11). Rachishisis exists in most cases, but defective spinal cord and column are usually covered dorsally by brain cerebellum and skin so that the open neural plate and vertebra are not seen on the surface.

HYDRANENCEPHALY

Differential diagnosis of hydrocephalus includes primarily hidranencephaly and holoprosencephaly. The first anomaly results from the occlusion of the internal carotid arteries

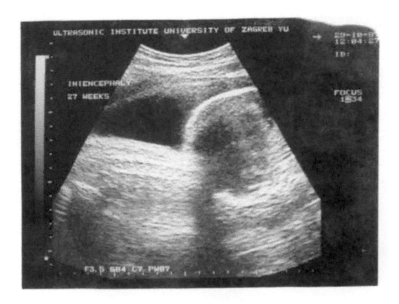

FIGURE 10.   Extreme retroflexion of fetal head in a case of iniencephaly.

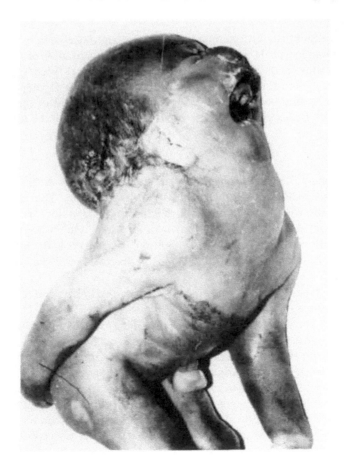

FIGURE 11.   Iniencephalic fetus after termination of pregnancy.

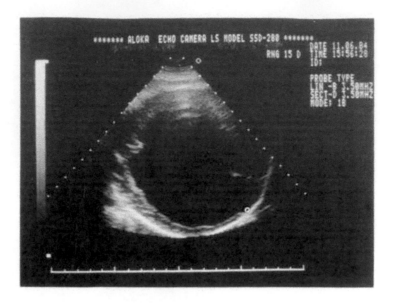

FIGURE 12.   Entirely fluid-filled intracranial cavity in hydranencephaly.

in utero with consequent cerebral hemisphere necrosis and liquefication. The sonographic appearance of hydranencephaly is characterized by the visualization of the midbrain, the brain stem, and posterior fossa structures surrounded with fluid-filled space (Figure 12). The choroid plexus is occasionally visualized floating in the fluid. Hydranencephaly can be distinguished from hydrocephalus because of the complete absence of the cortical mantle, while in most severe hydrocephalus cases, some cortical mantle can be identified.

HOLOPROSENCEPHALY

Holoprosencephaly is a developmental brain abnormality. The defect refers to the formation of the diencephalon and, subsequently, the telecephalon. The head is smaller on ultrasound examination. The most important feature in this condition is the absence of a midline falx, a point differentiating it from hydrocephalus and hydranencephaly. Facial anomalies are usually associated with this condition. When hypotelorism is found in conjunction with absence of midline echo, the antenatal diagnosis of alobar holoprosencephaly is almost certain.

There are three types of holoprosencephaly: alobar, semilobar, and lobar. The prenatal sonographic diagnosis has been described by Chervenek et al.[28,29]

More recently, Green et al.[30] presented a series of ten cases of alobar holoprosencephaly ranging from 16 to 38 weeks of gestation. The disorder was diagnosed according to two criteria: (1) a large central fluid collection in the fetal head, with no visible midline structures, but with the presence of a mantle around the fluid collection and fusion of the thalami and corpus striatum, and (2) sonographic abnormalities of the face, including hypothelorism, central clefts, facial asymmetry, and abnormal orbits. Indeed, hydrocephalus and hydranencephaly can often be confused with holoprosencephaly, and, therefore, careful examination of fetal face will help to reliably diagnose alobar holoprosencephaly *in utero*.

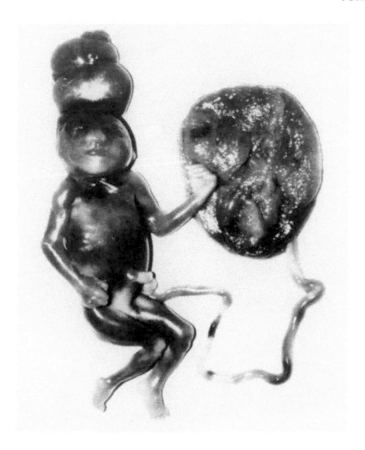

FIGURE 13. Typical occipital encephalocele after termination of pregnancy.

ENCEPHALOCELE

Encephalocele are the hernias of the brain protruding through defect in some part of cranium. They occur occasionally in the parietal, frontal, nasal, or nasopharyngeal region, but the majority, about 70%, are found in the occipital area (Figures 13 to 16). Encephalocele are recognized sonographically as brain filled such extending out of calvarium. One must always take care not to mistake fetal small parts for herniated brain.

Encephalocele should be differentiated from lesions with similar appearance, like cystic hygromes, hemangiomes, teratomes, and branchial cleft cysts.[31]

An abnormality may occur as an isolated lesion or as part of various syndromes like amniotic band syndrome (Figure 17). The polycystic kidney disease, encephalocele, and polydactyly suggest Meckel's syndrome, which has an autosomal recessive pattern of inheritance. Encephalocele may be part of Roberts', Chemkes', and Knoblock's genetic syndromes.

OTHER INTRACRANIAL DEFECTS

In the recently published literature, there have been numerous reports on precise ultrasound delineation of the rare congenital CNS anomalies, such as agenesis of corpus callosum

FIGURE 14.   Same fetus in Figure 13 from the back.

(Figures 18 and 19), porencephaly, intracranial arachnoid cysts, choriod plexus cyst, aneurysm of the Vein of Galen, etc.[32,33]

A successfully detected intracranial tumor in a large-for-date fetus of a 28-year-old woman has been also reported.[34] A rare case of Kleblattschadel syndrome, a rare form of congenital hydrocephalus, was also described.[35] This paper is important because it demonstrates the possibility of misinterpreting this finding, since it is similar in appearance to meningoencephalocele.

Kleblattschadel syndrome, or cloverleaf skull syndrome, is an unusual and rare form of congenital hydrocephaly caused by the premature fusion of the coronal and lambdoidal sutures. The resultant increased intracranial pressure causes the formation of a grotesque trilobed skull. A healthy pregnant woman was examined by ultrasound at 18 and 32 weeks by menstrual dates. The head was normally shaped and no other fetal abnormalities were appreciated in either examination in retrospect; 3 weeks later, the head measurements indicated 27 weeks rather than the expected 35 weeks by BPD. The head-thorax ratio measured 0.78, and the lateral ventricles were dilated. The last scan at 37 weeks of gestation showed a lateral ventricular enlargement and an abnormal head-thorax ratio. This rare form of cranial enlargement was given the name "Kleblattschadel syndrome" in 1960 with a description of 13 cases. Since then, sporadic case reports have appeared in the world literature, but this case is the first to present intrauterine ultrasonic appearance.[36]

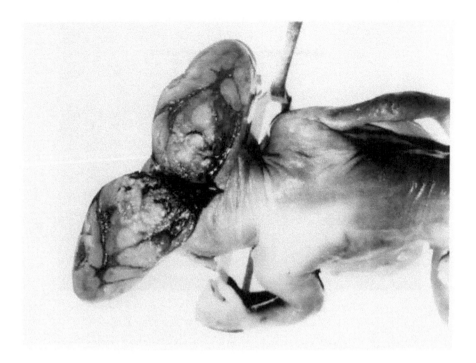

FIGURE 15.   Intracranial pathology within encephalocele is completely distorted.

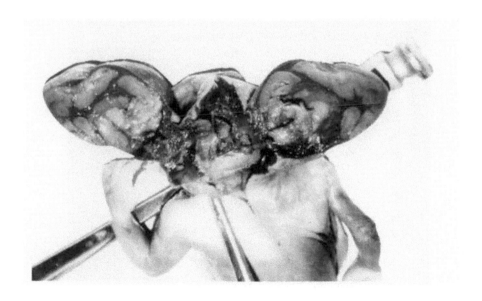

FIGURE 16.   Closer view into the intracranial cavity with large encephalocele.

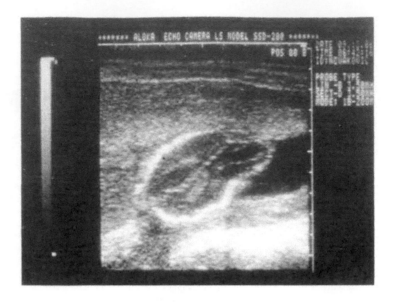

FIGURE 17.   Unusual case of frontoparietal encephalocele. Close contact of the bony defect with placental membranes suggested amniotic band syndrome. The finding was confirmed at autopsy.

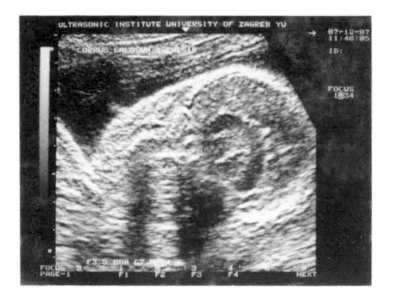

FIGURE 18.   Marked separation of the normal-sized lateral ventricle in agenesis of corpus callosum.

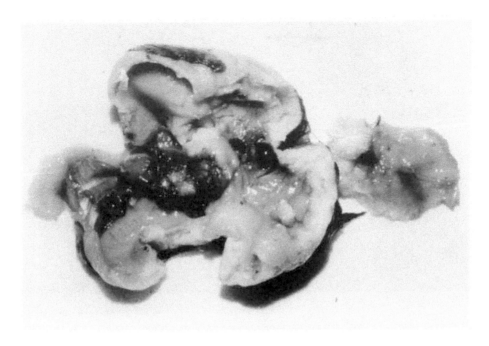

FIGURE 19. The autopsy finding confirmed the diagnosis of the case shown in Figure 18. Dilated ventricles with large communication due to agenesis of corpus callosum.

The examination of the fetal face should be a part of a routine ultrasound examination in the second trimester. Some facial details could be visualized as early as the 12th week of gestation.[33] For complete assessment of forehead, orbits and their distance, nose, lips, and ears, sagittal, axial, and coronal planes should be used (see chapter on normal fetal anatomy).

Anomalies of the orbits and nose are usually associated with severe intracranial and other fetal anomalies. Increased or decreased interocular distance (hyper- and hypotelorism) are diagnosed using nomograms of fetal interorbital distance.[37] They can be uni- or bilateral, isolated, or, as a rule, associated with other anomalies.[33]

Anomalies of the nose are rarely diagnosed *in utero*. Proboscis is a trunk-like appendage usually associated with arhinia (absence of the nose). It is almost always associated with holoprosencephaly (Figures 20 and 21).[33]

The fact that facial clefting is the second most common congenital malformation (13% of congenital anomalies) stresses the importance of face examination *in utero*. Facial clefts usually involve upper lip, the palate, or both (Figures 22 to 24). They are often associated with other anomalies (up to 60%). Usually, no specific syndrome can be established, although association with well-described syndromes could also be found.[33]

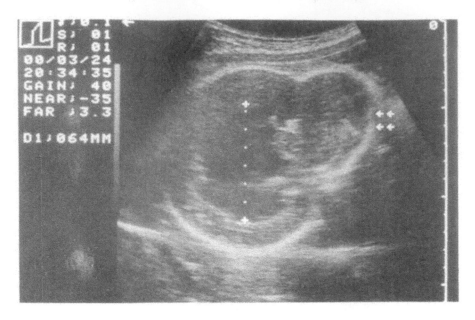

FIGURE 20.   Holoprosencephaly (single ventricle is marked with calipers) with proboscis (arrows) detected in the second trimester of pregnancy.

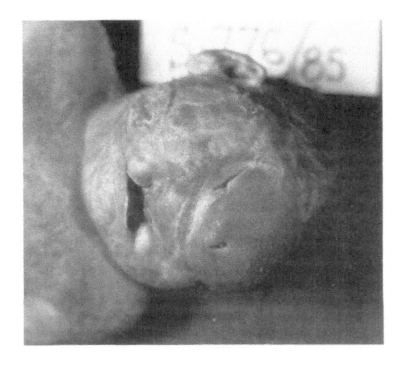

FIGURE 21.   Same fetus in Figure 20 after termination of pregnancy.

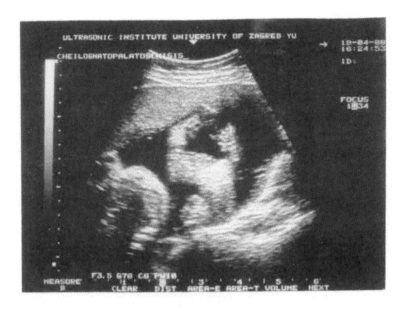

FIGURE 22. Coronal scan of the fetal face with large cleft lip.

FIGURE 23. Cleft lips immediately before surgical repair.

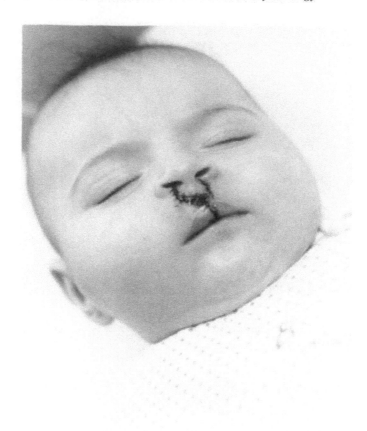

FIGURE 24.   Successful surgical repair of bilateral cleft lips shown in Figure 23.

REFERENCES

1. **Harwood, S. J. and Pinsker, M. C.,** Detection of fetal anencephaly using real-time ultrasound, *South. Med. J.,* 72, 223, 1979.
2. **Kurjak, A., Kirkinen, P., Latin, V., and Rajhvajn, B.,** Diagnosis and assessment of fetal malformations and abnormalities, *J. Perinat. Med.,* 8, 219, 1980.
3. **Hansmann, M.,** Sonar in prenatal diagnosis, in *Prenatal Diagnosis,* Proc. 3rd European Conf. Prenatal Diagnosis of Genetic Disorders, Murken, E., Ed., Ferdinand Enke, Stuttgart, 1979, 183.
4. **Robinson, H. P.,** The role of ultrasound in the prenatal diagnosis of neural tube defects, in *Prenatal Diagnosis,* Proc. 3rd European Conf. Prenatal Diagnosis of Genetic Disorders, Murken, E., Ed., Ferdinand Enke, Stuttgart, 1979, 179.
5. **Campbell, S.,** Early prenatal diagnosis of fetal abnormality by ultrasound B-scanning, in *Prenatal Diagnosis,* Proc. 3rd European Conf. Prenatal Diagnosis of Genetic Disorders, Murken, E., Ed., Ferdinand Enke, Stuttgart, 1979, 183.
6. **Mannes, E. J., Crelin, E. S., and Hobbins, J. C.,** Sonographic demonstration of fetal acrania, *Am. J. Roentgenol.,* 139, 181, 1982.

7. **Johnson, M. L., Dunne, M. G., Mack, L. A., and Rashbaum, C. L.,** Evaluation of fetal intracranial anatomy by static and real-time ultrasound, *J. Clin. Ultrasound,* 8, 311, 1980.

8. **D'Addario, V. and Kurjak, A.,** Ultrasound investigation of the fetal cerebral ventricles, *J. Perinat. Med.,* 13, 67, 1982.

9. **Sabbagha, R. E. and Shkolnik, A.,** Ultrasound diagnoses of fetal abnormalities, *Semin. Perinatol.,* 4, 213, 1980.

10. **Sabbagha, R. E.,** Abnormalities of pregnancy, in *Ultrasound in High-Risk Obstetrics,* Zuspan, F. P., Ed., Lea & Febiger, Philadelphia, 1979, 69 and 76.

11. **Sabbagha, R. E.,** Congenital anomalies, in *Ultrasound Applied to Obstetrics and Gynecology,* Sabbagha, R. E., Ed., Harper & Row, New York, 1980.

12. **DeVore, G. and Hobbins, C. G.,** Diagnosis of structural abnormalities in the fetus, *Clin. Perinatol.,* 6, 293, 1979.

13. **Garret, W. J., Kossoff, G., and Warren, P.,** Cerebral ventricular size in children, *Radiology,* 136, 711, 1980.

14. **Ben-Ora, A., Eddy, L., Hatch, G., and Solida, B.,** The anterior fontanelle as an acoustic window to the neonatal ventricular system, *J. Clin. Ultrasound,* 8, 65, 1980.

15. **Hyndeman, J., Johri, A., and Maclean, E.,** Diagnoses of fetal hydrocephalus by ultrasound, *N.Z. Med. J.,* 91, 385, 1980.

16. **London, D. A., Caroll, B. A., and Enzmann, D. R.,** Sonography of ventricular size and germinal matrix hemorrhage in premature infants, *AJNR,* 1, 296, 1980.

17. **Haber, K., Wachter, R. D., and Christenson, P. C.,** Ultrasonic evaluation of intracranial pathology in infants: a new technique, *Radiology,* 134, 173, 1980.

18. **Warren, P. S., Garret, W. J., and Kossoff, G.,** High resolution imaging of the neonatal brain, in Proceedings of the 24th Annual Meeting of the American Institute of Ultrasound in Medicine and the 8th Annual Meeting of the American Society of Ultrasound Technical Specialists, August 27, 1979, Montreal, Oklahoma City, AIUM, 1, 104, 1979.

19. **Boog, G.,** Le diagnostic echographique des anomalies congenitales de l'abdomen foetal, *Ultrasons,* 1, 121, 1980.

20. **Callahan, S. and Wedel, V. J.,** Ultrasound detection of fetal anomalies, in *Proc. 24th Meet. AIUM,* American Institute of Ultrasound in Medicine, Oklahoma City, 1979, 152.

21. **Morrison-Lacombe, G., Monfort, G., and Cristofary, J.,** Diagnostic antenatal des malformations congenitales par l'echotomographie, *Chir. Pediatr.,* 21, 249, 1979.

22. **Jeanty, P., Dramaix-Wilmet, M., and Delbeke, D.,** Ultrasonic evaluation of fetal ventricular growth, *Neuroradiology,* 21, 127, 1981.

23. **Vintzileos, A. M., Campbell, W. A., Weinbaum, D. J., and Nochimson, D. J.,** Perinatal management and outcome of fetal ventriculomegaly, *Obstet. Gynecol.,* 5, 69, 1987.

24. **Kurtz, A. B., Wapner, R. J., Rubin, C. S., Beuglet, C. C., Ross, R. D., and Goldberg, B. B.,** Ultrasound criteria for in utero diagnosis of microencephaly, *J. Clin. Ultrasound,* 8, 11, 1980.

25. **Hirsch, J. F., Pierre-Kahn, A., Renier, D.,** The Dandy-Walker malformation: a review of 40 cases, *J. Neurosurg.,* 61, 515, 1984.

26. **Pilu, G., Romero, R., DePalma, L.,** Antenatal diagnosis and obstetrical management of Dandy-Walker syndrome, *J. Reprod. Med.,* 31, 1017, 1986.

27. **Campbell, S. and Pearce, J. M. F.,** Ultrasound visualization of structural anomalies, *Br. Med. Bull.,* 39, 322, 1983.

28. **Chervanek, F. A., Isaacson, G., and Hobbins, J. C.,** Diagnosis and management of fetal holoprosencephaly, *Obstet. Gynecol.,* 66, 322, 1985.

29. **Chervanek, F. A., Isaacson, G., and Mahoney, M. J.,** The obstetric significance of holoprosencephaly, *Obstet. Gynecol.,* 63, 115, 1984.

30. **Greene, M. F., Benancerraf, B. R., and Frigoletto, F. D.,** Reliable criteria for the perinatal sonographic diagnosis of alobar holoprosencephaly, *Am. J. Obstet. Gynecol.,* 156, 687, 1987.

31. **Chervanek, F. A., Isaacson, G., and Mahoney, M. J.,** Diagnosis and management of fetal cephalocele, *Obstet. Gynecol.,* 64, 86, 1984.

32. **Comstock, C. H., Culp, D., and Gonzales, J.,** Agenesis of the corpus callosum in the fetus: its evolution and significance, *J. Ultrasound Med.,* 4, 613, 1985.

33. **Romero, R., Pilu, G., Jeanty, P., Ghidini, A., and Hobbins, J.,** *Prenatal Diagnosis of Congenital Anomalies,* Appleton & Lange, Norwalk, CT, 1988, 1.

34. **Hoff, R. and Mackay, I. M.,** Prenatal Ultrasound of intracranial teratoma, *J. Clin. Ultrasound,* 8, 247, 1980.

35. **Brahman, S., Colonel, L., Jenna, R., Major, M. C., and Wittenbauer, H. J. U.,** Sonographic in utero appearance of Kleeblattschadel syndrome, *J. Clin. Ultrasound,* 7, 481, 1979.

36. **Brahman, S. H., Jenna, R., and Wittenhauer, H. J.,** Sonographic in utero appearance of Kleeblattschadel syndrome, *J. Clin. Ultrasound,* 7, 481, 1979.
37. **Mayden, K. L., Tortora, M., and Berkowitz, R. L.,** Orbital diameters: a new parameter for prenatal diagnosis and dating, *Am. J. Obstet. Gynecol.,* 144, 289, 1965.
38. **Gorlin, R. J., Cervenka, J., and Pruzansky, S.,** Facial clefting and its syndromes, *Birth Defects Orig. Artic. Ser.,* 7, 3, 1971.

Chapter 8.3

SPINAL DEFECTS

Asim Kurjak

Visualization of the *vertebral column* is simple with ultrasound. Recognition of anatomical defects, however, requires time and an experienced examiner. With real-time scanning, the entire length of the spinal canal can be visualized horizontally in less than 2 min, and anything questionable can then be studied in greater detail.

Campbell et al.[1] originally described the method for detecting spina bifida by performing a series of scans with a static B mode scanner along the entire length of the fetal spine at right angles to the long axis. The normal spine with an intact neural arch appears in tranverse section as a closed circle, whereas the incomplete neural arch appears as a saucer or V-shaped complex. Care is needed, however, as a similar appearance can be produced artifactually by failing to remain exactly at right angles to the long axis of the spine. Real-time scanners allow the entire length of the spine to be viewed in longitudinal section, as the transducer is not inhibited by a gantry as are static scanners and can be moved into such a position that the fetal spine appears anteriorly on the screen. This view is essential so that the dorsal aspect of the neural arch can be inspected, including the characteristic sacral curve. In practice, both longitudinal and transverse scans are always used.

Spinal abnormalities fall into two main categories: cystic and noncystic. Meningocele and meningomyelocele are included in the cystic group. The incidence of cystic abnormalities of the spine is approximately 2 per 1000 births and 1 meningomyelocele per 100 births. The ultrasonic appearance of meningocele or meningomyelocele is that of a cystic mass of varying size, adjacent to the spine (Figures 1 to 7).

The fetal vertebral column should lie directly against the placenta or uterine wall. If there is a defect such as meningomyelocele, a sonolucent space-occupying mass is seen pushing the fetal vertebral column away from the wall of the uterus or placenta. Limb structures below the defect may be visualized with real time to see whether or not activity occurs. Theoretically, if there is a minor neural herniation, limb motion may occur, but where there is a greater degree of neural involvement, limb motion distal to the defect may be decreased.[2] However, Campbell and Pearce[3] observed fetuses with major dorsolumbar lesions to have apparently normal limb movements and have only observed one case of urinary retention in a fetus with spina bifida. Thus, the assessment has to be made on the extent of the structural defect and the presence or absence of large cerebral ventricles.

By applying the techniques of maternal serum α-fetoprotein (AFP) and amniotic fluid, it is now possible to detect over 90% of open fetal neural tube defects in the second trimester of pregnancy. Unfortunately, AFP studies do not identify fetuses with closed defects, nor have there been enough reports on the ultrasonic diagnosis of such cases before 20 weeks. Thus, the paper of Hood and Robinson[4] was the first one describing two cases of closed neural tube defects diagnosed ultrasonically at 18 weeks.

In both high-risk cases, the analysis of the amniotic fluid AFP did not suggest a neural tube defect. After successful ultrasonic diagnosis (illustrated with high-quality pictures), both pregnancies were terminated. It should be stressed that this case would be missed by fetoscopy, since the appearance of the fetus is normal and the diagnosis can only be verified at autopsy. Over 10% of neural tube defects are covered with skin, and therefore there is no permeation of AFP from the fetal cerebral spinal fluid into the amniotic cavity. For this

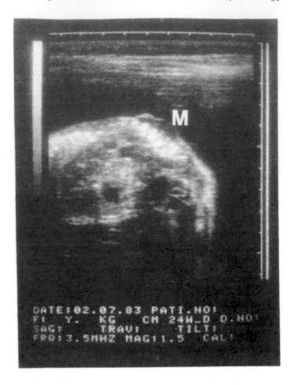

FIGURE 1.   Longitudinal section through the lumbar spina bifida. The defect is covered with a cystic extension of the meninges (m).

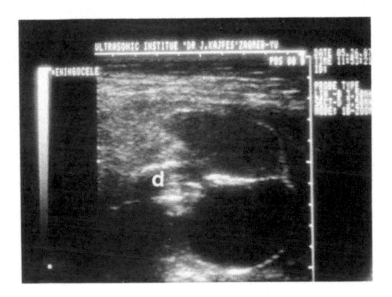

FIGURE 2.   Large cystic meningocele appearing as a bilocular cyst located closed to the fetal back. The spinal defect is also seen (d), thus enabling an accurate diagnosis.

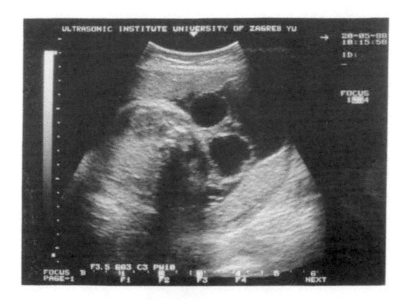

FIGURE 3.   Another case of myelomeningocele detected at the 29th week of gestation.

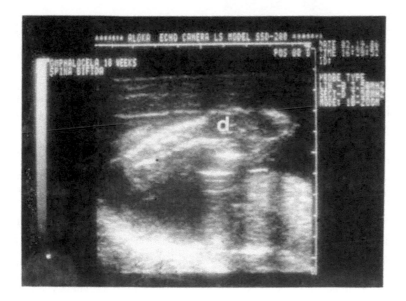

FIGURE 4.   Large defect in the cervical region of the fetal spine (d).

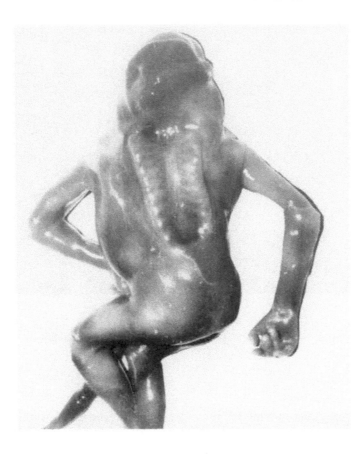

FIGURE 5.   The same baby in Figure 4 after delivery.

reason, AFP studies are not helpful in such cases, and diagnostic ultrasound offers the only practical alternative for their early detection. Undoubtedly, ultrasound has an important part to play in detecting major closed defects, and careful examination is made in all at-risk patients before amniocentesis.

There were several good papers on the first successful detection of spinal defects. Because of their pioneering roles, it is justifiable to review them briefly. In Robinson's series,[5] there were 15 cases of spina bifida and 1 encephalocele; 11 spina bifida cases were diagnosed at the first scan prior to amniocentesis (1 closed defect); 3 cases were picked up at the second scan after amniotic fluid results; and 1 spina bifida case was not visualized after 3 scans. The case of encephalocele was demonstrated at the first scan. There was one false positive diagnosis of an open spinal defect in a fetus in which the ultrasound examination showed a large exomphalos in addition. The amniotic fluid AFP in this pregnancy was only at the 4-SD level. At termination of pregnancy, the fetus appeared grossly normal, but the presence of the exomphalos containing the liver was confirmed.

Of the 321 patients in this series, 104 had been referred because of elevated serum AFP results. In 34.6% of cases, ultrasound showed an acceptable reason for the elevated levels. This includes underestimated gestational age, twins, and missed abortions. A further 39 patients (37.5%) were found to have a major abnormality, leaving 29 (27.9%) in whom no explanation was found.

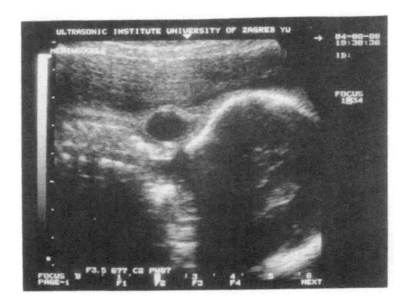

FIGURE 6. Longitudinal scan through the cervical spine and head showing cystic meningocele covered by the skin.

Christie[6] performed a systematic screening of all pregnant women during a 2-year period. Among the 3050 examined patients, 11 neural tube defects were correctly diagnosed at 18 or 19 weeks of gestation by ultrasound only. Remarkably, not one case of a neural tube defect was missed in this material during the first half of pregnancy. On the basis of these results, Christie concluded that ultrasound should be preferred over the AFP estimations for screening neural tube defects in early pregnancy and has now completed 15 years of total population screening. Overall detection rate is >95%, and no amniocenteses have been performed since 1979. A full report is currently being prepared.

The biparietal diameter (BPD) was measured by ultrasound mainly in the second trimester in 20 fetuses with spina bifida. The mean result was 0.83 cm (16%) less than the BPD for 186 unaffected fetuses at the same gestational age. The data suggested that growth of these fetuses was retarded. The practical consequence of this finding is that the routine use of ultrasound in pregnancy will increase the sensitivity of AFP screening for open spina bifida. The results indicating retarded growth were unexpected, since spina bifida, which is frequently complicated by hydrocephaly, is usually associated with BPDs which are larger.[7]

During a 3-year period in Queen Mother's Hospital, Glasgow, 16 pregnancies were terminated because of spina bifida, and in all but one, the defect was recognized by ultrasound. One lesion was not visualized; after termination, it was found that only one lumbar vertebra was involved. It may be extremely difficult to visualize clearly the lower portion of the spine, and it must be accepted that such small lesions may not be amenable to diagnosis at the present time. Amniotic fluid AFP levels were elevated in all but two of these pregnancies. In both of these two exceptional cases, the lesion was closed and termination was performed on ultrasonic evidence alone.[8]

In a paper by Miskin et al.,[9] the applicability of ultrasound in the detection of fetal spinal deformities between 16 and 20 weeks was illustrated by a model experiment and in a clinical examination of 121 high-risk pregnancies. The paper describes typical findings in spina bifida, but does not express the accuracy of the correct diagnosis in this material. In

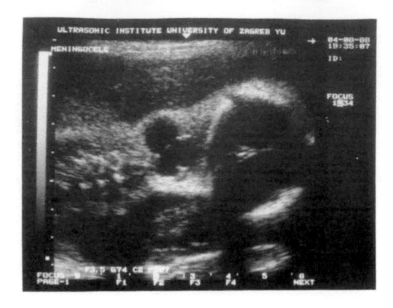

FIGURE 7.   Longitudinal scan of the same baby in Figure 6 in the frontal plane demonstrates multilocular appearance of meningocele.

spite of the normal finding of cervical flaring and widening of the fetal spinal canal, the authors found that in some normal cases, a minor degree of flaring can also be present in ultrasonography, sometimes in a unilateral shape. The cause of this perhaps is rotation of the fetal spinal canal either toward or away from the probe.

Wald et al.[10] has presented material of 6443 patients screened for neural tube defects in the Oxford area. Maternal serum AFP revealed 94% of the open neural tube defect. False positive values of maternal serum AFP were found in 3.8%, and in this group ultrasonography revealed in almost 50% either a multiple pregnancy or an underestimated gestational age.

Campbell and Pearce[3] have been successful in diagnosing 96 cases of spina bifida, of which 4 were skin covered. They have had two false positive diagnoses; one was in a fetus that had hydrocephaly and was thought to have a small sacral spina bifida. The other was a normal fetus. They have missed only six lesions. Two were in association with other major anomalies (hydrocephaly and iniencephaly) which were correctly diagnosed and for which the patients requested termination. The remaining four were early in their experience, were all sacral lesions, and were terminated because of a raised amniotic fluid level of AFP.

In a very recent and excellent paper from S. Campbell's group, cranial and cerebellar ultrasound markers of open spina bifida were evaluated in a prospective screening study of 436 pregnancies at high risk for this fetal abnormality. A total of 26 fetuses with open spina bifida were diagnosed. Values below the 5th percentile for gestation were found for BPD in 17 fetuses (62%) and for head circumference (HC) in 9 (35%).

The anterior horn of the lateral cerebral ventricle/hemisphere ratio was above the 95th percentile in 11 (42%), and there was ventriculomegaly of the posterior horn of the lateral ventricle in 14 (54%). Scalloping of the frontal bones, referred to as the "lemon sign", was present in all 26 cases and also in 5 (1%) of the structurally normal fetuses. A cerebellar abnormality was found in 25 cases (96%). In 9 fetuses (35%), the cerebellum was absent, and in 16 cases (62%), the cerebellar hemispheres curved anteriorly, producing the "banana sign". The predictive ability of each ultrasound marker to detect open spina bifida was evaluated by measuring the sensitivity, specificity, and predictive value of a positive and negative test. These findings demonstrated that certain cranial and cerebellar markers, in particular, the lemon sign and the banana sign or absent cerebellum, are consistent features of open spina bifida and are likely to improve the diagnostic accuracy of ultrasonography in the evaluation of pregnancies at high risk for this fetal abnormality.[11]

Similar results are produced at our institute in Zagreb. Unfortunately, the performance of ultrasound in the antenatal detection of fetal open spina bifida varies enormously, even among centers regarded as experts in this field.[1,4-6,9-12] It is our belief that advanced ultrasonic equipment combined with greater operator experience can completely replace amniocentesis. Since 1983, we have used high-resolution ultrasound to more reliable diagnosis of open spina bifida without performing early amniocentesis.

Althouse and Wald[13] showed that even with highly motivated treatment and care, some 50% of infants with open spina bifida die in the first 5 years of life, and of remainder only 6% were free from major handicap. As over 90% of infants with neural tube defects are born to mothers who have not previously had an affected infant, a screening test is necessary, and this exists in combined use of ultrasound and MSAFP.

REFERENCES

1. **Campbell, S., Pryse-Davies, J., and Coltart, T. M.,** Ultrasound in the diagnosis of spina bifida, *Lancet,* i, 1065, 1975.
2. **Gottesfield, K. R.,** Ultrasound in obstetrics, *Clin. Obstet. Gynecol.,* 21, 311, 1978.
3. **Campbell, S. and Pearce, J. M.,** The prenatal diagnosis of fetal structural anomalies by ultrasound, *Clin. Obstet. Gynecol.,* 10, 475, 1983.
4. **Hood, V. and Robinson, H. P.,** Diagnosis of closed neural tube defects by ultrasound in second trimester of pregnancy, *Br. Med. J.,* 2, 931, 1978.
5. **Robinson, H. P.,** The role of ultrasound in the prenatal diagnosis of neural tube defects, in *Prenatal Diagnosis,* Proc. 3rd European Conf. Prenatal Diagnosis of Genetic Disorders, Murken, E., Ed., Ferdinand Enke, Stuttgart, 1979, 179.
6. **Christie, A. D.,** Ultrasound screening for neural tube defects in early pregnancy, in *Abstracts, 3rd European Congr. Ultrasonics in Medicine,* Centro Minerva Medica, Bologna, 1978, 447.
7. **Wald, N. J., Cuckle, H., Borenham, J., and Stirrat, G.,** Small biparietal diameter of fetuses with spina bifida: implications for antenatal screening, *Br. J. Obstet. Gynecol.,* 87, 219, 1980.
8. **Neilson, J. P. and Hood, V. D.,** Ultrasound in obstetrics and gynecology: recent developments, *Br. Med. Bull.,* 36, 249, 1980.
9. **Miskin, M., Baim, R., Allen, L., and Benzie, R.,** Ultrasonic assessment of fetal spine before 20 weeks gestation, *Radiology,* 132, 131, 1979.
10. **Wald, N., Cuckle, H., Boreham, J., Brett, R., Stirrat, G., Bennet, M., Turnbull, A., Solymar, M., Jones, N., Bobrow, M., and Evans, C.,** Antenatal screening in Oxford for neural tube defects, *Br. J. Obstet. Gynecol.,* 86, 91, 1979.
11. **Campbell, J., Gilbert, W. M., Nicoladies, K. H., and Campbell, S.,** Ultrasound screening for spina bifida. Cranial and cerebellar signs in a high-risk population, *GBR-Obstet. Gynecol.,* 70(2), 247, 1987.
12. **Roberts, C. J., Hibbard, B. M., Roberts, B. E., et al.,** Diagnostic effectiveness of ultrasound in detection of neural tube defects, *Lancet,* ii, 1069, 1983.
13. **Althouse, R. and Wald, N.,** Survival and handicap of infants with spina bifida, *Arch. Dis. Child.,* 55, 845, 1980.

Chapter 8.4

THORACIC ABNORMALITIES

Asim Kurjak

The fetal thorax and its content are easily identifiable during ultrasound examination using the heart as a landmark. On transverse section, the heart is located anteriorly and occupies 20% of the thorax area during the last 2 months of gestation. Other organs that are regularly seen within the thorax are the lungs and great vessels located in the mediastinum. seen within the thorax are the lungs and great vessels located in the mediastinum.

The lungs appear as two moderately and homogeneously echogenic areas on either side of the heart. On longitudinal scan, the diaphragm can be recognized between lungs and liver as a relatively transonic line. Lung echogenicity is low as compared to the liver, but increases after 35 to 36 weeks, approaching that of the liver.

FETAL LUNG ABNORMALITIES

CONGENITAL CYSTIC ADENOMATOID MALFORMATION OF THE LUNG

Congenital cystic adenomatoid malformation of the lung is the most frequent congenital lung abnormality. The disease is caused by an excessive growth of terminal bronchioles and is usually unilateral. According to the morphological appearance of the lesions, the disease is classified in three types.[2] Type I is characterized by the presence of large pulmonary cysts. In type II, the cysts are much smaller, being less than 2 cm in size, while in type III, the cystic dilatation of the bronchioles is too small to be visualized by ultrasound. Helpful signs to detect type III disease are mediastinal shift and increased echogenicity of the lungs.[3,4]

Polyhydramnios is frequently associated with the disease and helps to make correct prenatal diagnosis. Typical ultrasonic finding is the presence of cystic lung tumor associated with fetal hydrops (Figures 1 to 3).

Prognosis of the congenital cystic malformation of the lung depends on the type of the disease, presence of fetal hydrops, and associated fetal anomalies. The worst prognosis is in type III of the disease. If fetal hydrops is present, it denotes uniformly fatal outcome. However, if other anomalies are present, e.g., hydrocephalus, renal agenesis, intestinal obstruction, etc., outcome will be also poor.[5,6]

LUNG SEQUESTRATION

Lung sequestration is a rare fetal anomaly characterized by the presence of an intra-thoracic tumor that arises from pulmonary parenchyma. It is classified in two types regarding the relation of the tumor to the normal lung. The intralobar type of the disease presumes that the tumor is developing within the visceral pleura of the lung, while in the extralobar type, the tumor is covered by its own pleura. Lung sequestration is diagnosed ultrasonically by demonstration of the solid tumor within the thorax that compresses the lungs and causes shift of mediastinal organs.[7] The prognosis of the condition is usually poor and depends, like in the case of cystic adenomatoid malformation of the lung, on the presence of the fetal hydrops and associated anomalies.[6]

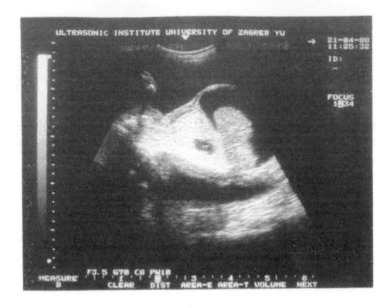

FIGURE 1. Longitudinal sonogram showing a marked polyhydramnios and fetal ascites at 26 weeks in a case of congenital cystic adenomatoid malformation of the lung.

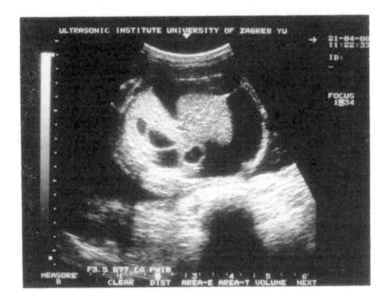

FIGURE 2. Transverse scan of the same fetus in Figure 1 showing four large cysts within the lungs, characteristic of type I of the disease.

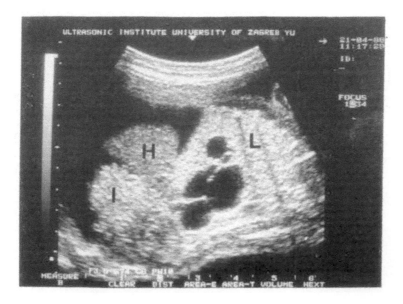

FIGURE 3. The cysts shown in Figure 2 are more clearly seen in longitudinal scan (L = lungs, H = liver, I = intestinal loops).

PLEURAL EFFUSIONS

Pleural effusions can be serous or chylous, very often associated with hydrops or congestive heart failure. Chylous effusions are usually the consequence of a lymphatic system abnormality. It is difficult to distinguish between isolated pleural effusion and chylothorax by ultrasound, but examination of aspirated fluid obtained by thoracocenthesis can help.

The management of patients with pleural effusions is still controversial. It is described in the chapter on fetal therapy.

Pleural effusions may be seen in hydropic fetuses and usually are manifested as crescentic areas of sonolucency in the subpulmonic regions. Some care must be taken to distinguish between true pleural effusions and small collections of subdiaphragmatic ascitic fluid. This differentiation is best accomplished by a coronal section through the fetal thorax and upper abdomen, seeking evidence of fluid tracking up along the lateral aspects of the fetal lungs (Figures 4 and 5).

Intrauterine pleural effusion is an uncommon cause of respiratory distress following delivery, but when present, it is associated with a mortality rate of 15%. If these effusions are diagnosed antenatally by ultrasound, the neonatal team can be informed and, thus, be prepared to institute early definitive treatment. The most frequent etiology is congenital chylothorax, which is constituted of the triad of polyhydramnios, pleural effusions, and the presence of a scrotum. Two cases are reported in which an antenatal ultrasound diagnosis of pleural effusion forewarned the attending neonatologist and was a factor in the favorable outcome of the case.[8,9]

ABNORMALITIES OF CHEST WALL SHAPE

Thoracic deformities of different degrees can be present in cases of chondroectodermal dysplasia, thanatophoric dwarfism, achondrogenesis, asphyxiating thoracic dystrophy, achondroplasia, and some other types of short-linked dwarfism.[10,11]

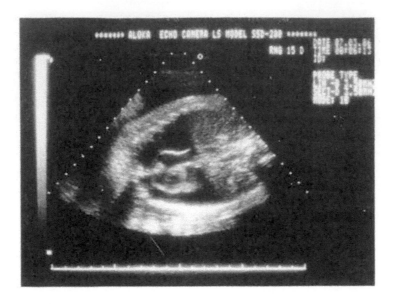

FIGURE 4.   Longitudinal scan of the fetus with chylothorax. The lungs are seen as floating within the fluid, while the abdomen appears normal.

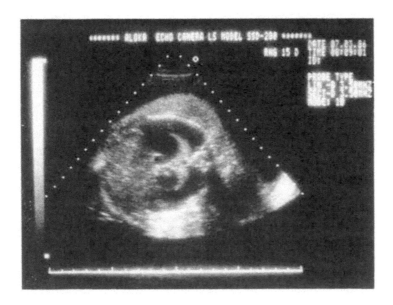

FIGURE 5.   Transverse scan of the same fetus in Figure 4.

REFERENCES

1. **Hattan, R. A., Rees, G. K., and Johnson, M. L.**, Normal fetal anatomy, *Radiol. Clin. North Am.*, 20, 271, 1982.
2. **Stocker, J. T., Madewell, J. E., and Drake, R. M.**, Congenital cystic adenomatoid malformation of the lung. Classification and morphologic spectrum, *Hum. Pathol.*, 8, 155, 1977.
3. **Graham, D., Winn, K., and Dex, W.**, Prenatal diagnosis of cystic adenomatoid malformation of the lung, *J. Ultrasound Med.*, 1, 9, 1982.
4. **Donn, S. M., Martin, J. N., and White, S. J.**, Antenatal ultrasound findings in cystic malformation, *Pediatr. Radiol.*, 10, 180, 1981.
5. **Kohler, H. G. and Rumer, B. A.**, Congenital cystic malformation of the lung and its relation to hydramnios, *J. Obstet. Gynaecol. Br. Commonw.*, 80, 130, 1973.
6. **Aslam, R. A., Korones, S. B., and Richardson, R. L.**, Congenital cystic adenomatoid malformation with anasarca, *JAMA*, 212, 622, 1970.
7. **Romero, R., Chervenak, F. A., and Kotzen, J.**, Antenatal sonographic findings in extralobar pulmonary sequestration, *J. Ultrasound. Med.*, 1, 131, 1982.
8. **Randolph, J. G. and Gross, R. E.**, Congenital chylothorax, *Arch. Surg.*, 74, 405, 1957.
9. **Deffort, P. and Theiery, M.**, Antenatal diagnosis of congenital chylothorax by gray-scale sonography, *J. Clin. Ultrasound.*, 6, 47, 1978.
10. **Knochel, J. Q., Lee, T. G., and Melendez, M. G.**, Fetal abnormalities involving the thorax and abdomen, *Radiol. Clin. North Am.*, 20, 297, 1982.
11. **Hobbins, J. C., Grannum, P. A. T., and Berkowitz, R. L.**, Ultrasound on the diagnosis of congenital anomalies, *Am. J. Obstet. Gynecol.*, 134, 331, 1979.

Chapter 8.5

CONGENITAL AND PERINATAL ANOMALIES OF THE GASTROINTESTINAL TRACT

Asim Kurjak

Many congenital and perinatal anomalies of the gastrointestinal (GI) tract may be responsible for partial or complete obstruction. The majority of the obstructions involve the rectum and anus; the remainder are predominantly in the small intestine. The important anomalies are as follows:

- Pyloric stenosis
- Duodenal atresia or stenosis (with or without annular pancreas)
- Jejunal or ileal atresia or stenosis
- Malrotation with or without volvulus
- Meconium ileus
- Hirschsprung's disease (aganglionic magacolon)
- Imperforate anus
- Duplications and diverticula

Ultrasonic examination of fetal abdomen is of utmost importance since it is common site of congenital anomalies. Normal ultrasound appearance of fetal abdomen is described in detail in Chapter 7.

Portions of the GI tract may be seen as fluid-filled structures within the fetal abdomen. The stomach is the most frequently seen portion of the tract. The normal fetal stomach, when visualized, appears as a small, fluid-filled structure, i.e., cystic density in the left upper quadrant. Demonstration of a mildly to moderately dilated stomach in the fetus is not necessarily abnormal because it is normal for the fetus to ingest amniotic fluid. Obstructive lesions of the GI tract are identified by the visualization of a distended, fluid-filled gut proximal to the site of obstruction.

Fetal bowel obstruction may be secondary to a congenital malformation such as intestinal atresia, but may also be caused by meconium ileus, duplication of bowel, volvulus, and rupture of bowel wall. Atresias are most commonly encountered type of fetal bowel obstruction, occurring in 1 of every 2700 live births. The site of obstruction is the ileum in more than one half of cases, followed by, in the descending order of occurrence, the duodenum, jejenum, and colon (Figure 1).

In general, the higher the obstruction, the greater is the likelihood of polyhydramnios and other obstetrical complications such as prematurity and higher perinatal mortality.

Atresia (complete occlusion) and, less commonly, stenosis (partial occlusion) of the GI tract account for about one third of cases of intestinal obstruction. The obstructive lesion (excluding anorectal lesions) is most frequently in the ileum (50%) and duodenum (25%), less frequently in the jejunum, rarely in the colon, and almost never in the stomach. There is an increased incidence of duodenal atresia as well as of imperforate anus in infants with Down syndrome. About 15% of intestinal atresias are multiple. The types of atresia are (1) a diaphragm-like occlusion with a distal segment, and (2) segments of bowel with cord-like connections.

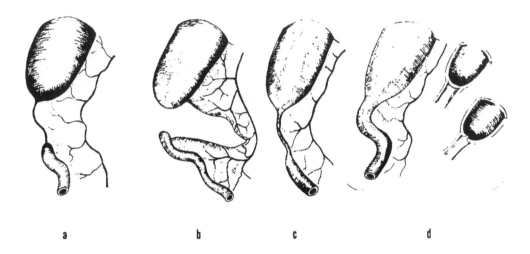

a   b   c   d

FIGURE 1. Forms of internal intestinal passage impossibility. (a) Complete intestinal atresia. Two segments are connected with fibrous band only. (b) Complete interruption of intestinal tube and a part of mesentery. (c) Strong stenosis of one intestinal part. (d) Impossibility of intestinal passage because of membranous barrier in intestine. Barrier can be complete (artresia) or with a small orifice (stenosis).

PYLORIC ATRESIA

Pyloric atresia is a rare anomaly accounting for approximately 1% of all intestinal atresias. Ultrasound visualization of a dilated, fluid-filled stomach associated with polyhydramnios is highly suggestive of this anomaly. However, diagnosis can be made with certainty only after delivery.

CONGENITAL INTESTINAL OBSTRUCTION

Intestinal obstruction is observed in approximately 1 in 1500 newborn infants. From an anatomic standpoint, congenital obstructive lesions of the intestines can be viewed as intrinsic, e.g., atresia, stenosis, meconium ileus, and aganglionic megacolon, or extrinsic, e.g., malrotation, constricting bands, intra-abdominal hernias, and duplications.

Duodenal obstruction, which is the most common form of GI tract obstruction visualized *in utero*, may be intrinsic as in duodenal atresia, or extrinsic due to annular pancreas or congenital peritoneal bands (Figures 2 to 5). The incidence of duodenal atresia ranges from 1 per 5000 to 1 per 15,000. The ultrasonic appearance of duodenal atresia *in utero* has been well described. The "double-bubble" seen on postnatal radiography has its counterpart ultrasonically as the "double cyst" within the fetal abdomen *in utero*.[1]

Ultrasonically, two round-shaped cystic structures are observed in the upper abdomen. The left cyst represents the dilated stomach, and the right one duodenum. Hydramnios is present in 50% of cases with duodenal atresia, and its absence does not imply clinical insignificance of abdominal finding. The "double-bubble" sign can be typically visualized from the 28th week onward. The situation is similar in other intestinal obstruction, and it should be emphasized that a normal early scan does not imply the absence of GI anomalies[2] (Figure 6). The "double-bubble" sign has to be differentiated from the "pseudo-double-bubble" sign which is occasionally seen in normal stomach with prominent insicura angularis.

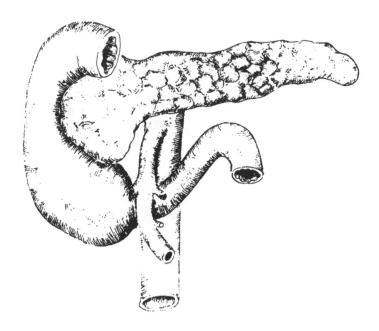

FIGURE 2.   Duodenal obstruction caused by pressure of mesenteric artery.

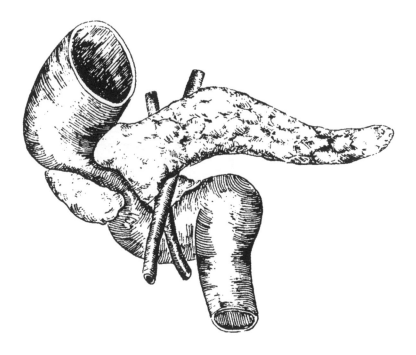

FIGURE 3.   Duodenal obstruction caused by annular pancrease. Annulus can be complete or partial.

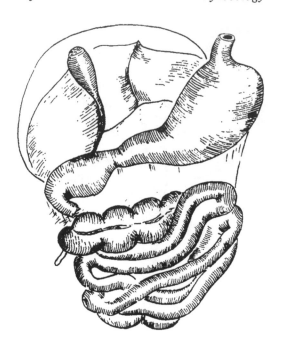

FIGURE 4.   Pressure on duodenum of incompletely rotated appendix.

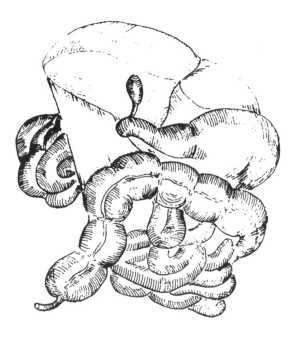

FIGURE 5.   Pressure on duodenum with peritoneal band.

The relation of right cyst to the gallbladder and the presence or absence of hydramnios serve as guidelines for diagnosis. As duodenal atresia is associated in almost 50% of cases with other fetal anomalies or chromosomal abnormalities, the fetus should be examined with extreme care[3-5] (Figures 7 and 8).

Duodenal atresia is associated with polyhydramnios, and this excess amniotic fluid is due to failure of the fetus to absorb ingested fluid from his or her gastrointestinal tract and thus exchange this fluid via its circulatory system with the placenta. Duodenal atresia may also result in elevated α-fetoprotein (AFP) levels in amniotic fluid.[4] The stomach is usually the larger of the two "cysts" and is seen in the posteriolateral aspect of the fetal left upper quadrant. The prenatal diagnosis of this condition is obviously useful since the obstetrician can be informed and subsequently alert a pediatric surgeon. Immediately after birth, a nasogastric tube should be inserted, air injected, and a plain abdominal radiograph obtained for confirmation. The surgeon can effect repair early and thus avoid the danger of aspiration. The repair is usually not difficult for a skilled pediatric surgeon, but it must be kept in mind that duodenal atresia is associated in 30% of the cases with mongolism and other severe congenital anomalies, so the parents should be counseled about these facts.[1,5]

In duodenal atresia or stenosis, the surgical procedures of choice are duodenostomy without dividing the pancreas, leaving as short a defunctioned loop as possible.

Other high GI tract obstructions, such as esophageal atresia, types A, B, and C, may be implied by the presence of polyhydramnios, although the actual lesion may not be identified *in utero* by ultrasound. Esophageal atresia occurs in about 1 in every 1500 live births, and 90% of cases have a tracheo-esophageal fistule, allowing fluid to enter atresia with no fistula to the trachea. Fluid is therefore unable to pass into the stomach which will not be detected ultrasonically. Lower GI obstructions have been demonstrated *in utero* by ultrasound, showing distended, amniotic fluid-filled bowel loops. These lower obstructions are not expected to be associated with polyhydramnios because the fetus uses most of its length of the GI tract for the absorption of ingested fluid.[1,2,6,7]

JEJUNAL OR ILEAL OBSTRUCTION

These obstructions may result from atresia or stenosis, meconium ileus, Hirschsprung's disease, intussusception, Meckel diverticulum, intestinal duplication, or strangulated hernia. The bowel in ileal or jejunal atresia ends blindly proximal and distal to an interruption in its continuity; there may even be a gap in the mesentery. With stenotic or "windsock" obstructions, the bowel and mesentery are in continuity. The large size of the proximal obstructed loop of bowel contrasts with that of the collapsed distal bowel (Figures 9 and 10).

Intestinal atresia or stenosis is regarded as always "secondary" to some other intrauterine disease process which results in mesenteric vascular occlusion. In approximately 25% of the instances of atresia, this is the responsible factor for the recognized disease state, i.e., meconium ileus, colon aganglionosis, gastroschisis, etc. In the others, however, only evidence for intrauterine intestinal infarction is present, i.e., mesenteric scars, granulomas adjacent to the intestinal defect, and histologic changes in the segments and the mesentery, which suggest prior infarction. It is believed that vascular insufficiency exists in the intestinal segments which are immediately proximal and immediately distal to the atresia. Associated anomalies are present in approximately 48% of patients. Approximately 30% have chromosome 21 trisomy syndrome. Malrotation of the colon with incomplete intestinal fixation occurs in approximately 22%, and congenital heart disease occurs in 20% of the patients. Tracheo-esophagel fistula and renal malformations are slightly less common.[1-3]

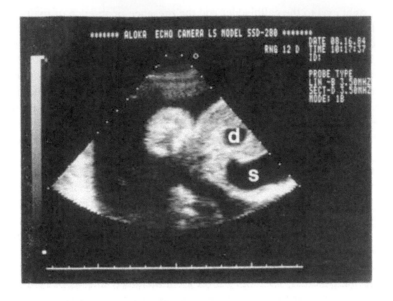

A

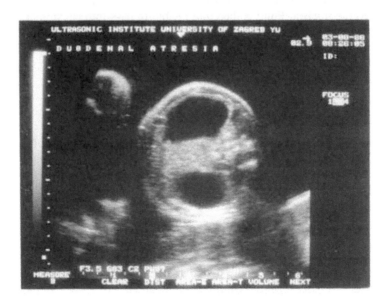

B

FIGURE 6.   (A) Duodenal atresia associated with hydramnios. The transverse scan, through the fetal abdomen illustrates the typical "double-bubble" sign. The left cyst in the upper abdomen represents the dilated stomach (s) and is usually larger than the right cyst, representing the dilated duodenum (d). (B) A case of duodenal atresia and polyhydramnios at the 27th week. Marked dilatation of the stomach and duodenum are visible. (C) Longitudinal scan of the same baby in B demonstrating the stomach (s), duodenum (d), heart (h), and bladder (b).

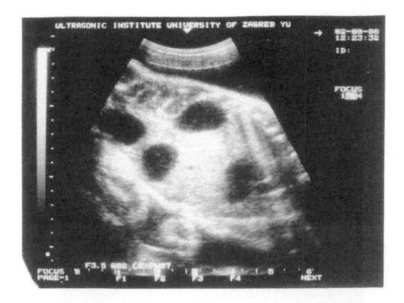

FIGURE 6C.

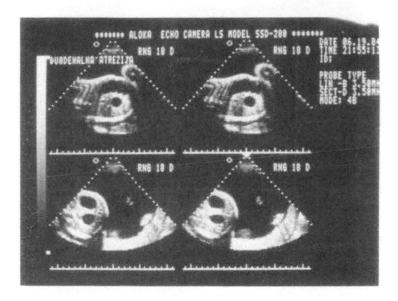

FIGURE 7. Another example of duodenal atresia with marked dilatation of the stomach.

Meconium ileus occurs in newborn infants with cystic fibrosis, but only 10% of patients with this disease develop meconium ileus. Volvulus, atresia, or perforation of the bowel may accompany meconium ileus. If the bowel perforates *in utero*, meconium peritonitis results: intraperitoneal meconium can cause dense adhesions leading postnatally to adhesive intestinal obstruction (Figure 11).

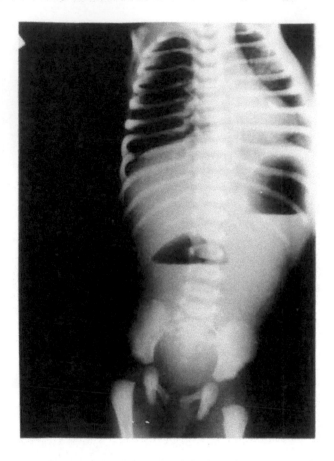

FIGURE 8.   The roentgenogram after delivery shows the same finding as in Figure 7.

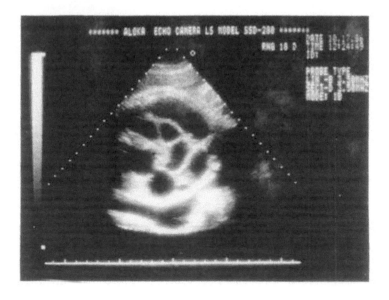

FIGURE 9.   Sonographic demonstration of markedly dilated intestinal loops in a case of fetal ileal atresia.

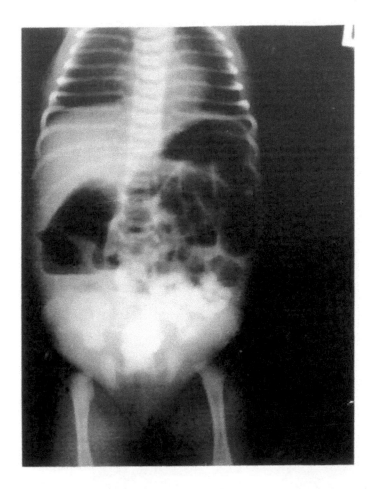

FIGURE 10.   Neonatal radiograph showing a finding typical of dilated loops.

CONGENITAL MEGACOLON (HIRSCHSPRUNG'S DISEASE)

This is the most common cause of intestinal obstruction of the colon and accounts for about 33% of all neonatal obstructions, although it is rare in premature infants. Occasionally there is a familial incidence of megacolon. Atresia of the colon is extremely rare (Figure 12).

There may be failure of migration of the cells of the embryonic neural crest into the bowel wall or failure of the myenteric and submucous plexuses to progress in a craniocaudal direction within the bowel wall. This disease results from absence of ganglion cells in the bowel wall, extending proximally from anus for a variable distance. The aganglionic segment is limited to the rectosigmoid in 80% of patients; in 15% the colon is aganglionic as far proximally as the hepatic flexure; while in 3% the entire colon lacks ganglion cells.

On ultrasound, jejunal and ileal atresias are characterized by several cystic structures in the upper abdomen representing dilated bowel loops. Hydramnios is seen less frequently, and its occurrence is reported in 25% of cases. More distal obstructions include colonic and anorectal atresias. In distal obstruction, there is a sufficient length of proximal bowel for complete resorption of swollowed fluid, and hydramnios does not occur.

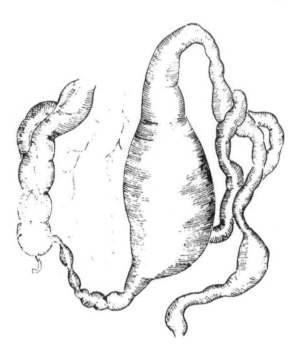

FIGURE 11.   Meconium ileus. Terminal ileum is maximally
dilated and filled with changed meconium.

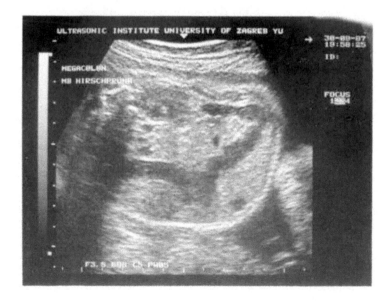

FIGURE 12.   Marked dilatation of the colon transversum at 36 weeks in a case of
Hirschspring's disease.

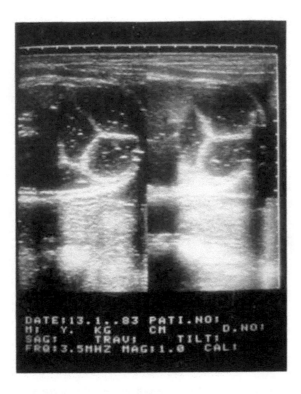

FIGURE 13.   Anorectal atresia. Dilated, fluid-filled bowel loops
are located caudally in the fetal abdomen.

Colonic atresia is associated in half of the cases with abnormalities of other, e.g., genito-
urinary or skeletal system, origin. Unfortunately, there is no reliable ultrasonic sign for their
distinction. Both conditions are characterized by large, fluid-filled, dilated loops, positioned
somewhat lower in anal atresia (Figure 13).

DEFECTS OF ABDOMINAL WALL

Congenital umbilical hernia, omphalocele, and gastroschisis may be demonstrated by
ultrasound *in utero*. These conditions involve a developmental abnormality of the abdominal
wall with variable external herniation of the abdominal viscera. In congenital umbilical
hernia, a portion of peritoneal sac and, occasionally, a short loop of intestine protrude
through the umbilical ring and are covered by subcutaneous fat and skin. The incidence of
congenital umbilical hernia is high; it is present in 10% of white and 40 to 90% of black
infants.

Omphalocele involves herniation of viscera into the base of the umbilical cord. In this
condition, the peritoneal sac is not covered by skin, as in an umbilical hernia, but Wharton's
jelly and amniotic membrane. Gastroschisis involves a defect in the abdominal wall lateral
to the umbilical cord without any layers of abdominal wall over the herniated viscera.
Omphalocele and gastroschisis fortunately are rare (approximately 1 in 10,000 births) and
over half are associated with other congenital anomalies (Figures 14 to 16).

In the case of omphalocele, sacular malformation of the umbilical cord containing various
portions of the intestinal tract occurs, with the umbilical ring widely open. This is generally

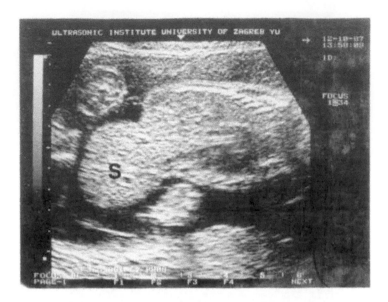

FIGURE 14. Omphalocele. Typical ultrasonic finding of a more solid sac (s) attached to the fetal abdomen at 24 weeks.

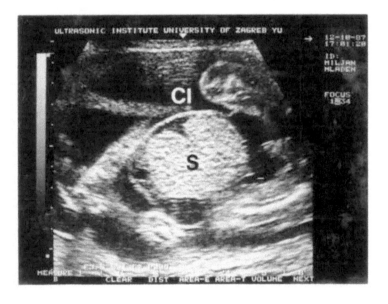

FIGURE 15. Cord insertion (CI) is clearly seen on its insertion on the surface of the sac (S).

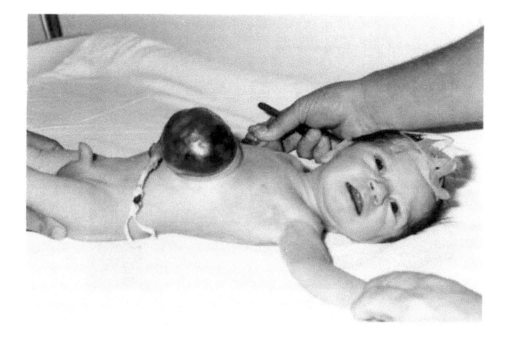

FIGURE 16.   The baby in Figure 15 after delivery. The sac and cord insertion are visible.

covered by a membrane made up of Wharton's jelly as an extension of the peritoneum. Elements of the umbilical cord may be present in the wall of the sac. The umbilical defect varies in size from small (1 to 2 cm) to massive and obliterating most of the abdominal wall. Contents of the omphalocele may be just one loop of bowel or the entire intestinal tract with the liver, spleen, etc. included. The membrane may be thin and translucent or substantial and opaque. The skin of the abdominal wall may extend up on the eviscerated intestine to make up one third to one half of the sac wall, or, in the case of congenital umbilical hernia, the mass will be covered with skin. The sac may have ruptured during or before birth, the remnants of the sac present or nonexistent. The difference between a ruptured omphalocele and gastroschisis remains in dispute.

Ultrasonically, these conditions manifest as a mass of tissue visualized adjacent and attached to the anterior abdominal wall of the fetus. The "mass" may contain loops of fluid-filled bowel, liver, spleen, and stomach. In the larger umbilical hernias, omphaloceles, or gastroschises, the herniated liver can be identified extraneous to the abdominal cavity; the umbilical vein and portal sinus within the organ aid in its identification. With careful technique and the skilled use of real-time equipment, one may be able to visualize ultrasonically a membrane covering the extended viscera and thus be able to diagnose umbilical hernia or omphalocele.[2,7-10] Although omphalocele and gastroschisis are both congenital defects of the abdominal wall, there are significant physical differences between them. The herniated sac of omphalocele contains, according to the degree of the defect, the intestines, liver, stomach, spleen, and in extreme cases, the heart. The sac protects the herniated organs from contact with amniotic fluid *in utero*, and they remain morphologically and functionally normal. An omphalocele containing the entire liver is extremely rare (1 in 10,000 births). The prenatal diagnosis of the hepato-omphalocele by means of ultrasonography and the subsequent team approach by perinatologists, neonatologists, and a pediatric surgeon are

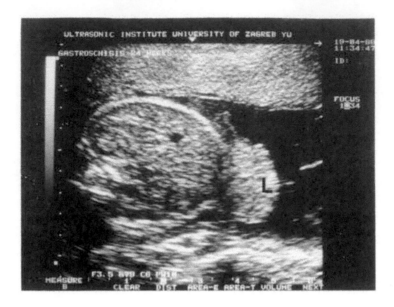

FIGURE 17.   Transverse sonogram showing intestinal loops (L) floating in the amniotic fluid in a case of gastroschisis.

the key factors in the successful management of these cases. Such a case is described with the emphasis on the team approach to ensure a successful outcome.[11] Another remarkable case in which omphalocele was detected in the first trimester of pregnancy is reported with interruption of pregnancy. This case is the earliest successful diagnosis of this malformation reported in the literature.[12]

Gastroschisis is a fetal abnormality consisting of a full-thickness anterior abdominal wall defect with a consequent evisceration of the bowel. Usually there is complete absence of any covering sac and, as opposed to omphalocele, there is a normal insertion of the umbilical cord, usually at the margin of the defect. In gastroschisis, the viscera floats uncovered in amniotic fluid, and the ultrasonic finding of bowel loops floating in the amniotic cavity is usually pathognomonic. A sonologist should always attempt to differentiate between omphalocele and gastroschisis, particularly because the former condition is associated to a high degree with cardiovascular and chromosomal abnormalities.[11-16]

Although the frequency of prenatally detected abdominal wall defects reaches almost 100%, a comprehensive approach to management has not yet been formulated. Pretemporary delivery undoubtedly minimizes the period of contact between intestine and amniotic fluid in gastroschisis and, thus, it may minimize the intestine inflammatory reaction which comprises functional recovery. Of course, the advantage of preterm delivery must be weighted against the risk of prematurity (Figures 17 and 18).

The other unsolved question is the role of Cesarean section (CS) in managing abdominal wall defects. The most compelling argument for CS is that it allows a planned delivery in a septic environment with everything in readiness for resuscitation and immediate surgical correction, but, still, it appears that the vast majority of cases can be safely delivered vaginally.[16]

Finally, the only possibility for survival of newborns with an omphalocele is immediate surgery. Antenatal diagnosis is, therefore, of vital importance. Primary repair of the umbilical hernia with closure of the umbilical defect is possible at any age. In larger defects, when

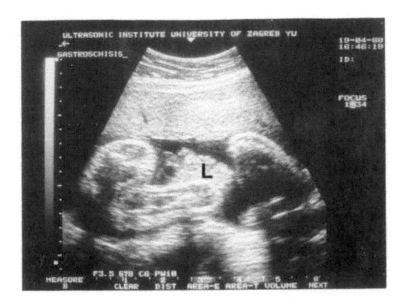

FIGURE 18.   Longitudinal scan of the same baby in Figure 17 (L = intestinal loops).

the return of the viscera to hypoplastic or underdeveloped abdominal cavity will result in respiratory deficiency, i.e., elevation of the diaphragm and diminished respiratory exchange, the fascia should remain open, the defect enlarged, and a staged repair employed using temporary synthetic material, i.e., silastic rubber sheeting. Ultimate closure can be accomplished in stages by 2 to 4 weeks of age. Skin coverage only with later abdominal wall repair is now infrequently employed.

Prognosis is excellent once the repair is accomplished and intestinal function established. Late obstruction due to adhesions are not a frequent problem in the larger lesions. Mortality rate is 20 to 30%. Causes of death are infections, inanition, or unrelated congenital abnormalities.

CONGENITAL DIAPHRAGMAL HERNIA (CDH)

Another very important congenital malformation involving both abdomen and thorax is CDH, an anatomically simple defect that is easily correctable by removing the herniated viscera from the chest and dosing the diaphragm. However, up to 80% of all infants with CDH die due to pulmonary insufficiency secondary to compression of the developing lungs by herniated bowels.[2,17]

Ultrasound diagnosis of diaphragmatic hernia is based upon three characteristic signs: polyhydramnios, mediastinal shift, and absence of normally placed stomach bubble. Polyhydramnios is a nonspecific sign of various congenital anomalies, and although its etiology in diaphragmatic hernia is not known, it seems that impaired fetal swollowing due to compression of esophagus may play a role (Figure 19).

Displacement of the fetal mediastinum is predominantly lateral, and it can be easily identified on the transverse section taken at the level of the fetal heart. The fluid-filled stomach and small bowel contrast dramatically to the more echogenic fetal lung, especially in left-sided CDH. In right-sided CDH, herniated viscera are more difficult to identify due

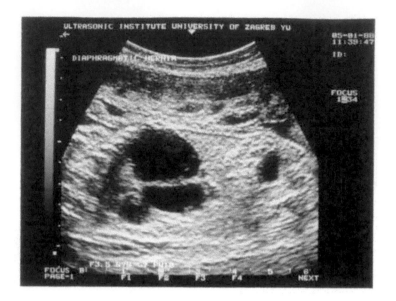

FIGURE 19.   A case of diaphragmatic hernia demonstrated on longitudinal sonogram at 25 weeks. Dilated bowel loop filling a large part of thoracic cavity is
clearly seen.

to the subtle difference in echogenicity between liver and lung. Generally speaking, it can
be stated that when abdominal organs are at the level of a four-chamber view, they lie within
the fetal thorax and CDH is present.

As far as a therapy is concerned, the principal advantage of prenatal detection is that
the mother can be transported to a neonatal unit where the baby can be electively delivered,
resuscitated, and operated. Unfortunately, despite all of our effort, 80% of CDH cases will
not survive.

Postnatal correction decompresses the lung and allows development to proceed, but no
new airways can be formed, because this stage of development was completed by 16 weeks
of gestation. The normal number of conducting airways is decreased, resulting in hypoplastic
lungs. Harrison's group have recently demonstrated that correction of CDH *in utero* is
physiologically sound and technically feasible. They have developed a successful *in utero*
surgical technique in fetal lambs which involves removal of viscera from the thoracic into
the peritoneal cavity, repair of the diaphragmatic defect, and enlargement of the abdominal
cavity by abdominoplasty by means of an oval silicone rubber patch.[17]

Although it looks like science fiction, CDH undoubtedly requires correction before birth,
and intrauterine surgery is the only logical step forward.

OTHER GASTROINTESTINAL MASSES

Other masses of different origin can less frequently be seen in the fetal abdomen. These
include duplications cysts, which are most commonly located in the ileum and esophagus,
meconium cysts, mesenteric cysts, and liver tumors such as hemangiomas and hematomas.
Cystic lesions can be confused with urinary tract abnormalities, and accurate evaluation of
normal urinary tract anatomy and function is required[1,2] (Figure 20).

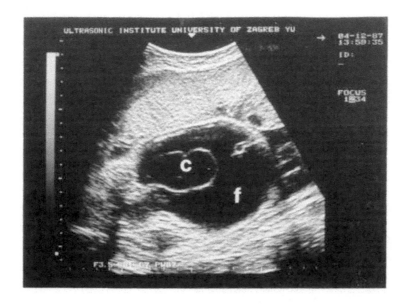

FIGURE 20.   Duplication cyst (c) surrounded by free fluid (f) in the fetal abdomen.

NONIMMUNE HYDROPS FETALIS

Hydrops fetalis is a general term describing the condition of a fetus that has generalized soft tissue edema (anasarca). This disorder is usually associated with scirrhose effusions within the peritoneum (ascites) pleural space (pleural effusion) or pericardial space (pericardial effusion).

When the fluid accumulation is longstanding, the normal contours of the viscera may become rounded, a change that may also be seen on ultrasound. With the early diagnosis of rhesus incompatibility, treatment by intrauterine transfusion, and early delivery, most hydropic fetuses are now caused by numerous maternal and/or fetal conditions. Table 1 lists the principal causes of hydrops fetalis.

The pathogenesis of hydrops entails any combination of anemia, cardiac failure, and mechanical obstruction to venous return. Since a variety of conditions, varying from those that are incompatible with life to those that are amenable to medical or surgical treatment, may result in hydrops fetalis, ultrasonography has an important role to play in the evaluation of this disorder.

Ultrasonic evaluation of the fetus with ascites and/or anasarca is helpful in distinguishing conditions, such as paroximal atrial tachicardia, which may be medically treated *in utero* or in the immediate postdelivery period, from those that are invariably fatal. Fetuses that have multiple congenital anomalies, large tumors that obstruct venous return such as mediastinal teratomas or neuroblastomas, can be sonographically distinguished from those fetuses that are anatomically normal. Fetal anemia or congestive heart failure are conditions that may produce fetal hydrops without a structural anomaly.

Serial sonographic examinations of the hydropic fetus are also helpful in determining the progression or resolution of this disorder. There have been at least three documented cases of resolution of fetal ascites *in utero*. This phenomenon was thought to be due to

TABLE 1
Causes of Hydrops Fetalis

Triploidy
Trisomy 18
Trisomy 21
Monosomy X (Turner syndrome)
Rhesus hemolytic disease
Thalassemia
Fetal red cell enzyme defects
Fetomaternal hemorrhage
Twin transfusion syndrome
Angioma of fetus or placenta
Renal or umbilical vein thrombosis
Cardiac malformation with conduction defect
Fetal tachycardia
Cardiac rhabdomyoma
Cystic adenomatoid malformation of the lungs
Pulmonary lymphangiectasia
Pulmonary hypoplasia
Lower urinary tract anomalies
Neuroblastoma
Maternal nephrotic syndrome
Congenital infection

intermittent episodes of congestive heart failure. If fetal ascites is proved to be secondary to immunologic hemolysis, real-time sonography can be used to guide attempts at intrauterine transfusion.[18,19]

The presence of fetal ascites and anasarca can easily be documented by ultrasound. In acute situations, sonography can be used to detect intrauterine fetal distress by indicating irregular or unusually slow heart rate. Sonography is also helpful to the obstetrician in determining the greatest abdominal dimension of the fetus and placental thickness, thereby assisting in the decision to perform a CS or allow a vaginal delivery.

The ultrasonic diagnosis of fetal ascites and generalized edema is usually straightforward. Some illustrative cases are shown in Figures 21 to 24. As Holzgreve et al.[20] pointed out, the complete antenatal and postnatal work-up may lead to a precise diagnosis in as many as 85% of infants with nonimmune hydrops fetalis. The most common etiologies are cardiac anomalies (20%), chromosome abnormalities (16%), recognizable syndromes (11%), and twin-to-twin transfusion syndrome (10%).

Because of the wide variety of etiologic factors that can be associated with nonimmune hydrops fetalis, the diagnostic steps should include complete blood count and indexes on both parents (to rule out hematologic disorders), hemoglobin electrophoresis (to rule out β-thalassemia), blood chemistry (to rule out the possibility of fetal red cell enzyme deficiency, i.e., glucose-6-phosphatase deficiency), Kleihauer-Betke stain (to rule out fetomaternal hemorrhage), serology for syphilis, toxoplasmosis, and cytomegalovirus (to rule out fetal infection), and oral glucose screen (to rule out maternal diabetes mellitus). A detailed ultrasound examination of the fetal anatomy is indicated to rule out associated malformations in an attempt to establish prognosis. The progression of nonimmune hydrops fetalis should be monitored by frequent ultrasound examinations. Amniocentesis for amniotic fluid bilirubin measurement has also been suggested.[21] Fetal echocardiography is an essential part of the antenatal work-up because the incidence of congenital heart defects is approximately 20%.

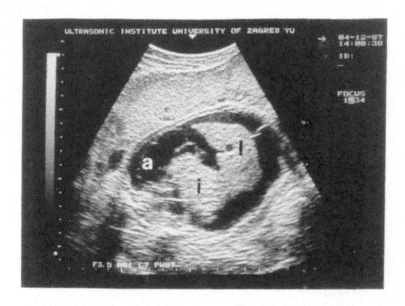

FIGURE 21. Typical ultrasonic appearance of the fetal ascites (a = ascites, l = liver, i = intestinal loops).

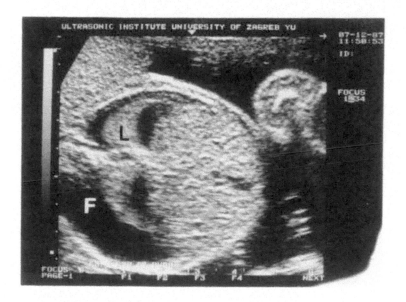

FIGURE 22. A case of bilateral pleural effusion (L = lung, F = fluid).

Amniocentesis for fetal karyotyping and amniotic fluid viral cultures are also indicated. The amniotic fluid sample may also be tested for specific metabolic disorders. Fetal blood can be obtained by percutaneous umbilical blood sampling.

In cases of nonimmune hydrops fetalis, the reported perinatal mortality rates range between 50[22] and 98%.[23] The highest mortality rate involves cases with other associated fetal abnormalities.

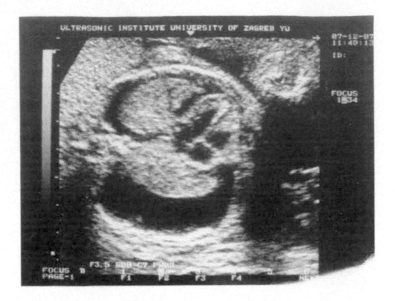

FIGURE 23.   Pericardial and pleural effusions in a case of nonimmune fetal hydrops.

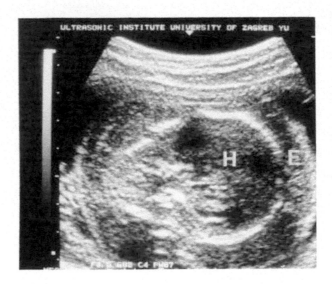

FIGURE 24.   Severe fetal hydrops. Thick edema is seen surrounding the fetal head (E = edema, H = head).

The management of the fetus with nonimmune hydrops fetalis should be dictated by the antenatal findings. If the antenatal findings are not sufficient to justify a poor prognosis, then the fetus should be managed aggressively. This management should include weekly sonograms to monitor progression of the hydropic changes and frequent biophysical monitoring (nonstress test/fetal biophysical profile). Fetal paracentesis to decompress the fetal abdomen and allow for a vaginal delivery has been performed.[24] In our department, we have done several paracentesis, but we would not recommend its routine use. Because hydropic fetuses are very vulnerable to the stress of labor and delivery, an elective preterm delivery, after documenting lung maturity, and liberal use of CS may be appropriate to improve the outcome of this group of infants.[19]

CONCLUSION

GI abnormalities consist of one fourth of major congenital abnormalities. Alimentary tract and the walls of the abdominal cavity are common sites of congenital abnormalities. Pyloric stenosis, different types of intestinal or esophageal atresias, and defects in abdominal wall or diaphragm have occurrence risks of 1 in 250 to 1 in 5000 live births.[25,26] In addition, there exist some more rare malformations inside the peritoneal cavity, such as biliary tract malformations and mesenteric cysts. Ultrasound is the best method for antenatal diagnosing of these abnormalities.[1,2,27]

The main problem in these pregnancies is the great risk of severe associated abnormalities. In particular, this is true with omphalocele, but also other types of GI malformations can be accompanied by severe malformations in other organs. For rational perinatal approach of a pregnancy with some fetal GI abnormality, fetal karyotyping is most important. For evaluation of the recurrence risk in these cases, the karyotype is also very valuable, because isolated GI abnormalities are mainly sporadic, but those cases with chromosomal aberrations have a real recurrence risk. Another very important point is a detailed echocardiographic examination of the fetus, so that in cases with fatal-associated abnormalities, unnecessary obstetric procedures, for example, can be avoided. Cases with isolated GI abnormalities or cases with nonfatal-associated malformations need hospital care for prevention of premature birth. Sufficient postnatal resources for intensive treatment of the newborn are necessary. Immediate postnatal surgical treatment reduces pulmonary complications in esophageal atresia,[28] and in abdominal wall defects, the risk of frank peritonitis increases after a delay of 6 to 8 h.[29] These facts stress the importance of prearranged and timed delivery for these cases.

Most cases of fetal GI anomalies can be safely delivered vaginally as near term as possible. Elective CS was recommended after the first reports concerning the antenatal diagnosis of omphalocele and gastroschisis, but nowadays, the need of individual consideration for assessment of the method of the delivery in these cases is stressed.[27] Kirk and Wah[13] could not find any benefit of CS in these abnormalities in their large series, even if the liver was extracorporeal. Our policy is to make, in cases with isolated abdominal wall defects, elective CS after establishment of pulmonary maturity, if liver or some other solid organ is located extracorporeally. Harrison et al.[10] refer to the need of preterm delivery for cases of ruptured omphalocele and gastroschisis due to the risk of chemical progressive peritonitis caused by harmful effects of amniotic fluid on uncovered intestine. Also, bowel ischemia and gangrene after perforation in cases with meconium ileus may experience prognostical use from preterm delivery and early surgical correction after the delivery. No wide clinical experience about these conditions exists yet, however, and the value of early delivery is still questionable.[2]

REFERENCES

1. **Kurjak, A., Latin, V., and D'Addario, V.,** Abnormalities of the fetus, placenta and umbilical cord, in *Progress in Medical Ultrasound.* Vol. 3, Kurjak, A., Ed., Excerpta Medica, Amsterdam, 1982, 87.
2. **Kirkinen, P. and Joupilla, P.,** The fetus with gastrointestinal abnormalities, in *The Fetus as a Patient,* Kurjak, A., Ed., Elsevier, Amsterdam, 1985, 181.
3. **Bovicelli, L., Rizzo, N., Orsini, L. F., et al.,** Prenatal diagnosis and management of fetal gastrointestinal abnormalities, *Semin. Perinatol.,* 7, 109, 1983.
4. **Weinberg, A. G., Milunsky, A., and Harrod, M. J.,** Elevated amniotic fluid alpha-fetoprotein and duodenal atresia, *Lancet,* ii, 496, 1975.
5. **Girvan, D. P. and Stephens, C. A.,** Congenital intrinsic duodenal obstruction: a twenty year review of its surgical management and consequence, *J. Pediatr. Surg.,* 9, 833, 1974.
6. **Dunne, M. G. and Johnson, M. L.,** The ultrasonic demonstration of fetal abnormalities in utero, *J. Reprod. Med.,* 23, 195, 1979.
7. **Eyheremendy, E. and Pfister, M.,** Antenatal real-time diagnosis of esophageal atresias, *J. Clin. Ultrasound,* 11, 395, 1983.
8. **Nakayama, D. K.,** Management of the fetus with an abdominal wall defect, in *The Unborn Patient, Prenatal Diagnosis and Treatment,* Harrison, M. R., Golbus, M. S., and Filly, R. A., Grune & Stratton, New York, 1984, 217 and 234.
9. **Seashore, J. H.,** Congenital abdominal wall defects, *Clin. Perinatol.,* 5, 61, 1978.
10. **Harrison, M. R., Golbus, M. S., and Filly, F. A.,** The management of the fetus with a correctable congenital defect, *JAMA,* 246, 744, 1981.
11. **Didolkar, S. M., Hall, J., Phelan, J., et al.,** The prenatal diagnosis and management of a hapatoomphalocele, *Am. J. Obstet. Gynecol.,* 141, 221, 1981.
12. **Schmidt, W., Gabelmann, J., Garoff, L., and Kubli, F.,** Ultrasonographische Diagnose einer Omphalozele im ersten Schwangerschaftsdrittel, *Geburtshilfe Frauenheilkd.,* 41, 562, 1981.
13. **Kirk, E. P. and Wah, R. M.,** Obstetric management of the fetus with omphalocele or gastroschisis. A review and report of one hundred twelve cases, *Am. J. Obstet. Gynecol.,* 146, 512, 1983.
14. **Sabbagha, R. E. and Shkolnik, A.,** Ultrasound diagnosis of fetal abnormalities, *Semin. Perinatol.,* 4, 213, 1980.
15. **Colombani, P. M. and Cunningham, M. D.,** Perinatal aspects of omphalocele and gastroschisis, *Am. J. Dis. Child.,* 131, 1386, 1977.
16. **Lenke, R. R. and Hatch, E. I.,** Fetal gastroschisis: a preliminary report advocating the use of cesarean section, *Obstet. Gynecol.,* 67, 395, 1986.
17. **Harrison, M. R., Golbus, M. S., and Filly, R. A., Eds.,** Congenital diaphragmatic hernia, in *The Unborn Patient, Prenatal Diagnosis and Treatment,* Grune & Stratton, New York, 1984, 237.
18. **Fleisher, A. C., Killam, A. P., Boehm, F. H., et al.,** Hydrops fetalis: sonographic evaluation and clinical implications, *Radiology,* 141, 163, 1981.
19. **Vintzileos, A. M., Campbell, A. W., Nochimson, D. J., and Weinbaum, A. J.,** Antenatal evaluation and management of ultrasonically detected fetal anomalies, *Obstet. Gynecol.,* 69, 640, 1987.
20. **Holzgreve, W., Holzgreve, B., and Curry, C. J. R.,** Nonimmune hydrops fetalis: diagnosis and management, *Semin. Perinatol.,* 9, 52, 1985.
21. **Maidman, J. E., Yeager, C., Anderson, V., et al.,** Prenatal diagnosis and management of nonimmunologic hydrops fetalis, *Obstet. Gynecol.,* 56, 571, 1980.
22. **Etches, P. C. and Lemons, J. A.,** Nonimmune hydrops fetalis: report of 22 cases including three siblings, *Pediatrics,* 64, 326, 1979.
23. **Hutchinson, A. A., Drew, J. H., Yu, V. Y. H., et al.,** Nonimmunologic hydrops fetalis: a review of 61 cases, *Obstet. Gynecol.,* 59, 347, 1982.
24. **de Crespigny, L. C., Robinson, H. P., and McBain, J. C.,** Fetal abdominal paracentesis in the management of gross fetal ascites, *Aust. N.Z. J. Obstet. Gynaecol.,* 20, 228, 1980.
25. **Bergma, D.,** *Birth Defects Compendium,* 2nd ed., MacMillan, New York, 1979.
26. **Jassani, M. M., Gauderer, M., Fanarott, A., et al.,** A perinatal approach to the diagnosis and management of gastrointestinal malformations, *Obstet. Gynecol.,* 59, 33, 1982.
27. **Campbell, S. and Pearce, M.,** The prenatal diagnosis of fetal structural anomalies by ultrasound, *Clin. Obstet. Gynecol.,* 10, 457, 1983.
28. **Louchimo, I. and Lindahl, H.,** Esophageal atresia: primary results of 500 consecutively treated patients, *J. Pediatr. Surg.,* 18, 217, 1983.
29. **Seashore, J.,** Congenital abdominal wall defects, *Clin. Perinatol,* 5, 61, 1978.

Chapter 8.6

GENITO-URINARY TRACT ANOMALIES

Asim Kurjak

INTRODUCTION

The ultrasonic diagnosis and assessment of urinary tract anomalies are currently of great interest, as indicated by the significantly increased number of reviews and detailed papers.[1-25] There are several reasons for this. First, with the gray scale and real-time systems, it is now easy to identify the fetal kidneys and bladder by their typical outlines. The normal fetal renal function is also well established, and this helps in the better understanding and assessment of some fetal urinary tract anomalies.[16,26-28] Furthermore, most of the fetal urinary tract anomalies are accompanied by fluid-filled masses in the fetal abdomen which are particularly easy to detect by ultrasound. Since fetal urine is a major source of amniotic fluid in late pregnancy, decreased excretion will result in oligohydramnios, a common obstetric indication for sonography. On the other hand, the possibility of prenatally diagnosing surgically correctable urinary obstructions has improved considerably in the last few years. Obstructive uropathy causing dilatation of the bladder and ureters, hydronephrosis, and oligohydramnios is an excellent example of a simple lesion that has a very severe effect on the developing fetus and may be prevented by correction before birth.[13] Successful and accurate antenatal diagnosis of urinary tract malformations could alter management. Some cannot be corrected, and most of the correctable lesions are best treated after normal term delivery. A few are amenable to treatment before term. Sonographic examination may aid conditions in classifying these patients as well as documenting the nature of certain urinary tract anomalies incompatible with life, precluding the need for continuation of pregnancy. Therefore, antenatal diagnosis of these disorders has practical clinical importance[2,3,8,15,29-34] (Table 1).

NORMAL ANATOMY AND PHYSIOLOGY

The fetal kidneys can be ultrasonically visualized as early as the 9th to 10th week,[25] but routine visualization is possible after 16 weeks. They can be recognized by their typical shape and position and by the presence of a central echo from the intrarenal part of the collecting system. In transverse section, they appear as two circular structures on either side of the spine; in longitudinal section, they show their typical bean-shaped appearance. The kidneys are generally hypoechoic, except for the capsule and the collecting system which are strongly echogenic. Sometimes a minimal dilatation of the renal pelvis can be observed; this should be considered a normal finding. The kidneys of fetuses between 15 and 17 weeks are seen less than 50% of the time. In fetuses between 17 and 22 weeks of age, one or both kidneys are seen in 90% of cases.[21]

The fetal adrenals can be recognized at the end of the first trimester; they appear as relatively hypoechoic ovoid or triangular structures located above the upper renal pole.[25] They are up to half the size of the normal kidney, and this may prove confusing.

The antero-posterior, transverse, and longitudinal diameters of the fetal kidneys increase linearly throughout pregnancy. The renal circumference in transverse section has been reported as 2.8 cm at 16 weeks and 8.4 cm at term, and the ratio of renal circumference to

TABLE 1
Urinary Tract Anomalies Detectable by
Ultrasound *in Utero*

Potter's Syndrome
  Bilateral renal agenesis
  Unilateral renal agenesis associated with contralat-
    eral dysplasia
  Rare syndromes (Meckel, Vater association, etc.)
Polycystic kidneys (Potter I)
Multicystic kidneys (Potter II)
Nonobstructive transient hydronephrosis
Obstructive hydronephrosis
  High (supravesical) hydronephrosis
  Low (infravesical) hydronephrosis
    Posterior urethral valve syndrome (Potter IV)

the abdominal circumference is remarkably constant in the second and third trimesters.[21,25,35-39] Identification of the normal kidneys is of great importance in evaluating a fetus, because the genito-urinary tract is the site of many developmental abnormalities. The primary function of the fetal kidney is to maintain water and electrolyte homeostasis. The kidney carries out this function by selectively excreting or retaining water and solutes as the condition dictates. In the fetus, body water and electrolyte balance are maintained largely by the placenta, so that renal maturation *in utero* is geared primarily to prepare the kidney for its extrauterine role. As a result, the functional capabilities of the fetal kidney are much greater than its normal functional requirements. Indeed, fetuses without functioning kidneys often manifest no water and electrolyte abnormalities. The major responsibility for water and electrolyte homeostasis is suddenly thrust upon the perinatal kidney as soon as the infant is born. However, renal maturation does not suddenly accelerate after the infant is born. The known facts on fetal urine may be summarized as follows:

1.   The urine is usually acid and hypotonic with a very low osmolar concentration (average 137 mosm/l).
2.   It usually contains slightly more Na than Cl.
3.   It contains little K and only the merest traces of inorganic P.

It follows that sodium chloride in excess of requirement must continually be entering the fetus and that free water must also in some way be made available. The character of the urine can be explained if the kidney before birth is outside the control of the antidiuretic hormone, the parathyroid hormone, and possibly the suprarenal hormone. The relatively high rate of urine production *in utero* is now generally recognized and has been confirmed using chronically catheterized preparations in the sheep and in the human fetus using the noninvasive ultrasonic technique.[16,16,28]

Assessment of renal size is important because certain abnormalities, such as infantile polycystic kidney disease, may present with nephromegaly. The ureters are usually not visualizable; however, a mild transitory dilatation can occasionally be seen in normal fetuses. Visualization of the fetal bladder is an important step in documenting the presence of normal renal functioning. The bladder is a dynamic structure, with constant filling and emptying in the normal fetus.

Measurements of the hourly fetal urinary production rate can be determined by noting the changes in the volume of the fetal bladder per hour. These vary from 2.2 ml/h at 22 weeks to 26.3 ml/h at term. Its volume does not normally exceed 10 ml at 30 weeks and 50 ml at term.[16] When higher values are detected, a repeat examination should be performed at 20-min intervals to demonstrate micturition, which generally occurs at intervals of approximately 40 min. Such measurements may be helpful in evaluating fetal welfare in normal and complicated pregnancies, particularly in intrauterine growth retardation (IUGR). Furthermore, they can be of help in the prenatal assessment of renal function in fetuses predisposed to renal disease.

Indentification of the fetal sex can be accomplished routinely in the second trimester if the fetus is in an appropriate position. The scrotum and the penis are easily recognizable floating in the amniotic fluid. Sometimes a mild hydrocele is detectable; in such a case, the testes are easily recognized in the tunica vaginalis. The female genitalia are slightly more difficult to visualize ultrasonically (see Chapter 7) can of the fetal perineal area from the 23rd.

GENITO-URINARY ABNORMALITIES

BILATERAL RENAL AGENESIS (BRA)

The estimated frequency of this syndrome varies from 0.1 to 0.3 per 1000 births. Most series show a marked male-to-female preponderance of 2.5 to 1.[25] About 40% of these infants are stillborn, but those born alive die soon after severe respiratory distress secondary to the pulmonary hypoplasia. If the diagnosis of BRA is made early, therapeutic abortion should be considered; if the diagnosis is made later, at least the management of the associated complications (including breech presentation and intrapartum fetal distress) could be facilitated, and the inevitably futile attempts at resuscitation might be avoided.

Potter described in her series of 50 cases the finding at autopsy that the adrenal glands, although of normal weight, did not conform to the usual shape. Instead, the adrenals took the form of an oval disc lying against the posterior abdominal wall, presumably due to the absence of a compressive effect by the normal kidney.[40]

In both fetus and infant, the adrenals may sometimes be confused with kidneys in a case of bilateral renal agenesis. Ultrasound can be useful here.

In the antenatal diagnosis of BRA, there is usually no problem in distinguishing a bladder which has just voided its total content from an absent or nonfunctioning bladder, a constant finding in BRA. Further evidence will be the absence of fetal kidneys and extreme oligohydramnios. However, severe oligohydramnios not only hampers imaging because of the absence of the fluid window, but also often results in an unusual lie of the fetus and significantly restricts movements. Therefore, the quality of the echograms is commonly substandard, so that it is seldom possible to confidently declare the kidneys absent.

More detailed functional and anatomic information can be obtained by aspiration of fetal urine under sonographic guidance. Urine production might be then measured directly, urine composition determined, and a fetal cystogram or pyelogram obtained.

In addition to oligohydramnios, the only other constant finding in all our cases of renal agenesis was the absence of a demonstrable urinary bladder. This was true despite repeated sequential ultrasound examinations and after the administration of a diuretic to the mother. Autopsy of patients with BRA usually reveals a hypoplastic and contracted bladder.

The absence of a fetal bladder would appear, therefore, to be a more reliable sign that the imaging of fetal kidneys in the diagnosis of BRA (Table 2).

It should be generally stated that between 20 and 24 weeks, the fetal bladder should always be observed to fill, and failure to see this over a period of 2 h following intravenous furosemide administration to the patient should allow a diagnosis to be made. However,

TABLE 2
Diagnosis of Bilateral
Renal Agenesis

Ultrasound findings:
  Kidneys: not visualized
  Bladder: not visualized
  Amniotic fluid: reduced
Outcome:
  Poor
Management:
  Termination of pregnancy

certain data do not support this view, claiming that a negative furosemide test cannot be used to diagnose renal agenesis.[25] Conversely, a normal urinary bladder would exclude this diagnosis.

The identification of reniform structures in the retroperitoneum does not exclude the diagnosis of BRA. If the unusual appearance of the adrenal glands in cases of BRA is considered, ultrasound of the fetal abdomen, particularly the fetal pelvis, may enable the correct diagnosis to be made.

Potter's syndrome is the eponym applied to the tetrad of nonfunctioning kidneys, oligohydramnios, and typical facies (low-set ears, prominent epicanthic folds, and hypertelorism) (Figure 1). Severe oligohydramnios is thought to be responsible for the sequela, since the infants with IUGR and premature rupture of membranes sometimes show a similar phenotype. Potter's syndrome should not be confused with BRA, which is the most common, but not unique cause of this fentype. Potter's syndrome has been proven to be present in polycystic kidney disease, Meckel syndrome, cerebro-oculo-facio skeletal syndrome, cryptophthalamus syndrome, VATER association, etc.[41]

INFANTILE POLYCYSTIC KIDNEY DISEASE

Infantile polycystic kidney disease (Potter type I) is due to dilatation and hyperplasia of collecting tubules. It is invariably bilateral and characterized by symmetric massive enlargement with maintenance of normal reniform contours (Figure 2A to F). Medullary ductal cysts in radial distribution, but no dysplastic elements, replace normal renal tissue. Although renal function is variable, it is generally incompatible with life beyond the neonatal period. Because most of the cysts, which lead to the polycystic kidney a "spongy" appearance, are difficult to discern with the naked eye, they are below the limits of resolution of sonography. The kidneys appear as very large, bilateral, reniform solid masses in the fetal flanks (Table 3).

The condition is inherited as an autosomal recessive disease and has a very high recurrence rate of up to 25%. The ultrasonic appearance is that of large and homogeneously solid kidneys with an increased ratio of kidney circumference to abdominal circumference (AC). Unfortunately, this diagnosis is often not made until the generalized abdominal distention draws attention to it. Furthermore, in the abortable period of gestation, the echogenicity of the kidneys may closely resemble that of the fetal liver and bowel. The bladder, when seen, is usually small, and there is associated oligohydramnios. There are several documented cases of prenatal recognition of adult polycystic kidney disease (Potter type III).[42,43]

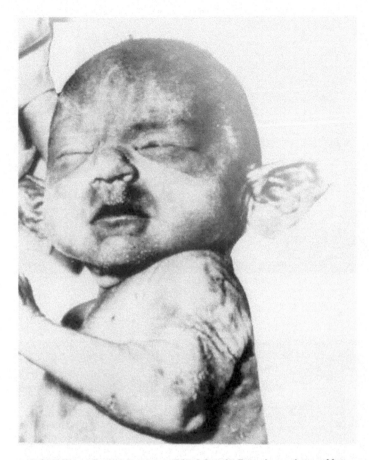

FIGURE 1. Typical fenotype of fetal face in Potter's syndrome. Note the hypertelorism, epicanthic folds, and low-set, big ears.

MULTICYSTIC KIDNEY DISEASE

Multicystic kidneys (Potter type II) are the most common of all neonatal abdominal masses. The condition represents 20% of all abdominal masses. As the unilateral lesion is no threat to life in the immediate neonatal period, accurate diagnosis by noninvasive means distinguishes it from other neonatal abdominal masses. The affected kidney is poorly organized, enlarged, cystic, and nonfunctional.

The diagnosis of a multicystic kidney is suggested by the presence of multiple cysts (Figure 3). The cysts are commonly of the order of 1 to 2 cm in diameter, but they can be up to 6 cm large. Generally, no such cysts will be seen in the opposite flank. In the rare case when multicystic kidneys are bilateral (the estimated incidence is 1 in 10,000[44]) and involve both kidneys completely, it is incompatible with a life expectancy greater than a few weeks. On the contrary, the unilateral condition is compatible with a normal life span.

The abnormality arises from the inability of the ureteral buds to divide properly and of the ampullae to induce differentiation of the nephrons.

Multicystic kidney disease may mimic hydronephrosis, but multiple cysts separated by distinct septa will be noted within the kidney. By contrasting fetal hydronephrosis, the entire kidney will be dilated by a single, large anechoic space, and the cyst will often have the

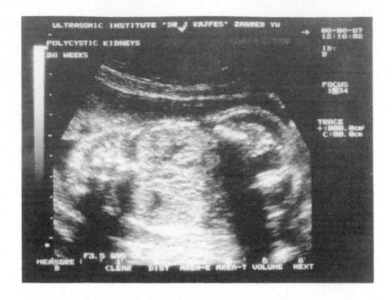

A

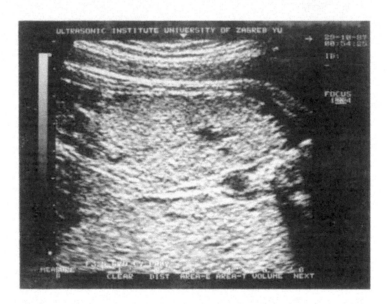

B

FIGURE 2.   (A) Longitudinal scan of fetal abdomen with typical polycystic kidneys. (B) Zoomed image of polycystic kidneys detected at 24 weeks gestation. Note the symmetrical enlargement and "solid" appearance of kidney tissue. (C) Autopsy finding in fetus with *in utero*-diagnosed polycystic kidneys. (D) Symmetrically enlarged "spongy" polycystic kidneys. (E) Longitudinal section of the same kidneys. (F) Whole kidney consists of numerous cysts covered with thin connective tissue.

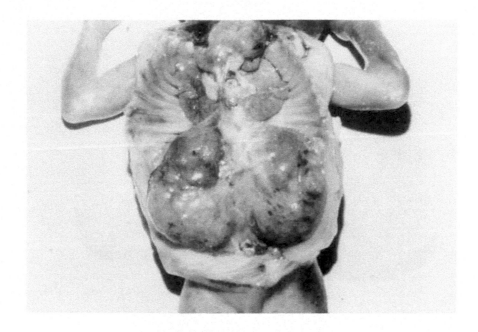

FIGURE 2C.

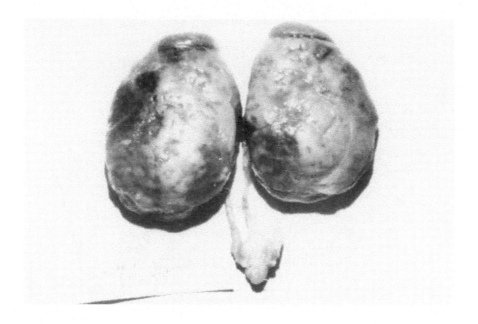

FIGURE 2D.

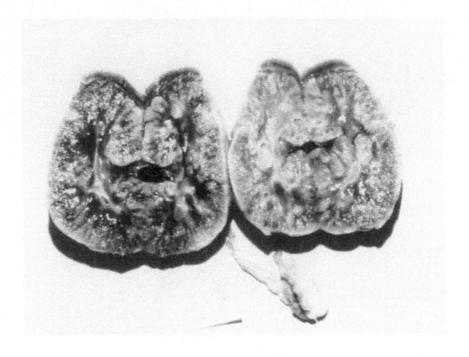

FIGURE 2E.

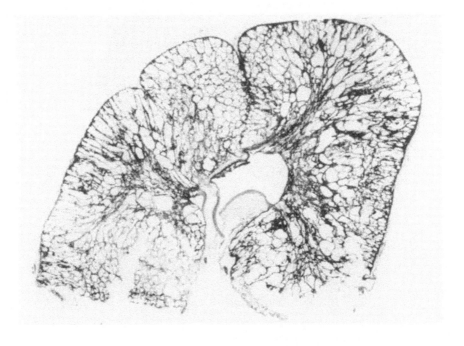

FIGURE 2F.

TABLE 3
Diagnosis of Polycystic
Kidneys

Ultrasound findings:
  Kidneys: symmetrically enlarged
  Bladder: usually small
  Amniotic fluid: usually reduced
Outcome:
  Poor
Management:
  Termination of pregnancy

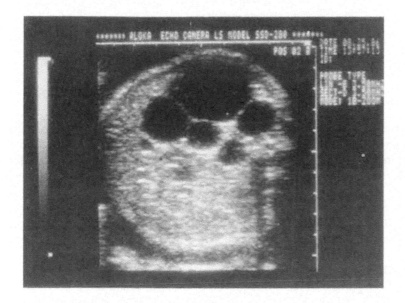

FIGURE 3.   Unilateral multicystic kidney with numerous noncommunicating cysts of variable size.

shape of a large "C". In addition, fetal hydronephrosis is more often accompanied by hydro-ureter than multicystic kidney disease, and the bladder may also be distended if outlet obstruction, anatomic or functional, is the cause. In hydronephrosis, especially when not massive, one sees sonographically smaller cysts (representing calyces) which radiate from a larger central cyst (the pelvis). Greater or lesser amounts of renal parenchyma border the lateral margins of the cysts (Table 4).

The differential diagnosis includes duodenal atresia, which presents the characteristic "double bubble" sign. It is further distinguished by the different locations of the sonolucent areas in relation to the fetal spine and by the presence of polyhydramnios, whereas renal malformations are characteristically associated with oligohydramnios.

Bilateral multicystic kidney would suggest bilateral hydronephrosis due to uretheral obstruction. Polycystic renal disease (infantile type) is always bilateral; the kidneys will be enlarged, but they have a solid appearance, being studded with innumerable small cysts,

TABLE 4
Diagnosis of Multicystic Kidneys

Unilateral
  Ultrasound findings:
    Kidney: multiple noncommunicating cysts
    Bladder: normal
    Amniotic fluid: normal
  Outcome:
    Good
  Management:
    Term delivery
Bilateral
  Ultrasound findings:
    Kidneys: multiple noncommunicating cysts
    Bladder: not visualized
    Amniotic fluid: reduced
  Outcome:
    Poor
  Management:
    Termination of pregnancy

rather than the echo-free areas typical of large cysts. The antenatal diagnosis of fetal multicystic kidney disease may be of great value to the pediatrician as well as to the obstetrician. Cases of extreme dilation of the collecting system may interfere with normal modes of delivery. More subtle degrees of dilatation may not be detected on physical examination of the newborn, and, therefore, sonography identifies these patients who are at risk for developing hypertension and infection.

Finally, 10 to 20% of patients with multicystic kidneys will have other associated urinary tract anomalies, most frequently hydronephrosis of the contralateral site.

OBSTRUCTIVE UROPATHIES

Fetal hydronephrosis is the consequence of the obstruction at the level of the urethra, the vesico-ureteric orifice, the uretero-pelvic junction, or associated with vesico-ureteric reflux (Figures 4 and 5).

The uretero-pelvic junction is the most common site of congenital urinary obstruction above the level of the bladder. The resulting hydronephrosis may be unilateral or bilateral. The level of obstruction may also be at the ureterovesicle junction, in which case there is hydronephrosis as well as dilated ureters. The distinction between the two is very difficult.

Congenital uretero-pelvic junction obstruction is a well-known clinical entity. The diagnosis is often made in late childhood when the patient presents with renal failure or a palpable abdominal mass. Known causes are extrapelvic adhesions, an abnormally situated junction between the renal pelvis and the ureter, aberrant vessels to the lower pole of the kidney, faults of the mucosa in the upper ureter, and intrinsic and functional abnormalities of the uretero-pelvic junction itself.

The ultrasonic finding of a normal-sized fetal urinary bladder associated with hydronephrosis and hydro-ureter is most commonly due to the vesico-ureteric reflux. However, before final diagnosis is made, the possibility of ureterocele with double ureter and duplex collecting system should be excluded (Tables 5 and 6).

Sometimes, hydronephrosis may produce large cystic lesions where little of the original renal structure can be identified. In these instances, differentiation from multicystic kidney may be impossible. The finding of dilated minor calyces may suggest multicystic disease,

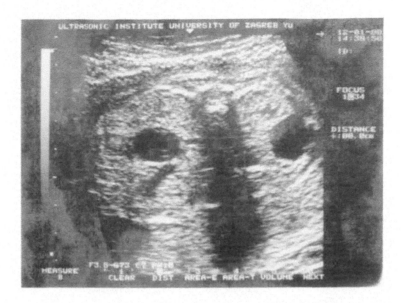

FIGURE 4.   Bilateral obstructive uropathy with mild dilation of both renal pelves.

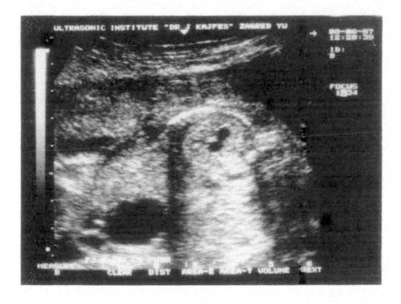

FIGURE 5.   Asymmetrical dilatation in a case of high obstructive uropathy due to utero-pelvic junction obstruction.

but the prominent and dilated renal pelvis is the key in such cases. There may also be obstruction of the urethra, in the posterior urethral valves, for example. Posterior urethral valves (Potter type IV) affects male fetuses almost exclusively (Figure 6). Here, one finds megacystis with secondary hydro-urethra and hydronephrosis. The anomaly is potentially treatable *in utero* and, therefore, discussed in detail in Chapter 3, Volume II.

TABLE 5
Diagnosis of High Obstructive Uropathy

Unilateral
    Ultrasound findings:
       Kidneys: communicating cysts
       Bladder: normal
       Amniotic fluid: normal
    Outcome:
      Good
    Management:
      Term delivery
Bilateral
    Ultrasound findings:
       Kidneys: communicating cysts
       Bladder: normal or small
       Amniotic fluid: normal or reduced
    Outcome:
      Variable
    Management:
      Dependent on gestational age and estimated renal function
      Term delivery
      Preterm delivery
      Correction *in utero*
      Termination of pregnancy

TABLE 6
Diagnosis of Low Obstructive Uropathy

Ultrasound findings:
    Kidneys: communicating cysts
    Bladder: enlarged
    Amniotic fluid: normal or reduced
Outcome:
    Variable
Management:
    Dependent on gestational age and estimated renal function
    Term delivery
    Preterm delivery
    Correction *in utero*
    Termination of pregnancy

If rupture of the renal collecting system occurs antenatally, the ultrasound appearance is that of fetal urinary ascites. When total urinary tract obstruction occurs, oligohydramnios usually follows, the fetus may acquire the nonrenal features of Potter's syndrome, altered *falcius* hand and foot development, fetal growth deficiency, and pulmonary hypoplasia.

There is no doubt that ultrasound is quite sensitive in diagnosing lesions that result in hydronephrosis in the fetus. Ultrasound cannot precisely delineate the exact cause of the hydronephrosis as to whether it is secondary to obstruction, reflux, or some other defect. Further confirmationary conventional studies are necessary in the postnatal period.

PRUNE-BELLY SYNDROME

The congenital triad of abdominal muscle deficiency, severe urinary tract abnormality, and cryptorchidism forms a rare but well-defined clinical condition popularly known as the

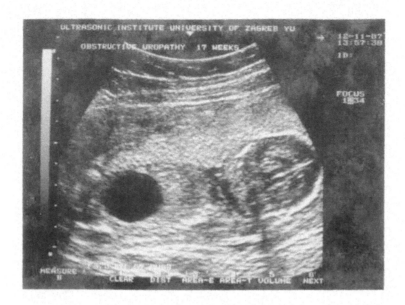

FIGURE 6. Low obstructive uropathy detected at 17 weeks gestation. Note the significantly reduced amount of amniotic fluid. The prognosis was estimated to be poor, and option of termination of pregnancy was offered to the parents.

"prune belly syndrome" (PBS) (Figures 7A and B). The term "prune belly" is descriptive of the characteristic wizened, dried plum appearance in the newborn and young infant. PBS is a rare congenital disorder, occurring in 1 in 35,000 to 50,000 live births. The first case of a newborn with a wrinkled abdomen devoid of musculature was reported by Frely in 1839. In 1895, Parker noted the association of abdominal musculature deficiency, urinary tract abnormalities (megaureter, cystic renal dysplasia, urethra obstruction, and megalocystis occurring in various combinations), and cryptohidism. In 1910, Osler reported such a case referring to the triad as the "Prune-Belly Syndrome". The triad is also known as the Eagle-Barrett-Syndrome and the Orbinski-Frely-Syndrome. Over 200 cases have been documented in the literature.[16] Survival with PBS depends on the degree of renal dysplasia and destruction as well as the significance of associated anomalies. Of these neonates, 20% are stillborn or die within 1 month and 50% die within 2 years, although one male patient lived to the age of 17 years.[16] There are several papers describing successful ultrasound diagnosis of this serious abnormality.[22,25,45-49]

ABNORMALITIES OF THE FETAL GENITALIA

Trying to determine the sex of an unborn child has always been of great interest to the parents. However, ultrasonic determination of fetal sex has been one of the less important functions of obstetric ultrasound. With the recent improvements in ultrasound technology it has become possible to differentiate, with a reasonable degree of success, between the male and the female fetus. Furthermore, some abnormalities in both male and female genitalia are ultrasonically detectable. During the 3rd month of gestation, the fetal testes begin to descend from their intra-abdominal position toward the scrotal pouch. In the seventh month, or later, this process is complete and the testes may be viewed within the scrotal sac. Between 36 and 40 weeks of gestation, fluid is occasionally ultrasonically detectable within the scrotum. In the past, this was considered as diagnostic of either a unilateral or a bilateral

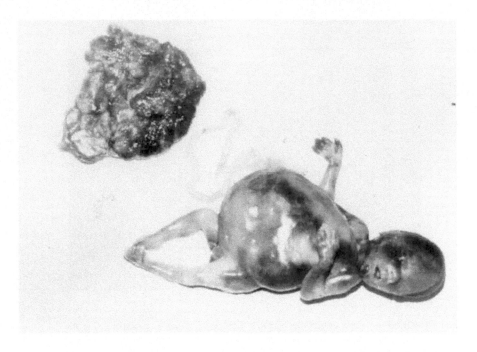

A

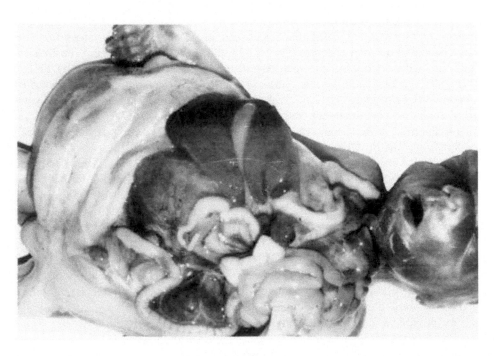

B

FIGURE 7. (A) Fetus with typical "prune-belly" syndrome. Note significantly distended abdomen with aplasia of anterior abdominal wall. (B) The marked dilation of complete urinary system was the reason for "prune-belly" appearance.

hydrocele. While this assumption is correct, it is not clinically significant in as much as most of the fetal hydrocele will be resorbed spontaneously. Medically, sex determination in the second trimester is of critical importance in patients whose fetuses are at risk for various severe X-linked disorders, and the possibility of obtaining this information quickly and without causing trauma can be of great benefit. Prenatal diagnosis is now available for many of these conditions including hemophilia, chronic granulomatose disease, and other diseases. Rapid sex determination by ultrasound can identify the male fetus, who will then require further study without delay. In addition, visualization of the fetal genital area can be useful in the diagnosis of pseudomosaicism or true mosaicism, when amniotic karyotyping shows both an XY-line and an XO-line. Ultrasound can also provide evidence of testicular function by demonstrating a masculine phenotype in fetuses at risk for testicular feminization syndrome.

Ultrasound sex determination may also be useful in resolving some of the more difficult renal tract anomalies such as low obstructive uropathy, which occurs exclusively in male fetuses. However, it should be stressed that this technique has no place as yet in the determination of fetal sex for patients at risk of producing an infant with a sex-linked disorder who have requested diagnosis and therapeutic abortion should the fetus be male.

FETAL OVARIAN CYSTS

The occurrence of fetal ovarian cysts is rare. The number of clinically verified cases published in the literature was 65 as of 1974,[50] and only a few of these were bilateral. This low frequency can be explained partly by the fact that only large tumors or tumors causing complications have been clinically diagnosed. The early diagnosis of cystic intra-abdominal masses in the fetus was accidental before the introduction of ultrasonic screening examinations for the gravid population, and consequently there was no adequately documented basis for discussing their real frequency, differential diagnosis, follow-up, or therapy.

The most probable alternatives in the differential diagnosis of palpable abdominal tumors in neonates include hydronephrosis and a distended urinary bladder. Of such palpable abdominal tumors, 50% are of renal origin, although some authors are of the opinion that ovarian cysts are the most common palpable abdominal masses observed in the female neonate.[50] A possible explanation for the rareness of fetal and neonatal ovarian tumors has, until recently, been the lack of reliable diagnostic methods. A suspicion of cystic tumors in the fetus is rare in routine obstetrical ultrasonic work, despite the improved resolution capacities of modern ultrasonic equipment (Figure 8A and B). The vast majority of authors support conservative surgical management as the method of choice in treating palpable cystic ovarian masses. The incidence of malignant lesions in ovarian cystic tumors in neonates is very low compared with the corresponding incidence of 40% in adults; therefore, in therapeutic considerations, the danger of some mechanical complication rather than the risk of an ovarian neoplasm must be taken into account. Prenatal and postnatal observation using the improved diagnostic capacities of ultrasound may partly replace operative treatment schedules in the future, especially in the case of smaller cystic ovarian tumors.

CONCLUSION

Almost all fetal genito-urinary abnormalities are detectable by ultrasound. The ultrasonographer has an increasing responsibility in the further management of these fetuses. Every possible attempt should be made to detect the most serious of these cases during the abortable period prior to 20 weeks gestation. With regard to other malformations, a fundamental distinction should be made, first of all, between unilateral and bilateral uropathies. In fact, if one has to manage a unilateral pathology and is sure that the other kidney is

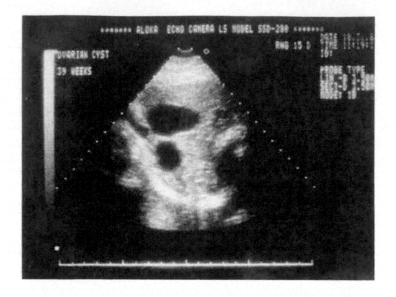

A

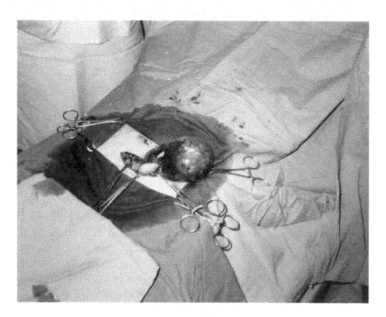

B

FIGURE 8.   (A) Ovarian cyst within fetal abdomen in the term pregnancy. No
intervention was indicated, and term vaginal delivery was allowed. (B) Surgical
removal of the cyst in the early neonatal period.

perfectly normal, there will be no indication for intervention either by treatment *in utero* or by early delivery. Weekly ultrasonographic checks will be sufficient. At birth, the newborn will undergo the usual examination and, of course, urography and cysto-uretography. These radiologic tests will be more profitable if performed 7 to 8 d after delivery to avoid errors due to the not yet normalized renal functions in the first few days. As soon as a certain diagnosis is made, surgical correction will be performed at the most appropriate time.

Finally, from our own experience, we would stress that a significant proportion of congenital uropathies were evident only after months or years had passed, when the affected organ is most often definitely compromised. This delayed postnatal diagnosis is due to the nonspecific symptomatology and often misleading symptoms, possibly referrable to the central nervous system or the gastroenteric apparatus.

Abnormalities of the genito-urinary tract are systematically underestimated as a possible cause of morbidity. The average delay between observation of the first symptoms and the discovery of the anomaly is as long as 16 months. Therefore, in 47.7% of patients with congenital uropathies, operation was performed within the first year of life, while only 18.6% of patients were operated on within the first month.[51] It should be mentioned that pyelonephritis due to congenital uropathies is responsible, according to various authors, for 21 to 54% of chronic renal failures in the pediatric age and 20% of those in adults.[51] The advantage of prenatal ultrasound diagnosis and proper perinatal management of these disorders is very obvious here.

REFERENCES

1. **Kullendorff, C. M., Larsson, L. T., and Joergenson, C.,** The advantage of antenatal diagnosis of intestinal and urinary tract malformations, *Br. J. Obstet. Gynecol.,* 91, 144, 1984.
2. **Fremond, B. and Babut, J. M.,** Obstructive uropathies diagnosed in utero — the postnatal outcome — a study of 43 cases, *Prog. Pediatr. Surg.,* 19, 160, 1986.
3. **Harrison, M. R., Golbus, M. S., and Filly, R. A.,** Fetal hidronephrosis: selection and surgical repair, *J. Pediatr. Surg.,* 22, 556, 1987.
4. **Suita, S., Ikeda, K., and Nakano, H.,** Antenatal diagnosis and pediatric surgery — an overview, in *The Fetus as the Patient, '87,* Maeda, K., Ed., Excerpta Medica, Amsterdam, 1987, 315.
5. **Kurjak, A., Latin, V., Mandruzzato, G., D'Addario, V., and Rajhvajn, B.,** Ultrasound diagnosis and perinatal management of fetal genito-urinary abnormalities, *J. Perinat. Med.,* 12, 291, 1984.
6. **Kurjak, A., Rajhvajn, B., Kogler, A., and Gogolja, D.,** Ultrasound diagnosis and fetal malformation of surgical interest, in *The Fetus as a Patient,* Kurjak, A., Ed., Excerpta Medica, Amsterdam, 1985, 243.
7. **Kurjak, A., Gogolja, D., and Kogler, A.,** Ultrasound diagnosis and perinatal management of surgically correctable fetal malformations, *Ultrasound Med. Biol.,* 10, 443, 1984.
8. **Berkowitz, R. L., Glickman, M. G., and Smith, G. J. W.,** Fetal urinary tract obstruction: what in the role of surgical intervention in utero?, *Am. J. Obstet. Gynecol.,* 144, 367, 1982.
9. **Collevecchio, G. and Angeloni, C.,** Pre-natal echographical diagnosis of fetal malformative renal pathology and treatment, *J. Fetal Med.,* 3, 108, 1983.
10. **Deter, R. L., Hadlock, F. P., and Gonzales, E. T.,** Prenatal detection of primary megaureter using dynamic image ultrasonography, *Obstet. Gynecol.,* 56, 759, 1983.
11. **Nicolini, U., Ferrazzi, E., Kustermann, A., Ravizza, M., Bellotti, M., Pardi, G., dell'Agnola, Tomaselli, G., Carmassi, L.,** Perinatal management of fetal hydronephrosis with normal bladder, *J. Perinat. Med.,* 15, 53, 1987.
12. **Dubbins, P. A., Kurtz, A. B., and Wapner, R. J.,** Renal agensis: spectrum of in utero findings, *J. Clin. Ultrasound,* 2, 189, 1982.
13. **Golbus, M. S., Harrison, M. R., and Filly, R. A.,** In utero treatment of urinary tract obstruction, *Am. J. Obstet. Gynecol.,* 142, 383, 1982.
14. **Hadlock, F. P., Deter, R. L., and Carpenter, R.,** Sonography of fetal urinary tract anomalies, *Am. J. Roentgenol.,* 137, 261, 1981.

15. **Harrison, M. R., Filly, R. A., and Parer, J. T.,** Management of the fetus with a urinary tract malformation, *JAMA,* 246, 635, 1981.
16. **Kurjak, A., Kirkinen, P., and Latin, V.,** Ultrasonic assessment of fetal kidney function in normal and complicated pregnancies, *Am. J. Obstet. Gynecol.,* 141, 473, 1981.
17. **Kurjak, A., Kirkinen, P., and Latin, V.,** Diagnosis and assessment of fetal malformations and abnormalities by ultrasound, *J. Perinat. Med.,* 8, 219, 1980.
18. **Kurjak, A. and Latin, V.,** Fetal and placental abnormalities, in *Progress in Medical Ultrasound,* Vol. 2, Kurjak, A., Ed., Excerpta Medica, Amsterdam, 1981, 77.
19. **Kurjak, A., Latin, V., and D'Addario, V.,** Abnormalities of the fetus, placenta and umbilical cord, in *Progress in Medical Ultrasound,* Vol. 3, Kurjak, A., Ed., Excerpta Medica, Amsterdam, 1982, 87.
20. **Kurjak, A.,** Fetal abnormalities in early and late pregnancy, in *Progress in Medical Ultrasound,* Vol. 1, Kurjak, A., Ed., Excerpta Medica, Amsterdam, 1980, 107.
21. **Lawson, T. L., Foley, W. D., and Berland, I. L.,** Ultrasonic evaluation of fetal kidneys, *Radiology,* 138, 153, 1981.
22. **Mariona, F. G., Bree, R. L., and Schwab, R. E.,** Prenatal diagnosis of fetal megabladder and urethral agensis, *Diagn. Gynecol. Obstet.,* 3, 259, 1981.
23. **Mendoza, S. A., Griswold, W. R., and Leopold, G. R.,** Intrauterine diagnosis of renal anomalies by ultrasonography, *Am. J. Dis. Child.,* 133, 1042, 1979.
24. **Sabbagha, R. E. and Scholnik, A.,** Ultrasound diagnosis of fetal abnormalities, *Semin. Perinatol.,* 4, 213, 1980.
25. **Romero, R., Pilu, G., Jeanty, P., Ghidini, A., and Hobbins, J. C.,** *Prenatal Diagnosis of Congenital Anomalies,* Appleton & Lange, Norwalk, CT, 1988, 255.
26. **Campbell, S., Wladimiroff, J. and Dewhurst, C.,** The antenatal measurement of fetal urine production, *J. Obstet. Gynaecol. Br. Commonw.,* 80, 680, 1973.
27. **Wladimiroff, J. W.,** Effect of frusemide on fetal urine production, *Br. J. Obstet. Gynecol.,* 82, 221, 1975.
28. **Wladimiroff, J. W. and Campbell, S.,** Fetal urine production in normal and complicated pregnancy, *Lancet,* i, 151, 1974.
29. **Colodny, A. H.,** Antenatal diagnosis and management of urinary tract abnormalities, *Pediatr. Clin. North Am.,* 34, 1365, 1987.
30. **Harrison, M. R.,** Fetal treatment, *N. Engl. J. Med.,* 307, 1651, 1982.
31. **Hately, W. and Nicholis, B.,** The ultrasonic diagnosis of bilateral hydronephrosis in twins during pregnancy, *Br. J. Radiol.,* 52, 989, 1979.
32. **Kurjak, A. and Degen, S.,** Legal problems and ultrasonically detected malformed fetuses, in *Ultrasound '82,* Lerski, R. A. and Morley, P., Eds., Pergamon Press, Oxford, 1983, 33.
33. **Matturi, M., Bruce, E., and Peters, R.,** Prenatal and postnatal sonographic demonstration of bilateral ureteropelvic junction obstruction, *Med. Ultrasound,* 4, 94, 1980.
34. **Pearson, J. F.,** Fetal surgery, *Arch. Dis. Child.,* 58, 324, 1983.
35. **Bernaschek, G. and Kratochwil, A.,** Fetal kidney measurements, in *Recent Advances in Ultrasound Diagnosis,* Vol. 3., Kurjak, A. and Kratochwil, A., Eds., Excerpta Medica, Amsterdam, 1982, 281.
36. **Bertagnoli, L.,** Systematic study of fetal kidney, in *Abstr. 4th European Conf. Ultrasound in Medicine,* No. 92, Latin, V., Ed., Excerpta Medica, Amsterdam, 1981, 35.
37. **Grannum, P., Bracken, M., and Silverman, R.,** Assessment of fetal kidney size in normal gestation by comparison of ratio of kidney circumference, *Am. J. Obstet. Gynecol.,* 136, 249, 1980.
38. **Jeanty, P. and Elkazam, N.,** Fetal kidney length and volume: normal values and their importance in the detection of multicystic kidney disease, in *Abstr. 4th European Conf. Ultrasound in Medicine,* No. 92, Latin, V., Ed., Excerpta Medica, Amsterdam, 1981, 35.
39. **Jeanty, P., Dramaix-Wilment, M., and Elkhazen, N.,** Measurement of fetal kidney growth on ultrasound, *Radiology,* 144, 159, 1982.
40. **Potter, E. L.,** Bilateral absence of urethers and kidneys. A report of 50 cases, *Obstet. Gynecol.,* 25, 3, 1965.
41. **Zerres, K., Volpel, M. C., and Weiss, H.,** Cystic kidneys, *Hum. Genet.,* 68, 104, 1984.
42. **Main, D., Menuuti, M. T., and Cornfeld, D.,** Prenatal diagnosis of adult polycystic kidney disease, *Lancet,* 2, 337, 1983.
43. **Pretorius, D. H., Lee, M. E., and Manco-Johnson, M. L.,** Diagnosis of autosomal dominant polycystic kidney disease in utero and in the young infant, *J. Ultrasound Med.,* 6, 249, 1987.
44. **Sanders, R. C. and Hartman, D. S.,** The sonographic distinction between neonatal multycystic kidney and hydronephrosis, *Radiology,* 151, 621, 1984.
45. **Farrant, P.,** Early ultrasound diagnosis of fetal bladder neck obstruction, *Br. J. Radiol.,* 53, 506, 1980.
46. **Garret, W. J., Kossoff, G., and Osborn, R. A.,** The diagnosis of fetal hydronephrosis, megaureter and urethral obstruction by ultrasound echography, *Br. J. Obstet. Gynecol.,* 32, 113, 1975.

47. **Garris, J., Kangarloo, H., and Sarti, D.,** The ultrasound spectrum of prune-belly syndrome, *J. Clin. Ultrasound,* 8, 117, 1980.
48. **Katz, Z., Lancet, M., and Kassif, R.,** Antenatal ultrasonic diagnosis of complete urethral obstruction in the fetus, *Acta Obstet. Gynecol. Scand.,* 59, 463, 1980.
49. **Lebed, J., Weiner, S., and Librizzi, R. J.,** Antenatal ultrasonographic diagnosis of the Prune Belly Syndrome, *JAMA,* 80, 399, 1981.
50. **Jouppila, P., Kirkinen, P., and Tounonen, S.,** Ultrasonic detection of bilateral ovarian cysts in the fetus, *Eur. J. Obstet. Gynecol. Reprod. Biol.,* 13, 87, 1982.
51. **Perreli, L.,** Prenatal diagnosis and congenital malformations of surgical interest, in *Prenatal Diagnosis and Surgical Treatment of Congenital Malformations,* Calisti, A., Astrei, A., and Piccin, G., Eds., Padova, 1983, 163.

Chapter 8.7

CONGENITAL SKELETAL ABNORMALITIES

Asim Kurjak

INTRODUCTION

The thalidomide disaster and the thousands of infants born with congenital limb defects during the early 1950s stimulated research in the area of limb defects. Ultrasonographers today continue to ask why, when, and how often limb defects occur. Skeletal malformations comprise, on the one hand, minor structure deformities, usually restricted to one or more bone segments, which do not cause particularly marked disability. There are, on the other hand, much more severe skeletal development defects, causing major pathologic changes which lead to intrauterine death or to death in pediatric age. These are mainly clinical entities in which the disordered bone formation may be isolated or else associated with malformation of other systems.

Skeletal malformations are not easily classified due to the different degree of expressivity of each disease and to the often arduous description of their pathologic features. The frequent observation of cases with low expressivity makes this task more difficult still. Prenatal diagnosis of skeletal defects requires primarily ultrasonography. Due to the ever-increasing sophistication of technical equipment, we are in a position to obtain more and more accurate diagnoses: the correct visualization of all four limbs, comprehensive of relevant bone segments, of the spine, and of the cranio-facial structure, made at proper gestational ages, is to be considered an essential part of a first-level ultrasound investigation.

Although the incidence of skeletal abnormalities in the general population is low, screening for these disorders is feasible, and the measurement of limb lengths should become a part of the physical examination of every fetus during the second trimester.[1-3]

ETIOLOGY

Small buds of tissue, representing the upper and lower limbs, first appear on the lateral body wall at about the 26th d after fertilization. Most of the limb defects develop during the embryonic phase, i.e., between the 3rd to the 8th week. Therefore, teratogenic factors will inhibit the rate of orderly differentiation of the part that is changing most rapidly and whose cellular components are highly sensitive at that particular moment. Like many others, limb malformations may be caused by genetic or environmental factors or by a combination of both. It has been estimated that 10% of malformations are caused by chromosomal aberrations, 20% by single-gene disorders, 60% by multiple-gene disorders, and 10% by environmental factors. These are agents like anoxia, irradiation, antivitamins, hormones, chemicals, and some viral infections.[4-8] The most common limb defect, phocomelia, is derived from the Greek phoke (seal) and melos (limb). The words describe the condition in which the upper or lower limbs or both are reduced to a "seal flipper" appearance. In strictest terms, the anomaly is characterized by the absence of the proximal portion of a limb or limbs; the hands or feet are attached to the trunk of the body by a single small, irregularly shaped bone. Recognition of its possible "epidemic" occurrence and the relatively easy association with a specific teratogen were possible only because of its previously extraordinarily rare spontaneous occurrence.

CLASSIFICATION

In the past, there was much confusion in using Greek and Latin names. Like in many other similar situations, the World Health Organization proposed a workable classification of limb malformations. This is currently being used all over the world as the standard nomenclature.[4] The seven major categories in the classification are

I.   Failure of formation of parts (arrest of development)
II.   Failure of differentiation (separation) of parts
III. Duplication
IV.   Overgrowth (gigantism)
V.   Undergrowth (hypoplasia)
VI.   Congenital constriction band syndrome
VII. Generalized skeletal abnormalities

Category I comprises congenital deficiencies characterized by either partial or complete failure of limb formation. It is further divided in two subcategories: transverse and longitudinal. Transverse deficits include all congenital amputation-type conditions (e.g., complete aphalangia, apodia, hemimelia, amelia). Longitudinal defects are all category I deficiencies not included in the transverse group and are characterized by a deficiency in the longitudinal axis of the skeletal structures and associated tissues (e.g., complete paraxial hemimelia, partial adactylia, phocomelia). The most profound longitudinal limb reduction is phocomelia. This anomaly may be complete (the hand or foot is attached directly to the trunk), proximal (the proximal segment is missing and the hand or foot is attached to the forearm or lower leg, which is attached to the trunk), or distal (the forearm or lower leg is absent, and the hand or foot is attached directly to the arm or thigh).

The category of failure of differentiation (or separation) (II) of parts includes all defects in which the basic anatomic units are present, but not completely developed. Examples are defects of shoulder and elbow, forearm and wrist, hand, and congenital flexion deformities like camptodactyly and clinodactyly.

Arthrogryposis is caused by failure of differentiation of the soft tissue of the extremities. Isolated muscles or groups of muscles are absent, and the joints they control may become stiff. The condition can affect one or all four limbs and usually causes spinal anomalies.

In the category of duplication of parts (III) polydactyly represents the most common example. The terms "overgrowth" and "gigantism" (IV) describe those conditions in which either part or all of the limb is disproportionally large. this may occur in the digit hand or forearm or in the entire limb. An illustrative example is macrodactyly.

Undergrowth or hypoplasia (V) may be manifested in the entire extremity or in its divisions. It may occur in either the upper or lower limbs. Digital shortening (brachydactyly) is the most common hand malformation seen in association with syndromes and systemic disorders.

Constriction bands (VI) are a result of focal necrosis along the course of the limb that occurs during the fetal stage of development. An area of necrosis involving the superficial tissues heals as a circular scar, creating the band. Amniotic bands have been implicated as a mechanical cause, but may actually be secondary to a healing limb injury. The defect is probably caused by a focal tissue defect that allows hemorrhage within the limb with resulting tissue necrosis. If the constriction bands are severe, intrauterine gangrene may develop and true fetal amputation occur.

A paralytic clubfoot deformity resulting from compression neuropathy of the peroneal nerve caused by a deep, below-knee constriction band has been described. For the ultrasonographer, it is useful to know that deformities occurring in association with the constriction band syndrome include cleft lip and palate, certain cardiac anomalies, meningocele, hemangioma, and idiopathic clubfoot.

Generalized skeletal abnormalities are grouped in the category VII. There is still much confusion in the presentation of the skeleted dysphasias, because over 55 distinct syndromes are delineated.

In an attempt to provide uniform nomenclature, the International Nomenclature for Constitutional Diseases of Bone was proposed in 1970 and revised in 1977 (with some changes, particularly in the classification of dysplasias with newborn presentation).[9]

The international classification divides the skeletal dysplasias into two major groups: the osteochondrodysplasias (abnormal growth and development of cartilage and/or bone) and the dysostoses (malformations of individual bones, singly or in combination). The osteochondrodysplasias are further divided into

1. Defects of growth of tubular bones and/or spine (e.g., achondroplasia), which are frequently referred to as chondrodystrophies.
2. Disorganized development of cartilage and fibrous components of the skeleton (e.g., multiple cartilaginous exostoses).
3. Abnormalities of density and/or cortical diaphyseal structure and/or metaphyseal modeling (e.g., osteogenesis imperfecta).

Most of these anomalies are recognizable by ultrasound, but precise identification is very difficult. For better understanding, it can be useful for a practicing ultrasonographer to know the differential diagnosis of the fetus bone dysplasias.

The achondroplasia is characterized by rhizomelic short-limbed dwarfism, with a large head and bulging forehead, depressed nasal bridge, and relatively prominent mandible. The proximal segments of the limbs are covered with fatty folds of skin, and the fingers are short and broad, giving the hand a three-pronged (trident) appearance. The chest is smaller than normal, and there may be slight respiratory distress.

Thanatophoric dwarfs are smaller than achondroplasts (birth length 36 to 47 cm), but larger than newborn infants with achondrogenesis. They also have a prominent forehead and depressed nasal bridge, but eyes bulge. Their limbs are extremely short and are held extended from the body. They are also hypotonic and lack primitive reflexes. The chest is small and commonly described as pear-shaped. In babies with achondrogenesis I (Parenti-Fraccaro), the head does not appear significantly large compared with the trunk. These infants are frequently born prematurely with a birth length below 30 cm. The skull is extremely soft, appearing to consist of small plaques of bone in a membranous calvarium. The neck is very short, and the arms extremely short and stubby. The thorax is also small and barrel-shaped rather than pear-shaped.

The salient features of distrophic dwarfism are (1) extreme shortness of stature with micromelia; (2) progressive scoliosis sometimes associated with kyphosis; (3) characteristic hand deformities with short fingers, synostosis of the proximal interphalangeal joints, and proximal insertion of the thumb which is subluxed in the so-called "hitch-hiker" position; (4) severe biolateral club cartilage; (5) limitation of mobility and a tendency to subluxation and dislocation of the joints; (6) bilateral hip dysplasia; and (7) cleft palate in some cases. Intelligence is normal.

Babies with achondrogenesis II (Langer-Saldino) are also extremely dwarfed, with a birth length ranging from 23 to 38 cm. The head is large compared to the rest of the body, and the neck is short and hidden in skin folds. The trunk is short with a square appearance, in contrast to the pear-shaped appearance of the chest in thanatophoric dwarfism. The abdomen is distended, and fetal hydrops is frequently present. Limbs are, again, very short and held extended away from the body. There are at least four osteogenesis imperfecta syndromes which may present with neonatal fractures, and these have been designated osteogenesis imperfecta types I through IV. The most common variety presenting in the newborn period is the syndrome of lethal perinatal osteogenesis imperfecta. These babies have characteristic beading of the ribs (rosary sign) (probably because of grossly defective osteogenesis), virtual absence of calcification of skull bones (except for bone islands), and a distinctive, broad, crumpled appearance of the long bones (concertina or accordion appearance) with or without campomelia.

In the lethal perinatal form of osteogenesis imperfecta (osteogenesis imperfecta type II), the babies are also small for gestational age, often stillborn or premature. The head may be relatively large on measurement, and the nose is finely made and pointed. There may be a triangular appearance to the face, with temporal bulging, and the sclerae are usually deep blue-black. The cranium is soft and membranous, and the bones of the vault are replaced by multiple bone islands, similar to achondrogenesis type I. Apart from the ultrasound, early diagnosis of this condition can be made by measuring the amniotic fluid pyrophosphate level.

Severe hypophosphatasia can be distinguished from osteogenesis imperfecta, although it is important to confirm the diagnosis biochemically by finding decreased serum alkaline phosphatase and elevated urinary phosphoethanolamine. The skull similarly shows grossly defective ossification, although the face and base are as severely affected as the cranium. Ribs are thin and wavy, and long bones are thin, ribbon-like, and twisted as well as bent, and may show multiple fractures.

In this chapter we have attempted to provide an integrated clinical, ultrasonic, radiographic, and morphologic approach to the fetus and infant with a skeletal dysplasia. It is important to keep in mind that our knowledge of these disorders is continually expanding. Specialists in the field of skeletal dysplasias are aware of many cases which are presently unclassifiable. Here, the combination of complete clinical, genetic, radiologic, ultrasonic, and morphologic documentation of skeletal dysplasias should eventually allow their classification.

There are a numerous syndromes that may present with limb reduction or shortening.[10-14] However, in practice, cases may be divided into those which present as an unexpected finding on routine ultrasonography and those which have been actively sought in a family with a known history of a skeletal defect. Table 1 shows dwarfing syndromes. The interested reader can find a full description of all disorders listed in the excellent review given by Smith.[15]

ULTRASOUND EVALUATION

In gravides at high risk for skeletal dysplasia, the sonographer may be called upon to determine discrepancies in cephalic, trunk, and long bone fetal dimensions. Therefore, reliable standards for the length of fetal bones are being developed.[16-25]

Fetal limbs can be detected ultrasonically from the 11th week of gestation. Fetal long bones are highly contrasted to other intrauterine structures and can be accurately measured from the 14th week onward. Fetal fingers and toes are easily identifiable as of 16 weeks of

TABLE 1
Features Associated with
Limb Reduction or
Shortening

Macrocephaly
  Thanatophoric dysplasia
  Achondroplasia
  Hypochondrogenesis
  Camptomelic dysplasia
Microcephaly
  De Lange syndrome
  Roberts' syndrome
  Fetal aminopterin effect
Minimal vault ossification
  Hypophosphatasia
  Achondrogenesis I + II
  Osteogenesis imperfecta I
Cleft lip or palate
  Short rib polydactyly
  Roberts' syndrome
  Moebius syndrome
  Fetal aminopterin effect
Narrow thorax
  Thanatophoric dysplasia
  Achondrogenesis I + II
  Jeune syndrome
  Short rib polydactyly
  Ellis-Van Creveld syndrome
  Camptomelic dysplasia
Polydactyly
  VACTERL association
  Short rib polydactyly I + II
  Ellis-Van Creveld syndrome
  Jeune syndrome (sometimes)
  Grebe syndrome

Syndactyly
  VACTERL association
  Fraser syndrome
  Moebius syndrome
  Fetal aminopterin effect
Joint contractures
  Multiple pterygium syndromes
  De Lange syndrome
Cardiac defects
  VACTERIL association
  Ellis-Van Creveld syndrome
  Short rib polydactyly I + II
  Holt-Oram syndrome
Genital or anal anomalies
  VACTERIL association
  Fraser syndrome
  Roberts' syndrome
  Short rib polydactyly I + II
  Camptomelic dysplasia
  Sirenomelia sequence
  De Lange syndrome
Hydrops
  Achondrogenesis I + II
Fractures
  Osteogenesis imperfecta I

gestation (Figure 1). By using real-time equipment, one can visualize limb movements and gain a rapid orientation of limb position, making the examination much easier and faster than with static scanners. A complete examination of fetal limbs in a fetus at risk of having skeletal dysplasia should include all long bone measurements on both sides. When examining the hand and foot, one should be aware that metacarpal and metatarsal bones are ossified at 16 weeks, whereas carpal and tarsal bones (except for the talus and calcaneus) are cartilaginous until term and not demonstrable by ultrasound. The long bones of the arm are most simply recognized by a scan which transverses the short axis of the limb. The sonogram of the upper arm will then reveal one bone, and the section through the forearm two bones. The overall length of a particular bone is obtained in longitudinal section by rotating the transducer 90°. Foreshortening of long bones can easily occur, and, to avoid this, the characteristic posterior shadowing has to be noted, and soft tissue must be seen beyond both ends of the bone. The legs are examined best in longitudinal section, which demonstrates both femurs and the thigh. In extended leg position, the calf with the tibia and fibula is seen by following the long axis of the extremity in the same section. In the flexed position, the tibia and fibula are examined in the same way as arm bones. Measurements are generally performed by placing calipers at the lateral edges of the bone. The only exception is femur measurement, which is performed from the distal epiphysis to the beginning of the femur

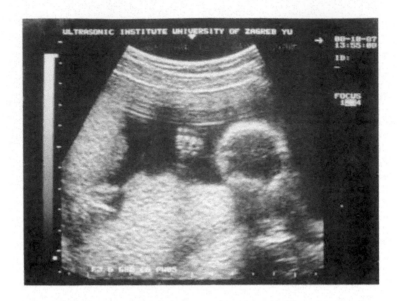

FIGURE 1.   Fetal hand at 16 weeks. The fingers are clearly seen.

neck. Numerous standards for long bone length vs. gestational age have been reported and are used for the detection of bone shortening in various types of skeletal dysplasia. Femur length (FL) measurement is usually made during routine scanning and serves as a good and reliable parameter for gestational age determination.

A wide spectrum of skeletal abnormalities has been diagnosed by ultrasound.[1,3,26-30] As it is possible to visualize clearly almost all fetal bones, ultrasound allows for the detection of any known skeletal defect. However, recognition of the anomaly, especially a minor one, depends mostly on the observer's skill, experience, and conscientiousness.

All systemic skeletal dysplasias can roughly be divided into two groups: mesomelic dwarfism, which affects more severely the middle part of the extremity (tibia, radius), and rhizomelic dwarfism, affecting the proximal part (femur, humerus). A common finding is the marked shortening of all four fetal extremities during the second trimester in an otherwise normal pregnancy (Figures 2 and 3). Although it is rarely possible and not necessary to differentiate between various types of systemic skeletal dysplasia, some anomalies present characteristic ultrasonic findings. Osteogenesis imperfecta is caused by disturbances in osteoid formation and results in bone hypomineralization. A pathognomonic finding *in utero* is the marked bowing of shortened bones or fractures. Hypomineralization can be seen occasionally as reduced bone reflectivity. Hypomineralization can also be observed in cases of achondrogenesis, but long bone shortening is regularly more severe than in osteogenesis imperfecta (Figures 4 to 7).

Thanatophoric dysplasia, which is the most common form of fatal neonatal dwarfism, also exhibits characteristic ultrasonic findings. Besides hydramnios, which is a constant associated symptom, there is marked thickening of soft tissue, and the thorax is abnormally small when compared to the large and protuberant abdomen and large head. The extremities are short and the proximal part is more severely affected (rhizomelic dwarfism) (Figures 8 to 11). Thoracic dysplasia is also noted in congenital hypophosphatasia, short rib polydactyly syndrome, osteogenesis imperfecta, or achondrogenesis and regularly suggests early neonatal death (Figures 12 and 13).

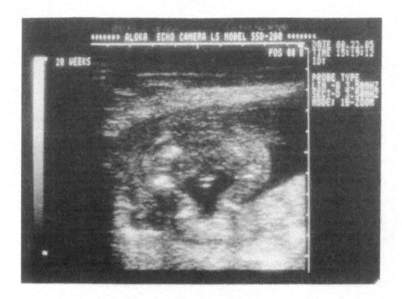

FIGURE 2. A case of achondrogenesis detected at the 20th week of gestation. The real-time sonogram shows both legs with hardly recognizable and extremely shortened long bones. Sex (male) is also observed.

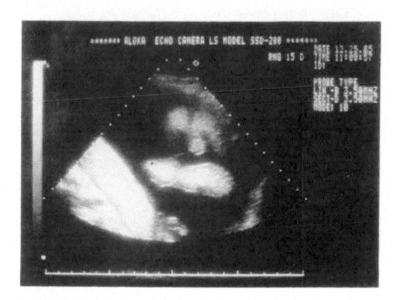

FIGURE 3. Short and deformed right leg in a male fetus at the 23rd week of gestation. Normal osseous structures are absent, and diagnosis of achondrogenesis was made upon pathohistological finding.

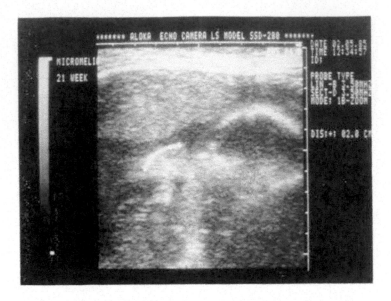

FIGURE 4.   Bowed and short humerus in a case of osteogenesis imperfecta at the 21st week of gestation.

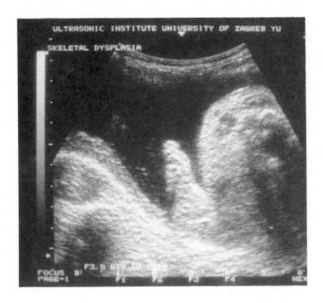

FIGURE 5.   Transverse section through the lower part of a 29-week-old fetus showing short and deformed leg.

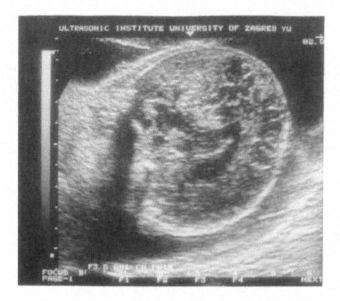

FIGURE 6. Sagittal section through the head of the same fetus in Figure 5 demonstrating an exceptionally clear image of intracranial anatomy due to demineralization of the skull.

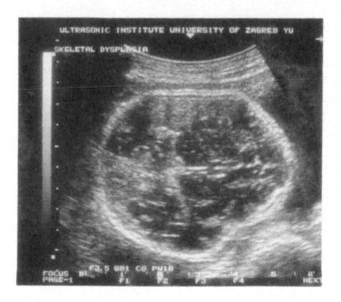

FIGURE 7. Transverse scan in the same case of Figures 5 and 6 illustrates distortion of the head caused by ultrasonic probe compression. Diagnosis of osteogenesis imperfecta was confirmed at pathology.

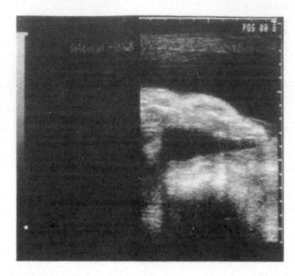

FIGURE 8.   A case of tanatophoric dysplasia diagnosed at 30 weeks. Longitudinal sonogram of the left arm shows marked soft tissue thickening, while the long bones are almost invisible.

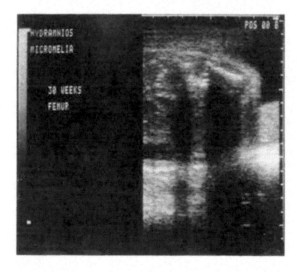

FIGURE 9.   Abnormally short femur in the same case in Figure 8.

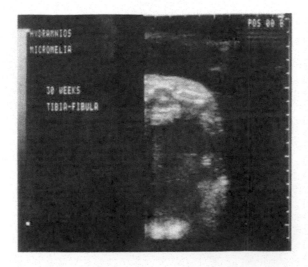

FIGURE 10.   Longitudinal section of the tibia and fibula also
shows abnormal appearance of shortened bones.

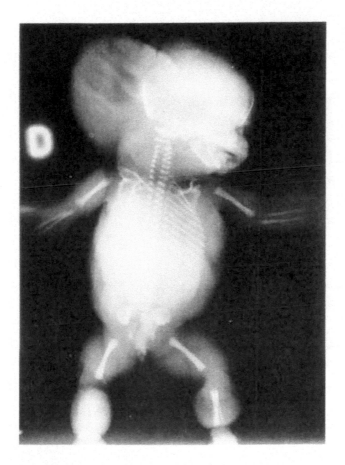

FIGURE 11.   Roentgenogram of the baby after premature delivery caused
by polyhydramnios. Note shortening of the bones and soft tissue edema.

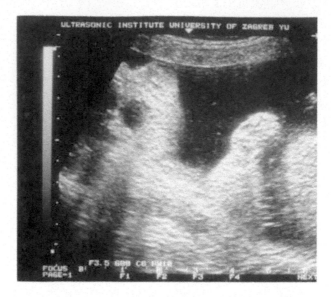

FIGURE 12.   A case of achondrogenesis detected at the 26th week of pregnancy. An oblique sonogram shows a part of the fetal face and an abnormally short right arm.

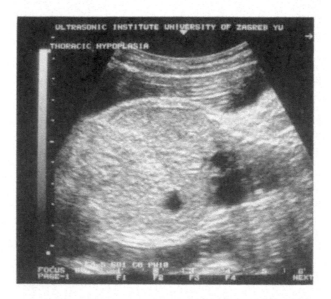

FIGURE 13.   Longitudinal scan through the fetal trunk demonstrates marked thoracic hypoplasia. The degree of thoracic hypoplasia is easily recognized by comparison between the thoracic and abdominal size in longitudinal scan.

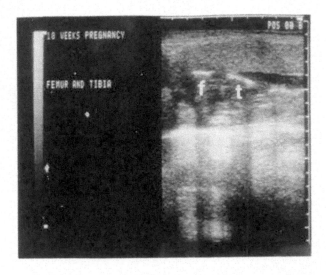

FIGURE 14.   A case of lower extremity hypoplasia detected at 18 weeks of gestation. The longitudinal sonogram of the right leg demonstrates the short femur (f) and tibia (t). Note that the femur is more severely affected, being even shorter than tibia.

Whenever there is a patient at risk of having a baby with skeletal dysplasia, ultrasound assessment of fetal limbs should start from the 14th to 16th week. Evaluation of long bone growth should be continued in 1-month intervals during the second trimester. In cases of achondroplasia, which is the most common systemic skeletal abnormality, displaying the dominant autosomal character of inheritance, the assessment of fetal limbs should be continued until 30 weeks of gestation, because the heterozygous form of the disease may not be apparent until 26 to 27 weeks of gestation.

Another group of skeletal anomalies involves limb reduction anomalies which can affect one or more bones and are rarely diagnosed by ultrasound. These anomalies are classified according to the embryonic somatic origin of the limb as amelia, hemimelia, phocomelia, etc. Ultrasonic diagnosis is easier in cases when patients are generally at risk of having a baby with a limb anomaly, e.g., Robert's syndrome, Fanconi anemia, etc., or when accompanying symptoms are present (Figures 14 to 18). A typical example is sympodia or sirenomelia, which is characterized by symmetrical fusion or soft osseous tissues of the lower extremities. A regular associated anomaly is aplasia of the genito-urinary system, which is responsible for severe oligohydramnios (Figures 19 and 20). However, when oligohydramnios is detected, the fetus should be carefully examined in order to detect possible limb anomalies. Arthrogryposis multiplex is an example of a limb anomaly which can be caused by mechanical intrauterine pressure in cases of severe oligohydramnios. Careful examination of the limbs is indicated, therefore, in all cases of oligohydramnios, regardless of the underlying cause, e.g., urinary tract anomalies, intrauterine growth retardation (IUGR), etc. Minor defects of the hand or foot are actually diagnosed only when the previous baby was malformed, and successful diagnoses of polydactyly, oligodactyly, syndactyly, and split hand and foot have been reported[31] (Figures 21 and 22). In evaluating the lower fetal extremities, the presence of clubfoot should also be ruled out. Clubfoot deformity may be

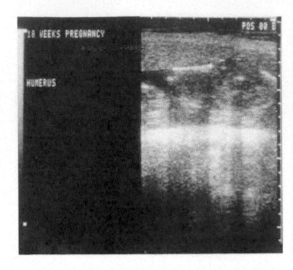

FIGURE 15.   Normal humerus in the same case in Figure 14.

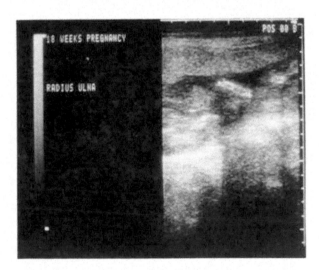

FIGURE 16.   The radius and ulna of the same baby of Figures 14 and 15 were also completely normal.

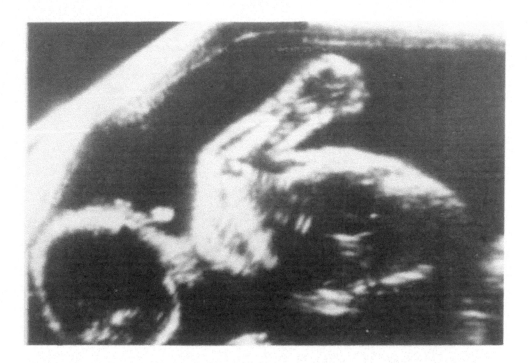

FIGURE 17. Sonogram of a 29-week-old fetus showing the right arm. The other arm and both legs were not visible, in spite of the slight polyhydramnios which facilitated examination.

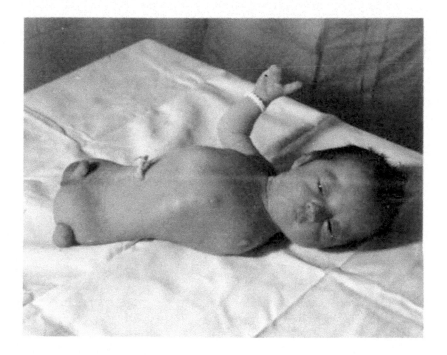

FIGURE 18. The same baby in Figure 17 after term delivery.

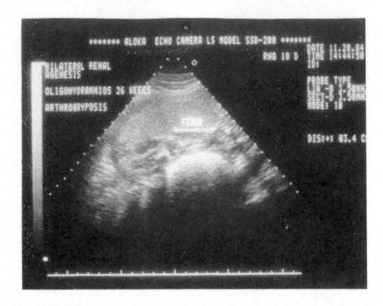

FIGURE 19.   Severe oligohydramnios in a case of bilateral renal agenesis at 26 weeks. Abnormalities of the lower extremities were seen, but were attributed to the complete absence of amniotic fluid.

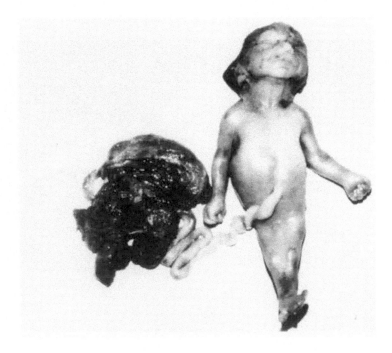

FIGURE 20.   The baby in Figure 19 after termination of pregnancy with typical phenotype of sirenomelia.

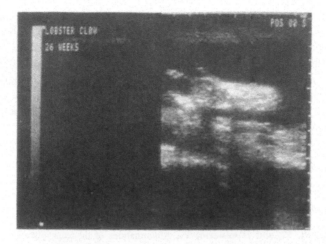

FIGURE 21. Lobster claw deformity (split hand) detected in a patient with high risk of having a baby with this abnormality. Longitudinal scan of the left forearm and hand shows the hand split between the 3rd and 4th fingers.

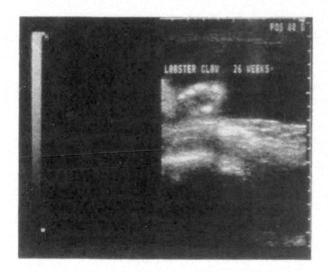

FIGURE 22. The sonogram of the right hand displayed a normal finding.

an isolated finding or it may be part of a systemic musculoskeletal disorder (e.g., arterogryposis, muscular dystrophies, diastrophic dwarfism), chromosome abnormality (i.e., trisomy 13), or spinal disraphism (spina bifida/myelomeningocele). To diagnose clubfoot sonographically, the tibia and fibula should be visualized simultaneously in their long axis. In this position, the ankle and foot are normally seen in short axis; however, in the presence of clubfoot, the foot deviates medially and lies at a right angle to the tibia and fibula. To avoid misdiagnosis, this abnormal position of the foot should be confirmed to be constant in subsequent examinations. Obviously, the ultrasonographer may be forgiven for despairing at the range of syndromes that may be present with limb reduction or shortening. It will take many more years to describe the full range of expression in individual skeletal dysplasias because of the relative rarity of these conditions. Significant help can be made by proper radiological and histological examination in the major referral centers. All material terminated for skeletal dysplasias should be X-rayed. In doubtful cases, copies of the roentgenograms and a representative unembedded sample of a long bone should be sent to a pathologist with an interest in these disorders.

REFERENCES

1. **Kurjak, A., Latin, V., and D'Addario, V.,** Abnormalities of the fetus, placenta and umbilical cord, *Prog. Med. Ultrasound,* 3, 87, 1982.
2. **Grannum, P. A. and Hobbins, J. C.,** Prenatal diagnosis of skeletal dysplasias, *Semin. Perinatol.,* 7, 125, 1983.
3. **Vintyileos, A. M., Campbell, A., Nochimson, D. J., and Weinbaum, D. J.,** Antenatal evaluation and management of ultrasonically detected fetal anomalies, *Obstet. Gynecol.,* 69, 64, 1987.
4. **Swanson, A. B.,** Congenital limb defects: classification and treatment, *Ciba,* 3, 3, 1981.
5. **Kricker, A.,** Congenital limb reduction deformities and use of oral contraceptives, *Am. J. Obstet. Gynecol.,* 140, 1072, 1982.
6. **Rafla, N.,** Limb deformities associated with prochorperazine, *Am. J. Obstet. Gynecol.,* 156, 1557, 1987.
7. **Freeman, R.,** Limb deformities possible association with drugs, *Med. J. Aust.,* March, 606, 1972.
8. **Schardein, J. L.,** *Drugs as Teratogens,* CRC Press, Boca Raton, FL, 1976, 132.
9. **Sillence, D. O., Rimoin, D. L., and Lachman, R.,** Neonatal dwarfism, *Pediatr. Clin. North Am.,* 25, 453, 1978.
10. **Kozlowski, K. and Beighton, P.,** *Gamut Index of Skeletal Dysplasias. An Aid to Radiodiagnosis,* Springer-Verlag, Heidelberg, 1984.
11. **Hwang, W. S., Tock, E. P. C., Tan, K. L., and Tan, L. K. A.,** The pathology of cartilage in the chondrodysplasias, *J. Pathol.,* 11, 127, 1979.
12. **Yang, S. S., Kitchen, E., Gilbert, E. F., and Rimoin, D. L.,** Histopathologic examination of osteochondrodysplasia time for standardisation, *Arch. Pathol. Lab. Med.,* 10, 110, 1986.
13. **Winter, R. and Thompson, E. M.,** Lethal, neonatal, shortlimbed platyspondylic dwarfism. A further variant?, *Hum. Genet.,* 61, 269, 1982.
14. **Little, D.,** Prenatal diagnosis of skeletal dysplasias, in *Prenatal Diagnosis,* Rodeck, C. H. and Nicqlaides, K. H., Eds., Royal College of Obstetrics and Gynaecologists, London, 1984, 301.
15. **Smith, D. W.,** *Recognizable Patterns of Human Malformation,* W. B. Sanders, Philadelphia, 1982.
16. **Queenan, J. T., O'Brien, G. D., and Campbell, S.,** Ultrasound measurement of fetal limb bones, *Am. J. Obstet. Gynecol.,* 138, 297, 1980.
17. **Jeanty, P., Kirkpatrick, C., Dramaix-Vilmet, M., and Struyven, J.,** Ultrasonic evaluation of fetal limb growth, *Radiology,* 140, 165, 1981.
18. **Wladimiroff, J. W., Jahoda, M. G. J., Laar Van Sabben, J., and Niermeijer, M. F.,** Prenatal diagnosis of skeletal deformities: early measurement of fetal extremities using real-time ultrasound, in *Recent Advances in Ultrasound Diagnosis,* Vol. 3, Kurjak, A. and Kratochwill, A., Eds., Excerpta Medica, Amsterdam, 1981, 273.
19. **Schlensker, K. H.,** The sonographic demonstration of fetal extremities in the middle trimenon, in *Recent Advances in Ultrasound Diagnosis,* Vol. 3, Kurjak, A. and Kratochwill, A., Eds., Excerpta Medica, Amsterdam, 1981, 227.
20. **O'Brien, G. D., Queenan, J. T., and Campbell, S.,** Assessment of gestational age in the second trimester by real-time ultrasound measurement of the femur length, *Am. J. Obstet. Gynecol.,* 139, 540, 1981.
21. **Le Lann, D., Keller, E., Heintz, M., Winisdoerffer, G., and Dreyfus, J.,** Identification des points femoral inferieur et tibial superieur en ecographie — interet dans la determination du terme gestationel, *Ultrasons,* 2, 17, 1981.
22. **Rauskolb, R., Jovanovic, V., and Rohlfing, W.,** Prenatal diagnosis of fetal limb deformities, in *Recent Advances in Ultrasound Diagnosis,* Vol. 3, Kurjak, A. and Kratochwill, A., Eds., Excerpta Medica, Amsterdam, 1981, 263.

23. **Mantagos, S., Weiss, R. R., Mahoney, M., and Hobbins, J. C.,** Prenatal diagnosis of diastrophic dwarfism, *Am. J. Obstet. Gynecol.,* 111, 139, 1981.
24. **Schlensker, K. H.,** Die sonographische Darstellung der fetalen Extremitatem im mittleren Trimenon, *Geburtschilfe Frauenheilkd.,* 41, 366, 1981.
25. **Filly, R. A., Golbus, M. S., Carey, C., and Hall, J. G.,** Short-limbed dwarfism: ultrasonographic diagnosis by mensuration of fetal femoral length, *Radiology,* 138, 653, 1981.
26. **O'Brien, G., Rodeck, C., and Queenan, J. T.,** Early prenatal diagnosis of diastrophic dwarfism by ultrasound, *Br. Med. J.,* 280, 1300, 1980.
27. **Shaff, M., Fleischer, A. C., Battino, R., Herbert, D., and Boehm, F. H.,** Antenatal sonographic diagnosis of thanatophoric dysplasia, *J. Clin. Ultrasound,* 8, 363, 1980.
28. **Sabbagha, R. E.,** Ultrasonic evaluation of fetal congenital anomalies, in *Clinics in Obstetrics and Gynaecology,* Gerbie, A. B., Ed., W. B. Saunders, Philadelphia, 1980, 103.
29. **Robinson, L. P.,** Prenatal diagnosis of osteogenesis imperfecta type III, *Prenat. Diagn.,* 7, 7, 1987.
30. **Gollop, T. R.,** Prenatal diagnosis of thalidomide syndrome, *Prenat. Diagn.,* 7, 295, 1987.
31. **Kurjak, A., Zergollern, S., Rajhvajn, B., Bujanovic, V., and Jurkovic, D.,** Ultrazvucno otkrivanje anomalija fetalnog skeleta, *Lijec. Vjesn.,* 108, 256, 1986.

Chapter 8.8

ABNORMALITIES IN MULTIPLE PREGNANCIES

Asim Kurjak

The perinatal mortality rate for twin pregnancies is about 10 to 15%, which is significantly higher than for a single fetus. Twin pregnancies should be followed with serial ultrasound examinations to document the viability of both twins as well as to examine the placenta, evaluate growth, and determine presentation and abnormalities[1-9] (Figure 1).

Twin transfusion syndrome, accardius, and conjoined twins may all be detected prenatally. Twin transfusion syndrome leads to intrauterine hydrops in the donor fetus or to death of one twin with a rise in the already increased α-fetoproteins (AFP) (Figures 2 and 3). Conjoined twins may be detected by ultrasonography and, like acardiac fetuses, carry a considerably increased risk of neural tube defects.[10] Conjoined twinning is an unusual occurrence (1 in approximately 50,000 live births) which, before the introduction of ultrasound techniques, was difficult to diagnose prior to delivery (Figure 4). The majority of these malformations were diagnosed at birth or roentgenographically. The Heidelberg group diagnosed conjoined twins at 12 weeks gestational age with separate hearts and joining of the two fetal bodies at the level of the thorax and the abdominal region.[11] The movements of the fetuses were very active, and it was noticeable that each of the two fetuses followed the movements of the other during the 30-min investigation. The authors have suggested that the period between the 15th and 20th week of pregnancy is the optimal time for the diagnosis of this serious malformation.

Conjoined fetuses are subject to high mortality. Practical chances for survival exist only in symmetrically conjoined twins. When the organs are not paired, the chances of survival are minimal.

Another remarkable case was diagnosed at 27 weeks, in which it was not possible to demonstrate separation of the twins in the lower sterno-abdominal area. A near-term elective Cesarean section (CS) was performed, and twin males were delivered, joined xipho-omphalopagus. The first twin had multiple malformations which included a large meningomyelocele in the sacral area. Separation surgery was performed the day of delivery. The fetuses demonstrated two separate and complete gastrointestinal tracts. The liver tissue was separated as well as the xiphoid. The first twin died 11 h after delivery. The second twin did well postseparation and was sent home after recovering from surgery. Throughout the patient's pregnancy the twins had remained in the breech presentation, and the sacral mass increased in size. With the knowledge of the presence of at least one fetal anomaly in one of the twins, a surgeon was available at the time of delivery, for prompt separation of the twins had become necessary in this case. This paper demonstrates that although conjoined twins are a rarity, their early diagnosis is essential to the welfare of the mother and the proper management of fetal delivery and postpartum care.[12]

Hansmann et al.[13] diagnosed first a thoracopagus pregnancy. At 37 weeks of gestation, two fetal head contours with two spines were recognizable by ultrasonography, but the differentiation of two hearts could not be made. The author recommends CS after a correct diagnosis in these cases and considers ultrasonography as the best diagnostic method. Regec and Bernstein described a case in which the biparietal diameter (BPD) of both twins was over 11 cm at term.[14] There were also incomplete falx development and excessive fluid filling of the intracranial vault. X-rays showed considerable enlargement of the fetal heads

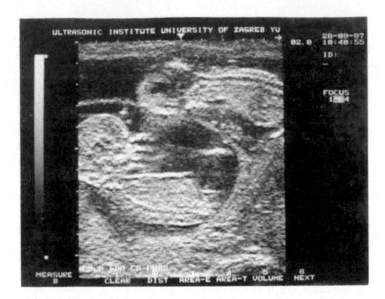

FIGURE 1.   Twin pregnancy. Longitudinal scan of both fetuses with amniotic band between them is clearly visualized.

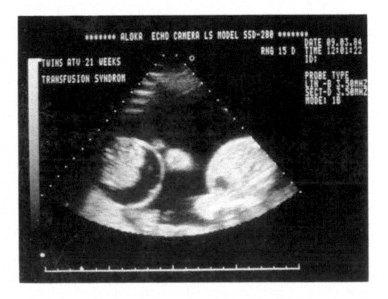

FIGURE 2.   Twin to twin transfusion syndrome detected at 21st week of pregnancy. Transverse sections of both fetal trunks are seen with fluid-filled abdomen of the left-hand side fetus.

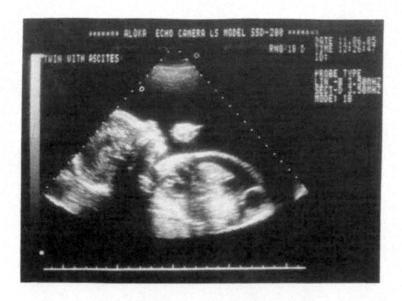

FIGURE 3. Longitudinal scan of the twin with ascites due to twin-to-twin transfusion syndrome.

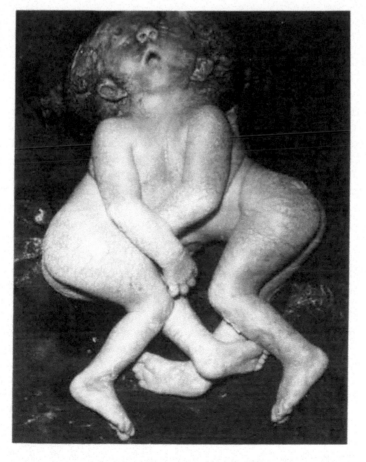

FIGURE 4. Conjoined twins after delivery.

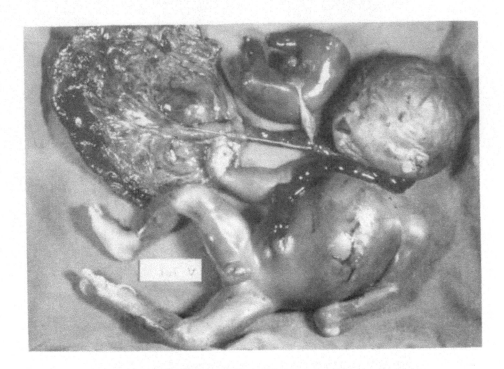

FIGURE 5.   Intrauterine death of both twins. First one presented as the fetus papyraceous, while the second one died due to strangulation of the umbilical cord.

without signs of other anomalies. CS was performed and CAT scan revealed hydroanencephaly in both twins who died at the ages of 9 and 11 d. At autopsy, the second baby did not have any cerebral brain tissue, while the other had just 5 g of cortical tissue. This is a very rare anomaly in twins, described only twice before (Spielmayer, 1905, and Haque and Glasauer, 1969). However, this was the first ultrasonic diagnosis.

Fetus papiraceus results when a blighted fetus is so compressed that all the fluid and most of the soft tissue except the skin are absorbed. This abnormality is associated with viable twins and is an unusual event occurring in approximately 1 in 12,000 live births. The diagnosis is usually made during labor or after delivery and rarely in the antenatal period.[15-16]

The etiology of fetus papyraceous in twin pregnancies is uncertain. Vascular anastomosis, placental infarction, placental insufficiency, velamentous cord insertion, and chronic maternal conditions may be responsible for fetal death and papyraceous formation. The death of a twin fetus is thought to present an environment hostile to the viable twin (Figure 5).

Most fetal deaths resulting in papyraceous formation occur during the second trimester. Out of the 300 pregnancies studied, 23 multiple gestations were found.[16] Of these, only three progressed normally to term as normal twin pregnancies. A fetus was lost in each of the remaining 20 pregnancies. In none of the patients with bleeding was the prognosis of the remaining fetus affected. Of the investigated patients, 75% were completely asymptomatic and might have been missed had the study not been carefully planned. Twin gestation is, thus, much more frequent than previously described, and the high morbidity affecting

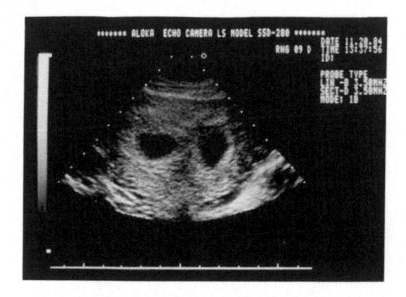

FIGURE 6. Transverse scan of the uterus with twin blighted ova.

this condition which readily manifests itself at the very beginning of the gestation may result in the disappearance of one of the twins.

Livnat et al.[17] described three cases of fetus papyraceous in twin pregnancies. In the first case, twins were diagnosed at 22 weeks of gestation. At the 38th week, ultrasound revealed only one normal growing fetus. The first baby was delivered spontaneously at term, followed by delivery of the second twin, a shrunken fetus within a sac. In the second case, twins were diagnosed at 12 weeks of gestation, and at 20 weeks, one fetus was alive and normal for this period of gestation, but the second one had a BPD corresponding to 15 weeks of gestation. At 29 weeks of gestation, it was shown that the first fetus grew normally, but the other had a decreased head size without signs of fetal life. Spontaneous labor took place at 35 weeks of gestation, and a stillborn baby and fetus papyraceous were delivered. In the third case, at 28 weeks of gestation, twins were diagnosed, but the BPDs of both fetuses were at the level of 19 weeks. At 30 weeks, only one fetus was seen. Because of the development of maternal hypertension, the patient was monitored carefully, and the spontaneous delivery took place at 34 weeks of gestation. A stillborn baby and fetus papyraceous were born.

This paper demonstrates the possibilities of ultrasound in the follow-up of twins. In spite of the fact that most of the losses of the second twin take place in early pregnancy, it is important to follow twin pregnancies, since the death of the other twin can also take place during the second or third trimester. A similar case in a triplet pregnancy has also been described and illustrated by our group.[18]

Kurjak and Latin[18] described 41 cases of abnormal multiple pregnancies. The most frequent was a normal pregnancy and a synchronous blighted ovum (20 patients). Others were twin blighted ova (nine patients) (Figure 6), blighted ovum and missed abortion (two patients), missed abortion in both gestational sacs (two patients), two embryonic echoes with the development of only one baby (three patients), normal fetus and an anencephalic twin (one patient), normal fetus and fetus papyraceous (two patients), and triplets with two fetuses papyraceous (one patient). The results suggest that one or more gestational sacs may

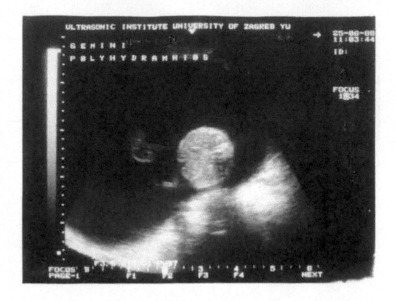

FIGURE 7.   Marked polyhydramnios of unknown cause in twin pregnancy.

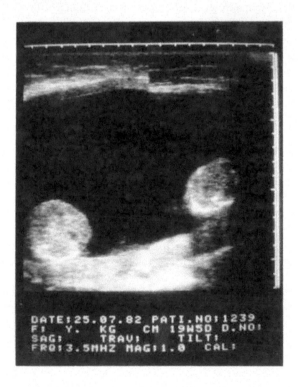

FIGURE 8.   Another case of marked polyhydramnios in twin pregnancy. Transverse section of both apparently normal fetuses is visualized.

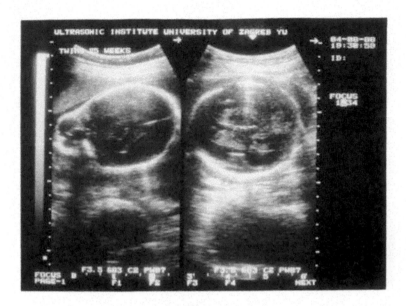

FIGURE 9.   Transverse sonogram of twins at 25 weeks showing a normal baby (right) and abnormal structure on the neck of the other twin, representing cervical meningomyelocele.

be resorbed during pregnancy without any adverse effect on the coexisting normal fetus. For most ultrasonographers, it is important to know such information before giving the final diagnosis of a multiple pregnancy to the patient. It is obvious from this paper that one of the important advantages of diagnostic ultrasound is its capability of examining early multiple pregnancy and of obtaining information which might otherwise be lost.

Discordant growth in twin pregnancy can be caused by monovular twin transfusion syndrome and fetal growth retardation of one fetus. Twin transfusion occurs only in monozygotic twins with one placenta and is caused by large, subchorionic vascular communications. Blood is shunted to the recipient fetus, which becomes volume overloaded, while the donor fetus becomes anemic and hyporolemic. As Whittmann et al.[19] pointed out, twin transfusion usually occurs in the second trimester. Overperfused twin is usually accompanied by hydrops fetalis and polyhydramios (Figures 7 and 8), while underperfused twin may have oligohydramnios. The hydropic fetus may become fetus papyraceous, with the underperfused twin surviving. When twin transfusion syndrome is suspected, the diagnosis may be confirmed by showing a differential of 5 mg hemoglobin or more between blood samples from each twin.[20]

A particular problem in ultrasonic assessment of multifetal pregnancy is diagnosis of fetal abnormalities. It has been estimated that the incidence of fetal anomalies in multiple pregnancy is twice as high as in singleton pregnancy.[21] A serious ethical and clinical problem is diagnosis of fetal abnormality in one twin, while the other is normal. In such a situation, selective feticide may be attempted by instillation of air or potassium chloride in the heart of the malformed baby.[22,23] However, careful evaluation of all relevant medical, ethical, and social factors is necessary before attempting this procedure (Figures 9 and 10).

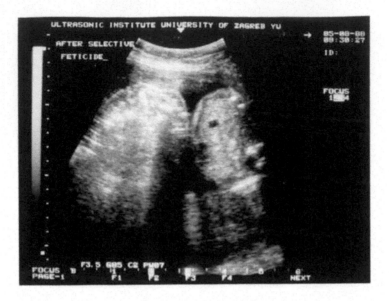

FIGURE 10.   Selective feticide was performed by installation of air in the heart of the abnormal fetus. Transverse sonogram shows normal appearance of the right twin, while visualization of the left baby is unclear due to presence of air in the fetal circulation and placenta.

REFERENCES

1. **Neilson, J. P.,** Detection of the small-for-dates twin fetus by ultrasound, *Br. J. Obstet. Gynaecol.,* 88, 27, 1981.
2. **Crane, J. P., Tomich, P. G., and Kopta, M.,** Ultrasonic growth patterns in normal and discordant twins, *Obstet. Gynecol.,* 55, 678, 1980.
3. **Hawrylyshyn, P. A., Barkin, M., and Bernstein, A.,** Twin pregnancies — a continuing perinatal challenge, *Obstet. Gynecol.,* 59, 463, 1982.
4. **Powers, W. F.,** Twin pregnancy complications and treatment, *Obstet. Gynecol.,* 42, 795, 1973.
5. **Finlay, D., Dillon, A., and Heslip, M.,** Ultrasound screening in a twin pregnancy with high serum alpha-fetoprotein, *J. Clin. Ultrasound,* 9, 514, 1981.
6. **Fink, R. S., Bowers, L. P., and Mackintosh, C. E.,** The value of ultrasound for monitoring ovarian responses to gonadotrophin stimulant therapy, *Br. J. Obstet. Gynaecol.,* 89, 856, 1982.
7. **Funduk-Kurjak, B. and Kurjak, A.,** Ultrasound monitoring of follicular maturation and ovulation in normal menstrual cycle and in ovulation induction, *Acta Obstet. Gynecol. Scand.,* 61, 329, 1982.
8. **Little, J.,** Congenital anomalies in twins, *Semin. Perinatol.,* 10, 50, 1986.
9. **Bryan, E. M.,** The intrauterine hazards of twins (editorial), *Arch. Dis. Child.,* 61, 1044, 1986.
10. **Schinzel, A., Smith, D. W., and Miller, J. R.,** Monozygotic twinning and structural defects, *J. Pediatr.,* 95, 921, 1979.
11. **Schmidt, E., Heberlong, D., and Kubli, F.,** Antepartum ultrasonographic diagnosis of conjoined twins in early pregnancy, *Am. J. Obstet. Gynecol.,* 139, 961, 1981.
12. **Wood, M. J., Thompson, H. E., and Roberson, F. M.,** Real-time ultrasound diagnosis of conjoined twins, *J. Clin. Ultrasound,* 9, 195, 1981.
13. **Hansmann, M., Schlacter, H., Goedisch, H., and Plotz, E.,** Prapartale Diagnose eines Thoracopagus mittels, *Ultrasonogr. Gynaecol.,* 12, 64, 1979.
14. **Regec, S. and Bernstein, R.,** Hydranencephaly in a twin pregnancy, *Obstet. Gynecol.,* 54, 369, 1979.

15. **Warner, R. W. and Bader, B.,** Ultrasound demonstration of fetus papyraceus in a twin pregnancy, *Med. Ultrasound,* 4, 141, 1980.
16. **Jeanty, P., Rodesch, F., Verhogen, Ch., and Struyven, J.,** The vanishing twin, *Ultrasons,* 2, 25, 1981.
17. **Livnat, E., Burd, L., Cadkin, A., Keh, P., and Ward, A.,** Fetus papyraceus in a twin pregnancy, *Obstet. Gynecol.,* 51, 41, 1978.
18. **Kurjak, A. and Latin, V.,** Ultrasound diagnosis of fetal abnormalities in multiple pregnancy, *Acta Obstet. Gynecol. Scand.,* 58, 153, 1979.
19. **Wittmann, B. K., Baldwin, V. J., and Nichol, B.,** Antenatal diagnosis of twin transfusion syndrome by ultrasound, *Obstet. Gynecol.,* 58, 123, 1981.
20. **Rausen, A. R., Seki, M., and Strauss, L.,** Twin transfusion syndrome. A review of 19 cases studied at one institution, *J. Pediatr.,* 66, 613, 1965.
21. **Levi, S. C. and Lyons, E. A.,** The sonographic evaluation of multiple gestation pregnancy, in *The Principles and Practice of Ultrasonography in Obstetrics and Gynecology,* Sanders, R. C. and James, A. E., Eds., Appleton-Century-Crofts, New York, 1985, 321.
22. **Alberg, A., Mitelman, F., and Cantez, M.,** Cardiac puncture of fetus with Huler's disease avoiding abortion of unaffected co-twin, *Lancet,* 2, 990, 1978.
23. **Rodeck, C. H., Mibashan, R. S., Abramowicz, J., and Campbell, S.,** Selective feticide of the affected twin by fetoscopic air embolism, *Prenat. Diagn.,* 2, 189, 1982.

Chapter 8.9

CONGENITAL TUMORS

Asim Kurjak

INTRODUCTION

The term "fetal tumor" should be used when it is evident that the tumor arises during the prenatal period.[1] As in adults, fetal tumors may arise from any tissue and are consequently characterized by a variety of pathophysiological findings. One of the numerous classifications divided fetal tumors into choristoma, hamartoma, embryoma, teratoma and malignant neoplasm. The first four masses may primarily be caused by faulty histogenesis and organogenesis, i.e., dysontogenesis or dysembryoplasia. Thus, their pathogenesis may, at least in part, be similar to that of congenital malformations. Malignant tumors may arise from faulty cytogenesis of normally developed organs. Obviously, fetal tumors represent a rare and heterogeneous group of abnormalities (Table 1).

However, a significant proportion of them can now be diagnosed by using modern, high-resolution ultrasonic equipment (Table 2). In this review, an attempt has been made to evaluate the role of ultrasound in the prenatal diagnosis and perinatal management of fetal tumors.

During the 15 years at our referral center, there were 57 fetal tumors detected prenatally (Table 3). For their evaluation, ALOKA ultrasonic machines were used (ALOKA SSD 250, 280, and 650).

HEAD AND NECK TUMORS

Hygroma colli is the most frequent fetal tumor in this group and in most cases carries poor prognosis to the affected fetus. Although usually classified as a tumor, it actually represents congenital malformation of the lymphatic system in which dilated lymphatic channels assume cystic proportion and form a poorly defined soft tissue mass. Cystic hygroma develops as a result of failure of the jugular lymphatic sacs to drain into the internal jugular vein.

Successful prenatal diagnosis of cystic hygroma has been extensively reported in the literature[30-32] and is usually based on the following criteria: cystic structure located in posterolateral neck, asymmetric multiple septa, and fetal hydrops. Fetal hydrops is frequently associated with hygroma and may be considered as a characteristic finding of this malformation (Figures 1 to 6).

Other pathological structures that should be differentiated from cystic hygroma are cervical meningomyelocele, encephalocele, and cystic teratoma of the neck. It is particularly important to distinguish encephalomeningocele and cystic hygroma on the basis of morphological criteria alone. These criteria have been described by Pearce et al.[33] and serve as a useful guide for differential diagnosis. Cystic hygroma is usually characterized by the presence of typical multiple septa, contains only fluid, and is located in the posterolateral aspect of the neck. They may sometimes extend over the trunk, back, or extremities. In more than half of our cases, the cystic hygromas were larger than the fetal head. On the contrary, encephalocele is characterized by the presence of the large cyst posteriorly to the

TABLE 1
Fetal tumors[2-4]

Head and neck tumors	Intracranial tumors (cont.)
Cystic hygroma	Systemic angiomatosis of the CNS and eye
Epignathus	(Van Hippel-Lindau's disease)
Goiter	Teratoma
Hemangioma	Tuberous sclerosis (Bournville's disease)
Neuroblastoma	Cardiac tumors
Proboscis	Bronchogenic cyst
Teratoma	Fibroma
Intracranial tumors	Hamartoma
Astrocystoma	Hemangioma
Cavernous angioma	Mesothelioma
Chordoma	Myxoma
Choriocarcinoma	Pericardial cyst
Choroid plexus papilloma	Teratoma
Colloid cyst of the third ventricle	Rhabdomyoma
Craniopharyngeoma	Chest tumors
Dermoid	Cystic adenomatoid malformation
Embryonal carcinoma	Intralobar, extralobar sequestration
Endodermal sinus tumor	Bronchogenic cyst
Ependymoma	Abdominal and pelvic tumors
Epidermoid	Appendiceal abscess
Germinoma	Cavernous hemangioma
Glioblastoma	Choledochal cyst
Glioma	Cystic hygroma
Hamartoma	Extrathoracic pulmonary sequestration
Hemangioblastoma	Hepatoblastoma
Hemangioma	Meconium pseudocyst
Lipoma	Mesenteric cyst
Medulloblastoma	Mesoblastic nephroma
Neuroblastoma	Neuroblastoma
Neurofibromatosis	Omental cyst
(Von Recklinghausen's disease)	Ovarian cyst
Papilloma	Ovarian teratoma
Pituitary adamantinoma	Retroperitoneal cyst
Retinoblastoma	Sacrococcygeal teratoma
Subependymal mixed glioma	Wilm's tumor

head. Although bony defect of the skull may not be seen in some cases, helpful signs which enable correct diagnosis are herniation of the brain tissue in the sac, smaller size of biparietal diameter (BPD), and presence of slight ventriculomegaly.

Hygroma colli is frequently associated with renal abnormalities, cardiac anomalies, single umbilical artery, and adrenal neuroblastoma. The most common associated anomaly in a case of cystic hygroma is fetal hydrops. Presence of hydrops has been documented[34,32] in 47 to 87% of cases and carries a uniformly bad prognosis, with a mortality rate close to 100%. Careful evaluation of fetal anatomy is always indicated. The most important part of prenatal diagnosis of fetal cystic hygroma is fetal karyotyping. Although previously considered as a characteristic anomaly of Turner's syndrome, cystic hygromas have also been found in association with other chromosomal abnormalities as trisomies 13, 18, and 21, as well as in one case of Syndroma Klinefelter.[31] Summarized data from the literature and our own experience showed normal karyotype in only 22.9% of cases (Table 4).

Because of that fact, standard obstetrical management of hygroma colli always includes fetal karyotyping. Information about fetal karyotype is also beneficial for management of

TABLE 2
Prenatal Ultrasound Diagnosis of Fetal Tumors

Type	Ref.
Head and neck tumors	
Cystic hygroma	2
	5
	3
Epignathus	6
	7
Goiter	8
Hemangioma	9
Neuroblastoma	10
Proboscis	11
Thyroid teratoma	5
Intracranial tumors	
Choroid plexus papilloma	2
Choroid plexus cyst	12
Craniopharingeoma	13
Glioblastoma	14
Teratoma	2
	15
	3
Cardiac tumors	
Fibroma	16
Rhabdomyoma	17
Chest tumors	
Bronchogenic cyst	18
Cystic adenomatoid malformation	2
	3
Extralobar sequestration	19
Abdominal and pelvic tumors	
Appendiceal abscess	20
Cavernous hemangioma	21
	22
Choledochal cyst	23
Extrathoracic pulmonary seques-tration	24
Meconium pseudocyst	25
	26
Mesoblastic nephroma	3
Neuroblastoma	27
Ovarian cyst	28
	3
Polycystic kidney disease	29
	28
Sacrococcygeal teratoma	2
	3

TABLE 3
Fetal Tumors Diagnosed by Ultrasound during a
15-Year Period

Type	Detected	Not detected
Cystic hygroma	20	0
Sacrococcygeal teratoma	9	0
Ovarian cyst	12	0
Neuroblastoma	3	1
Craniopharingeoma	0	1
Cystic adenomatoid malformation	2	0
Meconium pseudocyst	5	1
Facial teratoma	2	0
Facial fibroma	1	0
Rhabdomyoma	1	0
Choroid plexus cyst	2	0
Total	57	3

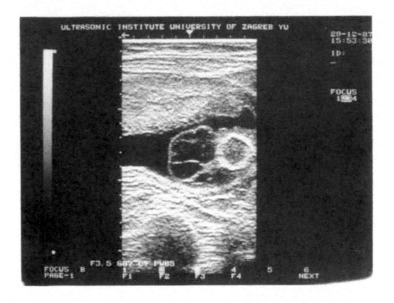

FIGURE 1.   A case of hygroma colli detected at 17 weeks of pregnancy. The hygroma appears as a large multilocular cystic structure at the level of the fetal neck.

further pregnancies. The option of pregnancy termination should always be offered to the patient before fetal viability. Later in pregnancy, rapid karyotyping should be performed. If hydrops is present, prognosis is extremely bad. It seems that in the group of cystic hygromas there is, although small, a certain number of cases in which prognosis is favorable. Those are fetuses with isolated unilateral or bilateral cystic hygroma, normal karyotype, and absence

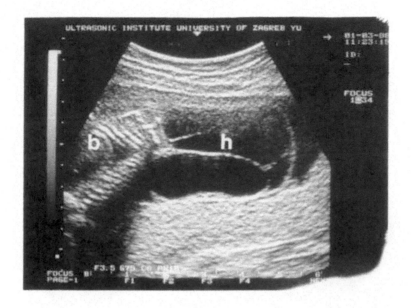

FIGURE 2. Oblique sonogram of a 22-week-old fetus with the large, cystic, fluid-filled hygroma arising from the fetal neck (b = fetal body, h = hygroma).

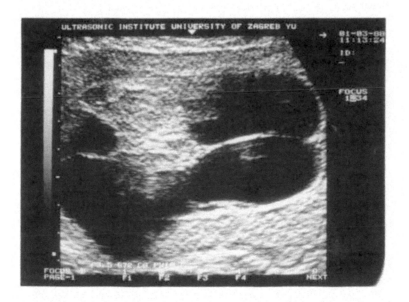

FIGURE 3. Different section of the same patient in Figure 2.

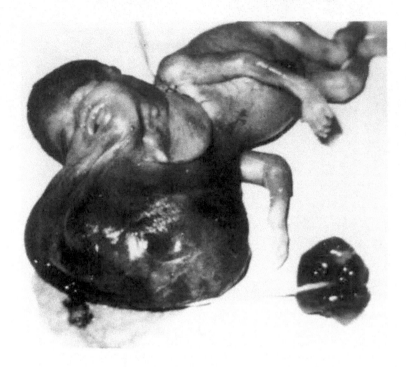

FIGURE 4.   The same fetus of Figures 2 and 3 after termination of pregnancy.

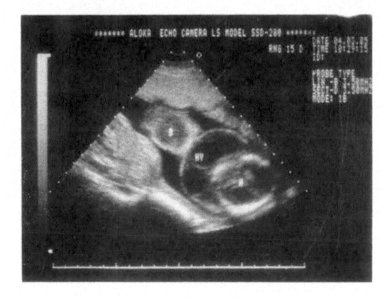

FIGURE 5.   Eccentrically placed cystic hygroma at the 19th week of pregnancy
(h = head, hy = hygroma, b = body).

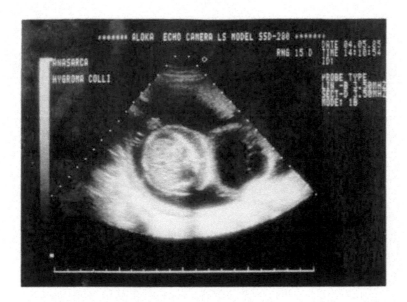

FIGURE 6.   A case of large cystic hygroma associated with fetal hydrops at the 18th week of pregnancy.

TABLE 4
Karyotype in 96 Cases of
Hygroma Colli[30,33,35-39]

Karyotype	No. (%)
Turner's syndrome 45 X	42 (43.8)
Trisomy 18	6 (6.3)
Trisomy 21	4 (4.2)
Trisomy 13	1 (1.0)
47 XXY	1 (1.0)
Normal	22 (22.9)
Unknown	20 (20.8)

of hydrops. If diagnosed after viability, these fetuses may be candidates for *in utero* puncture and aspiration of the hygroma. Such an intervention may be attempted before induction of labor on purpose to avoid potential mechanical problems caused by the presence of large neck tumor. During the last 5 years, our group had four such cases with active management and successful outcome. It has been described that on some occasions, cystic hygromas have been associated with prolongation of the second stage of labor, and in case of particularly large tumors, cesarean section (CS) has been indicated. By performing simple puncture of the tumor, which cannot cause any potential damage to the fetus, and by evacuation of tumor content, such complications could be effectively prevented and are potentially beneficial both to the mother and fetus. This is now a standard practice at our institute.

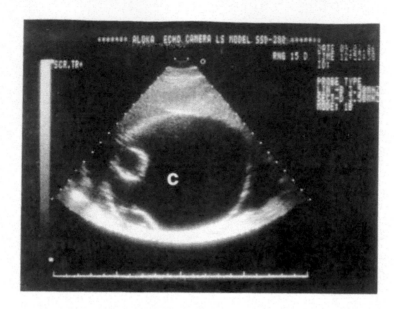

FIGURE 7.   Large, solid tumor (adenoma of the thyroid) in the neck region of a 17th-week fetus.

To conclude, it should be emphasized that cystic hygroma generally carries poor prognosis, and after an early diagnosis, termination of pregnancy is the most logical approach. Contrary to the general opinion, our own experience showed that there are cases in which prognosis could be much better, as illustrated with our four cases. All of the treated fetuses, after surgical resection, had normal development and are now at the ages of 5, 4, 3, and 2 years of life.

The most frequent fetal neck mass other than a cystic hygroma is a teratoma. In general, teratomas are benign in two thirds of patients.[40] Precisely at which point in gestation they arise is not clear, but their maximal growth is in the last trimester and thus may pass unnoticed on an early scan. Sonographically, they present as a variable echogenic mass arising from the sacrum, head, or neck, or within the thorax or skull.[41,42] These may be cystic, mixed, or solid in appearance and may continue to increase in size and grow more solid.[2] They can sometimes lie below the skin line, filling the anterior triangle of the neck. Thurkow et al.,[43] in 1983, described a case of malignant cervical teratoma.

Epignatus is a special type of teratoma arising from the sphenoid, pharynx, tongue, or jaw. Kang et al.[7] and Chervenak et al.[6] reported a successful antenatal diagnosis. Sometimes, a tumor can alter facial anatomy and grow into the cranium, stressing the importance for careful examination of both areas.

A fetal goiter is frequent in parts of the world where iodine deficiency is common. It may present as a solid neck mass with some echolucent areas. The usual cause is maternal ingestion of iodide preparations, and with proper maternal treatment, fetal goiter may decrease in size.[44] Our group diagnosed fetal thyroid adenoma with subsequent interruption of pregnancy[5] (Figure 7).

Gadwood and Reynes[10] diagnosed metastatic neuroblastoma of the neck with the nodules within or on the surface of most of the abdominal organs and the heart.

Hemangiomas can appear as solid mixed or cystic lesions. Identification of pulsations or flows can help in making an accurate diagnosis.[45]

INTRACRANIAL TUMORS

The most frequent intracranial fetal tumors are teratomas. Successful antenatal diagnoses were reported for choroid plexus papilloma, craniopharyngeoma, glioblastoma, and teratomas. The authors[15,46] described quite similar ultrasonic appearance: an enlarged head with the normal architecture completely replaced by a solid tumor containing cystic areas. These tumors grow rapidly, and, therefore, outcome is uniformly poor. A few survivors have been reported,[13] but with serious neurologic sequelae. In the one case from our population, the mass was confined to be craniopharyngeoma at autopsy. It was not identified antenatally, but there was massive polyhydramnios. Snyder et al.[13] reported an antenatal diagnosis of craniopharyngeoma as a calcified and lobulated mass surrounded by fluid. Riboni et al.[14] described ultrasonic appearance of glioblastoma. The mass was strongly echogenic, with a shift of the falx and hydrocephalus.

Choroid plexus papillomas are usually benign tumors attached to normal choroid plexus. Choroid plexus cysts uniformly disappear by 26 weeks, and, therefore, any cyst persistent beyond that age should be considered of different origin. They can possibly be a subarachnoid cyst or a porencephalic cyst.[12]

Tumors arising from the fetal face are even more rare. We have recently diagnosed a case of bilateral fibroma of the face in a fetus with multiple anomalies. It is important not to misinterpret this tumor as proboscis. Successful prenatal diagnosis of nasopharyngeal benign teratoma (epignathus) has also been reported.[6] Although appearing very impressive, this benign lesion might be successfully treated after delivery. However, prognosis depends on the size of the lesion, and it is important to prevent airway obstruction after delivery.

Diagnosis of intracranial tumor carries serious prognosis to the fetus, and in case of an early diagnosis, pregnancy termination is recommended. Specific diagnosis is not possible, and presence of the tumor may be suspected in a case of abnormal mass within the head or in the presence of hydrocephalus.[15]

CARDIAC TUMORS

The most frequent cardiac tumors in the fetus or neonate are rhabdomyomas. The diagnosis has been reported at 16[31] and 36 weeks.[29] The tumor is bruited, intramurally interrupting normal conduction, and, therefore, fetal arrhythmia is often the reason for referral. Since obstructing tumors can be successfully removed after delivery, prenatal diagnosis can increase chances for survival.[6,47,48]

Fibromas are also less frequent than rhabdomyomas. They may appear with similar symptoms and can be surgically removed after delivery.

CHEST TUMORS

The most frequent tumor identified in the fetal chest is a cystic adenomatoid malformation. There have been several reports[49-52] of successful antenatal diagnosis. Stocker et al.[53] and Comstock[54] described three types of tumor: Type I contains large cysts, 3 to 7 cm in diameter; Type II, smaller cysts, 1.5 cm in diameter; and Type III cysts are so small that they are not seen by ultrasound. Polyhydramnios is usual and hydrops frequent.

TABLE 5
Masses of the Fetal Abdomen and Pelvis[2]

Solid	Cystic	Mixed
Ectopic spleen	Hydrometrocolpos	Adrenal neuroblastoma
Normal gastrointestinal system	Choledochal cyst	Multicystic kidney
	Hemangioma of liver	Mesoblastoma — degenerating
Mesoblastic nephroma	Duplications of stomach	
Extrathoracic pulmonary sequestration	Cloacal dysgenesis	Normal small bowel
	Cystic hygroma	Meconium pseudocyst
Wilm's tumor	Mesenteric, omental or retroperitoneal cyst	Anterior myelomeningocele
Polycystic kidney		Ovarian teratoma
Chondroma	Meconium pseudocyst	Appendiceal abscess
Chordoma	Urachal cyst	Sacrococcygeal teratoma
Sacrococcygeal teratoma	Renal cyst	Mesenchymal hamartoma
	Adrenal cyst	Cavernous hemangioma of liver
	Sacrococcygeal teratoma	
	Myelomeningocele	
	Mesenchymal hamartoma of liver	
	Adrenal neuroblastoma	

Adzick et al.[55] and Clark et al.[56] performed decompression of the cyst, but the fluid reaccumulated rapidly. From the excellent reviews by Adzick et al.[55] and Comstock,[54] it seems that hydrops identified *in utero* is more predictive of outcome than the type.

Extralobar sequestration masses are usually left sided and lie near the diaphragm. In the four cases reported,[19,57-59] there were hydrops, pleural effusion, and no survivors. The prognosis is very poor if there is hydrops, although excision in children without hydrops is quite successful.[56]

Bronchogenic cysts may be single or multiple and may be located in the mediastinum or lung parenchyma. The two reported cases in the fetus[18,60] have both appeared as simple cysts surrounded by lung.

ABDOMINAL AND PELVIC TUMORS

Abdominal tumors may represent neoplasms or displaced or enlarged normal organs such as spleen, kidneys, or lung. Their proper prenatal identification is often difficult because they may appear as solid, cystic, or mixed solid-cystic (Table 5). Before any attempt is made, careful visualization of normal anatomy is necessary, including fetal sex determination.

Multicystic kidney is the most common of all neonatal abdominal mass. The condition represents 20% of all abdominal masses.[28] The affected kidney is poorly organized, enlarged, cystic, and nonfunctional. Multicystic kidney is consistently associated with ipsilateral segmented atresia of the ureter and uretero-pelvic junction occlusion. Occasionally, there may be a partial obstruction of the contralateral uretero-pelvic junction. The diagnosis of a multicystic kidney is suggested by the presence of multiple cysts. The cysts are commonly of the order of 1 to 2 cm in diameter, but they can be up to 6 cm large.[28] The contralateral tract is abnormal in up to 40% of cases.[61] In cases when multicystic kidney is bilateral and involves both kidneys completely, it is incompatible with a life expectancy greater than a few weeks, but the unilateral condition is compatible with a normal life-span. Sometimes bilateral multicystic kidney would suggest bilateral hydronephrosis due to urethral obstruction, since bilateral renal dysplasia is rare. Care should be taken because normally echogenic bowel can perfectly mimic a multicystic kidney. If there is massive enlargement of the fetal abdomen, elective CS should be considered to prevent the dystocia that may occur with vaginal delivery and to prevent further damage to these vital organs. If bilateral multicystic kidneys are demonstrated early in gestation, the obstetrician and parents may choose to terminate the pregnancy.

Infantile polycystic kidney disease is due to dilatation and hyperplasia of collecting tubules. It is invariably bilateral and characterized by symmetric massive enlargement with maintenance of normal reniform contours. Medullary ductal ectasia and innumerable ductal cysts in radial distribution, but no dysplastic elements, replace normal renal tissue. Although renal function is variable, it is generally incompatible with life beyond the neonatal period. The kidneys appear as very large, bilateral, reniform solid masses in the fetal flanks. The enlargement of the kidneys may not be visible by ultrasound until 24 weeks of gestation,[62] but has been reported[63] as early as 17 weeks. The ultrasonic appearance is that of a large and homogeneously solid kidney with an increased ratio of kidney circumference to abdominal circumference. Unfortunately, this diagnosis is often not made until the generalized abdominal distention draws attention to it. In the abortable period of gestation, the echogenicity of the kidneys may closely resemble that of the fetal liver and bowel.

Adult polycystic kidney disease has been identified in the fetus.[64,65] Kidneys are smaller in size than those of the infantile type.

Almost all fetal urinary abnormalities are detectable by ultrasound. The ultrasonographer has an increasing responsibility in the further management of these fetuses. Every possible attempt should be made to detect the most serious of these cases during the abortable period prior to 20 weeks of gestation. With regard to other malformations, a fundamental distinction should be made, first of all, between unilateral and bilateral uropathies. If one has managed a unilateral pathology and is sure that the other kidney is perfectly normal, there will be no indication for intervention either by treatment *in utero* or by early delivery. Weekly ultrasonographic checks will be sufficient. At birth, the newborn will undergo the usual examination and urography and cysto-ureterography. As soon as a certain diagnosis is made, surgical correction will be performed at the most appropriate time.

It is our belief that urinary tract surgery should only be considered if the baby is too premature to be delivered, if the baby is unlikely to survive unless surgery is undertaken, and if there is evidence of decreasing lung function or renal function as well as of lung compression. Before any surgical intervention is undertaken, other congenital abnormalities should be excluded, and this is not always easy. If bilateral multicystic kidneys or bilateral polycystic kidneys are demonstrated early in gestation, the obstetrician and parents may choose to terminate the pregnancy, because these conditions are not compatible with extrauterine life.

An ovarian cyst can be suspected if a fluid-filled structure is visualized next to a fetal kidney and female external genitalia are recognizable. These can be septated as in theca lutein cysts,[66] multiple small, round follicular cysts[67] or simple follicles with debris within them.[68] Cysts can sometimes be extremely large,[69] even causing dystocia. Our group was the first to point out that prenatal and postnatal observation may partly replace operative treatment schedules in the future, which is beneficial because even with microsurgical techniques it can be difficult to preserve the very small ovaries if they are firmly attached to the cystic wall.[28]

In the recent collaborative study from our three departments, 26 ovarian cysts have been described.[38] In our experience, ovarian cysts do not appear earlier than 30 weeks of pregnancy and may decrease in size throughout the remainder of gestation. Such a decrease in the size of the cyst may reflect the drop in gonadotropins, occurring at term, and presumably resulting from maturation of the hypothalamus to the negative feedback of estrogen.

Fetal ovarian cysts can be recognized by ultrasound. However, other intra- and retro-peritoneal fetal organs may appear as cystic masses or can contain cystic lesions; for this reason an absolute differential diagnosis may be difficult. The ultrasound finding suggestive of an ovarian cyst is that of a pelvic cystic or complex mass in a female fetus with normal kidneys and urinary bladder and a normal gastrointestinal tract.

In most cases, the normal course of fetal ovarian cysts is a spontaneous intrauterine or postnatal involution. Many of these cysts may therefore remain undiagnosed if routine ultrasound examination is not performed during late pregnancy. During intrauterine life, these cysts may undergo twisting and rupture or endocystic bleeding. Huge ovarian cysts may cause renal and bowel obstruction or dystocia at delivery. Prenatal diagnosis improves neonatal outcome by allowing an appropriate choice of the optimal time, mode, and place of delivery in order to avoid accidental and unexpected intrapartum and postnatal complications.

The management of a fetus affected by an ovarian cyst depends on the size and on the echo-pattern of the cyst. The management can be postulated as follows:

- When a fetal ovarian cyst is diagnosed, an ultrasonic examination should be performed weekly in order to evaluate modifications in the size and structure of the cyst. The cyst may undergo complete involution before delivery or may show structural changes suggesting complications, such as twisting or endocystic bleeding.
- The fetus may be delivered vaginally at term. A few years ago, the only indication for a CS was the presence of a cyst so huge as to be considered as a possible cause of dystocia. Recently, *in utero* treatment of the ovarian cyst modifies the management. The needle aspiration of the cystic fluid performed at term of pregnancy reduces the size, allowing a normal vaginal delivery.
- Serial ultrasonic examinations of the neonates are needed in order to evaluate the evolution of the cyst. The most likely evolution is a spontaneous resolution. Should the cyst persist or show an ultrasonic pattern suggesting a complication or a nonfunctional nature, laparotomy is indicated.

It remains unclear whether *in utero* puncture of the cyst and evacuation of its content should be justified in cases of particularly large ovarian cysts. In our opinion, intrauterine procedure can be attempted in the presence of large cysts filling the fetal abdomen.[28] We have actively treated two cases of large ovarian cysts by ultrasonically guided puncture before delivery, and both fetuses underwent surgery later without complications.

If properly performed, puncture of the cyst seems to be a low-risk procedure in comparison to the potential problems that a cyst may cause to the fetus or by causing dystocia.

In contrast to the relatively high incidence of 40% in adults, malignant tumors in neonates are rare, and there is only one report of a bilateral malignant ovarian dysgerminoma in a fetus.[70] Ovarian teratomas are usually more solid than benign ovarian cysts which are characteristically completely filled with fluid and have a thin, smooth membrane.

Ovarian cysts may be difficult to distinguish from hydrometrocolpos or cystic dilatation of the vagina and uterus secondary to mucous accumulation above an obstruction.[71,72]

Meconium pseudocyst is a sterile reaction when meconium is extruded from the bowel into the peritoneal cavity as a result of bowel atresia, stenosis, volvulus, or obstruction due to thickened meconium in cystic fibrosis. The wall is thickened, usually oval or tubular in shape.[25,26,73] An ascites and hydrops fetalis are often present. Samuel et al.[74] performed an

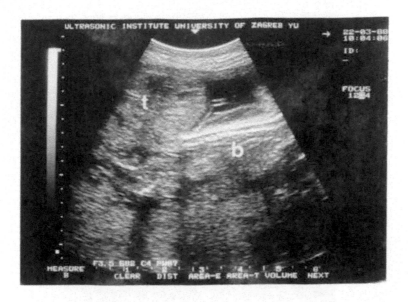

FIGURE 8.   Completely cystic appearance of presacral neuroblastoma diagnosed prenatally at the 23rd week of gestation (n = neuroblastoma).

antenatal treatment with a urograph in of what was perceived to be a bowel obstruction with impending perforation.

The most common malignancy in the newborn is a neuroblastoma. These tumors are unilateral, but 50% of infants have metastasis in kidneys, liver, subcutaneous tissue, and placenta. The mass usually arises from the adrenals, as in our own two cases (Figure 8). However, White et al.[27] reported one tumor which originated in the pelvis and two from the chest. They have different ultrasonic appearances and are often mistaken for a renal mass or for hydronephrosis.[75] Congenital adrenal neuroblastoma appears as a unilateral tumor of mixed and solid texture located in the upper pole of the kidney. Helpful diagnostic signs are calcifications within the tumor. This tumor may be suspected also when mother complains of nausea, vomiting, and hypertension.[76,77] These symptoms are caused by excessive production of catecholamine from the tumor which occurs in 75 to 90% of cases. Differential diagnosis of abdominal tumor has to include Wilm's tumor, although successful prenatal diagnosis of this tumor has not been reported as yet.

Mesoblastic nephroma is a benign solid mass contiguous with the kidney. There are several reports on prenatal diagnosis.[78-81] Polyhydramnios was present in most reported cases.

In all cases of abdominal tumors, expectative management is recommended, and definitive diagnosis and treatment are employed after delivery.

Sacrococcygeal teratoma represents the most frequent tumor in fetuses and newborns[40] Tumors are presumed to arise from pluripotential cells of Hensen's node, which explains the presence of tissues of all three germinal layers within the tumors.[82] In 80% of cases, tumor is seen as an external lesion protruding from the perineal or sacral region.

The majority of these tumors are small and of little consequence during pregnancy and labor. When the tumors are large, dystocia and hydramnios may be present. The tumor treatment involves extensive surgery, which should be performed early in the neonatal period because the likelihood of malignancy increases sharply if it is delayed. Thus, early diagnosis is very important for appropriate therapy.

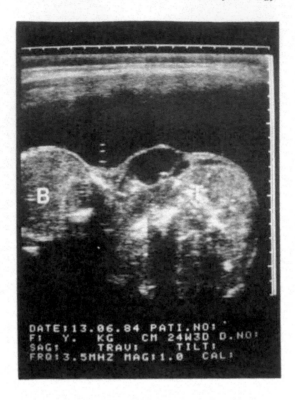

FIGURE 9.   Large predominantly cystic sacrococcygeal teratoma in a male fetus at the 23rd week of gestation (c = cystic teratoma).

Prenatal diagnosis is usually simple and based on the visualization of a tumor of variable size and internal structure.[83,84] Tumors may appear as completely cystic, mixed, or predominantly solid with obvious calcifications. Cystic and calcified tumors are most likely to be benign[85] (Figures 9 to 11).

There are several pathohistological classifications of sacrococcygeal teratoma. Most commonly they are divided in three groups: mature, immature, and malignant.[86] In the newborn, mature forms are most frequent, but the probability of malignancy rapidly increases with the age of the baby. However, a reliable distinction between malignant and benign lesions is not possible prenatally, but entirely cystic lesions are almost always benign, while solid tumors without calcifications should increase suspicion of malignancy. The size of the tumor is not usually an important prognostic factor, but in a case of an extremely large tumor, it may cause fetal cardiac insufficiency and hydrops.

Associated anomalies are not very frequent, but differential diagnosis between cystic tumor and myelomeningocele might prove to be difficult in certain cases.

Obstetrical management of sacrococcygeal teratoma depends on numerous parameters which include size and texture of the tumor and gestational age.

After an early diagnosis of solid-tumor pregnancy, termination would be most logical approach. In the case of a cystic tumor, which carries a pretty good prognosis, decision is more difficult. We have recently had two cases of cystic teratoma which were diagnosed before viability with active management and a successful outcome. In the first case, the mother was highly motivated to continue pregnancy, and her decision was strictly followed.

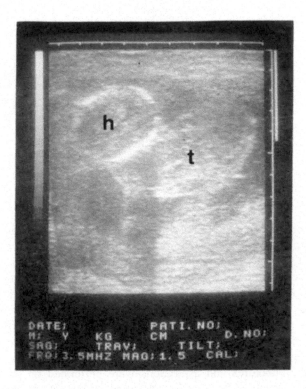

FIGURE 10. An extremely large solid sacrococcygeal teratoma detected at the 19th week of pregnancy. The fetal spine is visualized in the longitudinal section, enabling clear detection of the tumor insertion (b = body, t = tumor).

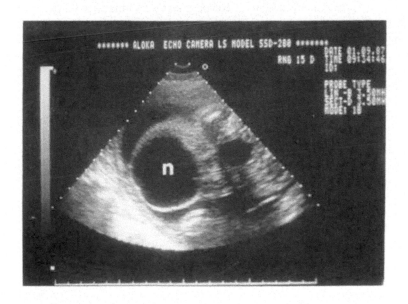

FIGURE 11. Another case of large, solid sacrococcygeal teratoma as seen on transverse scan through the lower part of the fetal body. Note inhomogenous texture of the tumor tissue (b = body, t = tumor).

TABLE 6
Neurobiochemical Analysis of
Aspirated Fluid from Sacrococcygeal
Teratoma

	Case 1	Case 2
Pandy reaction	+ + +	+ + +
Proteins (g/l)	2.13	5.06
Glucose (mmol/l)	2.30	2.37
Chloride (mmol/l)	114	126
Cells	Atypic	Atypic

Amniocentesis was performed for fetal karyotyping. During the procedure, the tumor was also punctured on purpose to increase reliability of prenatal diagnosis by analysis of tumor content. The puncture was repeated before intended vaginal delivery, and more than 2500 ml of fluid was removed. The baby was delivered, and surgical correction was successfully performed in early neonatal period. In the second case, diagnosis of cystic sacrococcygeal teratoma was made in a case of twins. One baby was normal, and in the other there was an isolated tumor. During amniocentesis, puncture of the tumor was also performed for diagnostic purposes. Both babies were chromosomally normal, and the pregnancy was allowed to progress. After a couple of weeks, fast growth of the tumor was observed, and several repeated tumor punctures and aspirations were performed on purpose to prevent premature delivery. Altogether, 8.5 l of fluid were removed by five repeated cystocentheses between 20 and 37 weeks of pregnancy. Babies were delivered at term by CS, and immediate successful surgical correction was performed. Both babies are now at the age of 18 months and are doing well.

These two cases illustrate that favorable outcome of cystic teratoma may be expected in most cases, and it should be seriously reconsidered whether an early diagnosis of this type of the tumor represents an indication for pregnancy termination. Puncture of teratoma increases the reliability of diagnosis of cystic teratoma vs. meningocele. This distinction might be difficult, particularly in case of breech presentation when a small spinal defect can be easily overlooked. The results of neurobiochemical analysis (Table 6) proved definitely that the aspirated fluid could not represent cerebrospinal liquor and confirmed the first ultrasound diagnosis.

CONCLUSION

There is still a lack of relevant experimental and clinical data to define a reliable and effective approach to prenatal management of fetal tumors. Taking into account the fact that these tumors are relatively rare pathological conditions, it seems that further experience will help to solve some of the problems already mentioned. It is concluded that each case of fetal tumor deserves a careful and individual approach, taking into account all relevant clinical, ethical, and social factors.

REFERENCES

1. **Nishimura, H. and Okamoto, N.,** *Sequential Atlas of Human Congenital Malformations,* Igaka Shoin, Tokyo, 1976.
2. **Comstock, C. H.,** Fetal masses: ultrasound diagnosis and evaluation, *Ultrasound Q.,* 6, 229, 1988.
3. **Romero, R., Pilu, G., Jeanty, P., Ghidini, A., and Hobbins, J. C.,** *Prenatal Diagnosis of Congenital Anomalies,* Appleton & Lange, Norwalk, CT, 1988.
4. **Warkany, J.,** *Congenital Malformations,* Year Book Medical Publishing, Chicago, 1971.
5. **Kurjak, A. and Latin, V.,** Fetal and placental abnormalities, in *Progress in Medical Ultrasound,* Vol. 2, Kurjak, A., Ed., Excerpta Medica, Amsterdam, 1981.
6. **Chervenak, F. A., Tortora, M., Moya, F. R., and Hobbins, J. C.,** Antenatal sonographic diagnosis of epignathus, *J. Ultrasound Med.,* 3, 235, 1984.
7. **Kang, K. W., Hissong, S. L., and Langer, A.,** Prenatal ultrasonic diagnosis of epignathus, *J. Clin. Ultrasound,* 6, 330, 1978.
8. **Barone, C. M., Van Nata, F. C., Kouridies, I. A., and Berkowitz, R. L.,** Sonographic detection of fetal goiter; an unusual case of hydramnios, *J. Ultrasound Med.,* 4, 625, 1985.
9. **McGahan, J. P. and Schneider, J. M.,** Fetal neck hemangioendothelioma with secondary hydrops fetalis: sonographic diagnosis, *J. Clin. Ultrasound,* 14, 384, 1986.
10. **Gadwood, K. A. and Reynes, C. J.,** Prenatal sonography of metastatic neuroblastoma of the neck, *J. Clin. Ultrasound,* 11, 512, 1983.
11. **Benacerraf, B. R., Frigoletto, F. D., and Bieber, F. R.,** The fetal face: ultrasound examination, *Radiology,* 153, 495, 1984.
12. **Chudleigh, P., Pearce, J. M., and Campbell, S.,** The prenatal diagnosis of transient cysts of the fetal choroid plexus, *Prenat. Diagn.,* 4, 135, 1984.
13. **Snyder, J. R., Lustig-Gillman, I., Milio, L., Morris, M., Pardes, J. G., and Yound, B. K.,** Antenatal ultrasound diagnosis of an intracranial neoplasm, *J. Clin. Ultrasound,* 14, 304, 1986.
14. **Riboni, G., DeSimon, I. M., Leopardi, O., and Molla, R.,** Ultrasound appearance of a glioblastoma in a 33-week fetus in utero, *J. Clin. Ultrasound,* 13, 345, 1985.
15. **Crade, M.,** Ultrasonic demonstration in utero of an intracranial teratoma, *JAMA,* 247, 1173, 1982.
16. **Schmaltz, A. A. and Apitz, J.,** Primary heart tumours in infancy and childhood, *Cardiology,* 67, 12, 1981.
17. **Standford, W., Abu-Yousef, M., and Smith, W.,** Intracardiac tumour (rhabdomyoma) diagnosed by in utero ultrasound: a case report, *J. Clin. Ultrasound,* 15, 337, 1987.
18. **Mayden, K. L., Tortora, M., Chervenak, F. A., and Hobbins, J. C.,** The antenatal sonographic detection of lung masses, *Am. J. Obstet. Gynecol.,* 148, 349, 1984.
19. **Romero, R., Chervenak, F. A., Kotzen, J., Berkowitz, R. L., and Hobbins, J. C.,** Antenatal sonographic findings of extralobar pulmonary sequestration, *J. Ultrasound Med.,* 1, 131, 1982.
20. **Hill, L. M., Breckle, R., and Avant, R. F.,** Sonographic findings associated with a sterile fetal appendiceal abscess, *J. Ultrasound Med.,* 1, 257, 1982.
21. **Nakamoto, S. K., Dreilinger, A., Dattel, B., Mattrey, R. F., and Key, T. C.,** The sonographic appearance of hepatic hemangioma in utero, *J. Ultrasound Med.,* 2, 239, 1983.
22. **Platt, L. D., DeVore, G. R., Brenner, P., Siassi, B., Ralls, P. W., and Mikity, V. G.,** Antenatal diagnosis of fetal liver mass, *J. Ultrasound Med.,* 2, 521, 1983.
23. **Dewbury, K. C., Aluwihare, A. P. R., Chir, M., Birch, S. J., and Freeman, N. V.,** Prenatal ultrasound demonstration of a choledochal cyst, *Br. J. Radiology,* 53, 906, 1980.
24. **Mariona, F., McAlpin, G., Zador, I, Philippart, A., and Jafri, S. Z. H.,** Sonographic detection of fetal extrathoracic pulmonary sequestration, *J. Ultrasound Med.,* 5, 283, 1986.
25. **Blumenthal, D. H., Rushovich, A. M., Williams, R. K., and Rochester, D.,** Prenatal sonographic findings of meconium peritonitis with pathologic correlation, *J. Clin. Ultrasound,* 10, 350, 1982.
26. **Lauer, J. D. and Cradock, T. V.,** Meconium pseudocyst: prenatal sonographic and antenatal radiologic correlation, *J. Ultrasound Med.,* 1, 333, 1982.
27. **White, S. J., Stuck, K. J., Blane, C. E., and Silver, T. M.,** Sonography of neuroblastoma, *Am. J. Roentgenol.,* 141, 465, 1983.
28. **Kurjak, A., Latin, V., Mandruzzato, G., D'Addario, V., and Rajhvajn, B.,** Ultrasound diagnosis and perinatal management of fetal genito-urinary abnormalities, *J. Perinat. Med.,* 12, 291, 1984.
29. **Hansmann, M., Hackeloer, B. J., and Staudach, A.,** Eds., *Ultrasound Diagnosis in Obstetrics and Gynecology,* Springer-Verlag, Berlin, 1986.
30. **Garden, A. S., Benzie, R. J., Miskin, M., and Gardner, H. A.,** Fetal cystic hygroma colli: antenatal diagnosis, significance and management, *Am. J. Obstet. Gynecol.,* 154, 221, 1986.

31. **Gustavii, B. and Edvall, H.,** First-trimester diagnosis of cystic nuchal hygroma, *Acta Obstet. Gynecol. Scand.,* 63, 377, 1984.
32. **Pijpers, L., Renss, A., Stewart, P. A., Wladimiroff, J. W., and Sachs, E. S.,** Fetal cystic hygroma: prenatal diagnosis and management, *Obstet. Gynecol.,* 72, 223, 1988.
33. **Pearce, J. M., Griffin, D., and Campbell, S.,** The differential prenatal diagnosis of cystic hygromata and encephalocele by ultrasound examination, *J. Clin. Ultrasound,* 13, 317, 1985.
34. **Chervenak, F. A., Isaacson, G., and Tortora, M.,** A sonographic study of fetal cystic hygromas, *J. Clin. Ultrasound,* 13, 317, 1985.
35. **Bluth, E. I., Maragos, V. A., and Merritt, C. R. B.,** Antenatal diagnosis of Turner's syndrome, *South. Med. J.,* 77, 1335, 1984.
36. **Chervenak, F. A., Isaacson, G., and Blakemore, K. J.,** Fetal cystic hygroma. Cause and natural history, *N. Engl. J. Med.,* 309, 822, 1983.
37. **Greenberg, F., Carpenter, R. J., and Ledbetter, D. H.,** Cystic hygroma and hydrops fetalis in a fetus with trisomy 13, *Clin. Genet.,* 24, 389, 1983.
38. **Jurkovic, D. and Kurjak, A.,** Fetal tumours, in *Fetus as a Patient,* Vol. 5, D'Addario, V., Ed., Excerpta Medica, Amsterdam, 1989, in press.
39. **Redford, D. H. A., McNay, M. B., and Ferguson-Smith, M. E.,** Aneuploidy and cystic hygroma detectable by ultrasound, *Prenat. Diagn.,* 4, 377, 1984.
40. **Donnelan, W. W. and Swenson, O. L.,** Benign and malignant sacroccygeal teratoma, *Surgery,* 64, 834, 1968.
41. **Campbell, S. and Pearce, M. J.,** The perinatal diagnosis of fetal structural anomalies by ultrasound, *Clin. Obstet. Gynecol.,* 10, 435, 1983.
42. **Trecet, J. C., Claramunt, V., Larraz, J., Ruiz, E., Zuzuarregui, H., and Ugalde, F. J.,** Prenatal ultrasonic diagnosis of fetal teratomas of the neck, *J. Clin. Ultrasound,* 12, 509, 1984.
43. **Thurkow, A. L., Visser, G. H. A., Ooterhuis, J. W., and Devries, J. A.,** Ultrasound observations of a malignant cervical teratoma of the fetus in a case of polyhydramnios: case history and review, *Eur. J. Obstet. Gynecol. Reprod. Bull.,* 14, 375, 1983.
44. **Weiner, S., Scharf, J. I., Bolognese, R. J., and Librizzi, R. J.,** Antenatal diagnosis and treatment of a fetal goiter, *J. Reprod. Med.,* 24, 39, 1980.
45. **Grundy, H., Glasmann, A., Burlbaw, J., Walton, S., Dannar, C., and Doan, L.,** Hemangioma presenting as a cystic mass in the fetal neck, *J. Ultrasound Med.,* 4, 147, 1985.
46. **Nicolini, U., Ferrazzi, E., Massa, E., Minonzio, M., and Pardi, G.,** Prenatal diagnosis of cranial masses by ultrasound: report of five cases, *J. Clin. Ultrasound,* 11, 170, 1983.
47. **Foster, E. D., Spooner, E. W., Farina, M. A., Shaker, R. M., and Alley, R. D.,** Cardiac rhabdomyoma in the neonate: surgical management, *Ann. Thorac. Surg.,* 37, 249, 1984.
48. **Riggs, T. W., Ilbawi, M., DeLeon, S., and Paul, M. H.,** Echocardigraphic diagnosis of right ventricular rhabdomyoma in two infants, *Pediatr. Cardiol.,* 3, 31, 1982.
49. **Diwan, R., Brennan, J. N., Philipson, E. H., Jain, S., and Bellon, E. H.,** Ultrasonic prenatal diagnosis of Type III congenital cystic adenomatoid malformation of lung, *J. Clin. Ultrasound,* 11, 218, 1983.
50. **Graham, D., Winn, K., Dex, W., and Sanders, R. C.,** Prenatal diagnosis of cystic adenomatoid malformation of the lung, *J. Ultrasound Med.,* 1, 9, 1982.
51. **Johnson, J. A., Rumack, C. M., Johnson, M. L., Shikes, R., Appareti, K., and Rees, G.,** Cystic adenomatoid malformation: antenatal demonstration, *Am. J. Roetgenol.,* 142, 483, 1984.
52. **Pezzuti, R. T. and Isler, R. J.,** Antenatal ultrasound detection of cystic adenomatoid malformation of lung: report of a case and review of the recent literature, *J. Clin. Ultrasound,* 11, 342, 1983.
53. **Stocker, J. T., Madewell, J. E., and Drake, R. M.,** Congenital cystic adenomatoid malformation of the lung. Classification and morphologic spectrum, *Hum. Pathol.,* 8, 155, 1977.
54. **Comstock, C. H.,** The antenatal diagnosis of diaphragmatic anomalies, *J. Ultrasound Med.,* 5, 391, 1986.
55. **Adzick, N. S., Harrison, M. R., Glick, P. L., et al.,** Fetal cystic adenomatoid malformation: prenatal diagnosis and natural history, *J. Pediatr. Surg.,* 20, 483, 1985.
56. **Clark, S. L., Vitale, D. J., Minton, S. D., Stoddard, R. A., and Sabey, P. L.,** Successful fetal therapy for cystic adenomatoid malformation associated with second-trimester hydrops, *Am. J. Obstet. Gynecol.,* 157, 294, 1987.
57. **Kristoffersen, S. E. and Ipsen, L.,** Ultrasonic realtime diagnosis of hydrothorax before delivery in an infant with extralobar lung sequestration, *Acta Obstet. Gynecol. Scand.,* 63, 723, 1984.
58. **Thomas, C. S., Leopold, G. R., Hilton, S., Key, T., Coen, R., and Lynch, F.,** Fetal hydrops associated with extralobar pulmonary sequestration, *J. Ultrasound Med.,* 5, 668, 1986.
59. **Weiner, C., Varner, M., Pringle, K., Hein, H., Williamson, R., and Smith, W. L.,** Antenatal diagnosis and palliative treatment of nonimmune hydrops fetalis secondary to pulmonary extralobar sequestration, *Obstet. Gynecol.,* 68, 275, 1986.

60. **Albright, E. B., Crane, J. P., and Shackelford, G. D.,** Prenatal diagnosis of a branchiogenic cyst, *J. Ultrasound Med.,* 7, 91, 1988.
61. **Kleiner, B., Filly, R. A., Mack, L., and Callen, P. W.,** Multicystic dysplastic kidney: observation of contralateral disease in the fetal population, *Radiology,* 161, 27, 1986.
62. **Mahony, B. S., Callen, P. W., Filly, R. A., and Golbus, M. S.,** Progression of infantile polycystic kidney disease in early pregnancy, *J. Ultrasound Med.,* 3, 277, 1984.
63. **Habif, D. V., Berdon, W. E., and Ming-Neng, Y.,** Infantile polycystic kidney disease: in utero sonographic diagnosis, *Radiology,* 142, 475, 1982.
64. **Main, D., Mennuti, M. T., Cornfeld, D., and Coleman, B.,** Prenatal diagnosis of adult polycystic kidney disease, *Lancet,* 2, 337, 1983.
65. **Pretorius, D. H., Lee, L. E., Manco-Johnson, M. L., Eingast, G. R., Sedman, A. B., and Gabow, P. A.,** Diagnosis of autosomal dominant polycystic kidney disease in utero and in the young infant, *J. Ultrasound Med.,* 6, 249, 1987.
66. **Nguyen, K. T., Reid, R. L., and Sauerbrei, E.,** Antenatal sonographic detection of a fetal theca lutein cyst: a clue to maternal diabetes mellitus, *J. Ultrasound Med.,* 5, 665, 1986.
67. **Sandler, M. A., Smith, S. J., Pope, S. G., and Madrazo, B. L.,** Prenatal diagnosis of septated ovarian cyst, *J. Clin. Ultrasound,* 13, 55, 1985.
68. **Preziosi, P., Fariello, G., Maiorana, A., Malena, S., and Ferro, F.,** Antenatal sonographic diagnosis of complicated ovarian cysts, *J. Clin. Ultrasound,* 14, 196, 1986.
69. **Tabsh, K. M. A.,** Antenatal sonographic appearance of a fetal ovarian cyst, *J. Ultrasound Med.,* 1, 329, 1982.
70. **Seeds, J. W., Mittelsteadt, C. A., Cefalo, R. C., and Parker, T. F.,** Prenatal diagnosis of sacrococcygeal teratoma: an anechoic caudal mass, *J. Clin. Ultrasound,* 10, 193, 1982.
71. **Hill, S. J. and Hirsch, J. H.,** Sonographic detection of fetal hydrometrocolpos, *J. Ultrasound Med.,* 4, 323, 1985.
72. **Abraham, D., Koenigsberg, M., and Hoffman-Tretin, J.,** The prenatal ultrasound appearance of hydrometrocolpos, *J. Diagn. Med. Sonogr.,* 1, 115, 1985.
73. **Hartung, R. W., Kilcheski, T. S., Greaney, R. B., Powell, R. W., and Everston, L. R.,** Antenatal diagnosis of cystic meconium peritonitis, *J. Ultrasound Med.,* 2, 49, 1983.
74. **Samuel, N., Dicker, D., Landman, J., Feldberg, D., and Goldman, J. A.,** Early diagnosis and intrauterine therapy of meconium plug syndrome in the fetus: risks and benefits, *J. Ultrasound Med.,* 5, 425, 1986.
75. **Atkinson, G. O., Zaatari, G. S., Lorenzo, R. L., Gay, B. B., and Garvia, A. J.,** Cystic neuroblastoma in infants: radiographic and pathologic features, *Am. J. Roentgenol.,* 146, 113, 1986.
76. **Giulian, B. B., Chang, C. C. N., and Yoss, B. S.,** Prenatal ultrasonic diagnosis of fetal adrenal neuroblastoma, *J. Clin. Ultrasound,* 14, 225, 1986.
77. **Newton, E. R., Louis, F., Dalton, M. E., and Feingold, M.,** Fetal neuroblastoma and catecholamine-induced maternal hypertension, *Obstet. Gynecol.,* 65, 49S, 1985.
78. **Ehman, R. L., Nicholoson, S. F., and Machin, G. A.,** Prenatal sonographic detection of congenital mesoblastic nephroma in a monozygotic twin pregnancy, *J. Ultrasound Med.,* 2, 555, 1983.
79. **Geirsson, R. T., Ricketts, N. E. M., Taylor, D. J., and Coghill, S.,** Prenatal appearance of a mesoblastic nephroma associated with polyhydramnios, *J. Clin. Ultrasound,* 13, 488, 1985.
80. **Romano, W. L.,** Neonatal renal tumour with polyhydramnios, *J. Ultrasound Med.,* 3, 475, 1984.
81. **Yambao, T. J., Schwartz, D., Henderson, R., Rapp, G, Anthony, W., and Denko, J.,** Prenatal diagnosis of a congenital mesoblastic nephroma, *J. Reprod. Med.,* 31, 257, 1986.
82. **Hatteland, K. and Knutrud, O.,** Sacrococcygeal teratoma in children, *Acta Chir. Scand.,* 119, 444, 1960.
83. **Horger, E. O. and McCatrer, L. M.,** Prenatal diagnosis of sacrococcygeal teratoma, *Am. J. Obstet. Gynecol.,* 131, 228, 1979.
84. **Gross, S. J., Benzie, R. J., Sermer, M., Skidmore, M. B., and Wilson, S. R.,** Sacrococcygeal teratoma: prenatal diagnosis and management, *Am. J. Obstet. Gynecol.,* 156, 393, 1987.
85. **Lees, R. F., Williamson, B. R., Brenbridge, A. N., Bushi, A. J., and Teja, K.,** Sonography of benign sacral teratoma in utero, *Radiology,* 134, 717, 1980.
86. **Valdiserii, R. O. and Yunis, E. J.,** Sacrococcygeal teratoma: review of 68 cases, *Cancer,* 12, 217, 1981.

Chapter 8.10

AMNIOTIC FLUID ABNORMALITIES

Asim Kurjak

The volume of amniotic fluid increases in a linear fashion until 38 weeks of gestation to a mean volume of 1000 ml, and then decreases to a mean volume of 250 ml at 43 weeks of gestation. Fetal anomalies which disturb fetal urine production cause oligohydramnios, while anomalies which inhibit fetal swallowing or absorption of amniotic fluid from the fetal intestine will cause polyhydramnios.

These gross changes in amniotic fluid volume are easily appreciated by the experienced ultrasonographer, but are less easy to quantify. Fetal urine plays an important role in amniotic fluid production early during gestation. The amniotic fluid is probably largely removed by fetal swallowing.

If either polyhydramnios or oligohydramnios is suspected, the fetus should be scanned carefully for the presence of congenital anomalies.

POLYHYDRAMNIOS

Of those pathological features associated with fetal anomalies, polyhydramnios is one of the most important. This condition carries a risk of 20 to 50% of fetal anomalies (Table 1). The etiology of this condition is not possible to elucidate in all cases. The regulation of amniotic fluid volume is a very complex system, in which the fetus is considered to take care of approximately 50% of the water exchange. A fetal fault, especially one affecting the function of the gastrointestinal canal, hemodynamics, and urination, as well as some disturbances of the exchange of material through the fetal, placental, and umbilical cord surfaces and the membranes, has a significant possibility of affecting the amount of amniotic fluid. Polyhydramnios, which has an incidence in a gravid population of 0.2 to 1.6%,[2] is considered to be associated with fetal esophageal and intestinal atresias in approximately 2 to 10% of the cases[3] if the atresy is in the proximal portion to the ligamentum Treitz. Anencephaly is associated in 40% of the cases with polyhydramnios,[1] and the connection of polyhydramnios with many other fetal anomalies, like omphalocele, gastroschisis, soft-tissue fetal tumors, and heart malformations,[4-6] has been reported. Fetal urine production is not usually increased in polyhydramnios, and some preliminary reports of the fetal stomach function have not described any pathology, if proximal duodenal atresias are excluded.[7] This complexity of the etiology of polyhydramnios is revealed by reports of its association to metabolic disturbances and miscellaneous fetal pathology like diabetes,[4] osteogenesis imperfecta, achondroplasia, and cephalothoracophagus.

Polyhydramnios is the rule in severe twin-to-twin transfusion syndrome cases. Excessive amounts of amniotic fluid may also accumulate in twin pregnancies complicated by an anomaly, or in pregnancies in which there is no apparent cause. Polyhydramnios in twin gestations, whatever the cause, results in an uncomfortable patient with an irritable uterus. Sometimes, therapy by amniocentesis is required, and the procedure is significantly facilitated by the use of ultrasound.

A qualitative diagnosis of unambicous polyhydramnios is easy in the ultrasonic examination: large, echo-free areas, increased fetal mobility, and distinct boundaries between intrauterine surfaces are suggestive of this condition (Figures 1 to 4). Attempts have been

TABLE 1
The Incidence of Fetal Malformations in
Polyhydramnios[1]

Author (year)	No. of cases with polyhydramnios	Incidence of fetal malformations
Macafee (1950)		(45%)
Barry	100	51 (51%)
Lloyd & Clatworthy (1958)		(43%)
Jeffocate & Scott (1959)	169	54 (32%)
Harris et al. (1961)	109	43 (40%)
Murray (1964)	846	186 (22%)
Lee (1967)		(45%)
Queenan & Gadow (1970)	358	72 (20%)
Gadd (1970)	100	33 (33%)
Hinselmann (1973)	50	22 (44%)
Pavlekovic et al. (1974)	299	14 (48%)
Kurjak et al. (1975)	260	91 (35%)
Kirkinen & Jouppila (1978)	60	18 (30%)

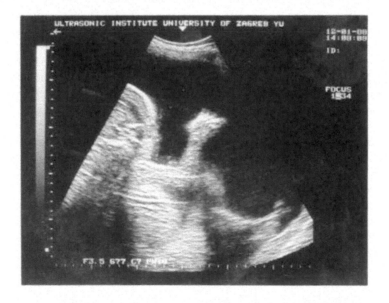

FIGURE 1.   Polyhydramnios at 26 weeks of gestation. Note the characteristic position of the fetus, which is lying on the posterior uterine wall separated from the anterior wall by a large amount of amniotic fluid. The arms and legs are also demonstrated as moving freely within the amniotic fluid.

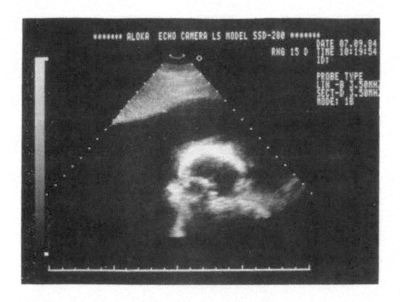

FIGURE 2. Extreme polyhydramnios at 25 weeks of pregnancy. Possibility of visualizing fetal anatomy in unusual detail is illustrated by fetal profile.

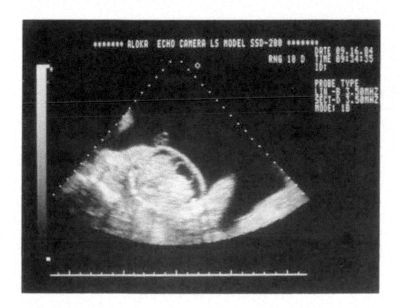

FIGURE 3. A case of polyhydramnios associated with fetal hydrops. Note the presence of fetal ascites, which is seen as an anechoic area within the fetal abdomen.

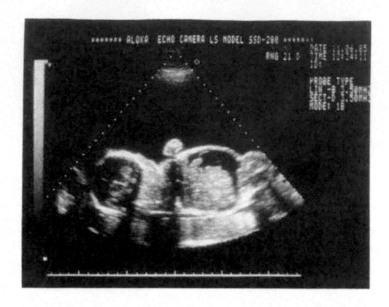

FIGURE 4.   Another example of nonimmune fetal hydrops associated with polyhydramnios. Note the typical position of the fetus, which is lying on the posterior
uterine wall.

made to quantify the degree of polyhydramnios by ultrasound, and the use of total intrauterine
volume estimation[8] and the ratio between uterine volume and fetal dimensions have been
presented.[4] However, in spite of the fact that in pregnancies complicated by polyhydramnios,
a high uterine volume correlates well with fetal risks, it does not necessarily correlate well
with the existence of fetal anomalies in these cases, because the main risk in polyhydramnios
is due to a premature delivery.

In most cases, polyhydramnios is suggested by a total intrauterine volume greater than
2 SD above the mean for a given gestational age. This measurement, however, should not
exclude polyhydramnios if the total intrauterine volume is less than 2 SD above the mean
(Figure 4).

Considering the high frequency of fetal anomalies and abnormalities in polyhydramnios,
the necessity of a careful ultrasonic evaluation of fetal, placental, and umbilical structures
must be stressed. When combined with other sophisticated methods, e.g., amniotic fluid
assays, fetal blood samples obtained by cordocentesis, as well as examinations of maternal
metabolism, ultrasonography will surely improve the possibilities for exact antenatal diagnoses in these high-risk cases.[9-13]

OLIGOHYDRAMNIOS

Oligohydramnios is a term which describes a gravid uterus with a very small amount
of amniotic fluid. There is still no uniform definition of this finding. Its presence has been
suggested by a total intrauterine volume 2 SD below the mean, as well by a scarcity of fluid
in the area of the fetal arms and legs, which produces an image of crowding.[10] Manning et
al.[13] have defined oligohydramnios if the largest pocket of amniotic fluid measures less than
1 cm in the broadest diameter. The criterion was later revised upward to 2 cm.[14] The third

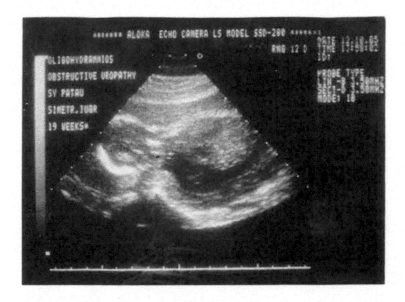

FIGURE 5. Severe oligohydramnios at 19 weeks. IUGR was diagnosed associated with low obstructive uropathy. Diagnosis of Syndroma Patau was made by amniocentesis.

and probably most widely used method is subjective of amniotic fluid quantity. Even the less experienced ultrasonographer can easily recognize significant oligohydramnios. Of course, in borderline cases, the reproducibility (and value) of such an assessment is doubtful.

The most important causes of oligohydramnios are fetal urinary tract malformations and intrauterine growth retardation (IUGR). Additional causes, more frequent in the third trimester of pregnancy, include premature rupture of membranes, chronic leak of amniotic fluid, and postmaturity.

URINARY TRACT MALFORMATIONS

It is well known that fetal urine is one of the major sources of amniotic fluid.[15-17] Therefore, the consequence of urinary tract obstruction or nonfunctioning renal tissue (multicystic kidneys, polycystic kidneys, renal agenesia) is a decreased amount or total absence of amniotic fluid. It seems that many of the pathologic findings which accompany renal pathology (facial and limb deformities in Potter's syndrome, hypoplastic lungs) are the consequence of oligohydramnios, i.e., intrauterine compression (Figures 5 and 6).

INTRAUTERINE GROWTH RETARDATION

Oligohydramnios is an accompanying finding in the majority of pregnancies complicated by IUGR. As postulated, one mechanism of underlying oligohydramnios in growth-retarded human fetuses may be a decreased production of fetal urine and lung liquid as a result of hypoxemia-induced redistribution of cardiac output. This hypothesis is supported by reports of decreased production of fetal urine and decreased fetal breathing movements in human fetuses with IUGR[15,16] (Figure 7). The recognition of an underlying pathology in the presence

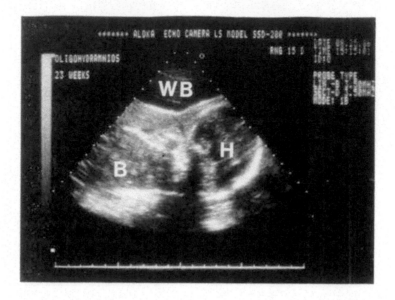

FIGURE 6.   Complete absence of amniotic fluid in a case of renal angenesis detected at the 23rd week of gestation. A water bag technique was employed to enable better visualization of fetal anatomy (WB = water bag, H = head, B = body).

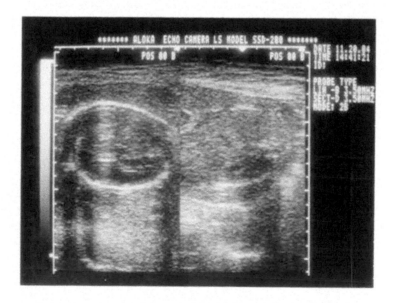

FIGURE 7.   Oligohydramnios at 28 weeks in a case of IUGR due to placental insufficiency. The fetal head and body can be recognized, but other anatomical details are not visible.

of oligohydramnios is often very difficult. The ultrasound image is poor, the biometry is rather inaccurate, and evaluation of fetal anatomy almost impossible. The major task is differentiation of renal anomalies and IUGR, as fetuses with renal pathology are often small for gestational age.[18] Doppler assessment of fetal circulation seems to be the diagnostic method of choice in such situations. IUGR significantly alters Doppler signals from fetal vessels (see Chapter 4, Volume II), in contrast to the normal finding if renal pathology is the cause of oligohydramnios.[19]

The instillation of normal saline, either into the amniotic cavity or fetal peritoneal cavity, in order to improve image quality and recognition of underlying pathology has also been proposed recently.[20]

REFERENCES

1. **Kurjak, A., Ed.,** Fetal abnormalities in early and late pregnancy, in *Progress in Medical Ultrasound,* Vol. 1, Excerpta Medica, Amsterdam, 1980, 107.
2. **Kirkinen, P. and Jouppila, P.,** Polyhydramnios. Clinical study, *Ann. Chir. Gynaecol.,* 67, 117, 1978.
3. **Wallenburg, H. C. S. and Wladimiroff, J. W.,** The amniotic fluid. II. Polyhydramnios and oligohydramnios, *J. Perinat. Med.,* 6, 233, 1977.
4. **Kirkinen, P.,** Intrauterine growth followed ultrasonically in normal and some complicated pregnancies, *Ann. Chir. Gynaecol.,* 68, 194, 1979.
5. **Kirkinen, P., Jouppila, P., Ylostalo, P., and Valkeakari, T.,** The antenatal diagnosis of congenital anomalies by ultrasound, *Duodecim,* 95, 22, 1979.
6. **Horger, E. and McCarter, L.,** Prenatal diagnosis of sacrococcygeal teratoma, *Am. J. Obstet. Gynecol.,* 134, 228, 1979.
7. **Vandenberghe, K. and Wolf, F.,** Ultrasonic assessment of fetal stomach function, physiology and clinic, in *Recent Advances in Ultrasound Diagnosis,* Vol. 2, Kurjak, A., Ed., Excerpta Medica, Amsterdam, 1980, 275.
8. **Phillips, J. F., Goodwin, D. W., Thompson, S. B., and Dempsey, P. J.,** The volume of the uterus in normal and abnormal pregnancy, *J. Clin. Ultrasound,* 5, 107, 1977.
9. **Gitlin, D., Kumate, J., Morales, C., et al.,** The turnover of amniotic fluid protein in the human conceptus, *Am. J. Obstet. Gynecol.,* 113, 632, 1972.
10. **Gohari, P., Berkowitz, R. L., and Hobbins, J. C.,** Prediction of intrauterine growth retardation by determination of total intrauterine volume, *Am. J. Obstet. Gynecol.,* 127, 255, 1977.
11. **Barkin, S. Z. et al.,** Severe polyhydramnios: incidence of anomalies, *Am. J. Roentgenol.,* 148 (1), 155, 1987.
12. **Landy, H. J., Isada, N. B., and Larsen, J. W.,** Genetic implications of idiopathic hydroamnios, *Am. J. Obstet. Gynecol.,* 157 (1), 114, 1987.
13. **Manning, F. A., Hill, L. M., and Platt, L. D.,** Qualitative amniotic fluid volume determination by ultrasound: antepartum detection of intrauterine growth retardation, *Am. J. Obstet. Gynecol.,* 139, 254, 1981.
14. **Moore, P. T., Mancini, R. A., and Spitz, H. B.,** Sonographic diagnosis of hydroamnios and olligohydroamnios, *Semin. Ultrasound CT MR,* 5, 157, 1984.
15. **Wladimiroff, J. W. and Campbell, S.,** Fetal urine-production rates in normal and complicated pregnancy, *Lancet,* 1, 151, 1974.
16. **Kurjak, A., Kirkinen, P., and Latin, V.,** Ultrasonic assessment of fetal kidney function in normal and complicated prognosis, *Am. J. Obstet. Gynecol.,* 141, 473, 1981.
17. **Seeds, A. E.,** Current concepts of amniotic fluid dynamics, *Am. J. Obstet. Gynecol.,* 138, 575, 1980.
18. **Hansmann, M., Hackeloer, B. J., and Staudach, A.,** *Ultrasound Diagnosis in Obstetrics and Gynecology,* Springer-Verlag, Berlin, 1985, 223.
19. **Hackett, G. A., Nicolaides, K. H., and Campbell, S.,** The values of Doppler ultrasound assessment of fetal and uteroplacental circulations when severe oligohydroamnios complicates the second trimester of pregnancy, *Br. J. Obstet. Gynecol.,* in press.
20. **Bradley, R. J. and Nicolaides, K. H.,** Ultrasound guided procedures in small for gestation fetuses, in *Intrauterine Growth Retardation — Diagnosis and Therapy,* Kurjak, A. and Beazley, J., Eds., CRC Press, Boca Raton, FL, in press.

Chapter 8.11

SURGICALLY CORRECTABLE DEFECTS

Asim Kurjak

When a successful diagnosis of malformation is made, the ultrasonographer should consider the following circumstances:

1. Whether the malformation can be relieved by surgery after birth.
2. Whether the size and shape of the fetus will lead to obstructed labor.
3. Whether a surgical procedure might be undertaken in pregnancy to relieve or ameliorate the problem.

In surgically correctable defects, the prenatal diagnosis of fetal anomaly can be life saving to the fetus, because the patient can be delivered in an institution where skilled pediatricians are prepared to institute appropriate resuscitative measures immediately and surgery can be performed within a short time after birth.

There were several papers on successful detection and improved perinatal management of surgically significant neonatal anomaly.[1-7]

A total of 5285 "high-risk" patients underwent ultrasonic examination, and among them, 41 fetal anomalies were diagnosed in the third trimester. Although 14 of the 41 patients carried a fetus with a potentially correctable anomaly, only 9 survived. This included four babies with hydrocephaly, two with meconium peritonitis, and each with duodenal atresia, a twisted ovarian cyst, and a "giant" omphalocele. The remainder were either stillborn or were in such poor condition at birth that infant survival was not possible.

Equally important, however, is the detection of certain surgically correctable anomalies where the prognosis for the newborn is significantly improved by antenatal recognition and the referral to an institution with a neonatal intensive care unit. Four of the six patients reported in the series were detected to have polyhydramnios, with the diagnosis of duodenal atresia made in two and meconium peritonitis and omphalocele in the others. The value of antenatal detection is obvious, particularly in babies born with meconium peritonitis or diaphragmatic hernia who are likely to develop severe respiratory insufficiency and acidosis immediately after birth.[8]

A total of 28 abnormalities have been diagnosed *in utero* by the use of ultrasound over $3^1/_2$ years. These include ascites, gastroschisis, omphalocele, sacrococcygeal teratoma, cystic hygroma, hydrocele, duodenal atresia, multicystic kidney, jejunal atresia, conjoined twins, uretero-pelvic junction obstruction, urethral valves, urethral agenesis, and hydronephrosis secondary to reflux.

Ultrasonic diagnosis has significantly improved perinatal management. Elective cesarian section (CS) has benefited infants with lesions causing distotia such as sacrococcygeal teratoma, omphalocele, and conjoined twins. Immediate notification of surgeons and neonatologists has reduced the delays of postnatal evaluation and treatment that contribute significantly to complications and death. In addition, the transfer of the pregnant mother carrying an infant with a significant surgical anomaly to a center with facilities for neonatal surgery, specialized in postoperative care, can be planned for in advance. In the near future, intrauterine fetal surgery or paliative intervention may provide increased salvage of patients with obstructive uropathy and diaphragmatic hernia, both of which carry high mortality rates secondary to *in utero* damage. Ultrasound has proved useful in following the dilatation of either intestinal or urinary tract structures *in utero*.

The knowledge in advance of a surgically correctable anomaly has the potential of benefitting the perinatal management of these pregnancies and also the postnatal and, perhaps, prenatal surgical management of these infants.[9]

In a very recent review, Suita et al.[4] presented 57 infants with 61 malformations detected antenatally by ultrasound. Of these, 22 malformations involved the alimentary tract, 5 the anterior abdominal wall defect, 3 diaphragmatic hernia, 27 genito-urinary tract, and 2 involved a cervical mass. Of 57 infants, 50 were surgically tracted; 45 survived with 2 late deaths at 33 d and 1 year. The antenatal diagnosis has significantly altered perinatal management, and it has done this in three ways: (1) by indicating the need for elective CS to avoid the risk associated with dystocia, e.g., large omphalocele, gastroschisis, large sacrococcygeal teratoma, and conjoined twins; (2) by enabling plans to be made for the baby to be born in or adjacent to a specialized center capable of fetal pediatric care once the baby is born (in this way the transport of the baby prior to birth is in the safest and best environment — in the gravid uterus); and (3) by enabling perinatal involvement of those who will be responsible for the postnatal care of the baby, specifically, the neonatologist and pediatric surgeons and, when considered appropriate, the team who will transport the baby and the pediatric anesthesiologist.

Counseling of the parents is essential, and the pediatric surgeon has a key role to play in this area. Only the ultrasonographer and pediatric surgeon together can give meaningful advice in reference to treatment and prognosis, and such advice should always be made available to the parents.[4] Experience from the author's department are presented elsewhere[5-7] and illustrated in Figures 1 to 27.

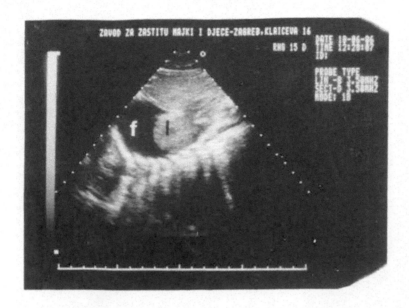

FIGURE 1. Postnatal sonogram of a neonate with congenital diaphragmatic hernia. Note the compressed lung tissue (l) due to presence of fluid-filled bowel loops within thoracic cavity (f).

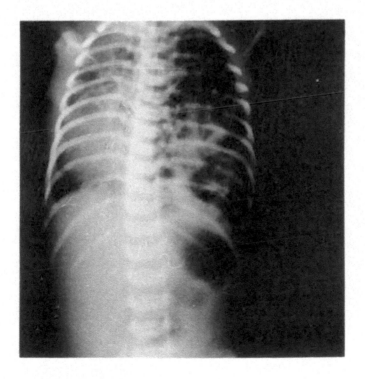

FIGURE 2. Postnatal roentgenogram of the same baby in Figure 1 showing bowel loops in the left side of the neonatal thorax.

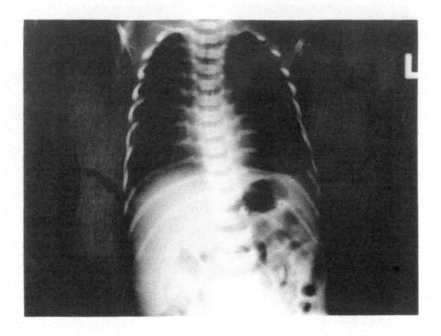

FIGURE 3.   Normal chest roentgenogram of the same baby of Figures 1 and 2 after successful corrective surgery.

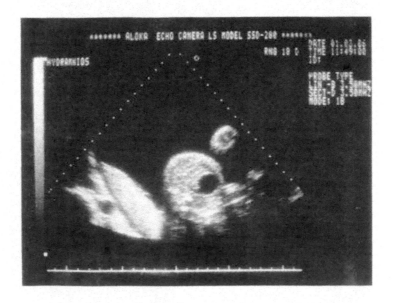

FIGURE 4.   Marked polyhydramnios in an otherwise apparently normal fetus at the 24th week gestation.

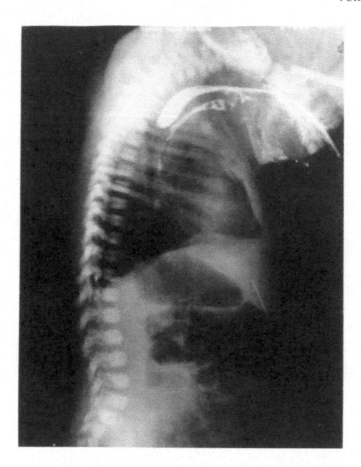

FIGURE 5. Contrast roentgenogram of the same baby in Figure 4 after delivery showed esophageal atresia, which was suspected, but could be confirmed prenatally.

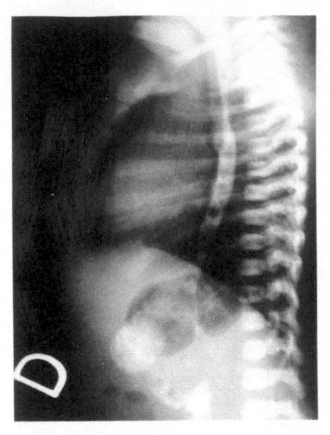

FIGURE 6.   Roentgenogram of the same baby of Figures 4 and 5 after surgery, demonstrating successful passage of dye through anastomosed esophagus.

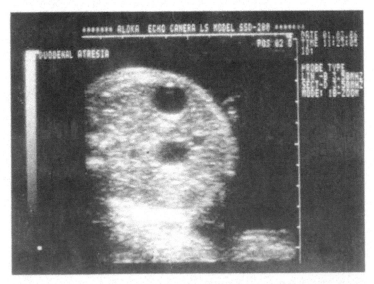

FIGURE 7.   Transverse section through the fetal abdomen at 26 weeks of gestation showing typical ultrasonic "double-bubble" appearance which represents a pathognomonic sign of *in utero* duodenal obstruction.

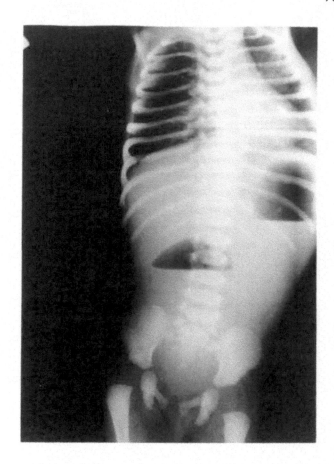

FIGURE 8. Confirmatory roentgenogram after delivery.

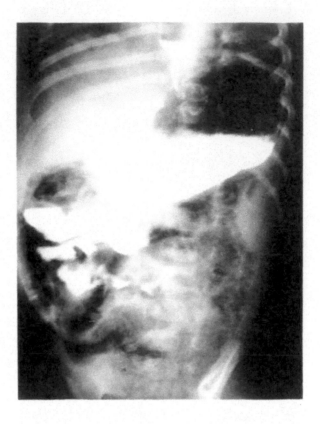

FIGURE 9.   Successful passage of dye after surgical correction.

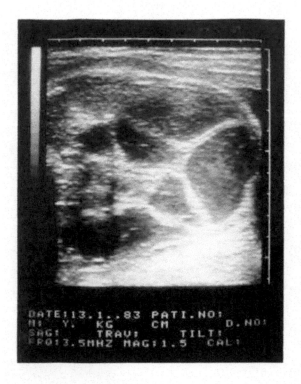

FIGURE 10. Transverse section through the fetal abdomen, demonstrating large fluid-filled bowel loops in a case of ileal atresia.

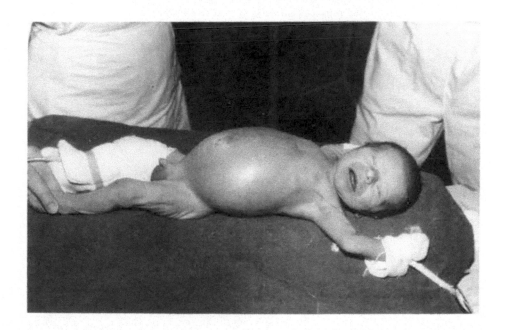

FIGURE 11. The baby in Figure 10 after delivery with marked distention of the abdomen.

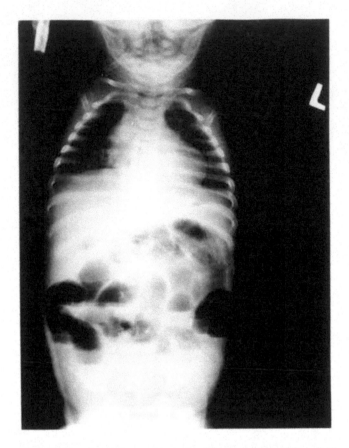

FIGURE 12.   Confirmatory radiograph of the same baby of Figures 10 and 11 showing pathological finding of fluid levels within the abdomen at the filled level.

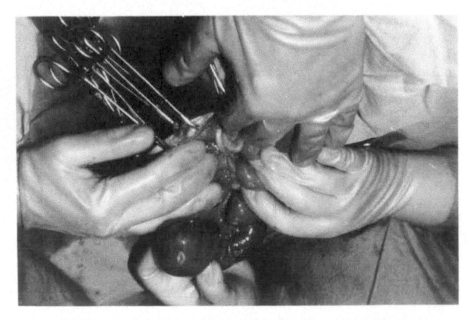

FIGURE 13.   Distended bowel loop and sight of atresia as seen during surgery.

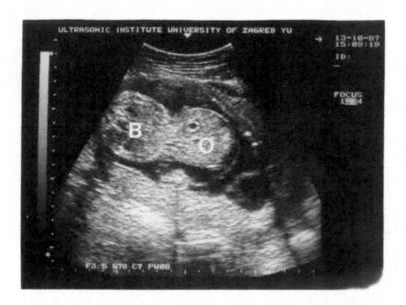

FIGURE 14. Transverse scan of the fetal abdomen with omphalocele (b = body, o = omphalocele).

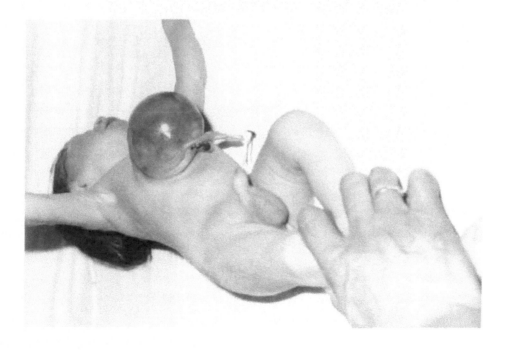

FIGURE 15. Same baby in Figure 14 after delivery. Note that the umbilical cord is inserted at the abdominal wall defect.

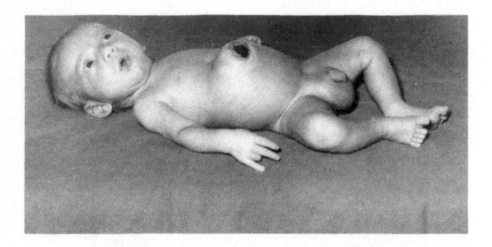

FIGURE 16. Healing of the wound during recovery period after initial surgical correction of the case of Figures 14 and 15.

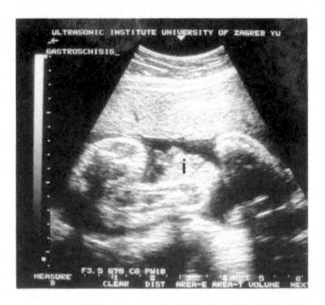

FIGURE 17. Gastroschisis detected at 26 weeks of pregnancy. Intestinal loops (i) are seen floating freely in the amniotic fluid close to the fetal abdomen.

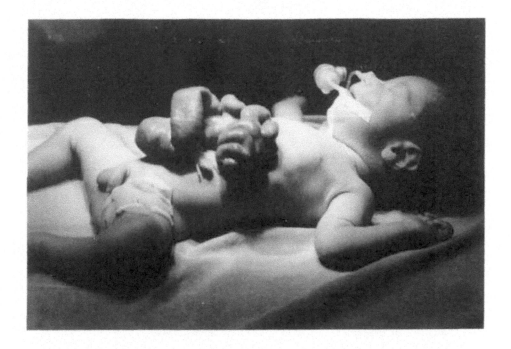

FIGURE 18.   The baby in Figure 17 after delivery, with the intestinal loops protruding from the anterior defect of the abdominal wall.

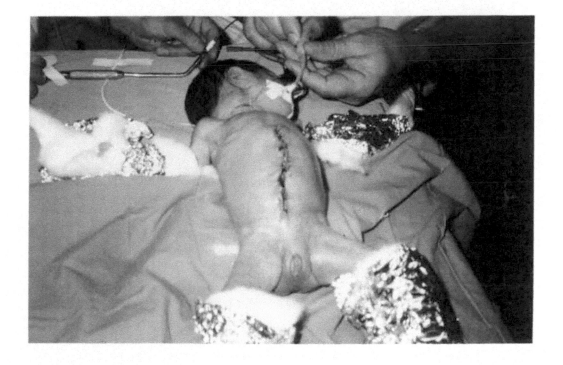

FIGURE 19.   The baby of Figures 17 and 18 immediately after surgical repair.

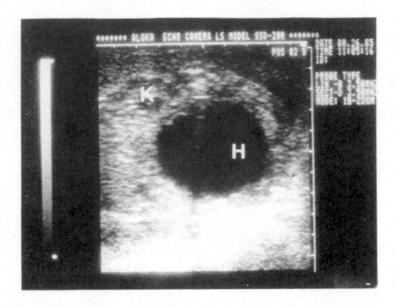

FIGURE 20.   A case of unilateral hydronephrosis detected at 34 weeks of gestation. Normal kidney is seen on the left (k), while the right kidney is completely fluid filled (h).

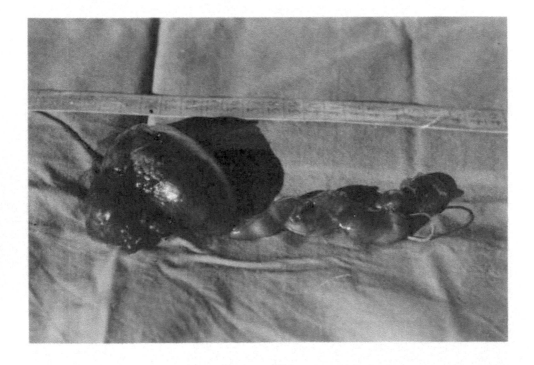

FIGURE 21.   Hydronephrotic kidney and dilated ureter after surgical removal.

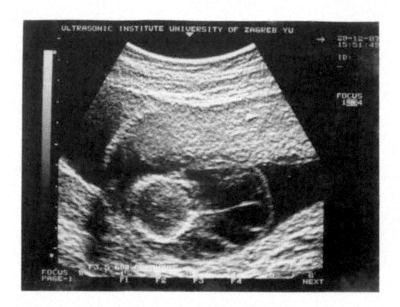

FIGURE 22. Large cystic hygroma detected in the second trimester in a chromosomally normal baby.

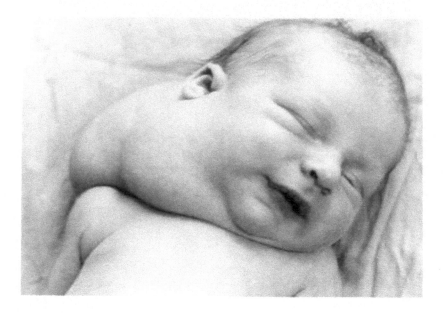

FIGURE 23. The same baby in Figure 22 after delivery, with a large tumor on the lateral side of the neck.

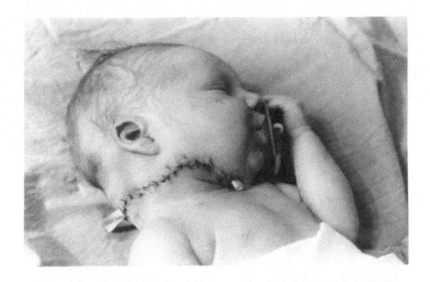

FIGURE 24.   The same baby of Figures 22 and 23 after surgical correction.

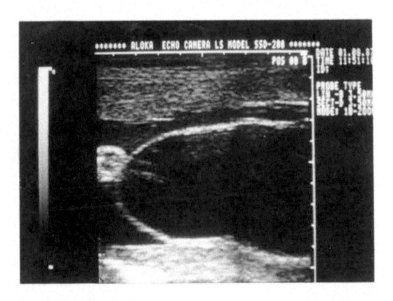

FIGURE 25.   Cystic sacrococcygeal teratoma as seen by ultrasound at the 34th week of gestation.

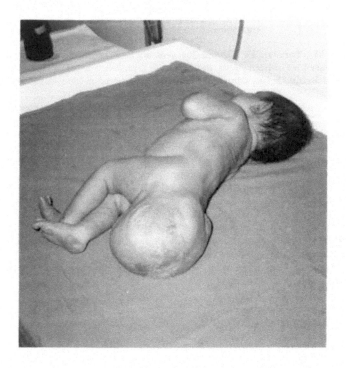

FIGURE 26.   The same baby in Figure 25 after delivery.

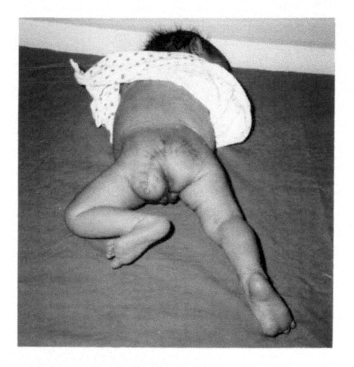

FIGURE 27.   Gluteal region of the baby of Figures 25 and 26 after complete surgical removal of the tumor.

REFERENCES

1. **Kullendorff, C. M., Larsson, L. T., and Joergenson, C.,** The advantage of antenatal diagnosis of intestinal and urinary tract malformations, *Br. J. Obstet. Gynecol.,* 91, 144, 1984.
2. **Fremond, B. and Babut, J. M.,** Obstructive uropathies diagnosed in utero — the postnatal outcome — a study of 43 cases, *Prog. Pediatr. Surg.,* 19, 160, 1986.
3. **Harrison, M. R., Golbus, M. S., and Filly, R. A.,** Fetal hydronephrosis: selection and surgical repair, *J. Pediatr. Surg.,* 22, 556, 1987.
4. **Suita, S., Ikeda, K., and Nakano, H.,** Antenatal diagnosis and pediatric surgery — an overview, in *The Fetus as the Patient, '87,* Maeda, K., Ed., Excerpta Medica, Amsterdam, 1987, 315.
5. **Kurjak, A., Latin, V., Mandruzzato, G., D'Addario, V., and Rajhvajn, B.,** Ultrasound diagnosis and perinatal management of fetal genito-urinary abnormalities, *J. Perinat. Med.,* 12, 291, 1984.
6. **Kurjak, A., Rajhvajn, B., Kogler, A., and Gogolja, D.,** Ultrasound diagnosis and fetal malformation of surgical interest, in *The Fetus as a Patient,* Kurjak, A., Ed., Excerpta Medica, Amsterdam, 1985, 243.
7. **Kurjak, A., Gogolja, D., and Kogler, A.,** Ultrasound diagnosis and perinatal management of surgically correctable fetal malformations, *Ultrasound Med. Biol.,* 10, 443, 1984.
8. **Touloukian, R. J. and Hobbins, J. C.,** Maternal ultrasonography in the antenatal diagnosis of surgically correctable fetal abnormalities, *J. Pediatr. Surg.,* 15, 373, 1980.
9. **Canty, T. G., Leopold, G. R., and Wolf, D. A.,** Maternal ultrasonography for the antenatal diagnosis of surgically significant neonatal anomalies, *Ann. Surg.,* 194, 353, 1981.

Chapter 8.12

ETHICAL AND LEGAL ISSUES

Asim Kurjak

INTRODUCTION

Several chapters in this book have shown our ability to diagnose fetal birth defects, which has achieved considerable sophistication. However, new scientific knowledge and resultant technologies create complex ethical dilemmas for society. Society is more critical both in the successful treatment of fetal disorders and in the maintenance of respect for the human dignity of the fetus. Therefore, fetal diagnosis and therapy raises not only scientific issues, but also ethical and legal ones which challenge many of our traditional concepts of the fetus. These scientific achievements in the coming years will force upon society unprecedented ethical questions concerning the value and the definition of the point of origin of human life.

Here we become involved in the juncture between legal, medical, scientific, and religious problems, all of which disciplines have moral standards of their own. The main question to be discussed asks when does life begin? Life has been defined as being terminated when brain activity ends. But if we were to say that life begins when brain activity starts, we would be admitting that the definition of the beginning of a life is dependent upon technology and not upon ethics or mortality.

Let us take, for example, the accepted definition of birth which some years ago was described as the complete expulsion of a fetus of 1000 g or 28 weeks of pregnancy. With advances in perinatal and neonatal intensive care, the line was drawn some years later at 500 g or 22 weeks of gestation. This meant that a 20-week-old fetus was not born by definition, even if it was viable. Today, the concept has changed. The same logic applies to a live fetus being accorded the term "life" if we use such definitions as the beginning of brain activity or ultrasonic proof of heartbeat and movement. The establishment of each of these parameters is shifted to an earlier stage year by year by improved technological refinements in electronic equipment. This leads us to the conclusion that to follow this line of reasoning means to give life, birth, and viability definitions determined by technology. The more advanced the technology, the earlier life begins. Thus, we will arrive at the ultimate point, which is parallel to the religious view, that life begins at the point of fusion of egg and sperm at fertilization, as happens in nature.

THE BEGINNING OF HUMAN LIFE AND ITS ASSESSMENT *IN UTERO*

In spite of the tremendous scientific advances in the world today, when, where, and how life began has still not been conclusively established. Some authors say that, in fact, life as such does not exist — no one has ever seen it. Szent-Gyorgyi says that the noun "life" has no significance, for there is no such thing as "life".[1] Le Dantez holds that the expression "to live" is too general, and that it would be better to say that a dog "dogs" or a fish "fishes" than to say that a dog or fish lives.[1]

Be that as it may, a definition of life should include not only life as it is today, but as it might have been in its primordial form and as it will be in the future. That is to say, all present forms of life are the fruit of an uninterrupted continuity from its very inception. Not a single form of life appears as something completely new: life, then, is transferred and not conceived in each new generation. Human life is no exception. Both the female ovum and the male sperm are human cells. Their merging, fertilization, is not the beginning of human life, but just one exceptionally important step in its continuity. True, the product of fertilization, the fertilized ovum or zygote, is a new form, but it is still not a new individual either by scientific or by general standards. This ovum still lacks any of the essential characteristics attributed to man. It does not have the rudiments of a central nervous system, nor does it react even to the simplest of stimuli. Life, in the true sense of the word, begins when the chemical matter gives rise, in a specific way, to an autonomous, self-regulating, and self-reproducing system. Life is connected with a living being, and it creates its own system as an indivisible whole. That is to say, it has individuality. Living beings transform matter, i.e., they create their own substance from matter obtained from outside, just as they break it down. The organism demonstrates a certain sensitivity in regard to some aspects of self-regulation. One of the most important characteristics of living beings is their reproduction, which is also connected with the inheritance of certain features.

Although the substance of living is composed of the same elements that go to make up inanimate nature, living beings have a specially complicated system of matter, such as does not exist in inanimate nature. Living beings demonstrate variability, individual development, and harmony. It is exactly this individuality which constitutes one of the most essential characteristics of the human being. It includes bodily features, special behavior, and the capability to recognize and adopt. These characteristics gradually develop into human fetuses.

Moral and litigious issues aside, let us consider the scientific information pertinent to any discussion of when life begins. Early on, at a time when the process of fertilization and early development was not understood, the position was held that life began with the movement of the fetus or "quickening". When it was appreciated that pregnancy occurred as the result of union of sperm and egg, many then defined the beginning of life as representing that event. As the physiology of the fertilization process is scrutinized in greater detail, however, it becomes evident that at the scientific level the issue is not quite so straightforward.

Can we then, as scientists, give to our legislators, based on our knowledge of fertilization, a clear-cut definition on the beginning of life? It has been doubted seriously that any scientist with genuine expertise in this field would be able to label one event or another in this complicated chain of events as the pivotal one on which to base a decision on exactly when "human life" begins. In response to this effort at legislation, the American Fertility Society's Public Affairs Committee drafted the following statement for distribution to the membership for approval: "Human life is a continuous process, and therefore, the exact moment at which a new person is formed cannot be defined in purely scientific terms. The definition of a person necessarily involves metaphysical (religious, philosophical) judgment." An overwhelming majority of the membership agreed with that position.

ASSESSMENT OF LIFE *IN UTERO*

The idea of a life *in utero* is by no means new. The Chinese, for example, have always considered themselves to be 9 months older than their European cousins. The Ancients believed that in each ovum or sperm there was a complete but tiny adult. They imagined that the body and soul came into simultaneous existence at the time of fertilization.

The theologians, however, introduced the idea that, *in utero*, we first existed in a prehuman, embryonic form, and subsequently after entrance of the soul, developed into the human fetus with which most people are familiar.

Hippocrates believed that the entrance of the soul into the male fetus occurred on the 13th d of intrauterine life. It entered into the female fetus on the 40th d. Actually, this idea was a considerable improvement on the scheme found in the book of Leviticus, where it is suggested that the soul does not enter even the male fetus until the 40th d and does not enter the female until 40 d after that.

With the development of embryological science, embryologists found themselves unable to confirm the notion that life *in utero* was divided into a prehuman and human era. Like the Ancients, they could discover only a continuum after fertilization. It now seems paradoxical that for centuries this idea of a continuum protected the early human fetus from violation by the unscrupulous until we, in our wisdom, saw such a liberalization in pregnancy termination.

The poets would have us believe that life *in utero* is a heaven of peace and quiet, and birth equivalent to "Paradise lost". But this is not so. We have our being there just as much as in the world we remember.

From the modern research of Sir William Lilley it is now clear that the uterus is not even a sound-proof box. The noise of the maternal heart and the rumblings of the maternal gut produce as much sound as a busy highway. It has been estimated that the sound level *in utero* may be as high as 90 dB.[2] Nor is the uterus completely dark. Though the developing baby may not see objects distinctly, the light intensity within the uterus has been likened to the glow which appears through the cheek when a torch is placed inside the mouth. It is also clear that the baby can taste the liquor which surrounds it. If chemicals are put into the liquor to render it bitter, the child swallows much less. By contrast, when the liquor is made sweet with saccharin, the child drinks much greater quantities.[2]

The remarkable individuality which we develop at an early stage of our intrauterine existence comes about by the wonderful integration of a series of complicated events. This beautiful intrauterine conformity, however, is subject to the malevolence of disease and chance, just as much as in life after birth. In fact, because of our vulnerability *in utero*, after pregnancy and delivery we are not again subject to such risks of mortality until our old age.

Very probably the Chinese are correct. Life does not begin with birth. When born, we are already 9 months old, and it is precisely because intrauterine life and neonatal existence constitute a continuum that medicine has a responsibility to learn how to study life *in utero* and, subsequently, how to care for it.

WHAT ARE THE MORAL ISSUES?

Morals are the practice of ethics, and ethics are the principles which govern man's duty to his neighbor. The concepts of natural and civil rights are included in such principles.[3]

NATURAL RIGHTS

One remarkable feature of modern history has been man's struggle to make manifest certain fundamental rights and freedoms which are so intimately connected with his nature that to be separated from them, would deprive him of a portion of his humanity. These natural rights are based on the idea that from conception, man has an inherent worth, an intrinsic dignity, a certain independence. He has an equal right to life, to liberty, to security of person, to freely exercise his mind, and to pursue contentment. These natural rights are independent of time, race, culture, or social development. Moreover, from these rights of being, from the rights of mind, from these fair, just, and due entitlements of all conceivable individuals, no man has the natural right to exclude another without his prior consent.

CIVIL RIGHTS

Less fundamental than natural rights are man's civil rights. Society depends for its survival upon an ordered liberty of the individual. Implicit in this concept are freedom from fear and from want, freedom of speech and to worship, and numerous basic cultural freedoms, including the right to be educated, to be safe within society, to work, to participate in the culture of life, and to share in its scientific benefits. To safeguard such civil rights, man has evolved the idea of civil liberties. These are the natural consequences of man's concern for every member of the human family, and civil liberties usually appear as the products of just government.

CONCERN FOR FETAL LIFE

Concern for fetal life has been expressed certainly since the time of Hippocrates. In the Hippocratic oath, it is written that "I will not give a woman a pessary to produce abortion." Here, concern is expressed not only for a potential human life, but also for a human life which cannot protect itself. In 1948, as mankind considered the horrors of a second world war, the Declaration of Geneva proclaimed "I will maintain the utmost respect for human life from the time of conception." However, present attitudes to early fetal life can be divided into three different categories.

1.   There are those who consider the early fetus as merely an organ of the mother and not a living human being. It has only those rights guaranteed to it by its mother, and no moral problem arises in regard to its removal. This view is obviously unjustifiable as it is not based on the nature of early fetal development. It takes no account of natural rights.
2.   There are those who consider all forms of human life, including fetal life, to be supreme. From the moment of conception, the fetus is a full human being with the same rights and same value as a baby at birth. This attitude accepts only one view of fetal life, considering all individuals as equal whether they be born or unborn.
3.   The view most commonly held is that a fetus is a potential individual, and that this potential increases throughout pregnancy, to become actual at birth. This opinion accepts that there may be times when fetal life is less important than other issues. In this context, fetal life would be presented as a phenomenon which, though it be of secondary importance on occasion, always has a value which should not be under-estimated.

Modern reproductive technology has raised many ethical issues. The increasing improvement of the techniques used will result in the earliest possible detection of even the smallest malformations. Some of these can be corrected *in utero*; but, as regards the others, where will the selection barrier fall? Before or beyond a harelip, a badly formed ear, a finger more or less? The horizon, perhaps as a treat, is that of a guaranteed child, the growth of which could be interrupted if any part should prove defective and the delivery of which, with everything in good working order and with all the expected accessories, would be guaranteed to the parents in advance. The requirements of desire correspond to the requirements of progress, and the present improvements instill into future parents the image, the possibility, and, therefore, the demand for a perfect child.

The ethical aspects of this work will continue to occupy the minds of those physicians and scientists who have chosen to work in these areas. *De facto*, they will be called upon to consider ethical issues into the foreseeable future.

LEGAL STATUS OF THE UNBORN CHILD

Following on from the above considerations is the problem of the legal status of the unborn child.[4,5] These rights do not extend by law to the previable fetuses. The problem is the line of demarcation. The cut-off point for viability is currently set at 24 weeks, but new medical procedures are rapidly shifting that point of viability to earlier and earlier dates. Predictably, there will be continuing controversy over the legal status of the previable fetus. Thanks to real-time ultrasound, we now have proof that human life begins much earlier than we believed. The criteria for the beginning of life, therefore, should not be taken as the day of birth, as specified in Roman law, but from the fact that the fetus is able to exist independently. However, with the advance of modern medical techniques, the fetus is capable of being born alive at an earlier and earlier age. The crime of child destruction is, therefore, expanding at the expense of what might otherwise be lawful abortion. Obviously, this situation needs legal reconsideration. Such reconsideration should make it clear that although the fetus in not invested with legal rights, when born alive, the child can bring an action retrospectively in relation to its intrauterine existence. Of course, a fault must first be proved, usually the fault of negligence, and a direct cause and effect must be shown between this fault and the substance of the child's complaint. Practically, an obstetrician need not fear such measures insofar as he acts with reasonable care and adheres to all the rules of his profession.

A further problem arises from the introduction of techniques for antenatal diagnosis. These techniques are complex and require considerable expertise. If a mistake is made, and the child is born with a serious deformity, are those individuals who carried out the tests likely to be the subject of litigation?

There is still doubt whether a child with an injury caused before birth by someone's negligence can sue for damages. A baby may be born and survive in an injured condition after damage caused *in utero* by surgical procedures. The injury may be evident at birth, or become so in childhood, or not appear until adult life. If the fetus has the right to sue, obstetricians will face a fresh risk of action for damages for negligence in the treatment given to a pregnant woman either for her benefit or for the benefit of the fetus. A further question to be argued in many cases would be the balance struck between benefit to the mother and risk to the fetus. To what extent is the mother responsible by accepting treatment? The life and health of the mother have traditionally always taken priority over that of the fetus if the circumstances of the case reach the extremity of choice. What, then, is the relation between a child who has been injured *in utero* by medical treatment and his mother? There are also a number of other problem areas. Two examples will help to illustrate them. What if high-risk patients are told of the possibility of amniocentesis and ultrasound examinations, but for religious or other reasons, take no action — would they have any defense against an action by an affected child? Where negligence, by an operator during amniocentesis, for example, causes harm to the fetus, the operator would be liable. Where the mistake results in an existing defect being missed, he would not, but in this situation, the parents themselves might have a case. The law seems inadequate in situations where by manipulation of the intrauterine environment or by other means, it might be possible to offer antenatal treatment as an alternative to termination.

Finally, it should be stressed once again that the problem is not that of determining when actual human life begins, but when the value of that life begins to outweigh other considerations such as the health or even the happiness of the mother. On the other hand, there is essentially no difference between euthanasia (terminating the life of a sick person) and teratothanasia (terminating the life of a malformed fetus), because in both cases life has been interrupted. Neither euthanasia nor teratothanasia have been legalized in any country in the civilized world, yet hundreds of pregnancies with malformed fetuses are interrupted annually.

In daily practice, it is important to differentiate between three levels of malformation: (1) incompatible for any type of independent life; (2) malformation requiring the lifetime aid of another person; and (3) malformation correctable by minor surgery or physical therapy. The first problem depends only on the decision of the mother. There should be no dilemma since, in the interest of the family, a child incompatible for life should not be born. Opinions vary in the second case since this type of malformed child can have a relatively normal life after habilitation. The third case causes the greatest dilemmas as to whether the pregnancy should be terminated or not.

FETAL THERAPY

Fetal therapy raises complex ethical questions about the rights of the mother and fetus as a patient.[5-10] Is the obstetrician to view the fetus or the mother as his patient? Usually there is no need to make the distinction; but what if the physician believes a procedure, such as fetal surgery, is indicated and the mother refuses to consent? To what extent is the mother responsible by accepting treatment? The life and health of the mother have traditionally always taken priority over that of the fetus if the circumstances of the case reach the extremity of choice. What, then, is the relation between a child who has been injured *in utero* by medical treatment and its mother? Whether we call the fetus a person, a patient, or a fetus, what rights will we accord to it? When will we leave all decisions regarding its health to its mother, and when, if ever, will we, as a society, decide to restrict the autonomy of pregnant women for the sake of their fetuses?[3] Undoubtedly, there is a need for involvement of not only individual patients, but also society as a whole in setting rules and priorities for fetal therapy.

FETAL ORGAN TRANSPLANTATION

Very recently, a new ethical and legal problem has arisen from the field of fetal organ transplantation.[11] Organ transplants could give an increasing number of children with fatal childhood diseases the chance of a full life. Anencephalic babies could be ideal donors because termination of pregnancy is justifiable, even in the third trimester, and vital organs other than the brain are usually normal. However, society has to decide what attitude to adopt towards the anencephalic fetus. One attitude is that an anencephalic baby is a product of human conception incapable of achieving "personhood", because it lacks the physical structure (forebrain) necessary for characteristic human activity and, thus, can never become a human "person". Another attitude is that the anencephalic fetus is a dying person, and that death is inevitable at or shortly after birth because of brain absence.

If the anencephalic fetus is considered to be equivalent to brain-dead subjects for legal purposes, the family should be able to allow organ donation delivery and to arrange the timing and place of delivery to facilitate transplantation.

CONCLUSION

The publicity accorded the thalidomide episode has increased the awareness of the public and the legal profession of the possibility that some human malformations are caused by nongenetic environmental influences. It is perfectly obvious that there has been an increase in the incidence of medicolegal cases involving malformed infants.[12]

Furthermore, these cases are receiving more attention in the lay press. The philosophy of some members of the legal profession and of the public is reflected in the concept that someone must be responsible for personal damages that have been incurred.[13]

Historically, the father or mother of a malformed infant was open to ridicule, criticism, or even prosecution. Folklore and superstition dominated the field, and the causes of malformations were attributed to evil spirits, fornication with animals, lewd thoughts, or other immoral acts. Certainly, in the 1600s no one would have thought of receiving compensation for the birth of a malformed child.

It is obvious that the problem of medicolegal litigation involving the unborn fetus will not be resolved without the active participation of the legal and medical profession and the national and state legislatures.

The medicolegal aspects of teratology have some unique problems that separate this field from other medicolegal problems. These problems include[12]

- Who can be the plaintiff?
- Multiplicity of defendants
- The legal rights of the unborn fetus
- Multitude of etiologies of congenital malformations
- The problem of available expert testimony

It is obvious that the problem of medicolegal litigation involving the unborn fetus will remain unresolved without the active participation of the legal and medical profession and national and state legislative bodies. In the area of human malformations, the physicians or pharmaceutical firms are extremely vulnerable to the plaintiff's attorney who actively solicits business. As an example, 1% of the 3 million annual pregnancies have some exposure to diagnostic radiation; 4%, or 1200, of these pregnancies will result in some type of congenital abnormality that is unrelated to the radiation. Therefore, by chance alone there are 1200 malformed infants born each year to mothers who received diagnostic X-ray exposure.

There are several factors or problems peculiar to the medicolegal aspects of teratology that separate it from the rest of the medicolegal field. These peripheral legal complications frequently consume much of the time of the courts so that the important issue of negligence and proof of causality may be ignored.

We have mentioned the necessity to hold interdisciplinary discussions, but those that have been held have not yet produced solutions. Are the morals of the lawyer above those of the scientists? One must on this point differentiate between morality and the law. It must be understood that a lawyer cannot draw up a legal document concerning the rights or conditions of a scientific or medical breakthrough before this discovery exists. Therefore, the scientists must be able to act according to an accepted code of ethics, before the lawyer is called to testify as to the legal standing of the results of the medical experiment.[13-16]

At the same time, the scientists and doctors must, in our opinion, realize the enormity of the responsibility in deciding to go ahead with a particular, as yet untried technique and accept discussion with broadly based public interdisciplinary bodies for the advancement of mankind by science in the service of nature.

REFERENCES

1. **Kurjak, A.,** The beginning of human life and its assessment in utero, in: Atti e Relazioni, Nuova Serie, Industria tipografica ditta ved., Trizio - Bari, XL, 1982, 269.
2. **Liley, A. W.,** The fetus as a personality, *Fetal Ther.,* 1, 8, 1986.
3. **Kurjak, A. and Beazley, J. M.,** Fetal therapy: ethical and legal aspects, in *The Fetus as a Patient,* Kurjak, A., Ed., Excerpta Medica, Amsterdam, 1985, 1.
4. **Kurjak, A. and Degen, S.,** Legal problems and the ultrasonically detected malformed fetuses, in *Ultrasound '82,* Lerski, R. A. and Morley, P., Eds., Pergamon Press, Oxford, 1982, 33.
5. **Crawford, M.,** Ethical and legal aspects of early prenatal diagnosis, *Br. Med. Bull.,* 39, 310, 1983.
6. **Barclay, W. R., McCormic, A., and Sidbury, J. B.,** The ethic of in utero surgery, *J. Am. Med. Assoc.,* 246, 1550, 1981.
7. **Dudenhausen, J. W.,** Historical and ethical aspects of direct treatment of the fetus, *J. Perinat. Med.,* 12 (Suppl. 1), 17, 1984.
8. **Martin, M. M.,** Ethical standards for fetal experimentation, *Fordham Law. Rev.,* 43, 547, 1975.
9. **Elias, S. and Annas, G. J.,** Perspectives and fetal surgery, *Am. J. Obstet. Gynecol.,* 145, 807, 1983.
10. **Harrison, M. R.,** *Perinatal Management of the Fetus with a Correctable Defect,* W. B. Saunders, Philadelphia, 1983, 167.
11. **Harrison, M. R.,** Organ procurement for children: the anencephalic fetus as a donor, *Lancet,* 11, 1383, 1986.
12. **Brent, R. L.,** The law and congenital malformations, *Clin. Perinatol. Teratol.,* 13, 505, 1986.
13. **Schedler, G.,** Women's reproductive right. Is there a conflict with a child's right to be born free from defects?, *J. Leg. Med. (Chicago),* 7, 357, 1986.
14. **Lister, D.,** Ethical issues in infancies of severely defective infants, *Can. Med. Assoc. J.,* 135, 1401, 1986.
15. **Serr, D. M.,** The ethics and morals of in-vitro fertilization, in *The Fetus as a Patient,* Kurjak, A., Ed., Excerpta Medica, Amsterdam, 1985, 12.
16. **Robertson, J. A.,** Legal issues in prenatal therapy, *Clin. Obstet. Gynecol.,* 29, 603, 1986.

INDEX